EDWARD II
THE MAN

About the Author

Stephen Spinks wrote his dissertation on Edward II while reading history at King's College London. He is a heritage professional, working for the National Trust managing three historic properties in Warwickshire with a team of 900 volunteers and around 150 staff. He publishes weekly articles about the fourteenth century on his popular blog, as well as giving writing and research advice. He is a columnist for *Midlands Zone* magazine, in which he writes a well received exploration of LGBT life today, partly political, partly personal. Stephen divides his time between Warwickshire, London and Birmingham. For more information, see www.fourteenthcenturyfiend.com.

EDWARD II
THE MAN

A DOOMED INHERITANCE

STEPHEN SPINKS

AMBERLEY

In loving memory of my sister Sarah, and grandmother Margaret.

Half-title page: The letter written by the papal notary Manuele Fieschi to Edward III sometime around early 1336, setting out a confession of the former Edward II explaining how he survived his alleged murder in 1327, moved to Ireland and then France, finally becoming a hermit in the region of Genoa in Italy. See Appendix 2. (© *Archives départementales de l'Hérault, Montpellier, France*)

Title page: The magnificent tomb and effigy of Edward II, designed in the court style. The alabaster effigy is one of the most decorative of all medieval tombs. It may well be an attempt at a lifelike representation of the king and was once adorned with colour, paste jewels and a gold ship, which sat upon the plinth. (*Author's Collection, by kind permission of the Dean and Chapter of Gloucester Cathedral*)

This edition published 2019

Amberley Publishing
The Hill, Stroud
Gloucestershire, GL5 4EP

www.amberley-books.com

Copyright © Stephen Spinks, 2017, 2019

The right of Stephen Spinks to be identified as the Author
of this work has been asserted in accordance with the
Copyright, Designs and Patents Act 1988.

British Library Cataloguing in Publication Data.
A catalogue record for this book is available from the British Library.

ISBN 978 1 4456 9445 0 (paperback)
ISBN 978 1 4456 6767 6 (ebook)

Typeset in 10.5pt on 13pt Sabon.
Typesetting and Origination by Amberley Publishing.
Maps and family trees by Thomas Bohm, User Design.
Printed in the UK.

Contents

Acknowledgements

In setting out on this journey I have since discovered that in order to write a book there are a plethora of people you have the privilege of meeting or working alongside to make it all happen. Here are just a few of the very many who have helped make this journey so special and to whom I owe a debt of thanks.

Firstly to Shaun, senior editor at Amberley, who took a punt on a first-time writer who had been itching to write a biography of Edward II for well over fifteen years and, in doing so, acquired the unenviable task of guiding me on that journey. He patiently listened to my questions, kept me calm when all else was stormy, and never flinched whenever he knew I would undoubtedly have a point of view on even the smallest of details. Also, Alex Bennett who wrestled with the many images I was determined to have in this book. We got there in the end.

My thanks must also go to the many and various staff and volunteers at the British Museum, the National Archives, the British Library, Christ Church Oxford, Corpus Christi College Cambridge, my dear friend Lucy Reid and many other teams at archives, libraries and national monuments up and down the country. They each, in their own way, gave me access to our nation's heritage, fielded my many and sometimes mundane or difficult questions, and thereby kept me on the journey and kept the history real. You all do sterling jobs and I cannot thank you enough. It takes certain care and determination to protect and preserve the nation's heritage for now and the generations ahead of us. Keep going, you're doing just great.

I also want to thank Ben Shipston, Assistant Director of Operations; Andy Beer, Regional Director, and the National Trust more broadly, for understanding the importance to me of bringing Edward II to a much wider audience, thereby granting me three months off the day job to focus on my writing. To have the support of an organisation such as this has made this book possible and I thank them wholeheartedly. As I do my many family and friends who have persevered and lived and breathed this book with me, whether they wanted to or not. They often put up with my trips to cathedrals, castles and windswept December battlefield sites, or simply listened from an armchair or a hairdressing seat because they knew how important the research is to me and, for the best part of a year, let me disappear into my study while I put all that research into this book.

Finally, and perhaps the most important thanks of all, must go to my mum, Christine, who had the patience and determination to teach her young son, from a very tender age, the history of the British Isles, about its people and its monarchs. I can still recite them chronologically in ascending and descending order thanks to many years of tests. The hours spent together poring over books and visiting sites, including Edward II's tomb at Gloucester as far back as 1995, inspired her son to always be curious, to seek out the past and to interrogate the evidence in order to share the knowledge of history with anyone who will listen. This is as much your book in spirit as it is mine.

A Note on Currency

The coinage of medieval England was measured, right up until 1971, in pounds, shillings and pence. The only coin in wide circulation in the fourteenth century was the silver penny, which was often broken in two to create a half-penny. A penny broken into quarters equated to a farthing. £5 had to be counted as 1,200 silver pennies; money was often transported in barrels. Money was also divided into units called marks, which equated to 160 silver pennies or two-thirds of a pound.

During the early fourteenth century, an unskilled labourer might earn between one or two pence a day. The earls, ranking highest in society after the king, could command an income of between £2,000 and £5,000 per annum. The only exception in this period, apart from the king himself, was Thomas of Lancaster who, at his height of power and influence, could command an income of £11,000 a year. A knight could earn £40 a year.

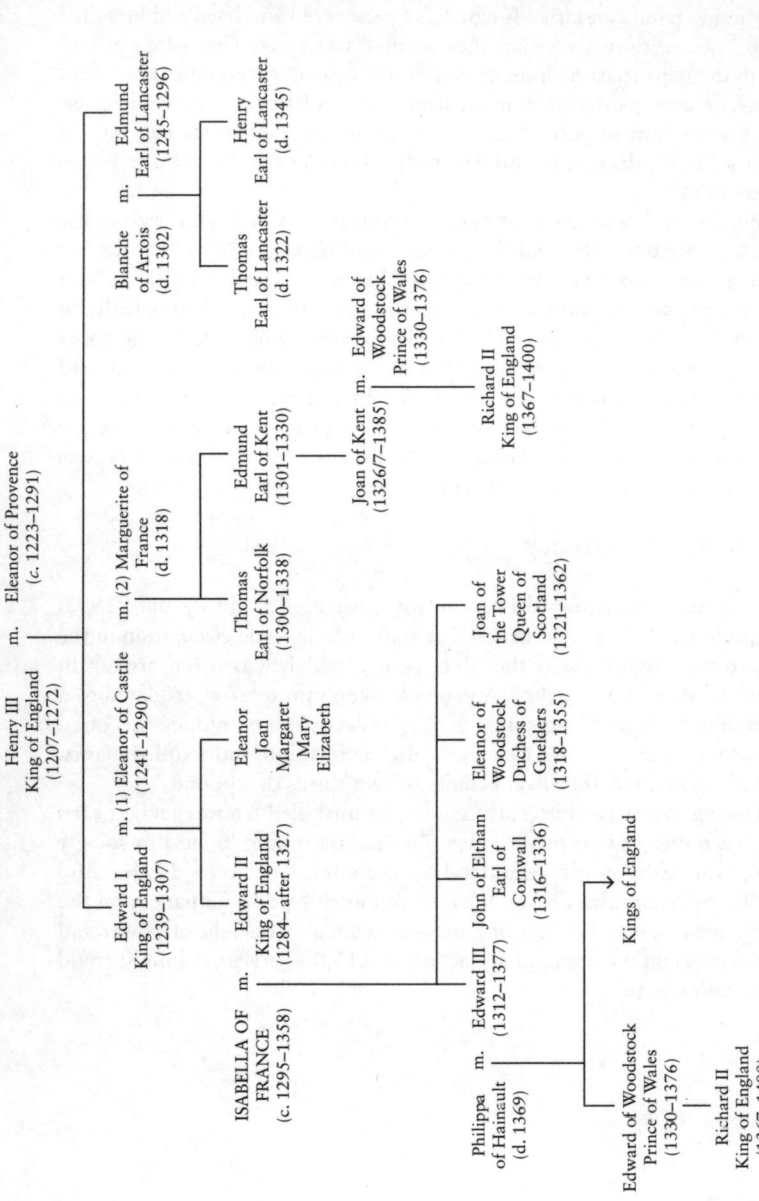

The House of Plantagenet. (© Amberley Publishing, Courtesy Kathryn Warner)

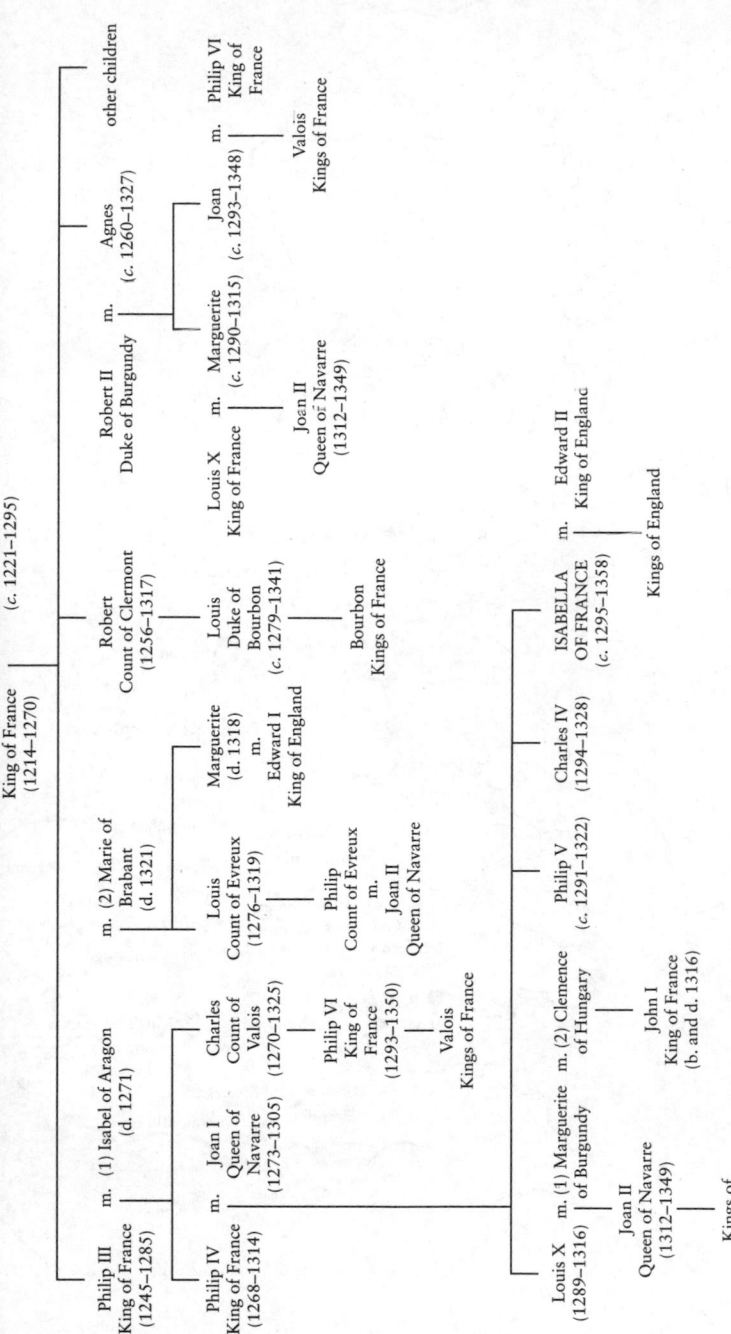

The House of Capet and Valois. (© *Amberley Publishing, Courtesy Kathryn Warner*)

England, Wales and Scotland

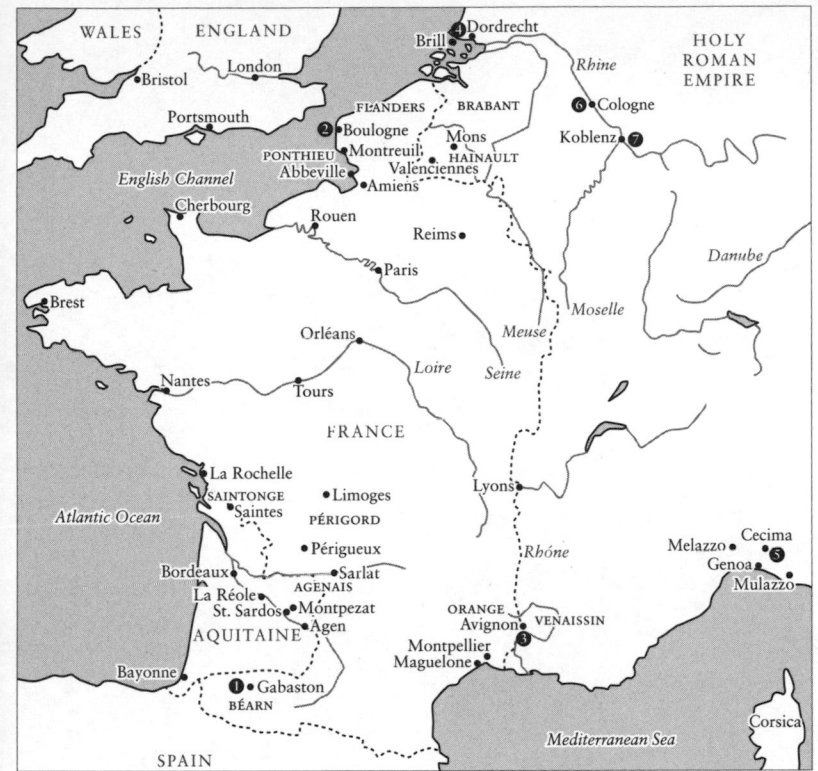

France and Western Europe

Preface

When I told people I was writing a book about Edward II, the first question was often a confused but simple one: 'Was that Longshanks?' Seeing my disappointment, there often quickly followed the second guess: perhaps he was the king who claimed the crown of France and started the Hundred Years War. On some occasions, I got the reaction: 'Oh, that one! The one in *Braveheart*.' This was often delivered with a knowing sense of disapproval at the silver screen's portrayal of a somewhat foppish prince who failed to show any backbone when confronted by hardship or his apparently violent father. Every so often, though, much to my excitement, I found someone who identified the man; however, his identity was usually encapsulated in tales of profound incompetence, personal weakness, an overbearing propensity for male favourites, tyranny and a dose of widespread misrule; with, of course, a good bit of gossip – rumours of red-hot pokers in dark corners of Gloucestershire generally dominated the conversation. We all like a good tale, and this one of an emasculated king put to death with a poetic nod to his alleged 'vices', even today, fills the popular imagination with gruesome images of perceived medieval brutality. I cannot blame anyone, of course. Edward II was, after all, living in the shadows of Titans. His twenty-year reign is wedged between those of his infinitely more successful father Edward I and his son Edward III, reigning for thirty-five and fifty years respectively, who dominate our nation's popular view of the medieval world. Edward I, strong and confident in his kingship, with imperial ambitions that could put Roman emperors to shame, forged the notion of a united set of kingdoms, despite falling short of actually delivering on this ambition. The gold lettering that adorns his austere polished Purbeck marble tomb in Westminster Abbey still proclaims him as *Scotorum Malleus* or 'Hammer of the Scots'. Unlike his son, and his own father Henry III (r. 1216–1272), Edward I kept his nobles in check, upheld and fiercely guarded the rights of the crown and championed the medieval ideal of kingship. On his death, the old leopard was compared by a contemporary to Alexander the Great. He was, in short, a tough act to follow.

Edward III was also to cast a shadow; three years into his reign he re-established royal authority, taking the English crown to new heights. Claiming the throne of France through lineal descent from his mother, Isabella of France, and his grandfather, the Capetian king Philip IV, despite French Salic law, Edward III was the champion of chivalry, the founder of the Order of the Garter, victor at Crécy and father to the legendary Black Prince. With *curricula vitae* like this, it is hard not to see the golden glow over the greater part of the late thirteenth and middle fourteenth centuries, luring the medieval reader like a moth to a flame.

So where does this leave Edward II? Out in the cold? More likely wrapped up in an almost impenetrable cloak of myths, legends, fantasies and the occasional nugget of truth. However, when you take the time to look beyond the rhetoric, the centuries of king bashing and the occasional bit of pub banter, using a good dose of thorough and sensible research, those multi-layered interpretations slowly begin to fall away. The notion of a foppish prince, moping about castles, being idle and generally good for nothing, quickly disappears. As do the reputations of some of those men said to be much greater than Edward II himself.

There is no doubt that the reigns of Edward I and III were highly successful and that Edward II failed ignominiously, but a closer look at the closing years of Edward I's reign reveals a king who was increasingly irascible and arbitrary, grasping for income as he fought the ever more difficult campaign to subjugate the Scots. He fiercely clashed with the Church and his Archbishop of Canterbury, oppressed his magnates towards the end, kept a tight control over patronage, held back baronial demands for reforms and almost reduced England to civil war in 1297.[1] At the time of his death, Edward I left administrative chaos, a burden of debt reaching a staggering £200,000 and a toxic legacy in Scotland brought about by his harsh and unrelenting policies after 1303. The rise of a defined Scottish nationalism rendered it impossible for any successor to complete the job. When Edward of Caernarfon came to the throne on 7 July 1307, this was his inheritance, which, in itself, was nothing short of doomed.

I first truly discovered Edward II at the tender age of thirteen. He has been there in the shadows ever since. The dissertation I wrote while reading history at King's College London was devoted to one of the high points in his reign in 1321–22. My first job in the heritage sector in 2007 was working for English Heritage at Kenilworth Castle, the place of Edward's unprecedented forced abdication. One of the houses I lived in was only a mile or two from Blacklow Hill, the poignant site of the brutal murder of Piers Gaveston in June 1312. With such daily reminders, it was only a matter of time before I began to put pen to paper. Along the way, I've become a lay member of the Finance Board at Gloucester Cathedral, the site of Edward's burial and magnificent tomb, and have been introduced to the Dean and Chapter through my research for this book. Edward has taken me on many a journey along the length and breadth of the British Isles, seeking out the monuments and records, following the breadcrumbs laid down by the king and his court some 700 years ago. In doing so, I have discovered the man as much as the king. To truly understand the latter, one has to understand the former. In an age when kings ruled instead of reigned, the personality of the king, his style of leadership and his approach to ruling his people would define his actions and policies, as well as impact on the behaviour and actions of those around him, and vice versa, to more broadly determine his legacy. Edward II was complex, full of contradictions and intense passions; and his passions, in all their diversity, combined with his difficult and somewhat doomed inheritance, would ultimately define his life and legacy.

As I began my research I quickly found myself standing on the shoulders of giants. There are three in particular. The first is Hilda Johnstone, Reader of History at my own university, King's College London, whose work in the 1940s first set out a picture of Edward in his apprenticeship and remains as valuable today as it was nearly eighty years ago.[2] Seymour Phillips, whose distinguished career continues to focus on Edward II, his reign and key individuals at his court such as Aymer de Valence, has produced such scholarly and comprehensive work that it creates the backbone for anyone seeking to set Edward II the in context of his time.[3] While I do not always agree with his findings, I am most indebted to his work, which has been a surefooted guide as I have travelled along this journey. The third giant is Ian Mortimer. Once in a generation, or in this case a century, someone comes along and asks the most curious of questions, constructed in the most breathtakingly refreshing way, which make us stop and think. Ian Mortimer is just such a person. His bold approach to interpreting history challenges us all to think about our own methods of research, how we may go about phrasing our questions of analysis and examining the facts before we can safely ascribe our individual understanding of the past. His challenges have set alight the modern approach to the reading of history.[4] As an undergraduate in 2003 who himself felt stifled by the rigidity and conservatism of the traditional approach to determining our historical record, I first read his work and it had a profound and lasting impact on me. His ongoing research on the survival of Edward II after September 1327 is ground-breaking and refreshing.

Lastly, you will not find in this book a confirmation or rebuttal of all those often hotly debated viewpoints held by historians past and present, as there are plenty of books on the reign where you can access those debates. This is consciously an account of the king himself. You will not find repetitious assumptions – 'they thought this', 's/he said that', 'they were wrong because'. Rather, this book is my view of Edward himself, his actions and the politics and machinations of his court as I see them garnered from, and formed by, the broad and varied evidence I have read over many years. The facts presented here are, therefore, allowed to speak for themselves and for you to judge accordingly.

I hope that in starting with a blank canvas I have created a window through which we can *all* peer, so at last we can see the man for who he was – a husband, a lover, a friend, an enemy, a tyrant to some, a king nevertheless, but above all a man just the same. I hope that as you look through this window, your curiosity is piqued and it encourages you to seek out more about his life and those who lived alongside him. Edward's dramatic biography, full of fierce loyalties, betrayals, personal revenge and survival against the odds, including the highly colourful circumstances surrounding his death, is ultimately a tale of the human condition. It has relevance to us all, in some way or another. If all I have achieved is to bring Edward's story to those who have never come across him before, or those who want to know more, then I have succeeded according to my own limited ambition.

Stephen Spinks
Stratford-upon-Avon
August 2017

PART ONE

Heir Apparent

The fourth squadron was commanded by young Edward, the king's heir,
Seventeen he was, and handsome, sensible and debonair.
Well his charger he could manage, and in this his first affray
Eagerly a chance he looked for, proof of prowess to display.

The Roll of Caerlaverock

1

Born on a Field
of Conquest

On Saint Mark's Day, 25 April 1284, the day on which the people of medieval England would parade through their villages carrying veiled black crosses while praying for good harvests, good weather and good health, a forty-three-year-old woman was in labour.[1] For hours, surrounded by some of the women of her household, headed by her trusted midwives, she lay in her dark, enclosed room, the air thick and oppressive with smoke from the fire. The windows in her lodging were boarded up to keep out light and fresh air, thought to bring evil spirits into the birthing chamber; the walls were adorned with tapestries of biblical scenes and calming flora and fauna. The decoration her ladies-in-waiting had chosen was deliberate. In the medieval mind, fear or moral distress during these tense hours in such a moment of lifegiving could be enough to physically damage the unborn child. Praying to St Margaret who had, as the legend goes, been swallowed by a dragon and disgorged again in an act of symbolic rebirth while clutching a crucifix during her ordeal, the women in the chamber called on the saint's heavenly powers to deliver the child safely. On this occasion St Margaret must have heard, for, eventually, after much painful labour, the mother gave birth to her fourteenth child. Childbirth in the medieval world was an uncertain affair both for the mother and the child; mortality was high during birth as well as in the days immediately thereafter. Despite the odds, the birth went well and a healthy baby boy was delivered in the confines of a wooden lodging, to the sounds beyond of masons carving stones and carpenters shaping great wooden beams; the great castle at Caernarfon, in which they both lay, was rapidly growing around them. Immediately the midwife reached out, cut the umbilical cord and threw it into the fire, a token of destruction to ward off the sinful accountability of the origins of his conception. She then promptly washed him down with wine and sugar water.

Within a week, on 1 May, the baby boy was presented to God through a baptismal rite by the principal midwife on behalf of his mother, Eleanor of

Castile, queen of England, and was given the name Edward in honour of his father, the great Edward I, king of England since 1272. The name Edward, despite its Saxon origins, was not entirely unusual; it had been resurrected by Henry III when he had named the baby boy's father some forty-five years earlier. Henry had been so taken with the cult of St Edward, the king who died in January 1066, sowing the seeds of Norman invasion later that year, and who was canonised in 1161, that he had spent a great deal of his fifty-six-year reign, and at great expense, reconstructing Westminster Abbey in the new Gothic style to shore up his ever-challenged kingship. News of the royal birth was celebrated widely at Caernarfon and beyond, and, as one chronicler noted, many rejoiced including the Londoners.[2] To mark this special occasion, on the day of the baptism alms of £10 were generously distributed to the people of the town to mark the birth of the king and queen's second surviving son.[3] It is here that our story really begins.

The baby was born onto a field of conquest. His father was in the final throes of achieving his imperial ambitions in Wales, which led to the death of the last ruling Welsh Prince of Gwynedd, Llywelyn ap Gruffydd, in a skirmish near Builth in 1282. Edward I systematically destroyed the remaining Welsh opposition and, in the following year, Llywelyn's brother Dafydd, briefly titular prince, was betrayed by his supporters. He was captured near Llanberis at the foot of Snowdon and sentenced to death for high treason, the first time the notion of treason had been expanded to include rebellion in which Dafydd's aim had been the death of the king. On 2 October, he was dragged through the streets of Shrewsbury, hanged by the neck for his crimes of murder, and disembowelled while still alive for crimes committed during Holy Week, with his entrails burned before him; finally his body was cut into four quarters for plotting the king's death, and the dismembered parts distributed throughout the realm as a warning to would-be renegades.[4] By the summer of the following year, the king was consolidating his power base through the construction of magnificent castles placed at strategic points around the former kingdom of Gwynedd. For Edward I, conquest was not just marked by removing troublesome individuals; it was made visible in buildings that would provide an indelible mark on the landscape and in the minds of the conquered. The people of Wales were left in no doubt about who now ruled them.[5]

It was by no means by chance, therefore, that the baby Edward was born at Caernarfon, a name with which he became forever associated. In fact, the place of his birth was positively planned for sound political reasons. By the start of 1283, it was only a matter of months before works at Caernarfon, Harlech and Conwy were underway after the king had commissioned the castle builder of the day, Master James of St George, to construct them using innovative architectural styles, initially overseen and carefully devised by the king himself. Once work began, it progressed at great pace – but not quickly enough to authenticate the tradition that

Edward of Caernarfon was delivered in the great, and still very imposing, Eagle Tower, which dominates the landscape and is full of medieval symbolism. As surviving records show, construction of the tower did not commence until 1285 and so a modest wooden lodging, removed in the 1280s, was the place of Edward's birth.

Nothing at the time recorded what the baby looked like. The recordkeeping for royal children was often fraught with problems. Inaccurate dates of birth and poor recording of names or locations, especially when the children were girls, were commonplace. We cannot even be certain whether Eleanor had fourteen or sixteen children by the time of her death. However, what is certain is that on this occasion at least the date and location of Edward's birth were accurately recorded by a royal official. In later life, Edward II was noted as being tall, well built and physically strong, much like his father who was known, then and now, as Longshanks. Edward I was 6 feet tall and physically active; he had a droopy eyelid, a slight lisp and long, curly Plantagenet blond hair that darkened to mousy brown as he grew into manhood.[6] Edward II would take after his father, albeit it without the droopy left eyelid and the lisp. Eleanor, his mother, born at Valladolid in Castile, in modern-day Spain, was known for her beauty, an astute sense of business and her devotion to her husband. The magnificent gilt bronze effigy made by William Torel in 1291 that adorns Eleanor's tomb in Westminster Abbey portrays the queen with long, flowing hair and a beautiful oval-shaped face. Both Edward's parents had fiery tempers, a trait they most certainly passed on to their son.[7] By standards then and now, Edward had two attractive parents and it is likely he was attractive too. Coins from his reign showing his profile look remarkably similar to that of his father, and to his son, Edward III, so it would seem the male Plantagenet genes were dominant even if images on coins were mostly stylised.

The birth of a son to the king in one of his new castles sent out a powerful message to the Welsh people that conquest was absolute and would be long-lasting. The statement was clear: the king continued to have children while the native royal Welsh dynasties had been extinguished. The tale told of Edward of Caernarfon's presentation to the people of Wales on a shield from the battlements of the castle as a prince born in Wales who could speak no English and was, therefore, fit to rule over them was most likely the invention of later generations; it first appears in the Elizabethan *Chronicle of England,* written by the antiquarian John Stow in 1584.[8] Yet despite this later colourful legend, the royal birth at a strategic castle during a period of conquest propelled the baby Edward into the political arena right from the start, which was what his father had planned with characteristic cunning.

Caernarfon, with its polygonal towers and walls lined with varicoloured masonry, was inspired by the great walled city of Constantinople in the ancient Eastern Roman Empire. Caernarfon was to remain central to the king's strategy to control the principality. Following the publication of the Statute of Wales at Rhuddlan in March 1284, which set out English administrative control over Wales, it became the political and administrative heart of English government until the seventeenth century.[9] Edward II was to have a lifelong connection to that country, which played out up until the end of his reign.

The baby Edward was immediately given a Welsh wet nurse, Mary Maunsel, whose task was to feed and care for him. Wrapped in swaddling cloth, great care was taken to keep the king's son safe and free from illness, especially as many, but not all, of his older brothers had already perished. However, Mary did not hold the position for long as she herself fell ill at Rhuddlan Castle before the year was out. Despite her short service, she had made an impression and continued in the household in a different role, for in 1312 Mary received 100s a year from the revenues from the king's mill at Caernarfon, and in 1317 Mary was in possession of 73 acres of crown land, where she lived rent-free for life as a result of her service.[10] Mary was replaced by Alice Leygrave, an English woman who was to remain close to Edward throughout her life. Alice would stay in Edward's household until his marriage to Isabella of France in 1308, whereupon she was transferred into the household of the new queen. Alice was with Isabella in France in 1313 and again in 1314, so her services were always useful to them.[11] Clearly a close bond had formed in Edward's childhood, made more poignant by his often absent, busy parents. Alice would therefore become his surrogate mother.

The royal children remained at Caernarfon for the summer as their parents consolidated their gains on progress through north, and later south, Wales. By early autumn, as the leaves over the huge forests began to turn and fall, the royal children, Edward, Joan and Elizabeth (the latter born at Rhuddlan Castle only two years earlier), were eventually bundled up and made the slow, winding journey back to England via Acton Burnell in Shropshire before heading south, finally meeting up with their parents at Bristol.[12] Edward was not to return to Wales until he was invested with the principality in 1301, when just shy of his seventeenth birthday.

2

A Happy Childhood

Every so often, we get brief glimpses of the life of Edward of Caernarfon as a child. Surrounded by his sisters, those in wardship to the crown as well as members of his extended family, his immediate circle created a busy, vibrant and substantial household. This household and the people within it did not remain in isolation either, being frequently visited by scores of other nobles and their families, as well as visiting dignitaries from the Continent. It is against this backdrop, therefore, that Edward grew up into the gregarious and sociable man we read about in later chronicles, someone who loved music, dancing, people from all levels of the social hierarchy, and life in general.

Edward's parents had a very happy and successful marriage. Married in Castile in 1254, Edward I was then only fifteen and his bride twelve. The royal couple went on to have a thirty-six-year marriage and at least fourteen children, possibly more. Edward was the fourteenth. By the time of his birth in April 1284, his elder brothers John (1266–71) and Henry (1268–74) were already dead, and his ten-year-old brother Alfonso would die before the summer of Edward's birth was spent. Before his death Alfonso, possibly Eleanor of Castile's favourite child, performed a final role. Following his father's confiscation of the Welsh regalia, the symbols that visually imbued sovereign power, Alfonso was given the task of presenting Llywelyn's crown and a ringlet, thought to have previously belonged to King Arthur, at the shrine of St Edward the Confessor, in Westminster Abbey.[1] It was a carefully crafted gesture designed to make yet another statement. Here was Edward I's heir making offerings to the Plantagenet royal saint; the family line would continue. Yet, however poetic and politically important this offering was, its benefit was short-lived; the spirit of King Arthur, it appeared, had extended enough grace because in August Alfonso died of fever, and a week later he was buried in Westminster Abbey next to the Confessor's shrine and in the shadow of his late grandfather Henry III.

Neither the king nor queen attended the funeral. They were in Wales, still consolidating their gains, but Eleanor had Alfonso's heart removed during the embalming process so that when she died she could be buried with it.[2] It may seem cold to us today that royal or noble parents were not present at the time of their children's deaths, but infant mortality was commonplace in the medieval world. The death of his older brother suddenly left Edward, now only four months old, as heir to the throne.

Despite the loss of his brothers, Edward had a gaggle of five healthy surviving sisters. The eldest, Eleanor, was born in 1269; Joan of Acre was born in 1272, the year of their father's accession to the crown, while he was on crusade in the Holy Land; Margaret was born in 1275; Mary in 1279; and Elizabeth, only two years her brother's senior, was born in 1282 at Rhuddlan in Wales. From the start, these sisters were a permanent feature of daily life; they shared the nursery and were bundled off together on royal visits, going from castle to castle, manor to manor. The royal family and their households in medieval England were peripatetic. Moving from place to place not only allowed the previous residence to be cleaned and aired while life resumed at the next, but it helped to protect the health of the royal family. In summer, London and other major towns such as York and Winchester were hotbeds of sickness and disease, and were best avoided. In 1290, the dowager queen, Eleanor of Provence, grandmother to the royal children, who always took an active interest in their welfare, wrote to her son who was planning to take the royal brood north, expressing her concern that they would be exposed to *le mauveis air* or the poor climate, to which the dowager queen had herself fallen victim while on her own travels.[3] The king, nevertheless, went north with his family without incident. Despite the loss of some of his siblings before 1284, Edward appears to have been in robust health, both then and throughout his life, although he did suffer from tertian fever in 1294, with his sister Margaret. A malarial fever, it reappears every three days, giving the sufferer a bad case of the sweats, which for Edward and Margaret was to last an uncomfortable full month.[4]

Given the age differences between the children, Edward would not spend all his childhood surrounded by his sisters. Royal daughters were politically expedient to their parents, who needed to build alliances and shore up relationships with European kingdoms and nobles in England. Five healthy daughters who would all grow into adulthood were royal pawns in the traditional marriage market, used for forging relationships that went far beyond the bedroom and were a cornerstone of medieval society. In an age where power and title was transmuted through children, marriage at the highest levels of society was not directed by personal feeling. For the children of Edward I and Eleanor of Castile, they could only have hoped that their own marriages would be as loving and as successful as that between their parents had become, but there was certainly no guarantee.

The first to leave the royal nursery in August 1285 was Mary, then only five years old. However, it was not marriage to a husband that called her away; instead it was marriage to God. On the insistence of her grandmother, sixty-two-year-old Eleanor of Provence, Mary was to enter the Convent of Amesbury in Wiltshire, an important religious settlement, which was the English daughter-house of Fontevraud in France. It was there, in France, that Henry II, his queen Eleanor of Aquitaine, Richard the Lionheart and the second wife of King John all lay buried. Eleanor of Provence was planning to retire to Amesbury, but before her entry there on 7 July 1286 the dowager queen built up a collection of royal and noble children who would share in her new religious life.[5] Edward may have lost a sister and his grandmother to God, but he was not an absent brother or grandson. Throughout his life he often visited his sister at Amesbury. Apparently, Mary was not all that well suited to a life of quiet contemplation. Much like her father, she was fiercely independent and lived life to excess, going far beyond the religious bonds it would be all too easy to think restricted her. Extravagant as her brother would become, Mary also shared in his love of gambling and on many occasions visited the court during its travels.[6] One such visit took place on 12 June 1293 when Mary made her way to see her then nine-year-old brother at Mortlake for two days, taking with her a group of nuns who may well have shared in her irreligious appetites. This was just one of many occasions that would punctuate Edward's life and it highlights their continued closeness.

By the spring of 1290, Eleanor of Castile was growing ill and there was a rush throughout that year to see some of her daughters married off as soon as possible; well-laid plans were suddenly sped up. The next to leave the childhood home was Edward's second-eldest sister, Joan, who on 30 April 1290 married the prickly Gilbert de Clare, Earl of Gloucester, one of the most prominent earls in the kingdom.[7] Two months later, Margaret followed her sister to Westminster Abbey and married John of Brabant, who would soon become the duke of that duchy located in the Low Countries.[8] It was an extravagant state occasion; at the banquet that followed, there were 426 minstrels.[9] Three years later, Edward's eldest sister Eleanor, then twenty-four to Edward's nine, was married to Henry, Count of Bar, at Bristol, and left England shortly afterwards. The marriage sadly only lasted a few years, for by 1298 Eleanor was dead.[10]

Edward did not escape the attention of his mother, who brought him into the centre of these marital considerations. Alexander III of Scotland, brother-in-law to Edward I, had died in 1286, leaving as his sole heir a young granddaughter forever known to history as the Maid of Norway.

Alexander had three children from his first marriage – two sons and one daughter called Margaret, all of whom predeceased him. Margaret had left Scotland for Norway, marrying its king, Eric, in 1281. Within two years Margaret gave birth to her namesake, and it was this little girl who by 1290 was sole heir to the Scottish crown.

Edward I, never one to miss a political opportunity, saw a chance to further his imperial ambitions. Negotiations began in earnest with King Eric of Norway and the slightly more cautious Scots, and by July 1290 the Treaty of Birgham set out plans for the marriage of Margaret to Edward of Caernarfon.[11] It would be a peaceful opportunity to combine the future of the two kingdoms. Papal dispensation was granted by Pope Nicholas IV as the youngsters were related in the third degree, and as 1290 approached the Maid of Norway was placed on a ship with her retinue and set sail for Scotland. In October 1290 news reached the king and queen of England that the Maid had died en route. Edward was back on the royal marriage market.

The last to leave the childhood home was Elizabeth, in January 1297. Edward, then twelve years old, watched his sister, the closest to him in age, marry John, Count of Holland, at Ipswich.[12] Elizabeth, who was her father's favourite, refused to leave England, nor was she persuaded by her father to do so. Eventually, her new husband prevailed in his efforts, but soon after, John died and Elizabeth returned to England. By 1302, her father had married her to Humphrey de Bohun, Earl of Hereford and Essex, which for Edward at least meant that another of his sisters was again within striking distance and a frequent visitor at both the royal court and to his personal household.[13]

Although in childhood and beyond Edward was surrounded by family, the year 1290 marked great change; he lost two influential figures. The early signs of sickness experienced by his mother Eleanor in spring that year only grew worse. By the summer, the queen looked to be ailing as she persevered with her work. By autumn, she was unable to travel. While in Nottinghamshire, Eleanor's party rested at Harby and it was there, at some time in the evening of 28 November, that she died, probably of some type of coronary disease.[14] Edward I, who in his thirty-six-year marriage had barely been without his wife at his side, was distraught at her loss. After her funeral the following month, he withdrew from public life. Moved by grief, he penned a letter to the Abbot of Cluny in which he wrote, 'Our consort, who we loved dearly in life, and whom we cannot cease to love now she is dead, has been prayed for constantly.'[15] Such an expression of devotion is in stark contrast to the strong, almost steely, leopard-like reputation of the king, which has become the stuff of legend.

As the body of the deceased queen was moved from Lincoln to London, wherever the cortege stopped each night, at places including Grantham,

Geddington and Dunstable, memorial crosses were later erected by order of the king – the now-famous Eleanor Crosses. Before her body was finally buried in Westminster Abbey, on 17 December 1290, the queen's viscera had been removed and buried in Lincoln Cathedral on 3 December. Her heart, with that of her son Alphonso that had been kept from six years earlier, were interred in the London Dominican Friary on 19 December. This triple burial was unusual, not widely practised in England at the time.[16] There is no record of the reaction of her younger son, who was six. We know Edward was with his sister Elizabeth at Laxton, where only two weeks earlier he had heard Mass in memory of his late grandfather, Henry III, who had died eighteen years earlier.[17] There is no record either that Edward attended his mother's funeral at Westminster Abbey or that his father sought him out in his grief. In the first six years of his life, his parents had been absent for nearly three years, from May 1286 to August 1289, spending their time in the English-held territories of Gascony in France.[18] Despite this, to assume there was not much of a bond between Edward and his mother is hard to substantiate with any certainty. In his later life, Edward would hear Masses and make other devotions to his mother so it seems she was not far from his mind many years after her death.[19] He must have also learnt much about his mother from his sisters, who were with him throughout his parents' long absence in the late 1280s.

Just over six months after the death of his mother, his paternal grandmother, the dowager queen Eleanor of Provence, also died and was given a solemn burial on 8 September at the convent she had entered a few years earlier. The young Edward could not have failed to notice that some of the most influential people around him were now gone. Yet, life continued. The king emerged from mourning in the early months of 1291 a somewhat changed man. In the absence of his wife, he threw himself into Anglo-Scottish affairs that would keep him and England busy for the rest of his reign. For Edward of Caernarfon, life within his household continued as before; his sisters came and went on their visits and his cousins and other noble families frequently visited.

The running of his household was expensive. The surviving expense rolls for the year 1288–89 report an expenditure of £2,140, while in 1292–3 this totalled around £3,900.[20] Between April and October that year, Edward left his favourite residence of Langley in Hertfordshire and travelled around the south of England. On the Feast of the Translation of St Thomas Becket, he was at Canterbury Cathedral. The great English martyr Becket, murdered in 1170, remained a favourite of Edward's throughout his life and significantly for him, this feast day would also mark, in years to come, the day of his father's death and his own accession to the crown.[21] In that summer of 1293, Edward stopped at

Winchester, Salisbury, Bath and the royal hunting lodge of Clarendon in Oxfordshire.[22] By 9 September, he was at Amesbury, visiting his sister Mary at the convent, possibly to pay his respects at the tomb of his late grandmother, praying for her soul. Already in childhood, Edward was being encouraged, and displayed, the conventional piety that he would show throughout his lifetime. By 20 September, he arrived at Bristol.[23] Despite his young age he was a busy heir to the throne and spent his summers seeing the country he would one day rule.

If not travelling with his household, then he would occasionally be visited by his father's court, at Langley or Mortlake. Langley was only a few miles south-west of the great cathedral town of St Albans and was held until 1290 by the queen from her husband's cousin, Edmund, Earl of Cornwall. In 1292, the manor underwent repair works in the great hall. Two chimneys were installed, replacing the central hearth that was commonplace in the late thirteenth and early fourteenth century. It was one of many evolutions that were taking place in architectural design in this period. The walls were redecorated in bright, rich colours such as vivid yellow orpiment and rich vermilion.[24] This is a reminder that the medieval world was full of colour and vibrancy, which today would be beyond most people's palette. Langley had stables, which not only housed horses but in the 1290s were home to a camel, a gift from a foreign ruler. There were gardens generously planted with fruits and vines, 8 acres of parkland filled with deer, 120 acres of arable land and meadows full of wild flowers.[25] There was a river and mill to and, given Edward's later interest in the practical side of land management such as digging and ditching – and swimming – it is not such a stretch to think he was exposed to these crafts and this pastime at a young age at Langley. It must have been a safe place and, when he became king, he would later purchase a small manorhouse in the grounds of Westminster Abbey, which he called Little Burgundy, as a retreat, perhaps recalling these early childhood days. The manor of Langley was very much a home for the king's children and Edward acquired it in his own right in 1302.

In January 1293 his sister Joan, now Countess of Gloucester, stayed for a number of nights. From 11 to 13 February, the brother of the Earl of Oxford, Hugh de Vere, stopped off and so did John de Brabant, as well as Edward's cousins Thomas and Henry of Lancaster, who arrived with a great company. The atmosphere must have been boisterous with many tales of bravado, as they had come from a recent tournament held at nearby Dunstable. Many more guests came and went. In April Joan returned, this time with her husband the Earl of Gloucester and a large company of knights and, shortly after, further lords arrived on 24 April, possibly to celebrate Edward's birthday the following day.[26] The pace kept up. In June his sister Mary was back again, seemingly not spending that much time at the convent at Amesbury, as were their royal cousins Thomas and Henry of Lancaster. The latter frequently visited the counties around London to take part in tournaments, this time at Fulham. Perhaps these ongoing visits were the inspiration in 1292 for an unnamed painter, who was paid 50s, to paint fifty-two shields and four knights on their way to a tournament onto the wall of the great hall. All this entertainment came at considerable cost; for twenty days in June alone, Edward's household had burned through £370, almost ten per cent of the whole year's budgeted expenditure.[27] Entertaining at his manors may have been an exciting and sociable daily ritual but his clerk, judiciously noting down the expenditure, appears far less enamoured of it. Over the course of the summer there are many comments next to expenditure details such as, 'they are staying', 'they are still here' and, on the last day before a host of guests moved off for yet another tournament, 'here they are still, and this day is burdensome'.[28]

The childhood of the young Edward was, therefore, one of great sociability and visibility. He spent the first ten years of his life travelling, entertaining and keeping up to speed, no doubt, with all that was going on around him and at his father's court. As he entered his adolescent years, Edward was clearly emerging with a sociable personality that is often commented on after he became king. Soon to become extravagant, a lover of fashion, horses, gambling and racing dogs, his life was rounded and energetic. As he grew, though, so did his father's need for him to step up to his duties. As he was leaving his childhood, life was soon to become even more complicated as demands were increasingly placed upon him as heir to the English throne.

3

Stepping out of the Shadows

In 1294 Edward I, now fifty-five years old, had ruled over England for twenty-two years. In that time the king had brought peace and stability to a kingdom that had previously witnessed civil war, which wrought devastation on a country then ruled by his father Henry III. However, the closing years of Edward I's reign would be marked by growing tension between an ageing and ever-more irascible king, his magnates, clergy and his domestic and European neighbours. War would dominate the agenda.

The relationship between England and France had, since 1254, been cordial, even friendly. Yet by the time Philip IV inherited the French throne in October 1285, relations with England had deteriorated, culminating in the confiscation of the remaining English-held territory of Gascony in a long-standing dispute. Edward I immediately responded, and the ensuing conflict would eventually last for nearly ten years. Shortly after the French confiscation, war broke out in Scotland in 1296, and faced with war on two fronts, the king marched an army north, culminating in immediate successes, most notably at Dunbar.

It was in this year, against the backdrop of war, that Edward stepped onto the political stage. His first taste of responsibility was a simple one. While his father was in Scotland bringing Scottish nobles to heel, Edward of Caernarfon was left in nominal charge of the defences of the south coast should Philip IV use the distraction in the north as an opportunity for invasion.[1] For twelve-year-old Edward there was little to do, his skills yet to be tested, for the threat of invasion did not result in anything other than fearful rumour. The ships simply did not come. Yet it was not long before things changed. By the summer of 1297, the king was determined to embark on a plan to forge foreign alliances with European powerhouses against his bitter enemy, Philip IV of France. It had always followed that when the king travelled beyond the sea he would leave a regent or lieutenant, styled *locum tenens*, who was vested with his authority to govern the kingdom during the king's absence.[2] Edward, now thirteen, was the natural choice to invest with such royal authority. In the month prior to the king's departure, a solemn ceremony was held at Westminster in which the Church and many of the leading nobles, such as the Earl of Norfolk and Earl of Hereford, swore fealty to his son, should Edward I die abroad. Without another heir, for Edward I this was more than just an occasion for pomp and ceremony. In the days that followed, more oaths were received.[3] For young Edward this must have been a memorable moment as the lords and barons of England knelt in front of him and proffered their unwavering support. It was the first time he really entered onto the political stage.

Edward was not expected to exercise royal authority on his own, of course. While the king's formal power rested with his son, Edward would be well advised, surrounded by some of the king's most loyal councillors including Richard Gravesend, Bishop of London; William Louth, Bishop of Ely; and Walter Langton, Bishop of Coventry and Lichfield. At the head of these ecclesiastical advisors was Henry of Newark, the Archbishop-elect of York. Joining them were Edmund, Earl of Cornwall, who was the king's cousin; the Earl of Surrey, who spent most of his time absent from London; and the Earl of Warwick. Finally, Edward also had the counsel of three barons: John Giffard, Reginald Grey and Alan Plonkenet.[4] Together, these men worked to ensure that the functions of government would continue while nominally overseen by Edward. For Edward, it was an opportunity to learn how it was done.

Unlike his 1296 appointment ostensibly defending the south coast, Edward's regency was a web of political tension in which he sat at the centre. Wars were costly affairs. Financing the recent military expeditions in Wales in 1294, Gascony, Scotland, and now an expedition to Flanders, was burdensome on the country. Taxation was essential; the king raised it directly through parliament, which he was bound to do since the time of Magna Carta, sealed in 1215 by King John, and subsequently re-issued under Henry III and Edward I at their coronations. In these three years alone, these crippling taxes had amounted to about £150,000 from the laity and £100,000 from the clergy, which was more than the total amount of the previous twenty years added together.[5] Despite this staggering sum, the exchequer struggled to balance the receipts. Making matters worse, not all of the king's army was made up from a feudal obligation, with the mainstay of his foot soldiers requiring payment. To provide for the army the king levelled his right of prise, by which his purveyors were able to requisition foodstuff and other victuals essential to feeding the men – without payment to the local population or, at best, at greatly reduced prices. The hated prise was increasingly not confined to periods of war. The Dunstable annalist noted of Edward of Caernarfon's household itself in 1294:

Two hundred dishes a day were not sufficient for his kitchen. Whatever he spent on himself or his followers, he took without paying for it. His officials carried off all the victuals that came to the market, even cheese and eggs, and not only whatever was for sale, but even things not for sale in the houses of the townsfolk. They scarcely left anybody a tally. They seized bread from the bakers and beer from the ale-wives, or if they had none, forced them to brew and bake.[6]

While the account may be exaggerated, the general feeling of the populace was all too clear.

The taxes continued. To further fill his coffers the king raised the maltote six-fold, a levy now of a fifth on the income from the sale of wool, which amounted to approximately half of the value of the land at the time. His officials confirmed that the sale of 8,000 woolsacks would generate an extra £50,000 for the royal revenues.[7] The clergy fared no better and in 1294 were forced to pay a half on their incomes. No one was spared the heavy burden; ecclesiastical, noble, merchant and peasant alike had to contribute. In the space of three years, the king had raised annual taxation but also removed the ability of many to pay those taxes because of the loss of goods his purveyors had already requisitioned. The result was a melting pot of dissent. It was not long before the pot began to boil over. The first refusal came from an enraged clergy, who attempted to enforce the bull *Clericis Laicos* in which taxation would require assent from the pope. Edward I was not moved and instead went further, demanding his nobles send their obligatory men in feudal service, traditionally raised only for conflict within England, to Flanders. Leading nobles refused. The king then levied a tax of an eighth, but with nothing more than the approval of 'the people who stood in his chamber'.[8] It was the straw that broke the camel's back. The result was outright opposition from the Marshall of England, Roger Bigod, Earl of Norfolk, and the Constable of England, Humphrey de Bohun, Earl of Hereford, claiming that the recent aid, tallages and prises levied without payment, had impoverished them and the people of the kingdom, so that they and others could not serve the king in his campaign.

During the thirteenth century there were two charters that enshrined the rights of the nobility, the Great Charter, otherwise known as Magna Carta, and the Charter of the Forest. Both had increasingly become the bedrock of limitations imposed upon an otherwise free royal hand. In times of crisis the nobility would unfurl their parchments and remind the king of his divinely sealed duties. When backed into a corner, kings of England had been forced to reissue the charters to calm the storm. As in times past, the demands for a reissue were promptly made. The regency council promised to reissue the Great Charter and the Charter of the Forest but, by now, this was not enough. As Edward I had boarded his ship for Flanders a week earlier, the earls subsequently drew up the Remonstrances, in which they attempted to curb Edward's arbitrary taxation; which left Edward of Caernarfon and his advisors to deal with the crisis.[9] Such was the tension that Edward and his council sought shelter behind the walls of London, and the writs issued around this time were attested to at St Paul's.[10] The council was kept busy. Writs were sent out to keep the peace and mayors of sixteen towns and constables of royal castles were warned to not to embroil themselves in the hostilities, warning of the experiences learnt from the Baron's War under Henry III in which chaos had ruled the kingdom, bringing about devastation and civil strife. Gossip swirled around the city and reports came in of a man who had said he wished the king's head was sat next to that of Llywelyn's, rotting on London Bridge, only for the man to be promptly beaten to death by a loyal London goldsmith.[11]

Edward and his advisors, against a backdrop of deepening political tension, agreed to reconfirm the Charters on 10 October.[12] They went further and offered the opposition earls the abolition of the much-hated maltote. Although Edward was nominally in charge during the king's absence, this policy was that of his advisors and to which the young Edward was encouraged to agree to and seal using the seal of absence his father had sent to him on 27 August. Reluctantly, the reconfirmations, with their additions, were again sealed by Edward I, at Ghent, a month later. For Edward of Caernarfon this was his first real taste of the exercise of royal power and, during the time he acted in his father's absence, it had been during a period of great political unrest. He now had first-hand experience of dealing with magnates who, only a month earlier, had sworn fealty to him and his father yet shortly afterwards had appeared in open opposition and forced concessions from the crown. He also saw first-hand the policy that his father adopted, which was very much an 'accept now, rescind later'arrangement. The position Edward I was forced to accept in the late 1290s was not one he welcomed; he spent the next six years attempting to roll back his concessions despite his promises towards reform. It would be this practice that Edward himself would later adopt with his own overmighty vassals when he came to the throne. Edward must have learnt while regent that those loyal around him could be counted on, but there were also dangers at court which could, if pushed too hard, erupt into open confrontation.

As one crisis neared its conclusion, another charged headlong into the arena. The Scots, resentful of English occupation, began to chaff under Edward I's rule. It was not only English magnates that the king had turned to and demanded feudal service from in Flanders. All it took was the campaigning of Robert Wishart, the Bishop of Glasgow, and the activities of men like William Wallace, to bring to an end the recently secured Anglo-Scottish peace. William Wallace, the son of Alan Wallace, a minor landowner in Ayrshire, rose up and killed the English sheriff William Hesilrig at Lanark. At the same time, Sir Andrew Murray, who had been imprisoned in Chester Castle the year before and had subsequently escaped, launched a campaign driving the English out of Inverness, Elgin and Banff. Murray and Wallace joined forces in August 1297 at the strategically important castle of Stirling, which was the gateway to the Highlands, at the same time that Edward of Caernarfon and his advisors were busy dealing with English complaints about taxation in London. If Stirling were lost, it would only galvanise a more widespread Scottish uprising.

Defence of Scotland was left in the hands of John de Warenne, Earl of Surrey. Despite his steadfast loyalty to the king, Warenne had no interest in Scotland and spent most of his time offering the job to anyone who would take it. The unbearable weather, according to the chronicler Guisborough, was simply too much for him.[13] His neglect meant that urgent requests for help, demanded from the treasurer Sir Hugh Cressingham, took months to arrive and delayed his preparations to ride out. On 11 September, Warenne suffered a humiliating defeat at Stirling Bridge in which he fled the field, escaping back to England with his life.[14] Cressingham was killed, his corpse flayed, its skin tanned and cut into small pieces and used as sword belts on the orders of Wallace as macabre tokens of his victory.[15] Emboldened, Wallace then raided across the border during the winter and terrorised the people of Cumbria and Northumbria, before returning to Scotland. The only success for the English was that Sir Andrew Murray was mortally wounded at Stirling and died two months later. Had he lived, he may have been a significant player in the Scottish wars that were to follow.

The defeat at Stirling Bridge caused shock in England. News arrived in London in late September, which actually helped break the political tensions over taxation, enabling Edward of Caernarfon to confirm the Charters on 10 October. The nobility who had remained in England and not followed the king to Flanders were suddenly united in a common cause. Summonses were issued in the name of the young Edward for an army to assemble under his nominal command, but this was later postponed until the king himself returned to take charge of the campaign, so serious was the unfolding Scottish crisis.[16] The delay allowed for further preparation and, at the head of a large army numbering around 26,000 infantry and 3,000 cavalry, Edward I, bent on subjugation, defeated Wallace at the Battle of Falkirk. The night before the battle, the king's horse had broken two of his ribs as he lay resting on the ground, apparently in fear of a Scottish night-attack on the royal camp.[17]

While Edward of Caernarfon did not fight or follow his father to Scotland, his time as regent must have taught him something about the role of king. His regency had seen two major crises. Now that he was growing into adulthood, it would not be long before he would take on an even greater public role.

The ongoing conflict with France came to a head in early 1299. Edward I's failed attempt in 1297 to forge effective alliances with European powers to curb the authority of Philip IV deepened the Gascon crisis. Twice, in 1294 and 1297, Edward of Caernarfon had been bandied around the marriage market, this time it was with the intention that he should marry Philippa, daughter of Guy de Dampierre, Count of Flanders. The project was pressed again and, in January 1297, three proctors took oaths to the alliance on behalf of Count Guy and, a few days later, three appointed English representatives swore to the marriage.[18] Philip IV of France immediately took the bait and sought to undermine the contract. During the next two years both Edward I and Philip continued to confront one another while the recently elected pope Boniface VIII attempted to mediate.

By 1299, as success in Scotland was reached following Edward I's victories at Falkirk the year earlier, respite was achieved in the Gascon crisis. English and French envoys met in the summer at Montreuil and agreed to a treaty to bring about peace. Among the terms were two clauses that would have a profound impact on Edward. The first, and most immediate, was the proposal that his sixty-year-old father should marry Marguerite of France, the sister of Philip IV and forty years the king's junior. Edward I had been without a wife since 1290, following the death of his beloved Eleanor of Castile, and still, therefore, ran the risk of only having one surviving male heir. With the absence of a spare for the heir, should Edward predecease his father, the line of succession would be fractured by disputes and civil war. But the king himself was not the only one considered, for the treaty also proposed a marriage between Edward of Caernarfon and Philip IV's only daughter, Isabella, who was then three years old. Both father and son agreed to the proposals and the Flemish plan was simply abandoned.[19]

Preparations immediately got underway for the imminent marriage of the king. By September they were complete and a twenty-year-old Marguerite set sail from France and landed at Dover on the 8th of that month. She was received into her new kingdom by her soon to be stepson and his welcoming party, including the recently forgiven Earl of Norfolk, Roger Bigod.[20] Edward and Marguerite were much closer in age, only five years separated them, and it must have been an exciting, if not an apprehensive occasion, for the young Edward waiting patiently at Dover for his new stepmother to arrive. For the first time in nearly ten years, there would be someone in the royal family taking the maternal lead. Marguerite would help to soothe the temper of her ageing husband, something that must have been well received at court, as the king had long been the iron-fisted leopard of legend. They seemed to hit it off instantly. Edward escorted Marguerite to Canterbury and two days later she married Edward I in the great cathedral. Nine months later, on 1 June at Brotherton in Yorkshire, Marguerite gave birth to her first child, a son named Thomas. For the first time since 1284, Edward now had a living brother.

The new queen certainly had the chance to build a good relationship with her stepson. Between 2 and 20 November 1299, Edward and his sister Mary, the nun at Amesbury, spent time in the company of their new stepmother at their childhood home, the manor of Langley, while the king was absent. Supplies of apples, pears, nuts and other fruits were brought from London; a London apothecary provided 12*lb* of sugar. They were together again, on and off, at Windsor Castle between Christmas 1299 and February 1300; between visits, Edward was going to and from the Tower by barge, with his knights and clerks skilfully rowed by Absolon, Edward's barge master.[21]

By the end of February the king had re-joined the family and together they left for a pilgrimage to Canterbury, where Edward made offerings at the Shrines of St Adrian, St Augustine and St Mildred in the Church of St Augustine. In the cathedral, he did the same at the statue of the Virgin and at Becket's crown, the point of the sword with which the archbishop was martyred in 1170 and the tomb he was first buried in. In honour of his parents, and while still praying at Becket's shrine, Edward made an offering on behalf of his as yet unborn sibling.[22] The bond between stepmother and stepson, it seemed, was forged and real.

However, the idyllic winter of 1299–1300 was over all too soon and trouble in Scotland now took centre stage. For Edward this was his first opportunity to follow in his father's footsteps and step into the martial arena. Writs went out and by July, the army was assembled. On the way north, both the king and Edward rested at the Abbey of Bury St Edmunds. Edward, it appeared, enjoyed the occasion and remained for a week after his father left, having requested to be treated as 'our brother in chapter', observing the ritual of daily life in the abbey and taking only the food portions equal to those of others.[23] This is not as unusual as it sounds, for heading off to war for the first time, this act of humility and piety prepared Edward spiritually for what was to come in any martial conflict. Certainly such acts would later stand him in good stead, especially after 1327.

On 4 July 1300, the great host entered Scotland and headed to Galloway to inflict injury on the great Scottish families of Bruce and Balliol, who had substantial land holdings in the region. By mid-July the war machine stopped outside the walls of Caerlaverock Castle, positioned near the shores of the Solway Firth, and when the garrison refused to surrender, bedded down for a siege. The king gave his son command of the rear-guard and an able, experienced war veteran, John de St John, the king's lieutenant and captain of Westmoreland, Cumberland, Lancashire and Annandale, was positioned at his side to help him make his decisions. He was also accompanied by Robert Tony, Henry le Tyes, William Latimer, William de Leyburn, and Roger Mortimer of Chirk. Although not in the rear-guard, Edward had the company of his cousins, Thomas and Henry of Lancaster, and his new brother-in-law, Ralph Monthermer, second husband to Edward's sister Joan de Clare, the widowed Countess of Gloucester.[24] While this command gave Edward a taste of warfare, it was from a position of relative safety. Nevertheless, the herald who composed the Caerlaverock Rolls of Arms described the siege in great detail:

> The fourth squadron with its train, Edward the king's son led. A youth of seventeen years of age, and newly bearing arms. He was well proportioned and a handsome person, of a courteous disposition and well bred, and desirous of finding an occasion to make proof his strength. He managed his steed wonderfully well, and bore with a blue label the arms of the good king his father. Now God give him grace that he be as valiant and no less so; then may fall into his hands those who never expect to do so.[25]

Clearly, Edward made an impression, as did his new coat of arms, only recently awarded to him for the campaign.

The first taste of war proved successful when Caerlaverock Castle fell at the hands of the king's miners and under great bombardment and after much intense fighting. The wider Scottish campaign, however, was hampered by an increasingly common setback. Frustrated by lack of revenues in the latter years of his reign, Edward I had little to pay his infantry, many of whom had not attended through feudal obligation. In the face of unmet promises, most simply deserted. The Scots, after the pitched battle at Falkirk in 1298, knew their chances of success lay in guerrilla tactics and avoided outright confrontation with the English army. By November, both Edward I and his son were back in Carlisle and dined with the queen on the 6th, no doubt with conversation focussed on the king's frustrations, the excitements of Caerlaverock and talk of the little baby Thomas of Brotherton, born six months earlier.

4

Prince of Wales

Edward was high in his father's esteem following the recent Scottish campaign. Since his time spent as regent in 1297, he increasingly found himself taking on royal duties when the need arose. After returning from Scotland, he headed south and, on 12 January, arrived at Ashridge in Buckinghamshire as his father's proxy to attend the solemn interment of the body of Edmund, Earl of Cornwall. The late earl was the youngest son of Richard of Cornwall, Holy Roman Emperor and brother to the late Henry III, who had died in 1272. Edmund died without issue and his earldom, with all its appurtenances, reverted to the crown. By 1301, other than the king himself, the old guard of nobles was almost gone, including Edmund of Lancaster, the king's brother, who had died in June 1296. Following the interment, Edward met his father at Lincoln, where a fractious parliament was underway. The king, ever in need of money to further fund the Scottish war machine, faced confrontation with the nobility and clergy alike, each pressing him to observe the charters, in particular the Charter of the Forest and a promised preamble. In an air of charged conflict, Edward I was forced to concede.[1] Edward must have watched his father at work and learnt from him that even the strongest and most powerful of men could be backed into a political corner. It was an occasion that would have resonance in the next reign.

Despite events, Edward I made a very special gift to his son, now nearly seventeen years old. On 7 February 1301, during the parliament, he granted to Edward both his lands in Wales and the earldom of Chester with all its substantial lands, manors and respective revenues. The grant included all the lands taken from the defeated Welsh princes of Gwynedd back in the early 1280s. The charter gave Edward 'our whole county of Chester, with our manors of Maclesfeld (Macclesfield) and Overton and all our land of Maelor Saesneg, with all their appurtenances to hold wholly and as fully as the king himself has held them'.[2] The earldom of Chester was symbolic, having been given to Edward I by his own father in 1254 prior to his marriage to Eleanor of Castile. The manors had been part of the dower of Eleanor of Castile and so had a personal connection with both the king and his son. Until then, Edward held two other possessions of his mother's, the counties of Ponthieu and Montreuil, which Eleanor herself had inherited from her own mother, the Countess Jeanne.[3]

A second charter followed on 10 May and, crucially, referred to Edward as *Pro Edward filio regis, Principe Wallie et comite Cestrense*; or Prince of Wales and Earl of Chester.[4] This was the first time that an English lord, the eldest surviving son of an English king, had received the title, which had previously belonged solely to the native Welsh rulers of Gwynedd. The style of 'prince' was new in England and not used prior to this date. The sons of kings were titled 'lord' or 'the king's son' and the title of prince was not given to the sons of a king as a matter of course until much later. The title itself was vested in territory and only the holder of the Welsh principality had a right to claim the title of prince in England. Edward III, the future son of Edward of Caernarfon, was never referred to as prince for he was never invested with his father's lands in Wales and thus before 1327, was referred to as 'the Lord Edward' only.

Edward of Caernarfon's new titles gave him extensive Welsh holdings: lands in North Wales, Anglesey, Hope and the Four Cantreds, West Wales, South Wales, namely the counties of Carmarthen and Cardigan, the castles of Haverford and Builth, all lands forfeited by the 1287 rebel Rhys ap Maredudd and any lands held by his father.[5] The charter of 10 May also granted Edward the castle and town of Montgomery, originally excluded from the charter of 7 February as these were then held by Queen Marguerite.[6] However, it appeared that by May, Marguerite had agreed to give these lands to her stepson in exchange for others, no doubt to add a personal honour to the man of whom she had grown fond.

The charters and titles came with due ceremony. Although there are no records for it, it is likely that Edward would have been invested in a solemn, well-attended ceremony, were he would have been girt with the sword of the earldom of Chester. For Wales, it is likely that a circlet of gold was placed on his head, a ring placed on his finger and a silver rod placed in his hand, which followed the style of ceremony recorded in a surviving account in 1343 when the Black Prince, the second English Prince of Wales, was invested by his father in this way 'according to custom'.[7] It is also quite possible that the circlet used was once owned by the defeated Llywelyn ap Gruffydd, and part of the regalia confiscated from the Welsh after Llywelyn's death in 1282. Edward had become a prince.

Eager to establish himself in his new-found position, the prince got straight to work and filled two important posts, Justiciar of Chester and Chamberlain, the former going to William Trussell on 12 April, and the latter to William Melton on 17 April.[8] Melton had been in Edward's service since 1297 and would remain so, in various capacities, until 1326. Edward left court shortly thereafter and headed via Chester into Wales, the first time he had been there since his birth at Caernarfon in April 1284. The next month was busy, for he received the homages of those who now held land from him as their lord and prince, and so Edward chose to sit at Flint, Hope, Ruthin and Rhuddlan, the place of his sister Elizabeth's birth in 1282; and lastly Conwy. No doubt his enthusiasm began to wane as men in their hundreds headed to these towns to bend their knee, place their hands in his and pledge their service, using an established formula. At Flint on 22 April, Edward watched 170 Welshmen bend the knee and say the words. At Conwy, between 28 April and 5 May, the formalities were in progress every day except one, and the total number of tenants received was more than 250.[9] It comes as no surprise that as he celebrated his seventeenth birthday on 25 April, the prince had the day off. Yet before Edward headed back to England, he had achieved something important. For the first time since 1282, the Welsh now had a prince on whom they could focus their service and expect reward in return, and it is no surprise that it is in Wales where Edward would later find some of his strongest supporters, even after 1326.[10]

On 24 May, Edward re-joined his father and Queen Marguerite at Kenilworth Castle in Warwickshire; they had recently returned from a progress around the Severn Valley. His homage gathering was not yet over, for at Kenilworth the English lords, including his cousin Henry of Lancaster, as well as Fulk Fitz Warin and Roger Mortimer of Chirk did homage for their lands held from him in Wales.[11] As the new prince there was no guarantee that Edward would have a fondness for the Welsh, in whose principality he had been born in 1284 and been its liege lord from 1301. In fact, Edward's view of Wales was no different to any other of his contemporaries. He most likely neither loved it nor disliked it. In a letter to Louis, Count of Évreux, brother to the king of France in May 1305, Edward wrote,

> We send you a big trotting palfrey which can hardly carry its own weight, and some of our bandy-legged harriers from Wales, who can well catch a hare if they find it asleep, and some of our running dogs, which go at a gentle pace; for well we know that you take great delight in lazy dogs. And dear cousin, if you want anything else from our land of Wales, we can send you plenty of wild men if you like, who will know well how to teach breeding to the young heirs or heiresses of great lords.[12]

While on the face of it, the letter hardly espouses a great fondness for Wales or the significance of its people, Edward was writing to Louis whom he knew well and with whom he joked freely. It shows Edward's sense of humour and playful nature, and demonstrates the values and views of English contemporaries of the time. Wales, for him, was now a part of his landholdings and power, but not necessarily close to his heart. He was, though, fond of its music and in particular the musical stringed instrument the crwth. In 1305 he sent the aptly named Richard the Rhymer to Shrewsbury Abbey to learn how to play it.[13] He also kept a copy of Welsh poems, which may have been presented to him when receiving the homage of his tenants in the summer, but there is no evidence to suggest that he could read the Celtic language.[14] Edward also relied on Welshmen like Gruffydd Llwyd and Rhys ap Gruffudd, who would go on to feature throughout his reign. They would become steadfastly loyal to the king and it was to them Edward would look as his reign drew to a close at the end of 1326.

With titles and land, Edward's household began to swell. By the close of 1305, it had risen to 140 and included nine knights such as John St John who had stood at his side at Caerlaverock the year before, John Fitz Simon, Robert de Haustede the Younger, and his long-standing friend and master, the Gascon knight, Guy Ferre.[15] Formerly steward to his grandmother, Eleanor of Provence, Guy had worked with Edward since at least 1293 to guide him through his martial apprenticeship, and it is perhaps from Guy that Edward would learn such excellent horsemanship.[16] He was certainly a well-chosen individual, closely linked to the court, a crusader, a knight, a steward – he had also been an executor to the dowager queen's estates after her death. It is for these reasons that he was ordered by Edward I to stay 'continually in the company of Edward the king's son by the king's special order'.[17] Edward appeared very fond of him. In addition to these most senior members, were ten men who were similar in age to Edward and were from noble families or in wardship to the crown, as their fathers were dead and they not yet old enough to inherit their estates, such as Gilbert de Clare, Edward's nephew. Nine had masters assigned to them in the household, but a tenth, the Gascon Piers Gaveston, did not. Gaveston, who excelled in arms and had arrived in England after Edward I's campaign in Flanders, may well have been singled out by his fellow countryman Guy Ferre who appreciated his skills and encouraged him to support Edward as the two grew into adolescence together; they were only a few years apart in age. In addition to these men were fourteen clerks busily administering the prince's household, including Walter Reynolds who, like Gilbert de Clare and Piers Gaveston, was to play a significant role in the coming reign.

Yet despite his recent acquisitions, Edward was not free to do as he wished. While he was now a prince and no longer simply 'the king's son', he still languished in the shadow of his father, and under his watchful eye. He had ultimate control over his son's household, as he did with that of his queen. So much so that in 1305 Edward was forced to write to the Earl of Lincoln, who was preparing to go on a diplomatic mission to France and had requested a member of Edward's household to go with him, to tell him he would require his father's permission before he could grant the request:

> Know, sire, that we have no knight or squire in our household, pleasing to you, who could aid or serve you, whom we would not willingly give you. But to Monsire Miles, we have no power to give leave (of absence) without the order of our lord the king our father, who has commanded and charged him with our household and our business. Wherefore it will be advisable for you to talk with our lord the king on this matter.[18]

Edward I it seemed, and unbeknown to Lincoln until this moment, was still very much the dominating influence in the prince's household and this must have, at times, grated on the young heir to the throne.

5

A Taste of War

War continued to dominate the agenda. Following his sojourn through Wales and after re-joining his father at Kenilworth, it was not long before the army, instructed at the Lincoln parliament to meet for midsummer, was assembled. Royal writs issued in February made clear that Edward was to be given the chance to distinguish himself.[1] This time, therefore, the army was divided into two; the first, under the command of the king, had mustered at Berwick, and the other, under the command of the new Prince of Wales, was waiting for him at Carlisle. Edward was now trusted to lead in his own right. Acting as a pincer, both armies would enter Scotland from east and west and cut off the enemy in order to bring about absolute submission.

Edward's army was substantial; it was mostly made up of men drawn from his new territories of Wales and the March, with his infantry roughly twice the size of his father's.[2] His immediate circle included a mixture of trusted men. Two had formidable experience: Henry de Lacy, Earl of Lincoln, now fifty years old, and Richard Fitz Alan, Earl of Arundel. Three of Edward's circle were much younger and much closer to him in age – his cousin, Thomas, now Earl of Lancaster; Ralph de Monthermer, titular Earl of Gloucester through right of his wife, Edward's sister Joan; and another brother-in-law Humphrey de Bohun, husband of Edward's sister Elizabeth.[3] Humphrey had succeeded his late father in 1298, the recalcitrant Earl of Hereford who had opposed both Edward I and his son during Edward's regency in 1297. As in the year before, those young men who were part of Edward's household also attended the campaign, including Gilbert de Clare, Robert de Scales, Robert de Clavering, William Munchensi and Piers Gaveston.

The war machine was impressive. Amid the clamour of arms, tents, carts and various martial paraphernalia, the company kept magnificent warhorses. Piers Gaveston had a dapple-grey worth twenty marks, but the most striking, and indeed the one valued the highest at £80, belonged to the war veteran Sir Reginald Grey. The hobelars, men who made up the light cavalry or mounted infantry, were paid 6d a day, the squires 1s each.[4]

Shortly after reaching Scotland, Edward's army on the west coast paused at Newcastle-on-Ayr and was bolstered by 650 knights and 1,600 infantry from Ireland, led by the Irish Justiciar John Wogan. This was the first time since 1296 that the king had called on support from the English-held territories centred around Dublin. As the campaign got underway, the castle at Ayr quickly fell. Edward then turned his attention to Turnberry Castle, the birthplace of Robert Bruce – which fell by early September. The prince sent news to his father of his symbolically significant victory, for which the king immediately gave thanks in Glasgow Cathedral.[5] As Edward advanced north to close the pincer with his father, who had achieved limited success moving north from Berwick through Selkirk Forest chasing the ghostly shadows of William Wallace, news arrived that the Scots had outflanked the prince's army and were besieging the castle at Lochmaben. The prince turned his army south to avoid being cut off and subsequently retook it. Edward had quickly demonstrated that his father was right to give him command of half of the army.

However, despite these gains, nothing more came of the campaign. Again restricted by dwindling funds, the king's infantry deserted in their thousands and, by early November, unable to spring the trap and without a Scottish army to fight, Edward initially moved back to Carlisle, where on the 20th a physician was sent to London to collect items to treat him for an ailment. A month later, Edward joined his father at Linlithgow where the royal army bedded down for the winter. The king had had enough. Writs issued in late summer became more visibly irate with the last, written on 16 October, bemoaning his plight: 'But for a lack of money we would have bridged the Forth ... we are sure that we would have done such exploits against our enemies that our business would have reached an honourable and satisfactory conclusion'.[6] It wasn't to be. Enraged by Scottish guerrilla tactics and frustrated by the desertion of his men, the king was determined to hold out in the heartlands of his enemies while he brooded over his next move. The atmosphere at Linlithgow was tense, and made worse for the prince as Piers Gaveston had been taken ill and subsequently sent by the king to Knaresborough in Yorkshire to recover during November and December.[7] The queen joined them for Christmas with her recently delivered second son, Edmund, who was born at Woodstock, which must have helped to lighten the oppressive mood. Edward, who had for so long had no brothers, now had two in as many years.

The drum of war rolled, albeit to a different beat in 1302. Although wintering in Scotland, the remaining remnants of the English army eventually disbanded and the royal family decided to return south. Despite a truce drawn up to last until St Andrew's day, 30 November 1302, preparations again got underway for another campaign to commence in spring 1303. Edward spent most of December 1302 and January 1303 at Sir Roger Pedwaedine's manor at South Warnborough in Hampshire. The stay must have been raucous at times, for not only did Edward lose £32 on dicing to Henry de Beaumont, and make further losses on Christmas Eve to Sir Reginald Grey and William Leyburne, he was obliged to pay a further 20*s* to Sir Roger for damage done to his estates while the prince and his household were in residence.[8] However, during this time Edward did tear himself away from dicing and, as always, reflected at the end of a year on his family, both with him and absent. On 27 November he attended Mass offering prayers in memory of his mother Eleanor of Castile, now twelve years in her triple grave.[9] On 16 December, he visited his sister Mary at the convent at Amesbury and heard Mass for his late grandmother, Eleanor of Provence. Given Mary's taste for gambling, one can only imagine the prince took further opportunity for a game of dice while catching up with his sister. Always generous and enjoying his new status, Edward presented to the queen at New Year a gift of a gold ring with a large ruby set into it.[10] By February he was back at his favourite childhood residence of Langley, which was bequeathed to him in his own right and where he now entertained both the king and queen.

Winter turned to spring and the truce with the Scots lapsed on St Andrew's Day, as negotiated the previous year. In early March Edward headed for London and at Holborn took the time to inspect the work of John of Somerset and his troop of sixty-three tentmakers who had been busily making up twenty-eight tents that included a great hall, two stables, a chapel, a council chamber and a room for the prince to sleep in. They were carefully crafted and embroidered with the leopards of the prince's arms.[11] As well as tents, Edward needed weapons and the armourers of London, including a man named Manekin, supplied three steel bacinets (headpieces), two pairs of jambers (leg armour), and two helmets, one with visor and another without. Edward's personal armourer Hugh de Bungeye used the six ounces of fine and various coloured silks he had purchased to make two quilted aketons (cotton jackets) worn under chain mail for the prince, 'five pairs of gilt spurs, a mail collar or pisan extending over the shoulders and embroidered two gambesons', which were thick cloth jackets worn under a sleeveless coat of mail emblazoned with Edward's coat of arms. As well as new pieces, material was provided to allow for repairs. De Bungeye provided iron thread for repairing damage to chain mail, while William Conrad supplied glue and other items for repairs to weapons like crossbows and longbows at a cost of 13s 6d. Even the essentials were considered, and two leather coffers were made to carry Edward's urinals.[12]

Beyond the immediate paraphernalia of war, Edward concerned himself with his entertainment for the journey ahead. His wardrobe accounts reveal a keen interest, and minstrels, singers and players, whom he kept with him in his household, would no doubt have travelled with him to Scotland too. In early 1303 he purchased an illuminated copy of the life of St Edward the Confessor, his namesake. He ordered that his lion, kept by Adam of Lichfield, should travel with the army while they went north. The lion was given a new collar and chain to mark the occasion, at a cost of 2s 9d; as well as a new cart in which to travel, and it was fed at a cost of 4d per day – twice the daily wage paid to an unskilled labourer. Before he left to meet the army, perhaps the excitement of the forthcoming campaign kept his spirits high for, in February, Edward paid compensation to Robert the Fool for an injury he had sustained while swimming with the prince.[13] Throughout his life Edward would remain a keen and active swimmer, which was remarked on later by his enemies as proof of his unconventional behaviour, as conduct unbefitting a man of his status. Edward ignored his critics.

By the middle of March preparations were complete and the prince left London, arriving at Durham on 14 April. In that same month he made an offering for his late master Guy Ferre who had recently died, and had, since his childhood, probably represented something of a father figure to him. This time the king's advance into Scotland was designed to overwhelm his enemy, even if the Scots would refuse to commit to a pitched battle. Edward I had used 1302 to raise as much revenue as possible, calling in debts in return for arms, while merchants were given extra privileges in return for higher customs designed to fill the royal coffers. The army raised was large and again forces were brought in from all over England and Wales, with a further 3,500 men from Ireland delivered in 173 ships.[14] This time the army was in overall command of the king, who in May crossed the border. Together, Edward and his father pushed north, crossed the Forth and marched past the poorly garrisoned Stirling Castle, perched on its rocky outcrop, whose garrison had in 1297 witnessed the English massacre at Stirling Bridge. Determined to demonstrate their might, the king and his son marched further into the north of Scotland. Their campaign was to be brutal. As a contemporary Peter Langtoff noted: 'Hamlets and towns, granges and barns, both full and empty, he everywhere burns; so does the prince, without sparing anything'.[15] The Irish contingents arrived in August and opened a second front on the south-west, which caused yet further devastation. By the middle of September, the royal army reached its most northerly point on the shores of the Moray Forth. The king laid siege to Lochindorb castle, owned by the only surviving Guardian of Scotland, John Comyn, which fell that October.

By November, the army moved south again to Dunfermline Abbey, symbolically the burial place of Scotland's kings, where it bedded in for winter. The prince moved his men to Perth, remaining there until 7 March 1304. During his winter pause, Edward entertained the earls of Lancaster, Warwick, Ulster, Athol, Strathearn, John of Brittany, Hugh Despenser and others, as well as the delegation sent to treat with the Scots – both on their way to meet the enemy and on their return. Although not with his father, Edward kept in contact via letter and through those travelling between the armies. Nor did he rest idle, for as winter drew to a close, Edward sent out a small contingent of forty men-at-arms under the command of Alexander de Abernethy into Strathern and the surrounding area to follow up on a rumour that William Wallace was still lurking in the vicinity.[16] The king, pleased with his son's efforts, encouraged him to send more men to aid in the search. Whether Edward did or not is unknown but either way, Wallace remained at large for at least another year.

While no pitched battle had been given during the latest campaign, such a show of English strength eventually weakened Scottish resolve and, on 2 February, the king wrote to his son giving him permission to receive any Scots who wished to give up the fight and submit to the king's will. By 9 February it was all over and the exhausted and overwhelmed Scots, led by the Guardian John Comyn, surrendered. Over the coming two months, one by one the Scottish lords bent the knee and swore allegiance to the English king. The fight, for now at least, was won.

However, the king was determined to give one more show of English strength to drive the point home. With the Scottish lords resigned to Edward I's overlordship, the king moved to Stirling Castle, which still stubbornly held out. He ordered that his son strip the local buildings and churches in Perth and Dunblane of their lead, except immediately above the altars, so that the metal could be melted down and used as counterweights to the large trebuchets, which were now ordered into position.[17] After a battery of missiles lasting twelve weeks, the garrison finally surrendered. Yet Edward I was in no mood to return home; during the last two months he had invested fifty men and considerable expense in building a giant trebuchet, aptly named Warwolf. The king was not about to waste his investment. He himself had come perilously close to losing his life when riding too close to the walls; he had been targeted and struck by a crossbow bolt, which embedded into his armour. It did little to improve his mood and now he wanted revenge. Despite their surrender, the defeated garrison were told to sit it out in the castle while the king tried out his new war machine. After a bombardment, the king was eventually satisfied and the garrison were allowed to leave in procession, barefoot, and with ashes on their heads, as custom dictated.[18]

The closing of the Scottish war in the summer of 1304 marked what would prove to be a haitus in what had so far been a long campaign. The Prince of Wales had gained a real and relatively successful taste of war. Through the three summers, he had demonstrated that he was both capable and willing to fight the enemy. While there was no great battle, or ballad sung to mark the occasion, he had supported his father's efforts, hampered by a lack of income and the subsequent desertion of troops, to achieve enough to make him no less successful in war than his father had been in his Scottish efforts at this juncture.

As war in Scotland dominated the agenda, news arrived as Edward had crossed the border north with his father, that on 20 May at Paris, a further treaty was finally agreed between England and France, which brought all hostilities over Gascony to an end. Following on from the Treaty of Montreuil in 1299, the proposal that Edward should marry the daughter of Philip IV of France was now formalised. As a result, four English envoys – the Bishop of Winchester, Henry de Lacy Earl of Lincoln, Amadeus the Count of Savoy and Otto de Grandison – agreed to the formal betrothal on Edward's behalf. On 12 June 1303, after final assent was given by the king and his son, the Bishop of Winchester and the Earl of Lincoln stood proxy and affianced Edward and Isabella by placing their hands in those of Giles, Archbishop of Narbonne.[19] The betrothal ceremony was complete. Edward was to marry Isabella of France when she would come of age and the fateful course of history was set.

6

Knighthood

By the close of 1304, Edward had proven himself capable in military arms, as a commander at the head of an army, as a lord, Prince of Wales and heir to his father's throne. His relationship with his family remained close and genial, and since the marriage of his father to his second wife, Marguerite of France, the Prince of Wales had secured not only a stepmother, but also a friend and supporter. As a new year dawned, and the royal family kept Christmas at Lincoln, the future seemed set fair for the Prince.

Parliament had been summoned to meet at Westminster for the first Sunday in Lent and Edward set up his household in Kennington, at his father's expense.[1] During parliament, Edward, with his clerks, received and worked through the petitions from Wales accumulated since 1301, arranging for responses to be given or further enquiries to be sought. For his tenants in Wales, as the head of their principality it was his judgement they now needed to find in their favour. As the parliamentary session drew to a close, Edward returned to Langley, then on Trinity Sunday, 13 June, left to meet his father at Midhurst in Sussex. It was at this moment, as if from nowhere, that peace within the royal family was shattered.

From a surviving letter written by Edward to the Earl of Lincoln, the prince made clear that on the day after his arrival at Midhurst on 14 June, 'on account of all that was told him of what had transpired between us and the bishop...(his father) is so angry with us that he has forbidden us and our people, however bold we might be, to come into his household, and has forbidden all the officials of the Exchequer to give or loan us necessary sustenance for our own household.'[2] There was a royal falling out, and Edward, it appeared, was at the heart of it. He was to be stripped of his household boon companions including Gilbert de Clare, Piers Gaveston, and others. The reason for this sudden rupture in the filial relationship was apparently the prince's behaviour; it was alleged he had insulted one of his father's principal ministers, the treasurer Walter

Langton, Bishop of Coventry and Lichfield. After breaking into one of his woods, Langton had challenged the prince – only to be met with a barrage of insulting language, which he subsequently reported to Edward I. The king, never tolerant of criticism of any of his ministers, reacted in his ever-increasing irascible way and publicly supported Langton.

The king's reaction, on the face of it, feels a little extreme, so it is likely that behind this event are a number of issues that had built up, leading to the final outburst. Edward still relied heavily on the Exchequer for financial support, as his incomes from Wales, Chester and Ponthieu were not sufficient to cover his household expenses, which had increased over recent years due to the campaigns in Scotland. On 4 May 1304, John Droxford, the keeper of the wardrobe, wrote to Richard de Bremesgrave, that the prince was 'much annoyed' at Richard's refusal to deliver wine for the use of his household and at other acts 'done against him since he came to Scotland'.[3] It may well be that the relationship between the prince and Langton had been becoming increasingly strained before June 1305, and the final heated exchange between them was the last act in a much wider play. Langton, who may have criticised the prince for any perceived excesses as Edward's financial demands mounted at a time when the king was short of money, ended any measure of cordiality between the two men once Langton had approached the king.

The king was only too aware of his own financial vulnerability and had over recent years relied heavily on Langton's advice in administrative and diplomatic affairs, as well as more general policy. When Langton had been openly criticised at the Lincoln parliament in 1301, which sought his dismissal, the king dug in and refused it outright. Only a year prior to this exchange at Lincoln, Langton had been challenged as rumours circulated of misappropriated funds when he was keeper of the wardrobe, to which the king was forced to respond with a detailed audit of the bishop's accounts.[4] By 1305, with the king's reliance on Langton greater than ever, any criticism of the bishop from members of his own family, let alone his heir, was too close for comfort. Queen Marguerite herself described Langton in the closing years of the Edward I's reign as 'the king's right eye'.[5] Edward I's very public upbraiding of his son sent out a very clear message to any further would-be challengers of the bishop. For now, at least, Langton was untouchable.

The prince, however, was not. Cut off from the Exchequer, Edward was faced with the immediate dilemma of how to pay for his household expenses. Without financial assistance, he was soon to discover who his friends really were. The prince wrote to his treasurer of the wardrobe, Walter Reynolds, instructing him to find means to quickly provide him with money but on no account to make Langton or the Exchequer aware of his activities. Reynolds began his work and soon enough Edward received an offer of 100 marks from Henry Blunsdon, half of which was in the form of a debt from the executors of Richard of Gravesend.[6] It was enough to pay for a week's expenses, but others offered aid as well, perhaps without being asked as they themselves were only too accustomed to the king's bad temper. Sometime in mid-July, Edward received the seal and the use of property belonging to his sister Joan, Countess of Gloucester, allowing him to raise funds for the immediate future. On 21 July, just over a month since the rift began, Edward returned it to her via Ingelard of Warley, enclosed under his own seal, with a message stating that Joan had been misinformed as to the king's present attitude, for he was now allowed 'a sufficiency of necessaries', followed by royal letters issued by the king to his sheriffs allowing them to provide the prince with what he required.[7] The king's attitude was softening, but publicly Edward I and his son remained aggrieved. Edward was still not permitted into the king's presence and it seems from 14 June until early August, when the prince lodged at Windsor Park obeying his father's instruction, he began to follow daily in the shadow of his father's court, but keeping a distance of a few miles. The public discord continued.

On 23 August 1305, at Smithfield, William Wallace, that robust and enigmatic Scottish rebel, found his luck had run out. Betrayed by his own people and captured near Glasgow by John of Menteith's men, who was rewarded with land worth £100, Wallace was turned over to the king. Following a trial in Westminster Hall, he was strung up and executed. He was dragged from Westminster through the streets to London, then hanged until near dead, disembowelled, his entrails burnt; his head eventually cut off and set on London Bridge. His limbs were sent to Newcastle, Berwick, Stirling and Perth as a warning to others.[8] It may well be that through August, as Wallace's bloody execution became imminent, the king, about to subdue a longstanding personal enemy, found his spirits lifting.

As Wallace mounted the gallows, the king's attitude to his son softened further and two of his household valets were returned to him, John of Haustede and John of Weston. Writing to his sister Elizabeth, Countess of Hereford, Edward implored her to speak to the queen, who was best placed to gauge the mood of the king, and intercede for him so they could bring about the return of Gilbert de Clare and Piers Gaveston, as this would go far in relieving 'the anguish which we have endured, and still suffer daily, through the ordinance and pleasure of our lord the king'.[9] Edward continued to adopt a wise and cautious strategy. He was determined to demonstrate exemplary behaviour to his father, who had instructed him to remain at Windsor. Edward turned down invitations to visit his sister Joan, and later Mary, in September; he explained he might be needed at any time in the Westminster parliament. Despite his earlier summons, the prince's attendance was not required and he was still kept publicly at arm's-length by the king.

The need to find a resolution was becoming more pressing. The king could not go on for much longer with such a public display before it would become damaging. While his father had not made the prince's life too uncomfortable, and no doubt remained affectionate albeit aloof to him, the final public reconciliation came rather quietly on 12 October, when the prince arrived at Westminster, and the following day presided over a banquet representing his father, although he did not sit in the high seat.[10] Peace in the royal family had been restored, at least for the moment.

As the quarrel came to a close, thoughts again turned to Scotland. On a cold night, on 10 February 1306, at the Church of the Greyfriars at Dumfries, Robert Bruce, 8th Earl of Carrick, murdered one of the most powerful nobles in Scotland, his rival John Comyn, Lord of Badenoch. Six weeks later at Scone, the Bruce had himself crowned King of the Scots albeit without placing his feet firmly on that famous relic, the Stone of Destiny – now in England and fixed into the newly commissioned coronation chair. The recent peace in Scotland following the execution of William Wallace was abruptly ended and Edward I's grip on that kingdom was now yet again directly under threat. As writs went out on 20 February, forbidding tournaments and ordering a muster of arms at Carlisle for 8 July, the king fell ill at Winchester as his long-term health began to decline. In an early writ, Edward I made it clear that he intended to 'be with our army in person if God permits'. But God did not permit, at least initially, and as his health deteriorated further, the king issued subsequent instructions on 17 April to English officials supplying victuals from Ireland, proposing to send his son Edward to Scotland with a great company of men. Later, on 25 April, he declared that he would follow his son after the campaign had begun.[11] In the end, the king began to recover, but he left Winchester after an extended stay of two months, not on horseback, but instead in a litter, in early May.[12] The leopard was now not only once more on the road to war but also to his eventual demise.

In April, now bereft of the old guard following the death of his closest nobles, only the veteran Henry de Lacy was left with the increasingly ill Roger Bigod, Earl of Norfolk; the king knew the time had come for the next generation to lead and complete the Scottish conquest. He sent the young Aymer de Valence to counterattack Bruce's advance and announced at Whitsun that his son was to be 'adorned with the belt of knighthood'.[13] The sheriffs of England were ordered to proclaim that anyone whose father was a knight and who was able and wished to become a knight themselves, should head to London to receive both the necessary equipment from the king's wardrobe and the knighthood itself.[14] In all, up to 300 men responded to the summons and arrived in the capital, already bustling with vast numbers of people who were there with their retinues to attend the forthcoming parliament.

A month before the knighting ceremony, the king prepared his son and on 7 April granted him the Plantagenet 'duchy of Aquitaine, the island of Oléron and the Agenais'.[15] For Edward, not only did this increase his status, allowing him to reduce his reliance on the Exchequer, which had hindered him the previous year, it rather more importantly elevated his status for his forthcoming marriage to Isabella of France. For the king, this gift also resolved the delicate question of homage, for now this burden passed to his son, a duty he could perform without the symbolic and political difficulties presented to the king of England when he knelt in front of Philip IV of France. In later life, this difficult position would also dog Edward II as he reigned during the rule of five different French kings, each requiring homage for the same lands.

When the time for the knighting ceremony finally arrived on 22 May, it was full of chivalric symbolism, pomp and pageantry. The night before the event, the prospective knights were expected to attend an all-night vigil by their arms, in silent prayer. With such a number, the group was divided – the majority heading to Temple Church, just outside the walls of the city of London, where fruit trees had been cut down and walls demolished to make way for an array of brightly coloured tents and pavilions.[16] Those of higher rank were afforded the company of the prince, who was holding his vigil in Westminster Abbey. For the monks, who observed the rule of St Benedict governed by silence and solemn prayer save only for chanting their offices, they found their sanctuary and indeed their sacred rules breached by the heady young men talking, shouting and making trumpet volleys to such an extent that they could barely perform their offices at the respective hours. As dawn broke, Edward headed to the chapel of St Stephen, in the Palace of Westminster, where he was knighted, girded with the sword belt by his father and received his spurs from Henry de Lacy, and Humphrey de Bohun, Constable of England.[17] Now a knight, Edward headed with the party to the abbey, to personally dub the remaining men. The crowds were so numerous, great warhorses were ridden through the throng, up the nave, to clear a passage to the high altar.[18] The ceremony itself was marred when two knights were crushed to death by the weight of the crowd.

Edward knighted many men that day who were to play critical roles during his own reign. He dubbed Hugh Despenser the Younger, who had only days earlier married Eleanor, niece to the prince and sister to Gilbert de Clare, heir to the earldom of Gloucester.[19] His father Hugh Despenser the Elder, who was present at the ceremony, was a trusted baronial advisor to the king and who himself was to serve Edward II with exceptional loyalty throughout his reign. Gilbert de Clare was knighted, along with Humphrey de Bohun, the Earl of Hereford, and Edmund Fitz Alan, the young Earl of Arundel who would remain loyal to Edward right up until his capture in 1326, among others. At the same ceremony, others who would present a challenge in the subsequent reign were also knighted. Most notably Roger Mortimer of Wigmore; John Maltravers, who was one of the men responsible for holding Edward captive at Berkeley Castle in 1327; and William Trussell, who was to give Edward news at Kenilworth Castle in January 1327 that his subjects had withdrawn their allegiance to him.[20] Edward I no doubt hoped that the ceremony at Whitsun that year would bind men to both the Scottish cause and also to his son, and in many ways this was true. It was unfortunate that as Edward II's reign was shortly to get underway that sooner rather than later, some of these relationships were to be quickly tested. Four days after the ceremony in the abbey, on Thursday 26 May, Edward knighted Piers Gaveston.

The banquet that followed was sumptuous. The music that rang out across the hall was played and sung by eighty minstrels provided by the households of the king, queen, the prince and nobles across the country. Ceremonial oaths were taken to solemnise the occasion. The king took his oath over two goldcast swans, proclaiming that he would avenge the injuries committed by the Bruce to God and the Church and not raise his sword again, save only in the cause preached by the new pope Clement V to recapture the Holy Land. Edward, following his father's lead, announced that he would not sleep two nights in any one place until he had reached Scotland to help his father defeat Bruce.[21] This banquet became known as the Feast of the Swans. It is quite possible that many more oaths were taken that night, but they remain unrecorded or do not survive.

The whole event had served its purpose well. The almost 300 newly made knights, or 'tiroes' as they were called by the Westminster chronicler, drunk with the glories of the knightly code, clamoured to join the Scottish campaign.[22] Preparations were finalised, including a valuation of the war equipment. Among the list was a black charger with three white feet valued at £60, which was a personal gift from Edward to his friend Piers Gaveston.[23] After a brief visit to his stepmother at Winchester on 8 June, Edward set out north and reached the assembled army at Carlisle. His arrival bolstered the forces under the command of Aymer de Valence who had, a month earlier, met and routed Bruce in battle at Methven near Perth.[24] Bruce escaped and after a skirmish with Comyn supporters, fled west while sending his wife and sister north, under the protection of his brother Neil, with the hope that they would reach Orkney.

Earlier in the spring, the king had awarded the confiscated castle of Lochmaben, one of Bruce's strongholds, to his son-in-law Humphrey de Bohun and the king's daughter Elizabeth.[25] As Elizabeth's brother the Prince of Wales entered Scotland, he headed to Lochmaben with Humphrey to secure its possession, and received its surrender on the day they arrived, 11 July. By 1 August, Edward reached Perth and quickly moved on in hot pursuit of the Bruce's family, arriving at the siege of Kildrummy Castle, which fell before 13 September. Neil Bruce, who was shored up behind its walls, was captured with Isabella, Countess of Buchan, and Mary Bruce, Robert's sister.

This time the war was to be more brutal than ever before. In the king's mind, Bruce and his supporters were now legitimately seen as traitors and, as such, 'the king and council order that all present at the death of Sir John Comyn, or of counsel and assent thereto, shall be hanged or their heads cut off'.[26] This was to be a bloody war, and noble birth was not sufficient to save Bruce's supporters from the full penalty of the king's justice. Edward I was in no mood for clemency, and Aymer de Valence and the prince were happy to oblige him. So much so that in March 1307, the king was forced to write to Valence reminding him to spare the poor from harsh punishment.[27] War on the populace was not to be as exacting as Valence was meting out. Edward, though, while he was no doubt brutal too, did demonstrate clemency on various occasions and wrote to Valence on 1 August thanking him for giving protection to the abbot and convent of Coupar Angus. He also asked the soon-to-be Earl of Pembroke not to damage the crops and other goods.

Despite these small concessions, the king himself was in no mood to spare those who had directly opposed him and viciously levied his Plantagenet anger against the Bruce's family. Neil Bruce, captured at Kildrummy, was promptly sent by the Prince of Wales to the king, who dispatched him to Berwick, where he was hanged, drawn and beheaded. A further two Bruce brothers, Thomas and Alexander, were captured at Galloway on 17 February 1307 and were executed soon after at Carlisle.[28] The women captured at Kildrummy, while spared their lives, were nevertheless made examples of. The Countess of Buchan and Mary Bruce were held in specially designed cages, providing extra security, and kept inside rooms at Roxburgh and Berwick. (These cages were not positioned over the walls out in the poor weather, as suggested in recent years.) The bishops of Glasgow and St Andrews were sent south in chains, and locked away in castle prisons.[29]

By the close of September, Scotland was again under English control and the Bruce, it seemed, had fled further west than the Mull of Kintyre, mostly likely to the small island of Rathlin, off the Antrim coast of Ireland. There was not much to do other than to hunker down for the winter, which the king did at Lanercost Priory from 29 September. Edward left Scotland on 20 November and travelled to Langley, then on to Canterbury and Dover, finally resting for Christmas at Northampton, visiting his baby half-brothers Thomas and Edmund.[30]

During this time, twenty-two of Edward's companions, notably Humphrey de Bohun, Roger Mortimer of Wigmore, Gilbert de Clare and Piers Gaveston, left Scotland without royal leave to travel to a tournament overseas, almost certainly in France. The king, in his anger, sent out orders to sheriffs in twenty-four counties for their arrest and the subsequent confiscation of their property. The knights, fearful to approach the king on their return in January 1307, instead headed to Edward at Wetheral Priory near Carlisle to seek his help. The prince did what he had always done in moments like this, and sought the intervention of his stepmother, with her persuasive talent for queenly intercession, which resulted in the king issuing his pardon on 23 January to sixteen of the offenders, before parliament opened two days later at Carlisle.[31] Something of a scandal was avoided, but within a month, a greater drama was to unfold in the bedchamber of the king.

7

An Errant Son

'You base-born whoreson! Do you want to give away lands now, you who never gained any? As the Lord lives, if it were not for fear of breaking up the kingdom, you should never enjoy your inheritance.'[1] These are the colourful words reported by the chronicler Walter of Guisborough. As this fearsome attack was made, the king, so the story goes, consumed with apoplectic rage, lashed out, tearing handfuls of hair from the prince's head, only to fall back into his chair exhausted. Convinced that his apparently profligate son was about to despoil the realm, the king called his magnates to him and there they agreed to banish the prince's friend Piers Gaveston from England.

It would be all too easy to run away with this colourful scene of an ill and ailing king striking out at his wilful young son, marked down for posterity by a dramatic verbatim account. However, not all contemporary records are quite so dramatic, nor agree on the details. Yet what remains true is that on 26 February 1307, the king made his son and Piers Gaveston swear solemn oaths at the Priory of Lanercost upon the Holy Sacrament, on the *Y Groes Naid*, fragments of the True Cross confiscated from the Welsh in 1283, and other relics in the king's possession.[2] Gaveston pledged to leave England from Dover at the end of April, three weeks after an upcoming tournament, to head to Gascony via Wissant, and not to return to England without the king's express licence. The prince, sharing Gaveston's distress, swore not to receive Piers or keep him by his side, unless he was recalled by the king alone. The king for his part, promised to provide Gaveston with a pension of 100 marks, £66 13*s* 4*d*, to cover his expenses overseas once he arrived partway on his journey at Wissant. While outside the realm, the king would enquire into Gaveston's estate and, depending upon what he found, 'would either increase or decrease it according to his pleasure'.[3]

So what had brought about this quarrel between the king, his son and Gaveston? In a word, advancement. The bones of the matter are clear. By

February 1307 Edward felt that his close friend, who, if the chronicler of Lanercost is to be believed, had long since started calling him his brother, deserved an endowment of the type that was beyond his position to grant. With a difficult path to tread to achieve his burning desire, the prince threw down the gauntlet and either in person or through Walter Langton, suggested to his father that Gaveston be given the vacant, and extensive, earldom of Cornwall with all its appurtenances.[4]

Gaveston was well known to the king who thought well enough of him as a suitable role model, incredibly able and full of the necessary martial skill, to place him in his son's household from around 1300. There he had most likely come to the attention of his fellow countryman, Guy Ferre, Edward's teacher of military arts, which would only have further recommended him to the king's son. Edward I would have watched Gaveston grow both in capability and position but also in the affection of the prince and those around him. After all, Piers Gaveston and Gilbert de Clare were both removed from Edward during his earlier quarrel with his father back in 1305, knowing full well that their exclusion would strike at his son, allowing the king to drive his point home over the prince's disagreement with his treasurer Walter Langton. Only a month before this dramatic incident, Gaveston had received a pardon from the king, with fifteen fellow knights, for absconding to France to tourney in the lists. He appeared, until February 1307, to be, at least in the main, in the king's affection.

For Edward I, the suggestion of a grant of this size and importance was beyond what was reasonable for two simple reasons. Firstly, he intended to give the earldom to one of his remaining sons, Thomas or Edmund; and secondly, Cornwall was then, as it is today, associated with the more senior members of the royal family. Gaveston, while of Gascon noble stock, was nevertheless far short of the necessary credentials to qualify for such an award.[5] It has been argued for many years that Edward's request was, in fact, to grant Gaveston the county of Ponthieu in northern France, as noted by Guisborough; however, Cornwall, and not Ponthieu, was the likely prize. The earldom of Cornwall was vacant following the death of Edmund, whose interment the Prince of Wales had attended on behalf of his father back in 1301. Ponthieu was already in the prince's possession; it was his inheritance, bequeathed directly by his mother, and his oldest title. It was already marked out as a potential dowry for his future wife, Isabella of France. The finer details of the pending marriage were at this very moment being formally ironed out, therefore Ponthieu needed to be available to the English royal negotiators.[6]

For Edward, achieving this grant for Gaveston posed a new problem, as he could not use his usual approach to influence his father through the intercession of his stepmother Queen Marguerite, used so successfully and as recently as the previous month. He knew all too well that his father intended to grant the earldom to one of her two sons so, therefore, the queen was not able or willing to help. For Edward, with the absence of his best diplomatic negotiator, either he or Langton would have to suffice. On the face of it, Walter Langton seems an unlikely choice to procure something of such importance for Edward, given their clash two years earlier. However, the treasurer was close to the king, as Edward I had demonstrated on many occasions; he had his ear and confidence, as the prince knew only too well to his previous disadvantage. Yet it must have been increasingly apparent to the court that the king's health was rapidly deteriorating and Edward would have only a short time to wait before he would come into his greater inheritance. What better way for him to test the future loyalty of a man with whom he had previously clashed? In Edward's mind, with the inability to call upon the queen, this was the perfect opportunity for Langton to redeem himself and prove his worth to his future master. Whatever the truth of it, whether Langton was set this impossible task or not, or whether Edward asked his father himself, what is certain is that it failed spectacularly.

As long as the king lived, Edward was not going to be able to achieve his goal. Understanding the king's frustration with his own failing health, we can understand him lambasting his son and subsequently banishing Gaveston. The Annalist of St Paul's noted that 'the Prince of Wales had an inordinate affection for a certain Gascon knight'.[7] While this affection was not the reason for the king's reaction, the inappropriate request for major land grants had become too much for the ailing king, resulting in him acting publicly. In all likelihood, on this occasion the king was not targeting his anger directly at Gaveston but again, as in 1305, his growing intolerance was fixed firmly on his son.[8] The two-month window for when Piers was to exit England showed there was no immediate urgency set down for the start of his exile. It was, after all, organised around a tournament, which took place a few weeks after the oaths were taken. Had Piers been the main culprit in this latest quarrel, his departure would have been far swifter.

When the time came to leave, Edward accompanied Gaveston and his party to his waiting ship at Dover. On 24 April, the day before Edward's twenty-third birthday, they were still in London; one week later they passed through Badlesmere in Kent, and were at Canterbury on 2 May. By the 5th the party had arrived at Dover, a week later than Gaveston had promised in his oath; their slow progress no doubt indicative of their mood, made worse by recent news that one of Edward's sisters, the Countess of Gloucester, had died.[9]

Before Gaveston's departure, Edward lavished him and his small retinue with gifts. To Gaveston, the prince gave two quilted buckram tunics, sindon and silk, as well as four green and four yellow tapestries. Four more were given, coloured green and decorated with red rosettes. He also gave Piers thirteen swans and twenty-two herons.[10] William de Anne and Henry de Guildford, both yeoman in Piers' retinue, were given money, £2 6s 8d, while the sum of £13 6s was distributed to the rest of the party.[11] Two minstrels, attempting to lift the dour mood, who had played for them during their slow journey to Dover, were gifted 6s 8d. Gaveston had been able to retain some of his household men, including William and Henry plus five more yeomen, a chamberlain to run his household in exile, two knights for protection, two falconers and four lesser servants. At the last minute, as Gaveston was boarding the ship, Edward felt that this was not sufficient and gave Gaveston one of his yeomen, John de Baldwin, who received a gift of 20s from his master, as well as a further six grooms.[12]

On or just after 5 May, Edward stood on the white chalk cliffs and watched as Gaveston and his party set sail into exile. Breaking his oath to travel to Gascony via Wissant, on the prince's order, Gaveston headed instead to Crécy in Ponthieu to wait. With the king ailing fast, it was only too apparent that his stay in exile was not likely to last long and so open defiance of their enforced oath at Carlisle was a direct challenge to the king, but a relatively safe one. Had they not thought the king likely to die soon, it was more reasonable for Gaveston to have headed, as agreed, to Gascony. They must have calculated the risk. Gaveston lingered in Ponthieu, Edward sending further gifts; this time two outfits for the tournaments that Piers was scheduled to fight in through the late spring. The first was green velvet with pearls, gold and silver piping, embroidery bearing Gaveston's coat of arms; the other was also green and equally impressive. Five horses were sent, with the huge sum of £260 for Gaveston's expenses, and promptly put to good use.[13] Edward was characteristically demonstrating his generosity to those to whom he was fiercely loyal – Gaveston most of all. Piers did not sit idle. Between tournaments, he had the time to host a visit from Anthony Bek, Bishop of Durham and Patriarch of Jerusalem, so clearly those at the English court felt that despite his oath to the king some months earlier, he was not yet a pariah.

Edward, left behind without his closest friend, headed to Langley in mid-May and moved about south-east England for the following month, visiting Lambeth on 8 June. By the 16th he had moved north to Northampton to begin, at some stage and in no apparent rush, the ten-day march to Carlisle to re-join his father who had ordered the army to assemble for July for another season of campaigning in Scotland. The king was now dangerously ill but more determined than ever to finish the work he had started by bringing Bruce to heel. Bruce had spent his time at Rathlin regrouping, and with Edward's policy of brutal subjugation in force, many Scottish nobles who once would have turned themselves over the king, now feared his retribution.[14] Disgusted by the execution of the Bruce brothers and the treatment of the Countess of Buchan and others, the self-proclaimed King of Scots found men flocking to his banner. The murderer of John Comyn now looked like the safer bet and, with growing confidence, Bruce broke the illusion of English invincibility by defeating Aymer de Valence at the Battle of Loudon Hill, 2 miles east of Kilmarnock, on 10 May. Days later, the Earl of Gloucester was routed, and both Gloucester and Valence walled themselves up at Ayr castle. The English, despite their overall position of strength, were now, in the immediate term, on the defensive.[15]

The king could wait no longer and moved his half-assembled army north. The leopard, dogged by dysentery, was forced to slow his pace – managing only a few miles travel each day.[16] In early July, rumours began to circulate around the camp, after the king spent days in his tent, that he was already dead. On hearing it, Edward I was determined to prove he was still very much among the living. Forcing himself up out of his bed, at the head of the army he marched north on the 3rd and 4th, only to rest on the 5th. By the 6th he limped into Burgh-by-Sands, just short of the Scottish border and in sight of that troublesome kingdom that had, for more than fifteen years, occupied his foreign policy. However, on the following day, the feast of the Translation of St Thomas of Canterbury, while being lifted up in his bed to take food, the sixty-eight-year-old king fell back dead in the arms of his attendants.[17] The old leopard, exhausted at last, was finally at peace. His son was now king.

PART TWO

Love and Betrayal

*But I am certain the king grieved for Piers … for the greater the love,
the greater the sorrow. In the lament of David upon Jonathan, love is
depicted which is said to have surpassed the love of women. Our king
also spoke thus.*

Vita Edwardi Secundi

8

The King's Favour

The day after the death of Edward I, news was urgently dispatched south to the prince, Queen Marguerite and that stalwart friend of the late king, the Earl of Lincoln. Edward was at Lambeth Palace on 8 and 10 July and possibly back at Westminster on the 11th when riders rode in with the news, which most heirs to the throne must desire to hear in their lifetime. There is no account that records Edward's reaction, but there was a sudden rush of activity as he set out that day for Carlisle, which he reached seven days later. The next day, 19 July, the new king made the short journey to Burgh-by-Sands to view his father's body, no doubt making sure that the old man had indeed perished as well as mourning his passing.[1] Edward learned, as he entered the royal camp, that news of the late king's death had been kept a secret and anyone caught spreading malicious gossip had been imprisoned.[2] The fear of emboldening the Scots, with the now immobilised English army sat idle at the border, was clearly a real one. The next day, on the festival of St Margaret, Virgin and Martyr, the shroud of mystery was lifted and Edward, back at Carlisle Castle, was publicly proclaimed King of England and Lord of Ireland. Anthony Bek, Bishop of Durham, and Henry de Lacy, Earl of Lincoln, and the other barons present, all bent the knee and swore homage and fealty to their new king. News heralding this shift in power travelled out across the country, reaching London on the 25th. The new reign had begun.

The next week saw Edward gain control over the machine of royal government. Two days after the proclamation, he issued his first official document using the privy seal 'which we used before we undertook the government of the kingdom'.[3] By the 29th, Edward wrote to his late father's chancellor, Robert Baldock in London, urging him to send the great seal, essential for authenticating legal documents. On 2 August the chancellor responded by sending north two of his own clerks, Richard of Loughborough and John de Munden, and a chancery clerk, Hugh de Burgh.[4]

The new king was more determined than ever to deliver on his earlier enterprise, first mooted at the start of the year. With his father now dead, he could finally grant Piers Gaveston the very endowment that had brought about his exile. The seal arrived at Dumfries, where the king was receiving the homages of those few Scottish lords who had not turned their allegiance over to Bruce. Edward immediately sent it to a local Scottish goldsmith who altered it, adding on the majesty side two castles in the field, reminiscent of his Castilian ancestry. It is poignant to think that these additions were a nod to his long-deceased mother, Eleanor of Castile, who was clearly still close to him in his thoughts.

With the tools in place and his father no longer there to object, Edward issued a beautifully decorated charter dated 6 August, which his clerk Thomas de Newhay had drawn up, endowing the absent Piers Gaveston, his friend since 1300, with the earldom of Cornwall with all its appurtenances.[5] The charter was, rather significantly, witnessed by seven earls including Lincoln, Lancaster, Hereford, Arundel, Richmond, Pembroke and Surrey.[6] Unusually, no one below the rank of earl was included in the witness list – indicating Edward's cleverly designed piece of theatre. He wanted to be certain that the higher nobility now agreed to Gaveston's return and, more importantly, to his elevation to the rank of earl. The chronicler writing the *Vita Edwardi Secundi* noted that the Earl of Lincoln himself confirmed that the earldom had been given on two separate occasions to men not of the blood royal and thus Edward's wishes were supported by precedents.[7] The oaths the earls had made with the late king, on or before 26 February at Lanercost, were now effectively dissolved. But not everyone fell for Edward's theatre. The Earl of Warwick is conspicuously absent from the witness list and this is most likely the first indication of Warwick's opposition to Gaveston, which was to grow rapidly over the coming months.[8] Three further documents relating to the grant were issued, all four authenticated with Edward II's new great seal. They were the only documents at this time to be so sealed.

At the moment of his accession, Gaveston had been uppermost in Edward's mind. On the day he had heard of his father's death in London, on the 11th, he dispatched letters to Ponthieu recalling him. It was his first act as king. Gaveston equally responded with breakneck speed and was back in England sometime around early August, briefly staying at the London home of Walter Reynolds, collecting letters that had been sent to him there on 19 July. On 13 August, Edward made payment of 10*d* to one of Gaveston's yeomen, Robert de Rufford, who had been injured on the return journey from Ponthieu, suggesting that the party had returned certainly no later than this date and probably days earlier.[9] Gaveston headed north while the king prepared to ceremoniously invest him with his new earldom. Geoffrey of Nottingham was ordered to supply Piers with lengths of green and indigo silk to make his new coat of arms and was paid for his efforts on 12 August at Dumfries.[10] It was all done by the 17th when Gaveston, now reunited with the new king, held a lavish feast at Sanquhar, attended by the earls of Lincoln, Hereford and Lancaster; the latter paying one of his minstrels to entertain them.[11] After months of separation, their reunion must have been joyous.

Gaveston's elevation was considerable. Cornwall was one of the most lucrative earldoms in the kingdom, with an annual income of approximately £4,000 and its boundaries were far more extensive than the geographical county. The tin mines in this area, which had seen a significant upturn in production since 1305, created considerable wealth. The earldom also included lands across England. Gaveston received the honours of Wallingford and St Valery in the Thames Valley, and lands in Oxfordshire, Surrey, Wiltshire, Northamptonshire, the town of Chichester in Essex, and Old Shoreham in Sussex. The honour of Berkhamsted was excluded from the original grant as it was in possession of the dowager queen, as Marguerite now became after the death of her husband, forming part of her dower lands. Also excluded were Eye, Fordington and Bradninch, which were still held by the late earl's widow, Edward's second cousin by marriage. In the Midlands and the north, the earldom included the western half of Lincolnshire, as well as specifically Boroughbridge and Aldborough.[12] In order to best administer his new estates, Gaveston retained many of the men previously employed by the crown and set up his central administration at Wallingford.[13] Overnight he had become one of the premier earls in England.

At the end of August, Edward announced that he no longer intended to continue the Scottish campaign that year and began to withdraw, leaving Aymer de Valence briefly as Keeper of Scotland until he was replaced by the Earl of Richmond on 13 September.[14] While it would have been difficult to continue the campaign, the choice not to over-winter the army was partly financial. The state of the country's finances was toxic, worn down by nearly ten years of Scottish campaigning and a good dose of corruption. As well as inheriting a crown, Edward also inherited colossal debts – to the staggering tune of £200,000.[15] The royal treasury was bare and extensive loans had not been repaid in some time. These financial restrictions would overshadow a large part of his reign. Edward needed a scapegoat. It was the perfect opportunity for the king to enact his vengeance on the very man who had become his long-standing enemy. Walter Langton, treasurer and Bishop of Coventry and Lichfield, had been caught up in both quarrels between Edward and his father. Now he no longer had the ability to hide behind his late master. His fall was swift, personal and deliberate. The day after Gaveston's elevation on 6 August, the order for Langton's arrest, sent south with three loyal knights, was carried out. Imprisoned initially at Wallingford, then Windsor, and finally the Tower of London, Langton was firstly stripped of his office as treasurer and replaced by Edward's loyal friend and keeper of his wardrobe, Walter Reynolds. On 20 September, Langton was further stripped of his lands and personal possessions, which were paid into the royal treasury by 7 October, including deposits he had made at the Temple in London. Guisborough claims they amounted to £50,000, which was highly exaggerated but demonstrates the perceived corruption levied at Langton's door.[16] On 4 October Edward passed the baton to Gaveston, appointing him, with the Earl of Lincoln, to hear accusations of corruption to build the case against the bishop. For this, the St Paul's annalist pours scorn on Gaveston, but conveniently omits Lincoln, claiming Langton's fall was orchestrated by the Earl of Cornwall in revenge for his exile.[17] While Gaveston was not the cause of Langton's change of fortune, he certainly became tarnished by it as it was felt by those who witnessed it that both the king and Piers had settled an old score.

Edward did not linger in the north for long. The royal party moved south and by the 9th were at Knaresborough, where Gaveston parted from the king, heading to Cornwall to enter into his new lands, while the king moved on to Northampton. Parliament was summoned to meet there on 13 October and the main business – the late king's funeral, the forthcoming coronation, and the new king's marriage – were on the agenda. All this came at a cost, with parliament agreeing to a grant of taxation of a twentieth and a fifteenth. The clergy were now more forthcoming than they had been of late, possibly because Edward agreed to the return of the exiled Robert Winchelsey, Archbishop of Canterbury, who had furiously clashed with the late king and been suspended from office by Pope Clement V in February 1306.[18] Edward had stretched out the hand of forgiveness. He was also able to ensure that parliament confirmed Gaveston's endowment to the earldom of Cornwall and the gift was duly entered onto the rolls held in the chancery. For his first parliament, Edward obtained everything he required from it. Things were looking good.

After his death, the late king's body had begun its journey south in late July. It travelled via Richmond to Waltham Abbey, where it lay for two months, until it was transferred to London on 18 October, before interment at Westminster Abbey.[19] The funeral, overseen by the new king on 27 October, marked the closing of the final chapter of one of England's greatest kings. Edward I's body was dressed in a red silk tunic, his head covered by a red satin mantle and his lower body covered in cloth of gold. He wore an open crown, in his right hand was placed a sceptre with a cross, and in his left, a sceptre surmounted with a dove. The eulogy was delivered by Anthony Bek, Bishop of Durham, and candles, then and for centuries to come, were lit, and prayers said to ease the king's soul into Heaven. Over the coffin, Edward's grave was marked by a plain black Purbeck marble tomb but it did not include an elaborate effigy like that of his first wife, Eleanor of Castile, who reposed next to him. The plain, cold starkness of its appearance reflected its occupant. Although Edward I was a loving husband, he was a king who increasingly ruled with an iron rod and bent his detractors, through diplomacy or force, to his will.

With the late king buried, the royal party moved on to Berkhamsted, for, on All Saints' day, 1 November, Piers Gaveston was raised yet further in status by marrying Margaret de Clare, niece of Edward II, and sister to the young Gilbert de Clare, Earl of Gloucester. As they entered the church, coins were thrown over their heads to mark the beginning of their married journey together.[20] It was a pinnacle in Gaveston's career and a key part of Edward's strategy. Through marriage, Gaveston was brought into the royal family, which, for Edward, was a defining moment, reinforcing his closeness to his friend. Edward II, as generous as ever, spent £112 on jewels for the bride and groom and £20 on minstrels, music being important to him. Margaret was given a new palfrey as a present from her uncle, and her ladies-in-waiting all received gifts from the king, which included cloth worked with gold and pearls.[21] Edward was in a generous, giving mood.

Despite his recent marriage, Piers spent the latter part of November until January 1308 with Edward, as well as his new wife. On 2 December, to mark what had been an exceptional year for him, Gaveston held a magnificent tournament at Wallingford, now the administrative heart of his new power base. The promise of a tourney always appealed to the nobility and martial classes, and was a perfect opportunity for knights looking to prove their prowess to magnates in need of good fighting men. It ensured a good turnout. Arundel, Hereford and Surrey took to the field, but Gaveston, unable to muster another earl on his side, swelled his ranks with young knights looking to impress. As the established guard fought the new, Gaveston's side took the spoils but lost the field. As the author of the *Vita* noted, 'for it is a recognised rule of this game, that he who loses most, and is frequently unhorsed, is adjudged the more valiant and the stronger'.[22] The outcome was, therefore, a sour one for many. For those earls who had watched over the last six months as Gaveston had returned from exile, been elevated to one of the most lucrative earldoms in the kingdom, married to the king's niece and was now outshining them on the tourney field, their patience became strained. As the year drew to a close, the veneer of peace that sat over the kingdom since the accession was beginning to crack. It would not be long before it would break and bitter personal resentment would boil over into outright political opposition.

As the Christmas festivities drew near, Edward turned his attention to his forthcoming marriage. Finally the long-awaited royal union, first touted as far back as 1299, was to be undertaken. Eight long years of sensitive diplomatic negotiations had taken place, at times mediated by two popes, Boniface VIII and Clement V, to bring about the end of the long-standing and often bitter discord between Edward I and his rival Phillip IV of France over the disputed territory of Gascony. This royal marriage was the central bargaining chip, and the betrothal had taken place in 1303 as part of the terms set down in the Treaty of Paris. Gascony, long since part of the much reduced Angevin empire of the early Plantagenet kings, was held by the Dukes of Aquitaine since Eleanor of Aquitaine had brought the duchy into English control when she married Edward's great-great-grandfather

Henry II, then just Count of Anjou and Duke of Normandy, in 1152. Their tumultuous marriage and famous offspring included the legendary Richard the Lionheart and King John. Both sons managed to hold onto the Gascon territory, but the boundaries of the duchy were chipped away until a much reduced but nevertheless significant landholding was retained by successive English kings. Gascony made its wealth from its vineyards and it exported wine across the known world, swelling the coffers of its successive dukes. While the duchy had been returned, at least under formal agreement, to the English crown in 1303, this final piece in the diplomatic accord, cemented by marriage, would now be fitted more permanently. Edward had had many years to grow accustomed to the marriage proposal and by 1307 showed no signs of not honouring his father's earlier negotiations. Final plans to travel to France and marry his twelve-year-old royal bride were soon put in place. Edward wanted, and indeed needed, a wife. His intense affection for men like Piers Gaveston did not sway him from his sense of duty; Gaveston had, after all, married only two months earlier. A queen and the birth of legitimate heirs were essential to the continuation of the Plantagenet line and Edward, as seen through many of his actions throughout his life, clearly had an acute awareness of his royal dignity and the need to protect the rights of the crown. Not to marry would be out of the question. To repudiate the contract and overturn the Treaty of Paris at this stage would inevitably bring about a renewed conflict with England's age-old enemy. This was something the king knew he did not need when he was burdened with heavy debts and a battle-weary kingdom, which made up the larger part of his inheritance.

While he had been burying his father in Westminster Abbey, final marriage negotiations were undertaken, headed by Phillip IV's brother Louis, Count of Évreux, and Cardinal Peter of Spain. Edward, hopeful that such a union would bring a magnificent dowry to help ease his financial position, was to be sorely disappointed. Louis politely informed his soon to be nephew-in-law, that the king of France was not attaching any dowry to his daughter other than the Duchy of Aquitaine, as outlined in the Treaty of Paris. If the new king of England did not like it, the king of France could always confiscate it again. If Edward had inherited the legendary Plantagenet rage, which he appears to have done, as evidenced on occasion, now was not the time to show it – except to those in his immediate council. Whether advised or not, Edward was shrewd enough not to take the bait and was confident enough in his position to play the political game too. It must have been particularly vexing not to receive any financial gain from the union and may have soured the thought of it, but this did not halt proceedings. Through November, the finer details were settled, overseen by the earls of Lincoln and Pembroke and the bishops of Durham and Norwich. Edward had the royal lodgings at the Palace of Westminster refreshed, the queen's gardens returfed, and the fish ponds cleaned and restocked in preparation for Isabella's arrival.[23] By 25 November, he sent a small contingent of his household to Boulogne in France, now agreed as the location for the wedding ceremony, to help prepare for the union – set down for late January.

The king turned again to Gaveston. On 26 December, as the Christmas festivities were underway, Edward appointed Piers as *custos regni* for the duration of his absence from England the following month.[24] As in all times when the kings of England left the kingdom, the monarch would appoint a leading noble, often someone of blood royal or married into the royal family, to act on the king's behalf. Edward had himself undertaken this duty back in 1297, when his father was in Flanders, and it was his first taste of royal government. His second cousin, the late Edmund of Cornwall, had acted as regent for Edward I while the king and queen were abroad in France between 1286 and 1289. The powers granted to act in the king's absence were broad but still with necessary limitations. In effect, significant decisions that required the king's personal authority were delayed until his return or sent to him abroad.

That December, Edward decided to go one step further. Who better to trust than his friend, who was now part of the royal family through his marriage to Margaret de Clare, and one of the premier earls in the country? Gaveston's appointment as *custos regni*, at least in Edward's mind, was fitting and followed the tradition of granting such an office to senior earls. For Edward, Gaveston was the ideal choice. He had grown up with him since 1300, playing a leading role in his household when Edward was prince.

The nobles did not agree. On 18 January, Gaveston's authority was set out; and the powers granted to him were extensive, including the ability to grant licences, give royal assents, deal with wardships and marriages and to make key ecclesiastical appointments – far beyond any of the former powers laid out for his predecessors.[25] The position did not create any immediate outward opposition, but the sudden appointment of Gaveston over someone like the ancient and experienced Earl of Lincoln, or Edward's cousins, Thomas or Henry of Lancaster, was unusual – and noted by contemporaries. One chronicler wrote 'the kingdom was left in the hands of Piers, as regent. An astonishing thing that he who had lately been an exile and outcast from England should now be made ruler and guardian of the realm.'[26] It did nothing to ingratiate him with his peers.

So why did Edward do it? In the most simple terms because he loved and trusted Piers. Edward and Piers Gaveston were lovers and this union created an intimacy that would bind them together for years to come and far beyond Gaveston's death in 1312. Seen in this light, Edward's actions become all too clear and while no evidence explicitly states that they were lovers, the actions and policies of the king over the next few years give a clear indication as to motivations. In the fourteenth century, homosexuality was condemned by the Church as a sin, an act which denied creative union and brought about the wrath of God as set out in stories like Sodom and Gomorrah. (Though it would be another 560 or so years before the term 'homosexuality' came into use.) Offenders were put beyond the Church through excommunication, and those more unfortunate offenders could be tortured, castrated or burned. The act of same-sex intimacy was not tolerated. However, Edward was a king and his position allowed him the freedom to express his intimate attachment to Gaveston in ways that many at the time were not able to do. For most of the nobility, what the king chose to do behind the closed door of his bedchamber did not concern them in the least; until, of course, the lover of the king, whether male or female, gained – or was perceived to have gained – royal favour and power to such an extent that it encroached upon their own traditional positions of influence at court.[27] Edward did not see the storm he was creating.

In the New Year of 1308, the St Paul's Annalist commented that since the start of the previous year, Edward 'loved Gaveston beyond measure' and that he 'strove to please him like one would a superior'.[28] The *Vita Edwardi Secundi*, a contemporary chronicle that closely charts the reign of the king and was likely written by John Walwayn, a clerk at court later in the employ of the Earl of Hereford, often commented on their intimacy. One of his entries for 1312 says that Edward lamented for Piers like 'David upon Jonathan' and that their love is said 'to have surpassed the love of women'.[29] The St Paul's Annalist goes further, citing Edward's behaviour when he first recalled Gaveston back to England when he overturned his father's policy of exile, claiming he behaved like the Old Testament king Reheboam, son of King Solomon, who cast off the advice of his father and chose to surround himself with and take the advice of younger, more unsuitable members of court. Those who know their biblical history will remember that Reheboam was also accused of promoting the cult of male prostitutes and to the readers of the time, the reference was probably clear.[30] While chroniclers often apply biblical stories to drive their points home, falling back on the teachings of the Church and adopting its moral code in their judgements, this statement is as close as we can get to a direct contemporary reference to the king's behaviour. To say we cannot know what Edward felt or exactly define his sexuality, misses the point; we do not, but what we can see are his actions and these, taken together, are compelling in understanding the nature of his relationship with Piers Gaveston. Their intimacy was so intense it would dominate the early years of Edward's reign, up until 1312, and cast a long shadow over the rest of it. Edward's appointment of Gaveston as *custos regni* was a personal one, and one given to his lover because he, at the time, was the one Edward trusted most. In the king's eyes it also confirmed Gaveston's elevation and reinforced his position as a member of the royal family, which had been Edward's plan since late 1306. Marriage to Margaret de Clare, of course was part of the process.

As Edward headed to Dover to set sail for France, resentment towards Gaveston was growing. This tension, not yet shown as outright opposition, was not brought about by his sexual intimacy with the king, but by his closeness to the political heart of royal government. Chroniclers like Walter of Guisborough pour scorn on Gaveston and his heritage, claiming he had been raised from the dust.[31] It would be all too easy to think that he was made from nothing and overnight had secured not only the most lucrative gifts in the land, but also the heart and bed of the king. This is inaccurate.

Born in the village of Gabaston, in Béarn, on the southern border of Gascony, Piers Gaveston was the younger son of Arnaud Gabaston and Claramonde de Marsan, who were landowners; his father was Lord of Gabaston and their family had held these lands since the 1040s. Arnaud owed fealty and homage to the Viscounts of Béarn and often gave service to the Dukes of Aquitaine, who were then kings of England. Gaveston's parents had substantial landholdings throughout the region, thanks to the successful marriage of the Gabaston and de Marsan families.[32] To say they were from the dust belies their position in Gascon society. By the 1280s, Arnaud had already begun more than twenty years of service to Edward I, initially in the Welsh Wars of 1282–83, just prior to Edward II's birth at Caernarfon. Gabaston impressed, fighting bravely in a contingent of men alongside three knights, seven mounted archers and 120 foot. He was a royal hostage for his new master Edward I, in 1288. This time he and others were sent to King Alfonso III of Aragon as security against a promised ransom of 70,000 marks for Charles of Solerno.[33] Arnaud was back again two years later in his role as royal hostage, only this time sent by Edward I to Philip IV, with others, in February 1294. This latest diplomatic hostage exchange came to an abrupt end when Gabaston escaped on 13 November 1296 and sped back to England to be subsequently well-received by the king. As Arnaud fled France, he gathered up at least three of his five sons, took his key possessions with him, and set out on a journey that would have life-changing implications for his surviving family. Those sons included Arnaud-Guillaume de Marsan and Guillaume-Arnaud de Gabaston, as well as Piers Gaveston, who was about fourteen years old. Piers was in the king's service in Flanders in 1297 when Edward, then his father's regent, was nominally looking after England. By 1300, impressed by Gaveston's martial ability and manners, Edward I placed him in his son's household and they seemed to quickly become friends. Both had lost their mothers while young, Gaveston in 1287 when five years old, and Edward in 1290, when he was six. Both their fathers were often absent, fighting in wars, so they clearly had things in common that bound them together. Both were sharp-witted, were versed in the complexities of *courtoisie* and loved to gamble and take risks, as the alleged break-in to the woods of the royal treasurer Walter Langton in 1305 shows.[34] At some point between 1300 and 1306, Gaveston and Edward's friendship spilled over into something more intimate and binding.

On 18 January at Dover, Gaveston's role as *custos regni* was set out, as well as writs that were issued in Edward's name commanding the senior clergy, earls and barons to attend Edward's coronation at Westminster

Abbey on 18 February.[35] The king set sail on the 22nd, arriving at Boulogne on the evening of the 24th.[36] In his flotilla was *The Margaret of Westminster*, a newly commissioned ship built to bring Isabella to England. Two days later, Edward increased the size of Isabella's dowry from £4,500 (18,000 *livres tournois*) to £5,000 (20,000 *livres tournois*) funded by revenues from the county of Ponthieu, which had always been intended to support the dowry. Reluctantly satisfied with the last minute adjustment, Philip IV agreed to allow the ceremony to proceed.

On 25 January, at the doorway of the Cathedral of Boulogne, the twenty-three-year-old Edward met his twelve-year-old bride. Isabella was richly dressed in blue and gold, the colours of France, and had a red mantle lined with yellow sindon. Edward wore a satin sleeved surcoat and a cloak decorated with jewels.[37] The king towered over his bride as they swore to bind themselves in marital union before God and the glittering assembly. Many of the leading figures in north-western Europe were present, including Isabella's three brothers, Louis, Philip and Charles, all later kings of France. The bride's father, the calculating and clever Philip IV, his brother, Charles of Valois; and half-brother, Louis Count of Évreux, were present. Edward II's sister Margaret and her husband John, Duke of Brabant as well as the Count of Hainault (whose daughter would later marry Edward and Isabella's son, the future Edward III) were in attendance. Other dignitaries included the Count of Savoy, the Count of Dreux, Robert of Artois, Louis of Nevers, Edward's stepmother Queen Marguerite, Isabella's aunt; Anthony Bek, Bishop of Durham; the earls of Pembroke, Lincoln, Surrey and Hereford, as well as barons of note including Hugh Despenser and Robert Clifford.[38]

There is nothing in the record that the bride and groom were ceremonially put to bed, as custom dictated. This is not unusual given Isabella's age and if it did not occur, this thankfully spared both of them what could have been a traumatic public experience. After the ceremony, eight days of celebrations and tournaments were held, Edward hosting on 28 January. On the 30th, as the ceremonies were drawing to a close, the King of France presented the royal couple with lavish gifts of more than 21,000 *livres tournois* as well as luxury furs, jewels and furnishings for Isabella's household. Edward gave Isabella an illuminated manuscript, which he had especially commissioned.[39] When the formalities were complete, the royal couple departed Boulogne – Isabella taking with her, her uncle, Louis of Évreux, and her French household – and headed to the coast. The new queen went separately from her husband, sailing on *The Margaret of Westminster*. Both landed at Dover on 7 February. As Edward arrived and disembarked in front of the assembled English court, he was seen to 'run to Piers ... giving him kisses and repeated embraces, he was adored with a singular familiarity'.[40] Whether Isabella witnessed this is not known, but she must have soon heard about it. This special familiarity, already known to the magnates, added yet further fuel to their jealous fires.

9

A Pariah at Court

Gaveston's time as *custos regni* had been spent carefully looking after the kingdom. During the nineteen days he held office, he had exercised the royal prerogative sparingly. In all, he dealt with twenty-nine pieces of business from wardships, financial and judicial matters, to the more mundane preparations of arranging for the king's return. On 27 January, he granted to Alexander Cheveral the property and person of John Walraund, listed as an idiot.[1] His decisions were modest, such as appointing Stephen de Abingdon and Richard de Montpellier the Younger as purveyors of Edward's wardrobe.[2] However, if the polistoire at Christ Church Canterbury is to be believed, while his exercise of the royal prerogative was in check, his behaviour was not. Riding high on what had been a glorious six months for him, Piers played the part of *custos regni* with *hauteur*; those who entered his presence were expected to kneel as they made requests of him, considered unusual in this role.[3] Malicious gossip began to swirl around the court that Gaveston had engineered the election for the successor to the recently deceased Walter de Wenlock at the Abbey of Westminster, taking bribes and backing Wenlock's choice of successor, Richard de Kedyngton. Gifts amounting to £6 13s 4d in coin, a gold cup and two pitchers changed hands sometime before he formally became *custos regni*, but whether through caution brought on by the mood at court or not, Gaveston did not approve the appointment – although he had the power to do so – waiting instead for the king to make the decision on his return to England.[4] Gaveston formally gave up his role on 9 February, two days after Edward landed at Dover when William Melton, keeper of the wardrobe, arrived at the castle with the great seal. Gaveston handed over his regent's seal to Edward in the presence of the Earl of Lancaster.[5]

The gossip continued. Gaveston, they said, had appropriated the income gathered from the burdened populace following the grant of taxation at the parliament at Northampton. Gaveston, with the king's knowledge, was taking part of the royal share of Walter Langton's estate confiscated in the autumn of 1307.[6] Gaveston, they said, had taken for himself the queen's wedding gifts and jewels bestowed on her by her father at her wedding – although Edward had simply sent them to Piers, as chamberlain of his bedchamber, for storage. The mood soured further. As gossip spilled over into hysteria, Gaveston, they said, had become a sorcerer and held the king under a spell who was bewitched and beholden to his evil council and now forsaking all others.[7] It was said there were now two kings in the kingdom, and by implication Edward and the crown, which were one and the same, were in peril.[8] As the king returned and showered Gaveston with kisses on the dockside at Dover the gossip, to the onlookers, must have seemed based on fact.

Of the earls and barons of England, most had inherited their titles from their forebears during the mid- to late part of the reign of Edward I. Only the Earl of Lincoln had lived through the better part of the reign and as a stalwart friend of the late king, had enjoyed favour during the high and lows of Edward's I iron rule. The former king had never been one to lavish great gifts upon his nobles, but chose instead to keep their individual power in check, their gifts small and, when forcing through his will, was confrontational and unbending.[9] This is what they knew, and if the nobility of England wanted change, a bigger slice of freedom and a place in the inner everyday royal circle, they must have pinned their hopes on his successor. As the new guard of earls and barons gave way to the old, Edward II was their ticket to becoming the Lincoln of the future.

As Edward recalled Gaveston and granted him the earldom of Cornwall with the earls' consent, they must have looked on eagerly thinking they were next. At last, after years of small gift-giving and the odd royal favour, now was their time. Yet they waited still and watched as Edward brought Gaveston into the royal family through marriage to Margaret de Clare, one of the best marriage catches of the day. Waiting, still nothing came their way. By December, as Gaveston was growing into his new-found status and outshining his peers at Wallingford, a rising sense of frustration became manifest. The realisation began to dawn that this was not going to be their time after all, and it must have seemed to the earls and barons that their long-hoped-for moment to gain a greater slice of the king's patronage was fast slipping away. They could not get close to him. Before Edward left for France, the king had appointed Gaveston as chamberlain of his bedchamber, meaning that anyone who sought an audience with Edward had to go through the chamberlain first.

So was the resentment well-founded? Apart from the question over the election of Richard de Kedyngton to the Abbey of Westminster, it seems Gaveston was guilty of nothing more than a touch of haughtiness.

Gaveston's role as chamberlain of the bedchamber allowed the pair the closeness they needed to live out their relationship. This was the first time they both had the freedom to enjoy it without the shadow of Edward I looming large. But in doing so, Edward miscalculated the mood. When he sought to emulate his father, as no doubt he had been taught, he did not recognise the need to exercise his patronage to the earls and barons whom he saw as already comfortably endowed. His father hadn't, so why should he?

Edward inherited the weight of his father's policies in war; a burden that had drained the treasury, over-taxed his people and relied on loans from foreign Italian bankers, like the Riccardi. The king's reliance on taxation granted in parliament, while still essential, had been eased with his foreign sources of coin. The nobility, who were able to use parliament to hold the king in check since Magna Carta in 1215, were increasingly losing their financial influence at key moments when their predecessors had not.[10] The war machine, necessary to complete the conquest of Scotland, was a runaway wagon – with the wheels in danger of coming off. In the nobles' mind, the accession of the new king was an opportunity to redress the balance, offer him support through suggested and careful reform and they, as the traditional body to bring about this change, were the natural wellspring of such reform.

During the lavish feasting that followed Edward and Isabella's marriage at Boulogne, the Earl of Lincoln and Anthony Bek, Bishop of Durham, assembled a group of nobles with the aim of helping to guide the king through the necessary reforms to help alleviate the financial burden and place him in the best possible position to solve the Scottish problem once and for all. With Edward's knowledge, Bek, Lincoln and eight others including the earls of Surrey, Pembroke, Hereford, Robert Clifford, Payn Talbot, Henry de Grey, John Botetourt and John de Berwick, attached their seals to a document promising reform. The Boulogne Agreement was at last the nobles' way to gain a footing into the king's inner circle which would, in their minds at least, prove mutually beneficial. So strong was the feeling that the Bishop of Durham was asked to excommunicate anyone of them who failed in his duty to help the king.[11] So reform could be initiated and, no doubt, rewards from a grateful king would flow from it.

What happened next changed everything. Preparation for the forthcoming coronation began shortly after Edward's accession. The date, 18 February, was purposely chosen to heighten the sanctity of the occasion as it was the feast of the translation of St Edward the Confessor, the Plantagenet royal saint. On 22 January Robert Winchelsey had been reinstated as Archbishop of Canterbury, following his exile and long-standing feud with the late king Edward I. Yet despite months of planning, at the last minute the date of the coronation was postponed for a week, falling instead on the feast of St Matthias the Apostle, 25 February. The archbishop was not making good progress on his return, dogged by illness, so he appointed Bishop Woodlock of Winchester to administer on his behalf, with the help of the bishops of Salisbury and Chichester. However, it may well be that something else was afoot.

Working with the king, Lincoln, Pembroke, Hereford and Robert de Clifford, as signatories to the Boulogne Agreement, began the process of reform. The coronation oath acted as the sacred compact between the king, God and his people. Bound by tradition, it set out that the king would uphold the laws, customs and liberties granted by his ancestors; preserve and protect the Holy Church; and render justice to the people of the kingdom. However, the earls suggested a fourth clause binding Edward to uphold 'the rightful laws and customs which the community of the realm have chosen'.[12] If anything, this curious addition built on the agreement that the king, unlike his father before him, would uphold decisions made between the king and his nobles. Only three years earlier, Edward I had secured agreement from Pope Clement V to release him from concessions made to the nobles in the Confirmation of the Charters in 1297 and the *Articuli super Cartas* of 1300. There was always the risk that Edward II would adopt a similar policy. The addition of a fourth clause gave the nobility some security that they could redress what they saw as the imbalances set in place by Edward I once and for all. In short, it was a move designed to avoid the problems of the previous reign. They may also have voiced their concerns over Gaveston, which Edward would not hear, and deferred this to the next parliament.[13] In this confused time, the addition to the coronation oath was not initially well received by the king, but in the spirit of a new beginning Edward eventually agreed. What he was signing up for would soon come back to haunt him and go far beyond his already doomed inheritance.[14]

The coronation went ahead on 25 February and was a lavish affair. Like the knighting ceremony that was held at the abbey two years previously, the crowds were immense and a 500-foot-long timber hall was erected so enough people could watch. As before, a wall came crashing down, this time killing John Bakewell, former seneschal of Ponthieu.[15] In the purpose-built stands sat many foreign guests, some of whom had attend Edward and Isabella's wedding the previous month. The queen's uncles, Charles of Valois and Louis, Count of Évreux, were present with her brother, Charles. As before in Boulogne, the Duke of Brabant attended with the Duke of Brittany, the counts of Pol and Savoy and Count Henry of Luxemburg, who was soon to become the Holy Roman Emperor. Two of the king's sisters were also in the abbey that day, Margaret, Duchess of Brabant, and Mary, the gambling nun who had met her brother and his new wife at the Tower of London the day before.[16] The king's stepmother, Marguerite of France, was present with her two sons, Thomas and Edmund.

Leading the procession into the abbey, dressed in the customary cloth of gold, was the Earl of Hereford, who carried the sceptre. He was followed by the Earl of Lancaster, who carried *curtana*, the Sword of Mercy, and the earls of Lincoln and Warwick, who each carried another sword. Hugh Despenser, Roger Mortimer of Wigmore, Thomas de Vere, Earl of Oxford, and the Earl of Arundel carried Edward's vestments. Gaveston, though, stole the show, taking the most prominent position. He was dressed in a gown of royal purple trimmed with pearls. Edward appointed Gaveston to carry the crown of St Edward the Confessor. He entered the abbey immediately before the king giving him precedence over all the other earls and barons. While Charles of Valois put the boot and spur on the king's right foot, the Earl of Pembroke was permitted to only place the boot on the king's left foot – Gaveston fastened the spur, placing him equal to the king of France's brother.[17] Bristling, the nobles watched as Gaveston 'redeemed' the *curtana* after Edward had ceremoniously placed a pound of gold on the high altar.[18]

It didn't get any better. At the banquet that followed, as the assembled party entered Westminster Hall, hanging on the walls were tapestries emblazoned with the arms of Edward and the Earl of Cornwall, which had been commissioned on 6 October at the cost of £5 from London upholsterers, John Engayne and John le Tapyter.[19] The queen's coat of arms were not recorded so it can only be assumed they were not displayed or, if so, not prominently. As the meal got underway, the food was cold and the king spent much of his time talking to Gaveston. For the nobles, any vestiges of royal favour or building a close relationship with the king while Gaveston was at court now seemed remote, perhaps impossible. By the time the night was through, one of the earls, according to the St Paul's annalist, wanted to kill Gaveston.[20] The road to reform was to collide with what the nobles now saw as the intolerable position of the king's favourite. One would be permanently muddied with the other. The peace was at an end and outright opposition lay ahead.

Confrontation was quick in coming. Parliament opened on the first day of Lent, 28 February 1308, at Westminster – three days earlier than planned. It did not open well. The nobles, present in London since the coronation had spent the intervening days laying their plans. The king, who had deferred their matters and concerns prior to the coronation, knew that the road ahead was going to be anything but easy. Holding his nerve and in a spirit of compromise, Edward declared at the start of the session that he wished to be 'counselled on the state of the Church, the state of the crown which he had only eight months earlier assumed, and more importantly how best to govern according to God, to justice and how the land might be preserved for his people'.[21] The nobles seized upon his words and declared that if the king was so interested in their advice, then he ought to grant them a written commission, the terms of which would bind Edward to uphold his promises and accept their proposals. Edward had inherited enough of his father's political astuteness to see through this. Agreeing to such a policy would hamstring him, given that the nobles at this point failed to outline what their formal proposals might be. He was being asked to sign a blank contract. Edward's cousin, Thomas of Lancaster, one of the leading earls of the time who still stood with the king, refused to agree to the proposal, as did Edward himself. Deadlock ensued, the king held firm and the nobles refused to bend. On or about 10 March, Edward had had enough. Parliament was prorogued and the nobles told to reconvene again at Westminster on 28 April. Round one went to the king.

The mood turned uglier. Edward clearly understood that he was fast losing the support of his nobles, and it must to have been clear that this was laid firmly at Gaveston's feet given the hysteria swirling around the court since the start of the year. Aware of the growing tension, Edward showed a core element of his character – loyalty to his friends. As the nobles, with the exception of the earls of Lancaster, Arundel and Oxford, moved north from London to the Earl of Lincoln's castle at Pontefract in Yorkshire to consult and plan their next steps, Edward left Westminster for Windsor Castle. As tensions grew and gossip swirled inside and outside the court, a real threat of civil war loomed. Edward was quick to act. Between 12 and 18 March, the custodians of key strategic royal castles were promptly replaced, including Robert Clifford at Nottingham, John Botetourt at St Briavels and Payn Tibetot; all three men had attached their seals to the Boulogne Agreement only two months before. Clifford and Tibetot were also removed from influential positions as Justices of the Forest north and south of the Trent. Edward's mood turned defiant and any predilection for friendly and consultative reform was now dissipated.[22] The tense political climate must have reminded him of his experiences when he was regent for his father in 1297.

King's men were promptly ushered in to new strategic posts. Keeping his cousin close, Edward granted to Lancaster the office of Steward of England, which the earl had long coveted.[23] Castles were given into safe hands including Gaveston himself, Hugh Despenser the Elder, John Chandos, Alexander Cheveral and Henry de Percy, among others. At the gateway to England, the mighty fortress of Dover Castle, built by Henry II, and the Cinque ports along the south coast, were placed in the custody of Robert de Kendal, one of Piers Gaveston's retainers.[24] Repairs were ordered to Windsor and the large quantity of wood used for temporary buildings at Westminster for the recent coronation was requisitioned and rowed upstream for repairs to the Tower of London.[25] Edward was preparing for open conflict.

On 28 April the second parliament of the year reconvened at Westminster, the nobles arriving armed, as they claimed, in self-defence.[26]

The roll call for the parliament included the Archbishop of York, the Archbishop of Canterbury still abroad; fifteen bishops, twelve abbots, three priors, eleven earls, forty-six barons and thirty-eight royal judges and clerks.[27] The nobles, now led by the stalwart Earl of Lincoln hunkered down in the abbey, the king remained apart in the palace of Westminster while Gaveston was safely ensconced at the Tower. Go-betweeners, most likely Lancaster, Hugh Despenser the Elder and other royal officials, moved between the parties.

Edward soon discovered that as he had anticipated, Lincoln and the others, like himself, had been busy. The gauntlet was thrown down almost immediately. Three baronial articles were read out, which in themselves must have made Edward furious. Firstly, the nobles, for the first time, radically declared that their homage and oaths of allegiance made at the coronation were more to the crown itself than to the individual who wore it. Further, that if the king who happened to wear the crown was not guided by reason, and in some way diminished the dignity of the crown, then they, the nobles, conveniently obliged by their oaths to uphold and serve the crown, were duty bound to intercede in order to reinstate its dignity. Lincoln went on. As the judges belonged to the king, they were unable to take recourse through legal action and so, if the king is evilly counselled, then they have the right to resort to remove the said evil. These were revolutionary words and for the first time separated the notion of the person of the king from the office of king.

Secondly, Lincoln declared in no uncertain terms that a 'person', meaning Gaveston, had come between the king and his nobles and by his counsel withdrew the king creating discord between both parties. Edward had disinherited and impoverished the crown, in reference to the patronage Gaveston had received since August 1307, although conveniently omitting that they had themselves sealed the charter of ennoblement granting Piers the major part of his substantial estate. The claim went further, suggesting that through his access to the king and the men he had built up around him at court, Gaveston had set himself up as an equal to the king, thereby enfeebling the crown.

Finally came the sting in the tail. Edward, they said, was blind to this and that he had shown his determination to maintain his favourite 'without regard to reason'. In the eyes of the people of the realm, Gaveston was a robber and a traitor, and therefore was adjudged and attained by the people. Lincoln finished by pointing out that only two months earlier, the king in his revised sacred coronation oath had promised to uphold the rightful laws and customs which the community of the realm had chosen.[28] The people, Lincoln triumphantly declared, had chosen that Gaveston must go.

The gloves were off. Edward refused to agree to any of it, in particular to the suggestion of a second exile for Piers. The nobles dug in their heels, a standoff ensued, punctuated, no doubt, with bitter exchanges. Events got uglier. In the spring of 1308, the abbot of Saint-Germain-de-Pres, Pierre de Courpolay, accompanied by three knights, sent by Edward's father-in-law Philip IV of France, arrived in England with a simple message. If Edward did not give Gaveston up, the King of France would treat all of the Earl of Cornwall's supporters as his enemies. Rumours circulated that Isabella's father, with support of his sister Marguerite, the dowager queen and late wife of Edward I, had sent 40,000 *livres tournois* (£10,000) to the earls to support their campaign to remove Edward's favourite.[29] Marguerite saw first-hand the influence Gaveston had over Edward and was keen to see her niece Isabella rise in her husband's affections. In the Capetian mind, this was not possible if the current situation did not radically change. Marguerite was also put out over Gaveston's elevation to the earldom of Cornwall the previous year, now out of reach for one of her two sons, Thomas or Edmund, despite her late husband's attempt to block such an ennoblement.

Edward remained defiant, yet by the middle of May, with almost everyone against him, the pressure became unbearable. On the 14th he made concessions to appease his father-in-law and agreed to assign the revenues and debts associated with the county of Ponthieu over to Isabella as her dower, giving the queen her promised income. That evening Edward dined with the earls of Lancaster, Richmond and Oxford, who continued to stand by him, and perhaps with their counsel, saw his untenable position for what it was.[30] Four days later, the king reluctantly agreed to Gaveston's exile.[31] Given his characteric inclination to protect those closest to him, and the intensity of their intimacy, it cannot have been anything but a heart-wrenching decision that Edward was forced into taking. Backed into a corner, he was rendered powerless to protect those closest to him.

The deadline was set. Gaveston had to relinquish to the crown all his lands held as Earl of Cornwall and leave England by 25 June. Driving the point home, the following day the newly returned Archbishop of Canterbury, Robert Winchelsey, threatened to excommunicate Gaveston should he return.[32] Edward's conciliatory act of burying his father's turbulent relationship with the archbishop, which he had inherited, had come back to bite him.

Yet Edward would not be entirely beaten. If Gaveston had to go, then in Edward's mind he was still able to ensure that his favourite was endowed with lands and gifts befitting his status. On 4 June, Piers relinquished the lands held by him as Earl of Cornwall in the presence of the Earl of Richmond, the chancellor and treasurer, but retained the title, which was still used in royal letters of the privy seal; in other official documents though, he was simply referred to as 'Sir Peter de Gaveston, knight'.[33] Three days later, while Gaveston was still with the king at Edward's childhood manor of Langley in Hertfordshire, the king granted Gaveston and his wife Margaret as a gift of good service various castles and manors including Skipton, the castle and honour of High Peak in Derbyshire, Cockermouth in Cumbria, manors in Northampton and Yorkshire and all of Edward's lands in the Isle of Wight including Carisbrooke Castle, which amounted to an annual income of £2,000.[34] While Margaret had not been cited in the parliamentary demand for exile, probably out of respect to her brother the Earl of Gloucester and as niece to the king, Margaret was nevertheless determined to accompany her husband.[35] Edward's gifts went further still. The couple were awarded an additional £2,000-worth of lands in Aquitaine, which included the county of Gaure, close to Gaveston's ancestral home of Gabaston. The two land grants resulting in a combined annual income of £4,000 was equivalent to the size of a large English earldom. Edward had marked out his Duchy of Aquitaine as a place of refuge for Piers and Margaret but as events unfolded, and with Edward's determination to hit back at his nobles, he changed his mind at the last minute. He was inadvertently inspired by a grant he authorised through letters patent to Richard de Burgh, Earl of Ulster creating him Lieutenant of Ireland. Sleeping on it overnight, on the next day, 16 June, Edward had his eureka moment and instead made Gaveston lieutenant, immediately displacing de Burgh.[36] In this, Piers was given regal power far exceeding his predecessors, including the right to present churches and benefices as he had been able to when appointed as *custos regni* in January that year, and to remove sheriffs and justices. The appointment was witnessed by the Earl of Richmond, Hugh Despenser the Elder, William Melton and Adam Osgodby.[37]

Gaveston's opponents were not best pleased with this final appointment and continued flow of royal patronage, but powerless to prevent the king from doing so, it did not at any rate change the will of Lincoln and the others. Gaveston was to go and this ensured they achieved their goal as well as creating the opportunity to have greater access to the king. In late June, Edward, Gaveston and their party moved to Bristol where, on or soon after the 25th, Gaveston and his wife set sail for Dublin in ships Edward had ordered John de Wyk to assemble.[38] For now, at least, the king was on the back foot, but much like his father, Edward had no intention of remaining so for long.

10

A Time for Tact

Edward had a plan. As he turned away from Bristol and headed east to Windsor, the king brought into play a clearly designed strategy. If Gaveston was to return, the king knew he needed to win over the opposition earls and this was going to take time and tact. Focussed and determined, Edward's strategy was a simple one – divide and conquer – and this by any means possible.

Using patronage as his principal tool, Edward began with his nephew, the seventeen-year-old Earl of Gloucester, brother to Gaveston's wife Margaret. Gloucester was barely in opposition so, in July, he received several grants and the release of rights to lands in his possession.[1] If he had wavered before, he didn't after. Quickly Edward moved on to his brother-in-law, the Earl of Hereford. By the start of August, he widened his net, ordering Gerard Salvayn, escheator north of the Trent, to restore to the earl any goods taken from him when Skipton Castle had been handed to Gaveston in June that year.[2] Conciliatory gestures such as this worked, and shortly afterwards brought the Earl of Lincoln over to his side. Lincoln, whose whole career had been in direct service to the crown, and the king more specifically, was keen to return to his natural role of counselor. Edward also worked on Warwick who, since the king's accession, had stood in opposition to Gaveston, most notably by his seal being absent from the charter granting the earldom of Cornwall to Piers at Dumfries in August 1307.[3] Warwick would take longer but, nevertheless, eventually showed signs of support for the king.[4] Pembroke was last to return to the fold. By the late summer, the names of these earls began to appear on witness lists on royal charters clearly indicating their closer co-operation and their being more frequently in the presence of the king. Edward's plan was starting to work.

On 4 August, the king made a more formal gesture of reconciliation. Acting as conciliator, he held a meeting at Northampton with the earls and barons. Although not a parliament, the king nevertheless sought the advice of those assembled and agreed to abide by their decisions at the next parliament, summoned on 16 August when Edward was at Langley, and set to meet at Westminster on 20 October.[5] He also swore an oath to remove six of his counselors as the earls had requested. These included the loyal Hugh Despenser the Elder, William Inge and William de Bereford, as well as Lancaster's retainer Nicolas de Segrave.[6] It was a tactical gesture and one the earls readily accepted.

Lancaster, however, was not so pleased. Within a few months, Edward and his cousin had a disagreement that created a rift that was to last a lifetime. The evidence for it is frustratingly absent. Given the earl's later reactions when challenges were made against his retainers, or more specifically when they were removed from their offices, it is not too hard to accept Segrave's dismissal as a bone of contention for the earl. Edward was not willing to protect one man when weighed in the balance against a much bigger plan. While Segrave's removal might not have been the breaking point in Lancaster's support for Edward later into the year, it must certainly have been a factor leading to the start of their troubles. Trivial matters, as noted by his modern biographer, were often exaggerated in their import by the stubborn, brooding earl. Edward was also wrestling with other disputes involving one of Lancaster's knights, who held the manor of Wilton in Pickering, Yorkshire so an accretion of minor matters confounded Lancaster's expectations.[7] Whatever the cause, Lancaster was not present at Northampton and by autumn, after the close of parliament, no longer appears on the witness lists of charters until March 1310. This would become a critical longer-term oversight in Edward's immediate plan.

For now, at least, things were tentatively looking up. Not fond of the joust, Edward nevertheless organised a tournament for the earls, barons and knights of England, held at Kennington in the early autumn. The earls shunned the event, sending out a clear signal that all was not yet forgiven.[8] It was however a litmus test and did not perturb the king enough to change his approach. Edward was focussed and determined.

Parliament assembled, as planned, at Westminster on 20 October 1308 and although no parliament roll survives, reviewing the writs of summons issued by the king the body was probably made up of the archbishops of Canterbury and York, nine earls including Lancaster, Gloucester, Lincoln, Surrey, Warwick, Hereford, Arundel, Pembroke and Oxford; along with fifty-seven barons and thirty-five royal judges and clerks.[9]

Edward dutifully put his mind to business and listened to the earls' complaints. As further gestures of goodwill, the king agreed, first, to the release of Walter Langton from the Tower of London; Langton had been wallowing in various prisons since his arrest on 7 August 1307. After more persuasion, he ordered the release of Robert Wishart, Bishop of Glasgow, and William Lamberton, Bishop of St Andrews, held in captivity in Porchester and Winchester castles respectively since 1306.[10] In the end,

Wishart would remain captive until after 1314 but these actions, taken as a whole, were clearly designed to appease the pope, Clement V, who had sent Arnaud d'Aux, Bishop of Poitiers, and Bertrand Caillau, as papal envoys in response to a letter from Edward to help mediate between the king and his earls. Edward was hoping to curry favour with Clement who, if all went well, would lift Winchelsey's threat of excommunication on Gaveston. This was a fundamental part of Edward's plan, for if Gaveston returned without papal blessing he would become excommunicated and would be barred from receiving the Holy Sacraments, hearing the liturgy or, should he die, would be denied burial in consecrated ground, endangering his immortal soul. Overturning this terrible threat was Edward's greater preoccupation and again reinforced the intimate bonds that existed between him and Gaveston. Edward, conventionally pious, cared deeply about Gaveston's spiritual welfare. Even before Piers had set sail to Ireland, the king had been working to gain Clement's favour on his behalf, granting on 16 June the town and castle of Blanquefort to the pope's nephew and namesake Bertrand de Got.[11] The redirection of royal patronage was working. Clement's choice of envoys included Bertrand Caillau, who was Gaveston's nephew. With ecclesiastical concessions made, shortly after parliament was prorogued, Caillau headed to Ireland to treat with his uncle to discuss the best terms for his return.[12] The plan was starting to come together.

At the same time Edward was working on the pope, he was acutely aware of the need to re-build his relationship with his father-in-law, Philip IV. When the pope had sent envoys, so too had the French king. The Bishop Guy of Soissons and Edward's friend Louis, Count of Évreux, reached England in September; Louis dining with Edward on the 12th.[13] During parliament, Edward, at one stroke, curried favour with both France and the Holy See and finally agreed to the formal suppression of the Knights Templar. Philip IV's insatiable greed to secure Templar wealth had, since 1307, convinced Clement V to disband the knightly crusading order, originally formed in 1119 to protect pilgrims on the roads to the Holy City of Jerusalem.[14] The pope resisted the charges of heresy, which Philip demanded, but nevertheless agreed to suppress the order for diverse malpractices. Up until this point, Edward had shown no real appetite to order the suppression in England and had held out since the papal decree. Changing his approach at this strategic moment only helped to further demonstrate his commitment to good government in the eyes of his foreign detractors, even if he was making concessions through a policy that he had otherwise chosen not to follow. Gaveston's return was Edward's principal aim at this moment and if it meant compromising on his political viewpoint to bring this about, he would.

Parliament, in return for concessions, was somewhat receptive to Edward's demand for a vote of taxation. While not immediately granted, any levy was made conditional on further reforms, which Edward agreed to hear at the next parliament. In October, at Canterbury, the king attended the consecration of his treasurer and long-time friend Walter Reynolds as the Bishop of Worcester, after the former had exercised influence both with the chapter of Worcester and the papal curia to bring about Reynold's election.[15] A month later, the French envoys secured a truce with Robert Bruce in Scotland, whose resurgence was a threat to Edward's hold over strategic castles won by him and his father up until 1307. By the close of 1308, with the absence of Gaveston and no reason for direct opposition to the king, Edward had clearly begun to regain his position, as astutely noted by the writer of the *Vita*:

> When the king saw that his barons stood against him like a wall, by reason of which he could not carry out his intentions, he tried to break up their confederacy and draw over the more powerful to his side. Therefore, relying on inherited and native caution – for the English flatter when they see their strength is insufficient for the task – he bent one after another to his will, with gifts, promises and blandishments, with such success that scarcely a baron remained to defend what had already been decided upon and granted.[16]

Edward, encouraged by his gains, upped the stakes. In January the king was ready to show some, if not all, his cards and ordered an assembly to meet at Westminster, which it duly did on 28 February. In attendance were Lincoln, Surrey, Gloucester, Hereford, Pembroke, Richmond, Warwick, Arundel, forty-two barons and others.[17] Although records from the assembly do not survive, it is likely that this was the occasion when Edward first mooted the idea of Gaveston's return. The king may have offered in return further reforms. Although no formal agreement appears to have been made at the assembly, the path was laid out – for on 4 March, Edward sent out writs for parliament to assemble at Westminster on 27 April. On the same day, the king wrote to Clement V informing him that he was sending an embassy to the papal curia at Avignon and although their business was not specified, the choice of diplomats made it clear: Walter Reynolds, now Bishop of Worcester; the royalist Bishop of Norwich; Edward's long-standing supporter and first cousin, the Earl of Richmond, who was a pro-Gaveston supporter; and the reconciled Earl of Pembroke.[18] Their principal task must have been the annulment of Winchelsey's sentence of excommunication. Wasting no time, the party departed in early March, stopping at the French court to seek Philip IV's support before heading on to Avignon.[19]

Edward, however, suffered a setback, as despite his strenuous efforts, he had not completely secured agreement at home. Lancaster, Lincoln, Gloucester, Hereford, Warwick, Surrey and Arundel gathered at Dunstable, under the pretext of a tournament, sometime in late March, nervous or angered at the suggestion of Gaveston's return. Most likely at this gathering, possibly headed by Lancaster who was now detached from

Edward, they set the reform agenda in motion once more; the product of this was a document containing eleven articles, which was presented to the king at Westminster when parliament opened in late April.[20]

The earls announced that the country was not being governed according to Magna Carta and outlined within the eleven articles various concerns including five age-old complaints. The king, they rightfully claimed, was abusing his rights of purveyance as Edward I had done, including excessive requisition of goods for use in the king's household. His officials were widely undertaking purveyance, often without warrant. Purveyance, taking goods at greatly reduced prices or for nothing, and burdening the populace as a consequence, had been a bone of contention when Edward first acted as his father's regent, as far back as 1297. The problem had never really been resolved and, if anything, had grown worse as a cash-strapped king sought to requisition goods. It was a policy that was deeply unpopular with his subjects. Articles four and five alleged that the jurisdiction of the steward and the marshal of the household had been unjustly extended and that the king's use of the privy seal offering royal protections was delaying the course of the common law. These issues had all been discussed by the nobles as far back as 1300 when Edward I had reluctantly granted the *Articuli super Cartas* to address them; but the king was then able, with papal approval, to avoid enacting change.

Among these eleven articles were four new additions, which included a demand to better control the issue of pardons to criminals, who had often been all too easily reprieved if they fought in the late king's armies; the abolition of new customs; an end to the depreciation of the coinage and, lastly, the provision of receivers of petitions to parliament to deal with unheard petitions. Given that most of the parliaments so far in the reign had been taken up with debate and conflict over Gaveston, many petitions from the knights and burgesses had simply remained unanswered.[21] As in April 1308, the assembled earls declared that these reforms had been agreed 'by the community of the realm', a phrase that Edward was becoming all too accustomed to hearing; his innovative coronation oath, born out of his inheritance, now dogging him at every turn.

Waiting no longer, the king made his move. He wanted Gaveston back and so asked parliament directly, which, despite all the royal patronage and currying of favour, was refused. Edward declared that he would not give his answer in relation to the eleven articles until the next parliament. The king, after all, could afford to hold out. It is hard to know what Edward was thinking at the time with regard to parliament's refusal but he still had his trump card to play; the embassy to Avignon was yet to finish its work. On 15 May, the English envoys granted the right of justice in Budos to another of Clement's nephews, Raymond Guillaume de Budos, and this it could be said had the desired effect.[22] On 21 May 1309 pope Clement V issued a bull annulling the sentence of excommunication on Gaveston, because as he chiefly declared, Edward had assured him that he was now reconciled with the earls and they were happy for Gaveston's return. The pope also made it clear that the Archbishop of Canterbury had failed to follow the appropriate procedure in canon law and so on the grounds of a technicality, the sentence was annulled. While Winchelsey was left spitting feathers after Edward had the bull read out to the archbishop and the bishops of London, Winchester and Chichester on 11 June, the bishops, faced with a *fait accompli*, broke ranks with Winchelsey and decided to back the king.[23] Aware that tensions would mount as parliament had refused Gaveston's recall, Edward made conciliatory concessions and ordered on 12 June that the sheriffs throughout the country uphold the Statute of Prises, ensuring goods could not be unduly taken by a lord from his tenants. Six days later, Edward ordered that outstanding crown debts as a result of purveyance be settled.[24] On 14 June, fearing a regrouping of opposition from some of his earls, the king ordered that Lancaster, Surrey, Hereford and others were not to engage in tournaments.[25] The Dunstable tournament had clearly set Edward's nerves on edge and he meant to control the earls he had worked hard to bend, in part, to his will. With tournaments banned, concessions made, and Gaveston's mortal soul no longer in danger, without waiting for parliament, Edward headed to Chester to meet Gaveston and Margaret who had sailed from Dublin by order of the king, travelling through Wales to meet them at the old Roman town on 27 June.[26] Gaveston had only been in exile for a year.

Edward had shown how he could play the political game and bend his nobles partly to his will through the careful application and redirection of patronage and royal favour when he was committed to something that he wanted. Acceding in part to the demand for reform as a concession for Gaveston's return was an astute policy, particularly as many of those reforms were simple repetitions of those demanded from his father in the last decade. For those who had only a year previously opposed Gaveston and the king after the coronation, this must have been intensely frustrating; while Edward had achieved the return of his lover and gained the support of the crown's traditional advisors, two things had been revealed. Firstly, that he was capable of good government and could lead in the business of running the kingdom when he was focussed on a cause. Secondly, that without Gaveston present the nobles could secure their traditional positions as counselors to the king; royal patronage flowed their way and they enjoyed greater access to the crown. In their minds, Gaveston's removal and Edward's improved focus on government only reinforced their view that Gaveston's presence threatened their positions and ability to work with Edward. As they saw it, reform was not likely to be achieved while Piers was with the king. Everything now rested on how Gaveston, Edward and the nobles could make his return work. The focus now, of course, was on how Gaveston would position himself back at court.

11

The Ordinances

Gaveston returned from Ireland with some determination to work more openly with his peers in a way not seen prior to his forced departure. Parliament convened at Stamford on 27 July, following writs of summons which had been issued by the king on the day Clement V's bull of absolution had been read out to Winchelsey and his three assembled bishops.[1] The mood must have been uncomfortable and full of weary suspicion as Edward and Gaveston were supported by the now outwardly sympathetic earls of Lincoln, Gloucester, Pembroke, Richmond and Hereford. The bishops of Durham, Chichester, London, Worcester, Winchester and Norwich with the Bishop-elect of Bath & Wells also stood by them. Gaveston was back – and those who remained in opposition to his return had little choice but to grudgingly accept it.

Edward granted concessions to help ease the mood, agreeing to uphold the eleven articles that had been presented at Westminster earlier in the year. He reconfirmed the *Articuli super Cartas*, promising to limit excessive purveyance and prises in particular, as well agreeing to the remaining demands to limit the authority of the steward and marshal of the royal household. On 20 August the county sheriffs were ordered to proclaim the Statute of Stamford across the kingdom and with it, Edward must have hoped he had reached a turning point.[2] In return, a relieved parliament granted the promised taxation it had held back as a bargaining tool, but more importantly for Piers, consented on 5 August to his restoration to the earldom of Cornwall, both in land and title. Lancaster's seal, however, is conspicuously absent from the charter of enfeoffment, he himself being absent at Stamford. Only two days earlier Piers had been careful to surrender the lands he held in exile, amounting to £4,000.[3] Edward's strategy had played out well.

Gaveston, perhaps on the king's advice, was careful to build relationships and was seen through the remaining year working more closely with his fellow peers, whereas in the past he had remained principally in isolation. In joint partnership, Gaveston, Gloucester and Lincoln presented a petition to Edward on 10 December requesting that the king cease collecting the agreed tax of a twenty-fifth from 21 December until 10 February 1310 as the terms of the Statute of Stamford were not being fully observed.[4] Gaveston continued his excellent relationship with the Earl of Richmond, who, according to Richmond's chaplain John of Canterbury, Piers 'loved beyond measure', calling each other father and son.[5] The author of the *Vita* noted,

> ...the earl of Lincoln, who the year before had been foremost of the barons in bringing about Piers' exile, now became a friendly go-between and mediator. At his repeated and anxious requests the earl Warenne who, ever since the conclusion of the Wallingford tournament, had never shown Piers any welcome, became his inseparable friend and faithful helper. See how often and abruptly great men change their sides.[6]

But not everything was hail fellow well met. In fact, what is striking throughout this time is that Gaveston worked with these few earls only, and does not appear to have forged any positive relationships with his remaining peers. Whether he tried, was shunned and afterwards reacted more defensively, or he felt he was unable to reach out to them because he resented them for bringing about the shame of his second exile, is not clear. Edward too was being more circumspect with his patronage, but perceptions that Gaveston held sway over gifts of lands, wardships and offices, both for himself and for his followers at the expense of everyone else, still persisted at court. When he had one of Lancaster's retainers removed and replaced with one of his own choosing, rumours swirled and, of course, offended Lancaster.[7]

The uneasy restraint on both sides once more began to crumble. Gaveston lashed out and foolishly created nicknames for some of his greatest detractors, calling Lancaster 'the churl' or 'the fiddler', Pembroke 'Joseph the Jew', Lincoln 'burst belly' in reference to the size of his waist and Ralph de Monthermer, the second husband of Edward's deceased sister Joan, 'whoreson' on account of his illegitimacy. For his longest serving critic, the Earl of Warwick, Piers reserved the title of 'the black dog of Arden', to which, if the Lanercost chronicler is to be believed, Warwick replied 'if he call me a dog, be sure that I will bite him so soon as I shall perceive my opportunity'.[8] That bite would one day injure the Earl of Cornwall and the result would bring about such devastation that it would cast a shadow over the larger part of Edward's reign.

Those earls singled out by Gaveston did not need much encouragement to set out their protests more openly, refusing on 18 October to attend a *secretum parliamentum* called by the king to meet at York on account of Gaveston's presence.[9] Any semblance of harmony achieved at Stamford was quickly evaporating. Edward was furious and eight days later, sent out writs altering the date parliament should meet to 8 February 1310. Again, those in opposition refused to attend, protesting about Gaveston and arguing that parliament should be located somewhere more convenient. Edward changed the summons once more on 12 December, this time to meet at Westminster in two months time.[10] With a growing sense of unease, Edward and Gaveston, with Isabella and Margaret, headed to the king's manor at Langley to see out Christmas and 'fully made up [their] former absence by their long wished for sessions of daily and intimate conversations'.[11]

The mood at the start of 1310 deteriorated rapidly. On 19 January Edward banned tournaments, again attempting to keep opposition to him and Gaveston in check. The earls sent word to Edward refusing to come to parliament because Gaveston 'was lurking in the king's chamber', that their 'approach would be unsafe' and 'if it was absolutely necessary to present themselves before the king, they vowed that they would make their appearance not unarmed as they were wont to do, but armed.'[12] This, they added, was not to threaten the king, but to protect themselves from Gaveston. Quite what Piers was expected to do is not clear, nor is there any evidence to suggest that either he or the king planned to seize any of their opponents. Edward responded on 7 February ordering Lancaster, Warwick, Pembroke and Hereford to attend but on no account to appear armed. They ignored the latter.

Fearing the worst, at the same time the king ordered Gloucester, Surrey and Richmond to provide safe conduct to those attending parliament and to arrest anyone who broke his explicit commands, as well as settling any quarrels that arose during the session; a job they must have dreaded.[13] To best protect Piers, Edward sent him away for his own safety, the location still unknown, fearing that his armed nobles may attempt to take matters into their own hands.[14]

The purpose of parliament outlined in the writs of summons was to discuss what action needed to be taken against the 'enemy, rebel and traitor' Robert Bruce, whose resurgence was undermining English gains in Scotland while Edward and the court were preoccupied by domestic and personal politics.[15] This topic never entered the discussions. As another hostile parliament got underway, Edward was presented with a damning petition outlining his rule to date by the Earl of Lancaster.[16] Lancaster, now more than estranged from his cousin, had taken up leadership of those in opposition. Edward listened as Lancaster accused him of being guided by evil counsel; that he had improvised the crown and was unable to maintain his household except through extortion, breaching Magna Carta as a consequence; that he was losing Scotland, and was dismembering crown lands in England and Ireland; that taxes granted to him by 'the community of the realm' in the last parliament and at Northampton in 1307 to fight in Scotland and act as relief against the hated prises through the king's policy of purveyance, were being wasted and the people remained burdened. Finally, Lancaster announced that the war in Scotland, a question of national pride and a necessity in the north of England, was not being pursued. He ended by demanding that the king look to the ordinance of his barons to avoid these further dangers and, calling upon them, as they were faithfully bound to him by allegiance, to address such issues and concern on his behalf.[17]

As in April 1308, the king refused outright. Parliament held firm, with those few not in agreement unable to aid the king in his defence.[18] As the twenty-six-year-old Edward became further entrenched, the opposition became uglier and declared that if the king refused to stand by the decisions made by the community of the realm then he was in breach of his sacred coronation oath, and as such they were duty-bound to retract their oaths of allegiance. The threat, whether real or not, was one that Edward could not afford to test. Deposing a king with no son to succeed him was most likely never a serious option that parliament would pursue but, under immense pressure and faced with nowhere to go, Edward relented.[19] He must have felt embattled and overwhelmed.

On 16 March 1310 the king issued letters patent agreeing to the election of twenty-one Ordainers who were to have authority to review and reform the government of the kingdom and his royal household, so long as those reforms were not prejudicial to his sovereignty. Their term, Edward agreed, was to run for exactly one year starting on 29 September 1310.[20] In this the king, while forced into yet another political corner, was shrewd enough to ensure the letters patent protected his sovereignty, in effect creating a loophole through which he could repudiate anything he felt came too close to his royal dignity. Much like his father, Edward II had grasped the rules of the political game enough to know how to fight for his inherited rights, albeit in defence rather than attack.

The Ordainers wasted no time. Three days after Edward issued his letters patent, six preliminary Ordinances were drafted at the house of the Carmelites in the city of London and presented to the king. Although these would later be incorporated in the New Ordinances a year later, they demanded the ongoing protection of the liberties of the Church, that the Ordainers base themselves in London under the protection of the king and that the mayor and aldermen of the city were to have access to the records of the exchequer and chancery. The king was not to gift land, revenues, wardships and marriages without the Ordainers express approval; revenues from custom duties were to be paid directly to the exchequer and not the king's household; foreign merchants who had profited from the custom duties since 1307 should be arrested and their goods seized until they had accounted to the exchequer; and, finally, that the king uphold Magna Carta in its full form.[21] It was not a good omen as control over the king's household was handed over and prised open for review. Nevertheless, Edward strategically delayed giving his consent until 2 August, some four-and-a-half-months after he first received the petition.

On 20 March while Parliament remained in session until 12 April, twenty-one ordainers were duly elected, the composition of which was a fair balance between reformers and those more sympathetic to the king. The nineteen bishops who attended parliament elected Lincoln and Pembroke as the first two ordainers. Of the twelve earls at Westminster they elected two bishops, Ralph Baldock and Simon of Ghent. These four then together elected two barons, Hugh de Veer and William le Marshall. The six subsequently elected the remaining fifteen of their body, which included the Archbishop of Canterbury, the bishops of Salisbury, Chichester, Norwich, St David's and Llandaff. Of the earls, Gloucester, Lancaster, Hereford, Arundel and Warwick each found a seat, with the barons Robert fitz Roger, Hugh de Courtenany, William Martin and John Gray. Of the remaining earls, Surrey, and Oxford, who was a political nonentity, were not elected; nor, unsurprisingly, was Gaveston.[22] Edward was clearly frustrated by these forced concessions and the manner in which they had been granted. On 11 May, in a defiant mood, he had the Bishop of Chichester replaced as chancellor with his long-term loyal ally and treasurer, Walter Reynolds, Bishop of Worcester. Reynolds, in turn, was replaced as treasurer by John Sandal.[23] This was testing the waters, for the preliminary Ordinances had not yet been granted by the king, who only did so on 2 August. He was, in other words, technically free to make the appointment without first seeking approval. Nevertheless, it rattled the body, which distrusted the king's intent.

Although Scotland had not been discussed at the Westminster Parliament, Edward had been informed by Alexander Abernethy and Alexander of Argyll at a council meeting that he needed to act now or lose Scotland altogether.[24] Bruce had held his first parliament as king on 16–17 March at St Andrews, a pivotal moment in the wider Scottish acknowledgement of Bruce as their king.[25] The English were losing their grip on Scotland. This, coupled with Lancaster's damning criticism at parliament, accusing the king of neglecting the war, was enough to spur Edward into action. He also realised that a campaign north of the border could either slow down the work of the ordainers, who only had until 29 September 1311 to complete their commission, or give the king distance from them. The army was subsequently ordered to assemble at Berwick-upon-Tweed for 8 September but, hampered by limited finances, the assembled force was small – about 4,700 knights, infantry and archers. The arrival of a further 3,000 men mustered from Ireland was cancelled at the last minute, owing to bad weather and rough seas.

Lancaster, Hereford, Pembroke and Warwick all refused to attend, focusing instead they said on their work as ordainers, now undertaken in London, as the king knew all too well. Instead each sent the minimum number of men they were legally obliged to muster, which amounted to five knights' fees, and eight in the case of Lancaster. Success for Edward in Scotland was not something they openly relished, as it would give him a renewed platform on which to challenge any reform of his household or government more widely. The zeal for reform was so great that Hereford, Warwick and Pembroke, all of whom had lands to lose in Scotland, preferred to stay south. This exposes the dissatisfaction felt in attending a campaign that Gaveston was taking part in.[26] Gloucester, Richmond and Surrey accompanied Piers, but the Earl of Lincoln was absent on account of the fact that Edward had made him *custo regni* while he was out of England.[27]

Edward, relieved to be away, left London at the end of July and met up with Gaveston again on the 7 September; Gaveston had left court much earlier, in February 1310. They arrived at Roxburgh on the 16th. The king campaigned in earnest and was at Renfrew and Glasgow during the middle of October and at Edinburgh via Linlithgow by the end of the month. The campaign to bolster support for the many remaining English-held castles principally below the Forth was underway. Bruce, though, knew the game well and would not commit to open battle with the English, favouring instead the odd skirmish and guerrilla tactics, which had been so successfully employed during the first decade of the fourteenth century. Frustrated by the lack of any major success, the army bedded down for winter, Edward setting up his court at Berwick, Gaveston at Roxburgh, Gloucester at Norham and Surrey at Wark.[28]

In January the campaign continued. This time Edward, who remained at Berwick, ordered Gaveston to leave Roxburgh, which he did on the 16th, and headed for Perth via Dundee, which he passed through on the 21st: his aim, to crush any support for Bruce.[29] Gloucester and Surrey passed through Selkirk forest in February, looking for men who were willing to swear allegiance to the king of England. Sad news reached Edward on 15 February that the Earl of Lincoln had died on the 5th, removing at a stroke an earl who, still in Westminster, may have been able to moderate the ordainers as they composed their reforms. Edward replaced him on 4 March with Gloucester, who was sent south to take up the role of *custos regni* and who was given the justices William de Bereford and Henry le Scrope to advise him.[30] Gloucester, though, was no Lincoln and before long was at loggerheads with Lancaster. On 3 March the royalist Bishop of Durham Anthony Bek also died. For the king the death of Henry de Lacy meant that Thomas of Lancaster, already Earl of Lancaster, Leicester and Derby, would now inherit Henry's earldoms of Lincoln and Salisbury through right of Thomas' wife Alice, making Thomas by far the premier earl in England, as he now commanded a vast fortune of more than £11,000 a year. In contrast, Gaveston's lands from his earldom of Cornwall amounted to an annual income of £4,000, while Gloucester could boast £6,000 by 1314.[31]

It didn't take long for Lancaster to flex his muscles. He was now Edward's main problem. As the earl headed north to meet the king to swear fealty for his two additional earldoms, Lancaster refused to meet him in Scotland, wary that his fealty could be legally challenged if offered out of the kingdom. Edward refused to move south until eventually, after heated exchanges, he moved a few miles across the border to accept Lancaster, who was on bended knee.[32] On 27 May, he released the de Lacy lands to his cousin.[33]

In late March Gaveston, after a brief visit to Edward at Berwick, eventually gave up Perth in May to Henry de Percy and the pro-English Earl of Angus, who had an accompanying force of 200 men-at-arms, and headed instead to Dundee.[34] For most of the campaign Edward and Gaveston were not in each other's company, although they remained in regular contact by messenger. It is most likely that Edward hoped Gaveston, renowned for his martial ability, might secure great success and thus reputation while campaigning in Scotland independently of the king. It was not to be, as the Scots continued to refuse to commit to battle.[35] Had Piers done so, it would have been far harder for those who opposed him to continue to do so.

As money began to run out by the start of 1311, on 28 February Edward wrote to his treasurer, who was also a co-executor for Lincoln's late estate, urgently requesting the release of 4,000 marks owed to him to help fund the campaign.[36] The request bore no fruit. Edward knew he could not make any further headway in Scotland without the grant of additional parliamentary taxation and so, with great reluctance, by the start of summer he turned and headed south, just as Bruce, in Edward's wake, swept through the English border counties harrassing the local population. On 16 June, a week before he left Berwick, Edward sent out a summons for parliament to convene in London for 8 August, most likely with foreboding.[37] He had done his utmost to delay the ordainers in their work but this only antagonised them, most notably when he decided that the exchequer should relocate to York while he was on campaign. Even Lincoln before his death was so outraged by the proposal he had threatened to resign his position as regent if Edward did not change his mind.[38] To make matters worse, in October 1310, the king had appointed Gaveston as Justice of the Forest north of the Trent and constable of Nottingham castle; the former a lucrative position and one gained without the consent of the ordainers.[39] It was not a shrewd move. As ever, Edward was allowing his personal feelings to dictate his policy.

As they headed south, the king knew that Gaveston's safety was at risk, for in the previous year, a possible attempt was made on Piers' life, given that the earl and six others were later pardoned for killing Thomas de Walkingham of Yorkshire that September. The author of the *Vita* mentions that from 1310 the earl was in danger of assassination.[40] The country was becoming restless; burdened by taxation and prises inflicted on them, the presence of Gaveston was seen by many on the back of malicious gossip as the root of the problem. The king had Gaveston installed in the mighty fortress of Bamburgh in Northumberland, away from any who wished him harm, while he continued onwards to meet his parliament.[41]

In 1174 the beleaguered Henry II, who was fighting an internal war against his wife Eleanor of Aquitaine and his many sons across the Angevin Empire, walked through the streets of Canterbury barefoot to the tomb of the then recently murdered Archbishop of Canterbury Thomas Becket. Henry was responsible, whether wittingly or not, for his brutal demise. After Henry was whipped by the monks and spent the night in penitential prayer, his luck changed forever. God and Becket, it seemed, had heard his prayers and were satisfied with his act of humility and from that moment, Henry turned the tide of war to become one of the strongest kings of Europe. Just before Edward attended parliament in August 1311, he too went on pilgrimage to Canterbury to the shrine of Thomas Becket, as he was wont to do, to make his devotions and kneel before the saint's shrine, praying long and hard for divine intervention. Surely Edward hoped his great-great-grandfather, and Beckett, could offer the support that he sorely needed. For Edward had seen only weeks earlier a draft copy of the work with which the twenty-one ordainers had tasked themselves. Walking into parliament in London on 16 August he knew he was going to be fighting not only for Gaveston but now for something more far reaching; his own greater sovereignty. He would need God, St Thomas and the intercession of his ancestors to overcome what would be one of his greatest challenges.

The Ordinances of 1311 were, beyond question, one of the fundamental pieces of legislation laid in front of a medieval king – almost an equal to Magna Carta itself, in terms of the attempt to curb the power and authority of the king. The document contained a comprehensive set of forty-one clauses, mostly restricting the king's authority in some form or other. The king, they ordained, was not to exercise patronage without the approval of parliament; in clause nine he was forbidden to go to war or leave the kingdom without prior approval; clause ten abolished prises through purveyance altogether; customs were to be paid directly into the exchequer and not collected by others including the financier Amerigo dei Frescobaldi, whom Edward relied on for foreign loans; the king's household could no longer be financed directly, receiving its income from the exchequer, limiting Edward's ability to spend independently. Clause twenty-nine ordained that parliament was to meet at least once a year, twice if necessary, in a convenient location, no longer on the whim of the king. Clause fourteen removed the right for Edward to appoint his own royal administrators including the treasurer, chancellor, steward, chief justices and keeper of the privy seal. Clause thirteen demanded that all 'evil counsellors' were to be removed and replaced by suitable alternatives. These clauses and many more were so far-reaching that they effectively rendered the king subject to the community of the realm, meaning, as always at this time, the nobility.[42] It was a straitjacket calculated to curb entirely the power and independence of the king and a means by which the nobility could take control of his personal household. Such attempts to curb royal power had not been seen since Simon de Montfort put the Oxford Provisions before Henry III in 1258.

If this was not in itself shocking enough for Edward, there was the expected declaration that the Earl of Cornwall was one of the king's evil counsellors – being singled out in a comprehensive clause of his very own. The nobility's patience with Gaveston had come to an end. Clause twenty set out that Gaveston was 'evil' and had ill advised the king, detached him from his natural and loyal lieges and his people, had robbed the kingdom and the crown of land, and wealth which he had stowed abroad; that he had drawn to him men whom by oath supported him against all others, assumed royal dignity, taken offices for himself and his supporters displacing men of honour, even after the preliminary Ordinances had prohibited it; he had taken the king to war in Scotland without the consent of all the nobles thereby endangering him, and was so corrupt that he simply had to go. In fact they had decided and set out, learning from their previous experiences, not only had he to leave England, but he was to leave Edward's dominion altogether – England, Wales, Ireland and his lands held in France. Gaveston was, they declared, never to return under any circumstance and should he do so he would be excommunicate, and any persons aiding him would be treated as felons and face the full penalty of the law.[43]

Faced with such an overwhelming attack on his own royal sovereignty and his favourite, Edward did the only thing he could. He refused all the demands outright and declared that the authority of the Ordainers was to reform only things that did not touch upon his sovereignty. Parliament bullied the twenty-seven-year-old king hard and threatened outright civil war. Edward held firm but was counselled by those more moderate that he simply did not have enough men or money to fight back. In desperation he hit out, applying the strategy he had used more successfully between the summers of 1308 to 1309. The king reminded the assembled nobles that they had themselves allowed the earl to return and were agreed in restoring Gaveston to his earldom. It changed nothing. Edward then declared he would accept all forty clauses so long as they dropped clause twenty and stopped pursuing the Earl of Cornwall. This was, on the face of it, an act of desperation to hold onto his lover when exile this time would mean losing Gaveston altogether. However, Edward was not foolish enough to expect to agree to the Ordinances and then live with them. He, like his father, grandfather and many ancestors before him, undoubtedly would apply the same strategy in times of crisis; accept the terms now, keep Piers if he could and seek to undermine and overturn the Ordinances later, most likely through papal annulment.

The nobles, all too aware of this strategy, refused outright. Gaveston, they declared again, must go and all forty-one of the clauses were to be adopted. If not, they would be forced to defend themselves with arms. Under enormous emotional pressure and surrounded by very few, if any, counsellors who advised him to hold out, Edward had no choice but to accept the Ordinances in full, under duress, which he duly did on 27 September 1311; two days before the Ordainers' official commission ran out. The Ordinances were published in the churchyard of St Paul's by the Bishop of Salisbury, who was acting on behalf of the Archbishop of Canterbury, to an audience that included the chief leaders Lancaster and Warwick, as well as Hereford, Pembroke, Arundel and Oxford. On 10 October, copies of the Ordinances were sent out to every county across the country to be proclaimed as law by the sheriffs.[44] To commemorate their achievement and Edward's acceptance, Lancaster had a tablet erected in St Paul's churchyard to mark the occasion.[45] The king, furious and utterly exhausted, had lost.

12

Murder at Blacklow Hill

On the morning of 4 November, three days later than decreed in the Ordinances, Gaveston set sail into his third exile. The month before, Edward had written to his sister Margaret and her husband John, Duke of Brabant, seeking a safe haven for his favourite.[1] On 13 October he sent Gerard Salveyn, one of his household knights and possibly the man involved in the initial clash between Edward and Lancaster in 1308, to France, to seek safe conduct from Philip IV, allowing Gaveston to pass through his kingdom in order to reach his new home.[2] Hampered by limited means, the fifteen-year-old Queen Isabella offered financial aid from her revenues from the county of Ponthieu to help ease Gaveston's exile.[3] Isabella must have seen first-hand the emotional distress this situation was causing her husband, Piers, and Margaret de Clare, who was now seven months pregnant, and wanted to help reduce their suffering. There is little evidence that Isabella was openly hostile to Gaveston since 1308 and this act of kindness came at a moment of great need and was certainly a welcome gesture.

Edward, as expected, began to fight back. The king moved large chests of coin and jewels by barge from Westminster to his apartments at the Tower of London to help secure him a ready source of cash should he need to pawn them. The Ordainers may have thought they had immediate control over the king's financial resources but Edward wrongfooted them. Two days after the Ordinances were published, the king sent Robert de Newington and William de Lughtebergh to the pope seeking their annulment where Edward deemed them prejudicial to his crown. His envoys' commission also sought the support of the seven English representatives at the Council of Vienne, which included the Archbishop of York, the bishops of London, Winchester and Carlisle, as well as Master Adam Orleton, canon of Hereford.

With Gaveston in exile, the political tension at court did not get any better. During the second session of parliament, which began in

November, the earls of Lancaster and Warwick, spurred on by their recent success, set before Edward a further set of ordinances despite their commission having run out at the end of September.[4] These last-minute additions can barely be called reforms, but sought to build on clause thirteen of the Ordinances, which demanded the removal of evil counsellors. Edward had no choice but to read through the twenty-five names singled out for their apparent bad counsel and it is no surprise to find that eighteen of them were men directly connected with Gaveston.[5] Those doomed by association included Piers' yeomen John de Charlton and John de Knockin, his attorney William de Vaux, recently appointed for five years during Gaveston's expected absence, with Roger de Wellsworth who was his clerk and treasurer and John de Hothum.[6] Edward, it was also demanded, was to remove further close friends of his own including Henry de Beaumont and his sister Isabella de Vescy.[7] Edward was apoplectic with rage. This time he had truly been pushed too far. He decided to fight back, only now he would be unstoppable.

The tension at court was palpable. On 28 November an angry Edward ordered those earls who had come armed to parliament to remove their men and weapons.[8] Tournaments, such as the ones proposed at Northampton, were banned. Rumours began to circulate that Gaveston had not gone into exile at all but had ventured back to his lands in Cornwall and was hiding in remote places such as his former castle at Tintagel or worse still, lurking in secret in the king's bedchamber.[9] The former Ordainers themselves were concerned enough to send two of their band, Hugh de Courtenay and William Martin, through the west country to either capture him or at least dispel the rumours. They failed, of course, because Gaveston was in Flanders, made clear on 23 December when the king paid a messenger a pound for travelling from the continent bearing letters from the former Earl of Cornwall.[10] Gaveston hysteria was still in vogue. In this charged atmosphere, Edward bided his time and held his Christmas court at Westminster, gambling at dice and mulling over his plans. What he would do next would have life-changing consequences for all involved.

Royal defiance characterised 1312. Edward left Westminster shortly after the New Year, taking with him a heavily pregnant Margaret de Clare. She went to York, while the king arrived at Gaveston's former castle of Knaresborough on the 8th. Gerard Salveyn, who had again been dispatched to the Continent on 1 December, arrived through the castle gates shortly afterwards, this time with a companion, Gaveston. Whether this was a secret fleeting visit so Gaveston could be with Margaret for the birth of their first child, or a fully staged return, is not immediately clear. But given Edward's mood the latter is more likely. He was determined more than ever to have his way. The royal party immediately set out for

York, arriving on the 13th, the day after Gaveston's wife Margaret had given birth to a daughter named Joan.[11] Three days later, the king, in front of an assembled crowd of local knights and burgesses, declared that he had been forced under duress to accept the Ordinances, which were prejudicial to his crown. He was therefore, as law and custom allowed, revoking them forthwith. Whether the crowd shared the king's opinion is a matter of conjecture.

On 18 January Edward officially announced via a document he personally drafted that Gaveston's exile had been against 'law and custom' and now he had returned and justified himself to the king, Edward was satisfied that Gaveston was both good and loyal.[12] Two days later, the king restored the earldom of Cornwall in full.[13] On the same day, jubilant in his defiance, Edward gave forty marks to Margaret to celebrate her churching and threw a feast at the house of the Friars Minor at York. The packed audience were entertained by Edward's fool King Robert and his minstrels, with much drinking, merriment and dancing.[14] This jubilant atmosphere was the last they were likely to enjoy as opposition was growing more menacing in London.

Edward knew that his actions in January would have a profound impact and strike at the very heart of the Ordainers' agenda. That was always his intention. On 26 January, with Gaveston back in the royal camp, in an attempt to appease the strengthening opposition, the king issued an order declaring that he would uphold those clauses that were not prejudicial to his crown, perhaps misguidedly thinking that this might mitigate the anger of his earls.[15] Three days later, a formal proclamation of Gaveston's return and restoration to his estates was read out in the Guildhall in London and was received with general hostility.[16] Lancaster responded, sending a letter to the king demanding that he uphold clause twenty; Gaveston, he declared, must go into exile or hand himself over to the barons for judgement. Edward flatly refused.[17] The ensuing deadlock could now only be settled one way. Preparations for open conflict on both sides began in earnest.

Edward was again quick to act. Sending out orders to men such as William de Montacute and John de Percy, the king placed ten castles into a state of alert, ensuring they were provisioned and able to withstand assault.[18] No expense was spared; £30 was spent on the defences of York castle where the king was to base himself.[19] Through February, Edward and Gaveston continued their defensive preparations. By the end of the month they were briefly at Scarborough ensuring that the mighty fortress, in need of some repair, was made ready. Scarborough is a formidable castle, high up on the headland, so was a good location in which to sit things out. Accessible by land and sea, provisions could be brought into a besieged garrison or could equally provide an escape route by boat should the castle fall. They had decided that Gaveston, with his brother Arnaud-Guillaume de Marsan and their sister who arrived in March, were to weather the storm there.[20] They were further bolstered on 17 March by the arrival of forty-eight men-at-arms to swell the ranks of the much smaller garrison. If this was to be Gaveston's last stand, they were certainly wasting none of the time available to them. Edward took pains to build and maintain the support of the people of the town as well as at York, by reconfirming their charters of liberties.[21] Support of the local populace, surely reluctant to be swept up into this civil conflict, was essential to Edward's planning; without it, his opponents could march around the north unopposed. As pressure mounted, the king continued to use a double strategy, again seeking the intercession of the pope by sending his envoy, Gaveston's nephew Bertrand Caillau, to France. Securing papal absolution from his oath to uphold the Ordinances would in an instant render the opposition hamstrung. As Edward was all too aware, time was fast running out. The net was closing in on them and they knew it.

An indignant Lancaster and those earls who opposed Gaveston met at St Paul's in London on 13 March more determined than ever to bring about his destruction or removal. Ignoring Edward's revocation of the Ordinances, they declared them valid and swore by oath not to rest until they were enforced in full and Gaveston removed from the king.[22] The earls each took on a role to close in on Gaveston, hoping that they could detach him from the king, whom they were not willing to attack head on. The Earl of Gloucester, who decided to support whatever the earls agreed upon, was given the south to ward and was least likely to come into direct contact with his uncle, the king. Hereford was to protect the east, Lancaster Wales and the west, while Robert Clifford and Henry de Percy were to head north and close off the northern border. Fear and rumour had mounted as Edward and Gaveston unexpectedly moved from York to Newcastle for a period of three weeks. Allegations spread that Edward was in talks with Robert Bruce, who might place Gaveston in safe custody in return for a peaceful solution to the Scottish conflict. While there is limited evidence to support this claim in the chronicles, which may just be reiterating hearsay, the party were at Newcastle, stalled there by a sudden illness that meant Gaveston needed rest and to receive prolonged treatment from the doctor William de Burntoft.[23] Unlikely or not, the nobles clearly felt threatened by the idea. Pembroke and Warrenne, who in the last year had stood by the king, now moved into opposition to Piers and were given the unenviable task of bringing him in. Striding into the Exchequer in London, the chamberlains were told in no uncertain terms not to send any financial aid north, especially to those who were helping 'the enemy of the kingdom'.[24] With the lifelines cut, the trap was set. All they had to do was capture their quarry.

By the start of spring England stood on the brink of outright civil war. Edward was of a mind to fight for both Gaveston's right to remain by his side and his earldom of Cornwall, along with his own broader sovereignty. On 28 March the king granted to his favourite order, the Dominicans, 700 marks to be used by them to found a house at Langley to celebrate prayers 'for the souls of his ancestors, for himself and for his state'.[25] This gift, fulfilling an oath made years before, suggests that Edward may well have been prepared to accept, or at least had considered, that this could mean a fight leading to imprisonment or death. He was making preparations for his immortal soul. It is characteristic of his profound sense of loyalty to those closest to him that he would be willing to sacrifice himself to save others. On 4 April, after formally granting custody of Scarborough and Carlisle castles to Gaveston just days before, Edward commanded Piers on pain of forfeiture not to surrender himself or Scarborough to anyone, even if the king were brought before him a prisoner. If the king was to die, Gaveston should hold it still and for his heirs.[26] This was an extraordinary command.

By the start of May, news of Lancaster's approach a few miles outside Newcastle at the head of a large host reached the king, just hours before Robert Clifford and Henry de Percy swept into the town. Lancaster had travelled by night to avoid word getting out, but this subterfuge had failed at the last moment. Entering the castle without hindrance from the local populace, the magnates were disappointed to find it empty, their quarry fled in great haste to Tynemouth. In his determination to escape, the king had left a substantial part of his baggage train behind, including war horses, arms, a great stash of jewels and other valuables, which were a boon for Lancaster.[27] The treasure trove was just that and possibly made up of items Edward had shipped to the Tower of London from Westminster. Without it, Edward's finances were limited at the time of greatest need.

The royal party, with a now pregnant Isabella, quickly moved on from Tynemouth to Scarborough, which they reached on 10 May; Edward and Gaveston by sea and Isabella and her retinue by road, which was the much safer method of travel for her while she was in her first trimester. Leaving Gaveston behind the safety of the walls with his brother and sister, Edward continued on to York via Knaresborough, where he arrived on 17 May, meeting up with the queen who had arrived safely.[28] Edward was careful to ensure throughout these chaotic months that his wife was well cared for and they appeared close and working together in a tightly bound partnership. If the sixteen-year-old Isabella was hostile to Gaveston at this point, it is hard to find evidence for it.

Piers Gaveston holding out behind the walls of Scarborough did not have to wait long. Almost immediately after Edward left him on

10 May, Pembroke, Surrey and Henry de Percy arrived and began their assault. In a frantic bid to keep his earls in check, Edward wrote to them demanding that they break their siege lines.[29] They ignored him. Lancaster set up his men between York and Scarborough, effectively cutting the king off from his favourite, which the earls had always hoped to achieve. Edward became desperate. To stall for time while he awaited news from the pope and the king of France, the king sent letters that suggested favourable terms of surrender to Gaveston, who in turn persuaded the Earl of Pembroke to uphold them.[30] The terms were well considered on Edward's part. Pembroke, Surrey and Percy were to promise on oath and by the consent of the community of the realm to protect Gaveston while he was to be taken into custody and sent with them to meet the king and Lancaster, or his representative, at St Mary's Abbey in York. There they would formally present the terms of surrender to all parties. If Edward was unwilling to continue negotiations over Gaveston's future with the assembled opposition, then by 1 August Piers could return to Scarborough, at which point the earls' guarantee of safe conduct would come to an end. During his absence Scarborough was not to be further garrisoned or the grain stores restocked thus giving him an advantage. In return, Pembroke, Surrey and Percy promised to forfeit their lands if Gaveston came to any harm while he was in their custody and Piers in turn promised not to counsel the king to alter the terms of the agreement.[31] It was a generous offer and one each party readily accepted to prevent a protracted siege. Edward had secured at the eleventh hour both respite from the assault and also time. His attempts to raise men at York had failed, either because there was no appetite from the local inhabitants or because the king was now in financial difficulty without his baggage train. With the deal done, Gaveston subsequently opened the castle gates and placed himself into the custody of Pembroke, Surrey and Percy, as promised.

The party reached the king on 26 May at St Mary's Abbey. It is not clear whether Edward and Gaveston were permitted to see each other, as no reference is made of Gaveston being in attendance, so it is likely they did not and he was held nearby. The king gave promises that he would satisfy the demands of the earls at the next parliament, while they in turn renewed their oaths to protect Piers on pain of forfeiture.[32] As the charged meeting drew to a close, Piers was placed in the sole custody of Pembroke who, it was agreed, was to head south taking Gaveston to his castle at Wallingford while the king summoned parliament to meet at Lincoln on 23 July.[33] This was certainly a better outcome for the Earl of Cornwall, who, already hampered by low provisions at Scarborough had a chance of gaining time and was therefore likely to come out of this chaotic year with some form of political settlement that may be more in his favour. Edward too would have a platform on which to challenge and hopefully revoke the Ordinances, supported by international voices. Or at least that is how Edward saw it.

With the deal done, Gaveston and Pembroke moved south. On 9 June they reached Deddington in Oxfordshire and bedded down for the night. Leaving Gaveston under light guard because de Valence knew Piers would not flee, Pembroke went to visit his wife Beatrice at Bampton, 20 miles away. It was to be a fatal misjudgement. Next morning as dawn broke, Gaveston awoke to a nightmare. The 'Black Dog of Arden' had come to bite.

> Coming to the village very early one Saturday he [Warwick] entered the gate of the courtyard and surrounded the chamber. Then the earl called out in a loud voice: 'Arise traitor, thou art taken.' When Piers heard this, seeing that the earl was there with a superior force and that his own guard did not resist, he dressed himself and came down. In this fashion Piers was taken and led forth not as an earl but as a thief; and he who used to ride on a palfrey is now forced to go on foot.[34]

Warwick marched Gaveston 25 miles north to Warwick Castle and threw him into his prison. Eight days elapsed before Lancaster, Hereford, Arundel and John Botetourt assembled in the Great Hall of the castle. What followed was a mock trial in which the former Earl of Cornwall was not permitted to speak in his defence as accusations of breaking the Ordinances and his treachery were bandied around. The penalty for such treachery, they declared, was death and by mutual agreement sentence was passed. Piers had become, through no legal process, a condemned man. The trial had no legitimacy and the nobles were acting outside their jurisdiction. At the very least Gaveston had the right to be tried by his peers in parliament and more importantly, whether the nobles agreed or not, Edward had revoked the Ordinances which removed the platform on which Piers could be judged. If he was to die, this was calculated murder.

As dawn broke on 19 June, Piers Gaveston was forced out of Warwick Castle by Lancaster, Hereford, Arundel and Botetourt, while the Earl of Warwick himself stayed behind, lurking in his fortress. Two miles north of the town they came to Blacklow Hill, 4 miles from Kenilworth Castle and under the ownership of Lancaster, now the premier earl in England. Gaveston was handed over to two Welshmen who led him to the top of the hill. There, so all could see, one Welshman ran him through the body with a sword; while he collapsed there dying, the other eventually cut off his head.[35] The butchered body was left where it fell as the party of nobles separated and the onlookers dispersed.

According to the *Annales Londonensis* four shoemakers from Warwick gathered up the body parts and carried the mutilated corpse back to the Earl of Warwick who was still in his castle. He refused to receive them and promptly instructed them to return the body to Blacklow Hill.[36] Eventually the Dominicans travelled to the hill and collected up the bloody corpse, sewed the head back onto the body and transferred it to their house at Oxford. This act of kindness against such marked savagery could not extend to Gaveston's burial, for he had died excommunicate and therefore could not be buried in Holy ground.[37]

Piers Gaveston, thrice exiled favourite and lover of the king, had been brutally put to death with no sound legal process by a group of men bound by oath to uphold the Ordinances. Lancaster had taken responsibility for his murder by allowing the crime to take place on his land, but no earl, especially Warwick, was free from blame. They all had Gaveston's blood staining their hands. Everything now rested on what Edward would do next.

13

Fragile Peace

At the time of Gaveston's murder Edward was with Isabella at Burstwick, where he may have heard the news on the 20th. Most of the government rolls fall silent for six days after this date, which may be an indication that the king immediately took to his rooms following the news. His private reaction, of course, can never be known but given their intense, intimate relationship, it cannot have been anything but shock, anger and overwhelming grief. After Gaveston and Pembroke had left St Mary's Abbey in York the previous month, Edward had thought he had secured temporary respite and an opportunity to outmanoeuvre those magnates who opposed Gaveston and sought the full implementation of the Ordinances. Given the exchange of oaths in which Pembroke had promised to forfeit his lands as the price for protecting Gaveston, murder was simply not an outcome that any party had envisaged. Pembroke's folly in leaving Piers under light guard was a genuine mistake, the earl believing that his peers would not break his oath. Pembroke's lack of consultation with his peers over Gaveston's surrender left him standing at the edge of a precipice. Immediately after Warwick and his men entered Deddington, Pembroke frantically sought help to recover Gaveston; first appealing to the Earl of Gloucester and then to the university and burgesses of Oxford for aid. Neither party was forthcoming. Left with no other alternative and fearful of losing everything he owned, Pembroke headed with Warrenne to the king in July and begged his forgiveness. Edward magnanimously granted it.[1] The loyalty of any earl in this period was very fluid, based primarily on individual need and changed as each political crisis came and went. Pembroke, like Edward from now on, could not always count on support from those he expected to give it. From now onwards, he would remain loyal to Edward until his own death twelve years later.

The execution of an English earl was highly unusual, and while under royal protection, simply unprecedented. Since the Norman Conquest of 1066, only four members of the nobility had suffered what we may loosely describe as capital punishment. William the Conqueror had executed Earl Waltheof in 1076 on account of his part in a rebellion. Simon de Montfort, who rose in rebellion against Henry III and his son, later Edward I, was killed and butchered at the battle of Evesham in 1265 on the orders of the Lord Edward. It was usual practice to take knights and members of the nobility into custody for ransom during war, but Simon was sought out, killed and mutilated for usurping the royal prerogative. It was a very personal type of revenge. His head was sent to Maud Mortimer by her husband Roger as a trophy and displayed at a celebratory banquet. Dafydd ap Gruffudd, titular Prince of Wales, had been hanged drawn and quartered in early October 1282 as a result of English legal process and with the full authority of the king after he brought the Principality under direct English rule. The same can be said for the execution of the Earl of Atholl in 1306 by Edward I who despite his Scottish landholdings had turned his coat on the English king after promises of support. On these four occasions, death was meted out by the crown, in some fashion or other. Gaveston's death, while under royal protection, was not, and this action taken by Lancaster, Warwick and the others was unprecedented. Against such a backdrop, emotions were highly charged among all involved and the following sixteen months would take enormous negotiation and the tact of numerous mediators to bring about a fragile peace in England.

So how had it come to this? Piers Gaveston had not always been so hated. During his time in Edward's household before the king's accession, Gaveston had been a close, intimate companion of Edward's, which did not receive open censure from those around them until February 1307. With the exception of Warwick, Piers appears to have forged friendships with all those who would later become his peers. His elevation to the earldom of Cornwall was not opposed after his first exile, nor was his marriage to Margaret de Clare. He had, on the face of it, been accepted.

The opposition to Gaveston came from one principal issue, his control over royal patronage. After Edward's accession, while their intimate relationship still did not appear to overtly affront the nobles at court, Gaveston's inevitable closeness to the king, his ability to charm and influence, quickly became a bone of contention. In his role as Chamberlain of the Bedchamber, Gaveston had a direct access to the king that no other could hope to gain. This gave Piers far-reaching access to Edward's patronage, both for himself and those who sought the earl's favours, and sometimes at the expense of his peers. This influence is not always clear in the record – it is highly likely that Piers exercised an unwritten control over patronage. Under Edward I many of the nobles who would come to oppose Gaveston had waited for Edward's accession hoping for a greater slice of royal patronage, which brought influence and access. Land was power in the fourteenth century. They were to find early that Edward II did not think as they did, and while it was Edward's choice as to how he chose to distribute royal gifts, Gaveston became the scapegoat.

Edward showered Piers and his followers with gifts, which over time created widespread resentment and hostility. This was a key characteristic of Edward throughout his life – to make rich gifts but only to those he felt were deserving. Following Gaveston's death, his widow Margaret received nearly £2,000 in land grants making her a wealthy woman in her own right. Edward did not follow the traditional expectations of his age and this was critical in building opposition to both him and Piers. Gaveston's role as *custos regni* in 1308 dented the pride of senior nobles who were more suited by birthright to such an important office. In the eyes of the king, Gaveston's marriage into the royal family made him the perfect and most trusted man for the job but the earls felt otherwise. Although Piers exercised his authority conservatively, he was nevertheless marked out by holding the office at all.

The Wallingford tournament exposed growing resentment as the golden boy of the tourney demonstrated his military prowess, charm and wit, beating some of the earls in arms and inadvertently humiliating them as a consequence. It was rubbing salt into newly opened wounds. That wit, when on the defence, could be barbed and his role at the coronation drove the final nail into his coffin, which entrenched thereafter hostility to him. Following his return from Ireland, where he had governed well and demonstrated political aptitude, Piers sought to reconcile and build bridges, which he achieved with Lincoln and Gloucester, but against the hostility of Lancaster, Hereford, Arundel and most notably Warwick, he turned defensive and his creation of derisive nicknames for some of them only isolated him further.[2]

There was no going back after that point. He was the pariah at court and in the nobles' minds had to be separated from Edward if they were ever to gain access to and the co-operation of their king. They wanted reforms, long overdue since the days of Edward I, and this demand became mixed in a complex web of politics woven about the position of the Earl of Cornwall.

What no party foresaw was the murder at Blacklow Hill. Against such a backdrop where individual loyalties at court meant no one was bound together in a defined unified party, the rules of the game kept changing as people worked to their own advantage. Only Warwick was consistent in his long-standing opposition. As Gaveston lay dying on Blacklow Hill, Warwick and Lancaster had achieved a single outcome: Edward II would never again trust and work with the nobles who believed that by removing Piers they could take up their traditional positions of influence at court and become greater beneficiaries of the king's patronage. The next ten years of Edward's reign would be coloured by intense hostility, built around his desire for bloody vengeance on those who had brought about the death of Gaveston.[3]

As Edward left York on 28 June, he kept Isabella safe in the north. At this moment, the *Vita* records that Edward's anger fixed most heatedly on Warwick, whose exile he wanted at worst, his head at best.[4] Those in his council including Hugh Despenser and Henry de Beaumont suggested war, while moderation was encouraged from Pembroke and Warrenne who joined the king in mid-July.[5] On arriving in London in early July Edward gave a passionate speech at Blackfriars to the mayor and alderman to hold the city for him and to close the gates to the earls, who had moved to Worcester after Gaveston's death to plan their next steps. London's populace, while volatile in mood and more inclined to support Lancaster, agreed and promptly closed the gates to the city. Edward moved onto Dover and received the homage of the Cinque Ports, as well as fortifying castles and raising men throughout the south-east.[6] He meant to fight.

The pain Edward felt at Gaveston's death was not however shared by many around the country. Songs, poems and mock toasts sprung up in bawdy houses and taverns: 'Glory be to the Creator! Glory to the earls, who have made Piers die with his charms! Henceforth may there be peace and rejoicing throughout England! Amen.' Another, following a similar theme went, 'He who placed himself as a head above his equals loses his own head. Justly his body is pierced whose heart was so puffed up; Hand, sea, stars and world rejoice in his fall.'[7]

Despite raising 600 foot from Norfolk, Suffolk and the Forest of Dene, Edward's numbers remained too small for a direct assault on the Blacklow earls, so the king adopted a double strategy.[8] On the one hand he prepared for conflict, on the other to fall back on papal and French mediation to bring about a resolution, sending Pembroke and Henry de Beaumont to Philip IV on 6 August for aid. Edward knew Lancaster and Warwick in particular had sullied their hands with Gaveston's murder and Edward's own position had grown stronger now that Pembroke and the king of France would surely support him. In a strong enough position, Edward summoned the earls hunkered down at Worcester to meet with him.[9]

Lancaster, Warwick and Hereford responded as anticipated with arms, stopping north of London between St Alban's and Ware on 3 September, sending messengers instead to enquire why they had been summoned.[10] As tension made nerves raw, the young Earl of Gloucester stepped forward as mediator with the support of the Earl of Richmond, along with a delegation from France which arrived in late summer and that included Cardinal Arnaud, Bishop of Poitiers, Louis Count of Évreux and Cardinal Arnaud of Santa Priscia.[11] The task before them was an almost impossible one. Edward left for Windsor to be with Isabella, who was now heavily pregnant and had travelled to the castle from the north to be with her husband.

On 28 September the king issued safe conducts to Hereford, Robert Clifford, John Botetourt and others to meet the mediators at Markyate in Hertfordshire, while London remained closed to them. The following three months were drawn out by the earls' initial obstinacy, holding to their version of the truth that they had not murdered Gaveston but rather had removed a traitor from the realm and had acted according to the Ordinances. The king, they initially held, did not have the right to revoke them without the approval of the community of the realm. Edward understandably refused to acknowledge Gaveston as a traitor. Ultimately, the demands from those representing the earls were summed up best in the *Prima Tractatio*, in which they sought to have sufficient security to approach the king for a pardon. They offered to surrender the many valuable goods taken at Newcastle by Lancaster in May 1312. They also promised to secure a subsidy in parliament for war with Scotland as well as funding 400 men-at-arms at their own expense for the next Scottish campaign, which was becoming ever more pressing. In return, they expected that the Ordinances would be upheld, all evil counsellors would be removed, lands seized by the king from their supporters since Gaveston's murder be restored and Gaveston of course be declared a traitor.[12]

Within two months, after much wrangling, a peace treaty was finally engineered and settled on 20 December 1312 in which the Ordinances were not mentioned, nor Gaveston or his status at the time of his death. In return Edward would agree to grant his pardon, and those jewels, horses and other valuables taken at Newcastle would be restored to him on 13 January 1313 at St Albans.[13] Importantly for Edward, the barons also agreed not to pursue those associates of the late Earl of Cornwall, still at Edward's court, whom the king was doing everything he could to protect. He was in no mood to give up anyone. With the peace treaty agreed, Edward had secured his main aims, but the agreement itself was conditional on approval from Lancaster and Warwick, neither of whom were present at Markyate.

While negotiations were ongoing, Edward remained at Windsor, living out his intense grief quietly with Isabella. On 20 October he granted his permission for his queen, now nearing the end of her pregnancy to make her will, in which among many things, her executors were given power to buy land to the value of £1,500 to build a hospital for the poor and for the salvation of her soul and that of her husband.[14] Edward himself had lost sisters to the birthing chamber.

Yet thankfully their fears came to nothing. On St Brice's Day, 13 November 1312, Isabella safely gave birth to their first child – a healthy baby boy, named Edward after his father, despite the suggestion from Louis of Évreaux that he be named Philip after Isabella's father. Edward, who was overjoyed, granted to his son the earldom of Chester which the king himself had received in February 1301.[15] The baby was baptised three days later and given seven godparents, which included the envoy Cardinal Arnaud d' Aux, Louis of Évreaux, Pembroke, Richmond, Hugh Despenser and the bishops of Bath & Wells, and Worcester. Walter Reynolds, who had long served Edward since his time as Prince of Wales, would soon become Archbishop of Canterbury following the death of Robert Winchelsey in May 1313, which only further strengthened Edward's position.[16] London rejoiced at news of the birth and Edward and Isabella left the confines of the castle to visit the city in late January, attending a pageant held in their honour, staying at Eltham Palace, which Edward had granted to his wife in 1311.[17] The birth of an heir to the throne did much to lighten Edward's immediate grief, but it certainly did not heal it completely. It also created political stability and inadvertently helped Edward's position while the barons remained further than ever from his good offices.

The general mood at the start of 1313 did not improve. Lancaster failed to appear with the king's jewels as promised at St Alban's on 13 January and shortly afterwards he rejected the peace treaty on the grounds that Gaveston was a traitor and the king needed to acknowledge him as such. This time Lancaster had overplayed his hand. Edward, with support of the papal and French envoys, refuted all. The mediators began their work again, this time more forcibly. Lancaster and those who refused to accept the terms were quickly informed that if they continued to act as they did, the king would be justified in moving against them.[18] Their position had weakened considerably. Edward had gained the upper ground. On 23 February 1313 the jewels, horses and valuables seized by Lancaster at Newcastle were transferred by the Earl of Hereford, Robert Clifford and John Botetourt from Clifford's house in Fleet Street to the Tower of London where they were received by Walter Reynolds and John Sandale the Treasurer.[19]

The surviving inventory is impressive and includes among many items a gold cross with two balas rubies, three sapphires and four pearls. There were many rods or staffs listed on the inventory and one was encrusted with five 'beautiful' rubies worth £63. Along with the jewels were the valuable horses, forty-one destriers and coursers and one palfrey, with nine pack horses whose job it had been to pull the load. Those horses which had perished and items damaged since their capture in May 1312 were to be compensated for as agreed.[20] The most valuable item returned, a large ruby ring valued at a staggering £1,000, did not come from Newcastle but was rather poignantly confiscated from Gaveston when he was imprisoned at Warwick castle. He also carried an enamelled silver box containing three large rubies mounted in rings, as well as one emerald and one diamond.[21] Perhaps Gaveston had received them as gifts from Edward, especially the ring, or he may have intended to pawn them to raise support once he had headed south.

Despite the wrangling, all that now essentially remained was for Edward to give his earls the kiss of peace, and pardon the 350 associates who had been directly involved in working against him and in bringing about the death of his favourite. Parliament was summoned to meet on 18 March but Edward could not yet stomach granting forgiveness to the men who had brutally murdered Gaveston. He feigned illness, determined to bide his time and bring his rebellious magnates in on his own schedule.[22]

To add to the delay, on 23 May Edward and Isabella set sail from Dover for a two-month stay in France with Pembroke, Richmond, Hugh Despenser, Henry de Beaumont and 220 members of the court to celebrate the knighting of Isabella's brothers and uncle in Paris.[23] The stay would of course involve discussions with Philip IV about Gascony. The magnates left behind had to wait even longer for their pardons while Gloucester became *custos regni*.[24] The knighting ceremony on 3 June at Notre Dame in Paris was a lavish affair and reminiscent of Edward's own knighting at the Feast of the Swans in 1306 at Westminster Hall. Philip accorded Edward the honour of belting his eldest son, Louis, King of Navarre in his own right and future King of France, while his other sons and brother were also knighted. Edward, Philip and Louis then knighted nearly 200 more.[25]

On Tuesday 5 June, two days after the ceremony, Edward held a banquet in open tents at St Germain des-Prés. Dressed in one of the many beautiful items of clothing from the wardrobe the king had recently purchased for the sum of £1,000, Edward spared nothing on the feast, which included 94 oxen, 189 pigs, 380 rams, 200 pike, 160 carp and 80 barrels of wine.[26] The king had to pay 60s in compensation to a Parisian whose grass had been eaten by the oxen.[27] The following day, Edward and his father-in-law swore oaths to take the cross and go on crusade. Three days later Isabella and other members of the court took the oath to accompany their husbands on the perilous journey to Jerusalem. The feasting and carousing must have been a welcome relief for Edward after the previous twelve months of strife and loss. The following day, Godfrey of Paris noted in his chronicle that Edward and Isabella overslept and the king missed a meeting with his father-in-law that morning.[28] That evening he roused himself and headed to the shrine of the Crown of Thorns at the Sainte-Chapelle where he gave a pound in devotion.[29]

Edward and Isabella were close during their stay in France. After the birth of their first child the year before, it seems they remained sexually active. Isabella was now eighteen and Edward twenty-nine. After their return from France, Isabella's apothecary noted in his records the purchase and administration of pennyroyal on two separate occasions to the queen, so it is possible that Isabella miscarried.[30] Had Gaveston lived, Edward and Isabella's sexual relationship would probably not have changed. Edward was bisexual and while he more likely had a preference for male company given his ongoing closeness to male favourites, he and Isabella until at least 1322 maintained a close, intimate and supportive marital relationship. Their time in France shows how very close they were, and Isabella was no doubt a greater comfort and support to Edward emotionally and physically during these challenging times than anyone else could be. Isabella herself surely felt more secure now she had provided an heir.

The last three days of their two-month stay in Paris and Pontoise were spent with Philip IV at Poissy. The trip had been a great success and at no time during the talks with Philip over Gascony, which ended on 2 July, had Edward been asked to compromise or agree to anything. The king of France, seemingly content with a happy daughter and the birth of a healthy grandson had gone easy on his son-in-law. Edward agreed to enact a one-year truce with the Scots, which would run out on 20 June 1314; importantly, he had secured the support of the king of France in this. When and if Edward continued campaigning in Scotland, Philip had pledged not to support Robert Bruce, despite Scotland being a traditional French ally.

One evening as events drew to a close, the king and queen's pavilion caught fire in the middle of the night. Edward saved Isabella, both of them running out into the field naked to escape the flames. The queen burnt her arm and needed treatment in the months that followed.[31] It was a close call for both of them.

Edward, Isabella and the court returned to England on 15 July 1313. Sailing back across the Channel, the heady two months of celebrations and successful foreign negotiations behind him, Edward knew his next task was to pardon those who had murdered Gaveston. On 19 June, which marked the first anniversary of Gaveston's death, Edward paid to be entertained by Robert the Fool and fifty-four naked dancers.[32]

Parliament assembled on 8 July but had fallen apart without the king's promised presence, the delay unquestionably another of Edward's tactics. Lancaster, Warwick and those seeking pardon left in frustration before Edward finally arrived on 23 July.[33] Despite his ongoing reluctance, in the end he knew he would need to bring the situation to a close. On 14 October, almost sixteen months to the day since Gaveston's murder, Edward met his recalcitrant nobles in Westminster Hall. What he was feeling as he watched Lancaster, Warwick, Hereford and others bend their knee in front of him is impossible to pinpoint, but raising them up to give them the kiss of peace must have been hard. Two days later when the pardons were officially announced through letters patent, the king was invited to a banquet of reconciliation held by the earls; he, in turn, hosted one the following day.[34] Edward may have officially forgiven them but, in private, he had most certainly not forgiven nor forgotten their actions. He still had not achieved vengeance and his determination to do so remained very much alive.

PART THREE

Overmighty Vassals

Consider lord king ... the power of the barons; take heed of the danger that threatens; neither brother nor sister should be dearer to thee than thyself. Do not therefore for any living soul lose thy kingdom.

Vita Edwardi Secundi

14

Bannockburn

Once more the agenda turned to war. Only this time, rather than conflict among England's magnates, Edward focussed his sights on Scotland and Robert Bruce in particular. Since the last Scottish campaign nearly three years previously, beating back the crowned Bruce and advancing English gains hard-won since 1300, had taken a back seat during the ensuing political crisis brought on by the magnates' pursuit of Gaveston.

In the intervening years Bruce had not sat idle. As was customary with Scottish tactics at this time, Robert deployed his men in highly effective hit-and-run raids in areas loyal to the king of England in Scotland and, profitably, in northern England. This action proved devastating to the northern population huddled south of the border, and in 1311, 1312 and 1313, the people of Northumberland paid racket money to Bruce to keep his heavies at bay, the princely sum of £2,000 a year, which increased significantly in 1313.[1] Without an effective resistance from the king of England, Robert Bruce and his surviving brother Edward became so confident in their attacks that they harried as far south as York. By 1313 Scottish self-confidence was at its height and a well-devised strategy to seize back control of English held castles, financed from the money bullied out of the English, became the principal aim of the Bruce campaign in order to oust the enemy from Scotland altogether.

The first castle to fall in early 1313 was Perth, followed a month later by Dumfries. Linlithgow was lost when a loaded haywain was used to jam open the gateway, allowing the Scots to pour in and overwhelm the defending garrison.[2] The quick, sharp-witted tactics paid off and were again used to overwhelm Roxburgh in February 1314 and finally Edinburgh a month later, when attackers clambered up the steep, slippery volcanic rockface, scaling the walls at night. None of the garrison believed such a climb possible, yet Bruce and his men proved to the defenders' detriment that it most certainly was. With these dramatic losses, and in such quick succession, the Bruce brothers turned their attention to the remaining English-held castle that underpinned Edward's foothold in the country: Stirling.

Stirling Castle sat on top of a steep, rocky outcrop overlooking the valley below. It was the key to holding onto the Scottish Lowlands and provided the gateway to the Highlands. Possession of it was not only of strategic importance, it was also symbolic. It had been in English hands ever since Edward I, and Edward II, who was then Prince of Wales, had captured it in 1304. Recapturing it now, Bruce knew, would effectively nullify Edward's claim to the kingdom, he would be unable to base any English army that moved north of border in relative safety. In March 1314, after the fall of Edinburgh, and not in 1313, which is often incorrectly quoted by later historians, the Bruce and his brother began to besiege Stirling castle. The constable, Sir Philip de Mowbray, fearing the worst and knowing Edward was already on the march north, agreed in mid-May 1314 to surrender the castle to the Scots if Edward II did not appear in sight of its walls by Midsummer's Day, 24 June. With all due grace Robert Bruce accepted the terms, knowing full well that even if Edward arrived in time and re-garrisoned, they could attack the castle again within a year, when the king was likely to return south. At the same time, Edward Bruce harried the north of England and briefly attacked Carlisle Castle, attempting to distract Edward II's military preparations.[3]

Edward II's inheritance yet again came into play. The king needed money to continue the campaign that his father had started and spent the remaining few months of 1313 and the first half of 1314 sourcing income. Edward ordered a muster that would be large and well-equipped enough to finally overwhelm Robert Bruce, whom the king still referred to as the Earl of Carrick. With the Frescobaldi exiled and now bankrupt since the initial publication of the Ordinances in 1311 had removed them from England, Edward relied heavily on another Italian financier, Antonio Pessagno. His extraordinary wealth allowed Edward to borrow vast amounts of money to fund the campaign, with Pessagno providing more than half of the supplies and more than £21,000 in ready cash for the king's use.[4]

Still hampered by restricted funds and vast debts, Edward reached out to both his father-in-law and the pope, borrowing 160,000 florins or £25,000 from the latter.[5] Philip IV loaned Edward £33,000, and in order to seal the deal, Edward briefly travelled to Boulogne in France for eight days, from 12 December, to discuss terms and ongoing issues to do with Gascony. Philip remained supportive, and in early January 1314, Isabella was sent on a diplomatic mission to the French court to continue discussions over Gascon petitions, securing concessions from her father. Parliament played its part and following on from the settlement reached with the magnates over Gaveston in October 1313, the king was granted taxation of a twentieth and a fifteenth on moveable goods, which was to be collected by 24 June 1314.[6]

With his financial situation improved at least in the short term, preparations got underway. During parliament that November, Edward countermanded a recent demand from Robert Bruce that any Scottish landholders who had failed to swear allegiance to him within a year would find their lands forfeit. Edward announced his intention to muster at Berwick on 24 June and any Scottish followers loyal to his crown ought to muster there. It was a well-timed move, designed to build his Scottish support and welcome anyone who still held out against Robert Bruce, who by no means ruled over a united Scottish kingdom. On 23 December Edward summoned Lancaster, Warwick and six other earls, with eighty-seven barons, to attend with their military host on 10 June.[7] Purveyance, despite its unpopularity, was also ordered and the subsequent goods that were raised were to be stored at Berwick and Carlisle.[8] As rumours of further Scottish raids into England led by Edward Bruce began to trickle south, Edward sped up the plans to head north, commanding Lancaster and twenty-one magnates to be at Newcastle earlier than initially ordered, now 1 June.[9]

Edward was able to assemble an impressive number of men as he headed, for the sixth time in his life, to war with the Scots. In March and April, orders for 20,000 infantry from England and Wales went out.[10] While it is likely that not all these were assembled, the infantry lines were substantial. Edward himself took eighty-nine household knights, seventy of which he had recruited specifically for this campaign, as well as thirty-two bannerettes. Pembroke was accompanied by eighty knights and men-at-arms, and with the earls of Gloucester and Hereford swelled the numbers with their own retinues. With men provided by and accompanying Hugh Despenser, Robert Clifford and other barons, in all there were approximately 2,000 knights for the campaign. Although the exact final numbers are hard to determine, given that the muster roll is missing, it is likely that the total army of infantry, cavalry, archers and other men-at-arms amounted to between 15,000 and 20,000.[11] It was the largest army seen since Edward I's campaign at Falkirk in 1298 and drew comment from the author of the *Vita* who noted 'never in our time has such an army marched out of England'.[12]

Although not all of the English nobility marched to war, Edward's position since Gaveston's murder had improved significantly. Following the settlement in late 1313, there was no mention of Gaveston as a traitor or that the Ordinances should be reinstated. Edward had managed the diplomatic negotiation well and was adept at building the support of both the pope and his father-in-law. Exploiting the weaknesses of those nobles who opposed him was something that the king was very capable of doing, and it was this very fact that kept Lancaster and Warwick, in particular, away. They, with Surrey and Arundel, simply refused to turn up, claiming that they had not been summoned in the correct way and the campaign had not been agreed in parliament.[13]

It was utter nonsense, of course, because Edward had secured taxation for the campaign in the November 1313 parliament, and part of the settlement terms in that year confirmed that Lancaster, Warwick and others would go to war alongside Edward in Scotland and in all haste. The king's summons on 23 December was legal and in due form. So why the bluff? The simple truth was Lancaster and Warwick were afraid: afraid that a triumphant Edward in Scotland would give the king the confidence to seek his revenge on his return south for Gaveston's murder.[14] It was a calculated risk that they could not take, and rather than act in the interests of England, they chose self-protection. Surrey's motivations were different, as he was seeking an annulment from his wife Joan de Bar, who was Edward's niece and this had caused recent tension between the king and his earl. In any event, the four earls sent their minimum feudal obligations, which amounted to as little as sixty knights and men-at-arms in a campaign that mustered nearly 20,000 men.[15] Edward could work without their numbers and was possibly relieved that they stayed at home and out of his way.

The king was eager to reach the north as soon as possible. Parliament, which had originally been summoned to meet on 21 April 1314 at Westminster, was cancelled on 24 March.[16] By early May he had moved from London to York and had reached as far north as Durham by 21 May. On the 26th, Edward arrived at Newminster and it was here that word arrived via messenger that Philip Mowbray, constable of Stirling Castle, had come to terms with Bruce during the recent two-month siege.[17] The king now decided to meet those terms and be within sight of the walls of Stirling by Midsummer's Day. It was going to be a tall order given the previous commands to be at Berwick for that date. The following day, 27 May, Edward ordered the infantry to march in haste, which the *Vita* lamented, 'short were the halts for sleep, shorter still were those for food, hence horses, horsemen and infantry were worn out with toil and hunger.'[18] Moving such a number at speed was difficult. The baggage train alone stretched over 4 miles.[19] Despite the challenges, which included a last 50-mile march from Berwick, Edward's army came in sight of the walls of Stirling castle on the morning of 23 June. He had fulfilled the terms negotiated between Mowbray and Bruce and so the latter had lost this round.

Bruce was at Stirling when Edward's army arrived. The Scottish army likely numbered 500 cavalry and up to 6,000 infantry; potentially a third of the size of Edward's host.[20] Unlike their English counterparts, the Scottish army was equipped for and more accustomed to guerrilla tactics. Their weapons and armour were light, allowing for easy travel and a quick getaway. As the historian and senior lecturer in war studies Aryeh Nusbacher writes, 'open field warfare was just not their idiom'.[21]

Bruce had been careful to draw his men up on the west side of the valley, hidden in the New Park – which was covered by a dense woodland area, much larger than is seen today. Stirling Castle, perched on its rocky outcrop, sat to the north. To the south, just beyond Tor Wood, was a river called the Bannock Burn, which in most parts but not all, was steep sided and flowed east to join the tidal river Forth, which itself flowed into the much larger Firth of Forth. To the east of the valley, opposite Bruce and New Park, was 'the Carse', an open piece of land of mixed ground, some areas more dry and stable, others, especially further north and east, boggy and marsh like, becoming more waterlogged according to the tide. This meant that between the Bannock Burn and Stirling Castle, the valley was a relatively constricted horseshoe shape, bordered by rivers and woods. In order to reach the castle, Edward's army had to ford the Bannock Burn as they emerged from Tor Wood to continue their journey up the old Roman road.

As Edward's army travelled through Tor Wood he was met by Philip Mowbray, constable of the castle, who had been given safe conduct by Robert Bruce to meet with the king. There it was agreed that Edward would continue to ford the Bannock Burn and head towards Stirling. Mowbray must have made the king aware that over the last month, Bruce and his men had dug deep pits filled with upturned stakes either side of the road, then covered them up. Anyone walking over them, especially the cavalry, would founder, and thus a move north would restrict the army to a narrow column. This was typical Scots guerrilla tactics, designed to pick off any men they could before the English army moved on. It was now clear that the English needed to move north but away from the Roman road, in a space that was less constricted for an army of its size.

This changed the game and so Edward and his counsel, led chiefly by the Earl of Pembroke, Sir Giles d'Argentein, Robert Clifford and Hugh Despenser, decided to halt and plan out their next move. Pembroke, a veteran of the Scottish wars, had beaten Bruce at the battle of Methven in 1306 but subsequently lost to him at the battle of Loudon Hill a year later. It was the last open field battle fought between the English and the Scots up to that point. Giles d'Argentein, according to the poem written in the fourteenth century by John Barbour whose work championed Bruce, claimed d'Argentein was the third greatest knight in Christendom.[22] Clifford and Despenser, including Edward, had all fought in Scotland in previous campaigns and were more than capable in military planning and in fighting hand-to-hand.

The vanguard comprised mounted knights and men-at-arms. But all was not well. Command of the vanguard was disputed between the young Earl of Gloucester who claimed his family had always held the privilege, and Edward's brother-in-law, Humphrey de Bohun, Earl of Hereford, who was the hereditary constable of England. This office gave Hereford key responsibilities during times of war and so the two men were at loggerheads.[23] It was a matter of family pride and honour and would not help matters when the army came into open conflict with the Scots.

As the army, stretching miles back, began to appear out of Tor Wood the vanguard began to ford the Bannock Burn. As they crossed, Gloucester and Hereford saw a small contingent of men down on the slopes far below the woods of New Park and Bruce's banner flying. It was too good an opportunity to miss, and so without direction from Edward who had not yet emerged from Tor Wood, the vanguard led by its competing earls of Gloucester and Hereford, charged. Hereford's nephew Henry de Bohun reached the relatively isolated Bruce first and in the clash that followed, Bruce dodged de Bohun's lance and split his head open with his battle axe.[24] In the melée that followed Gloucester was thrown from his horse, possibly as a result of one of the pits. With the first skirmish turning quickly against them, Hereford, Gloucester and the vanguard beat a hasty retreat.

Edward and his counsellors decided the mainstay of his cavalry and men-at-arms would ford the Bannock Burn and set up camp on the drier areas of the Carse to the east side of the Roman road. The king's harbingers had discovered that there was sufficient hard standing for a camp that could accommodate at least the cavalry and archers. The infantry were to cross in the morning, camping instead on the south side of the burn due to limited space. It would be a fateful decision. Robert Clifford and Henry Beaumont had also crossed earlier in the day and attempted to reach Stirling Castle, possibly with the aim of looking for an alternative path to the castle for the army to travel rather than using the narrow Roman road hemmed in on either side by pits. However on their reconnaissance, they had been met by a band of Scots under the command of Thomas Randolph, Earl of Moray, who poured out of New Park wood and took up formation to the north between the small contingent of English cavalry and the castle. Kneeling in schiltron formation the Scots were able to repel Beaumont, Clifford and their mounted men.[25] A schiltron, meaning 'shield-wall', was made up of a line of men armed with 15-foot spears, whose assembled line would bend around forming a circular, oblong or square formation with each man facing outwards. The circular formation was by far the easiest to manoeuvre across the field. This 360-degree hedgehog of spears becomes impenetrable to a charge of mounted knights as their lances, let alone their swords, cannot get close to the defenders, while the attackers are heavily exposed and potentially impaled in the attempt. Schiltrons could also be made up of concentric lines; effectively creating hedges within hedges, with a wide-open centre where knights, commanders and hostages could position themselves in relative safety. It was a highly effective way of attacking infantry, and cavalry in particular, but was vulnerable to the arrows from enemy archers.[26] The schiltron, first used at Falkirk in 1298, could be a devastating tactic and almost outmanoeuvred Edward I during that confrontation.

The reconnaissance attempt did, however, prove more fruitful in other ways, as Clifford and Beaumont had identified that there was sufficient hard ground to travel north to Stirling without having to take the narrow Roman road. This allowed Edward and his counsellors the possibility of moving the army without falling into Bruce's pits. In addition, the Scots had not committed to an open battle for seven years, and when they had, had only done so because they were given no other option, which was not the case here. It is almost certain that as the evening of 23 June drew to a close, both Edward and his counsellors, and Robert Bruce himself, did not plan to meet for battle on the field the following day or any day soon after. Instead, Bruce would continue his long-established guerrilla tactics, perhaps sweep into the outer edges of the English camp overnight and kill enough men only to disappear into the night and from New Park altogether, heading as the *Scalacronica* suggests to Lennox.[27] This was the Bruce way, and used against both Edward I and II since 1300. Robert himself had seen the overwhelming numbers that Edward had brought with him. To fight and risk everything in a single battle – when Bruce had no son or direct heir other than his brother, who was also childless – was not a sensible option and both sides knew it.[28]

What happened next changed everything. At some point during the night, Sir Alexander Seton, a Scottish knight in English employ turned his coat and rode off to Bruce's camp, possibly reporting Edward's plan or more certainly imparting news that the English military council was divided in opinion about what to do in the morning.[29] Gloucester, with Sir Ingram de Umfraville, had sought to rest the following day given the army's long march from Berwick, while Edward, Pembroke and Giles d'Argentein expected to march ahead to the castle, at least securing a better and safer encampment where the whole army could come together. The debate had become heated and Edward rashly accused Gloucester of cowardice and treachery.[30] Edward appeared over-confident. It was a poor lapse of judgement on the king's part to offend one of the leaders of the vanguard, but it appears that Gloucester's view was still nevertheless in the minority. With Seton's betrayal, which Edward and his council were unaware of, Bruce had been given an unexpected advantage. Instead of withdrawing he could now risk an open confrontation as soon as Edward sought to move his cavalry in a show of force north to Stirling, knowing quite possibly that the English and Welsh infantry would still be on the south side of the Bannock Burn.

As planned, on the morning of 24 June 1314, Edward, Pembroke, his military council, mounted men and archers formed up and faced north towards Stirling. The battalions of cavalry were behind the vanguard, and archers were positioned either side of the left and right flanks. It was a strong formation. Should the Scots repeat what they had done the day before to Clifford and Beaumont and appear in front of them preventing their approach to the castle, the archers were well placed to shoot from left and right and decimate the schiltrons, without the need for injury to the cavalry, until the Scots broke ranks and fled under a hail of arrows. John Barbour records that the English looked like they had formed one single column, which is accurate from the view point of the Scots standing in the woods at New Park to the east.[31] Edward's formation, when viewed from this position on the left flank, would look like a single column. It wasn't. From the English perspective, the deployment was well thought out and had been tried and tested, plus in their minds, it was likely that Bruce had already disappeared overnight, which was his normal tactic.[32] As they set out no one in the English ranks could have expected what happened next.

Bruce's men came out from the woods of New Park and formed up to the English army's left flank and knelt and began to pray, reciting the *Pater Noster*. Edward, amazed, thought initially that they were kneeling in submission but soon realised his mistake.[33] Turning the army about to face west as a single entity was difficult in terms of repositioning the divisions in such limited space. The archers on the flanks were suddenly in the wrong place, effectively right at the front of the army, ahead of the vanguard, while the right flank of archers had now became stuck at the back. In a stroke, Bruce had ensured that his schiltrons, at least immediately, were safe so long as Edward's archers were blocked behind extensive numbers of mounted men. As the Scots took up their schiltron formations, uphill from the English, the archers could not effectively respond and were forced out of the way as the vanguard under Gloucester and Hereford charged the Scottish lines. They had no other choice.

The result was the same as Clifford and Beaumont's efforts the day before. Medieval mounted knights at this time had almost always seen lines of infantry break and run during a fullscale cavalry charge. Holding nerve and standing in situ was a likely death sentence and mounted men would simply have ridden over those standing still. But horses would not run into a schiltron, they would instead seek to leap over it or swerve out of the way. With all these things in mind, as Gloucester led the charge moments ahead of the main vanguard with Hereford behind, he fell foul of the months of training that the Scots must have undergone. The schiltron walls stood firm and Gloucester with the front line of knights ploughed headlong into a wall of spears as the Scots stood their ground. The twenty-three-year-old Earl of Gloucester, not wearing his surcoat because that morning he did not think he would be fighting in a battle and so was unrecognisable, was impaled or unhorsed and killed.[34] Hereford and the remainder of the vanguard arrived seconds later to plough into the same wall, now filled with dying bodies of knights and horses. The vanguard was broken up, scattered in confusion or impaled.

At this point Bruce's much smaller cavalry ran down the archers who had previously made up the left flank of Edward's army. Edward and his council were forced to commit the main cavalry and men-at-arms, including themselves who had been sited behind the vanguard. As they charged they too were to meet the unflinching power of the schiltrons. Bruce committed to battle himself, forming a fourth schiltron. Moving out of New Park wood, he headed to block off the English army's approach to the north to

Stirling castle. With the archers still restricted at the back of the column they could not find the range to reach Bruce's schiltron without risking the English knights. With Bruce in play to the north and Stirling almost cut off, the remainder of the Scots to the west, and the Bannock Burn behind with the bogs to the east, Edward and his cavalry were caught in a trap. As space became more constricted the chance to regroup the mounted men and reposition the archers became impossible and time was quickly running out. Panic broke out and the battle turned into a bloodbath as men attempted to pour back over the ford at the Bannock Burn or were trapped in the bogs trying to escape to the south-east of the castle.

In among the chaos, despite the king fighting hard 'like a lioness deprived of her cubs', Pembroke seized Edward's reins and gathered around them 500 mounted men forcing the king off the field for his own safety.[35] The fighting had become so intense that Edward's horse was killed. He was immediately remounted, but only after his shield bearer, Roger Northburgh was captured.[36] Edward protested and wanted to keep fighting, but Pembroke and Giles d'Argentein knew that his capture would be catastrophic and bring about the end of all hope of winning Scotland. A ransomed king was something they could neither stomach nor afford. They forced themselves through the carnage to leave the field, Edward himself killing men with his mace as he left, and headed initially around Bruce's schiltron to Stirling Castle.[37] There, Philip Mowbray rightly told the king to flee rather than be held hostage behind the walls of Stirling and so the king, Pembroke and 500 mounted men rode to Dunbar with the Black Douglas in hot pursuit, picking off knights who stopped to relieve themselves en route. From Dunbar, Edward took ship to Berwick, which he reached on 27 June.[38] Giles d'Argentein, knowing Edward was safe, left the king and rode back into the heat of battle to continue the fight. Sadly it was his last act of chivalry, dying in the carnage.

The battle for Stirling Castle, later known as the Battle of Bannockburn, was a great victory for Robert Bruce. He had for the moment won when he never expected to fight at all. The death toll is impossible to determine, given that the muster roll is missing, but what is certain is the Earl of Gloucester and Giles d'Argentein perished, along with Edmund Mauley who was the king's steward, Robert Clifford, Payn Tibetot, and William Marshall who was a former Lord Ordainer. At least forty knights were killed with many archers and other men.[39] Pembroke's nephew, John Comyn, son and namesake of his father who was murdered by Bruce in 1306, also died. Those wealthy enough, so worth taking alive for ransom, included the Earl of Hereford, the Earl of Angus and Ingram de Umfraville. Ralph de Monthermer, Edward's brother-in-law to his late sister Joan, was also captured along with Maurice and Thomas Berkeley.[40]

The king's extensive baggage train, which had previously stretched for miles, was looted and the king's seal and his shield were captured when

Northburgh had been taken hostage. Bruce was magnanimous in victory and showed an impressive degree of chivalry. Following the battle, he spent the night watching over the body of Robert Clifford and Bruce's dead second cousin, the Earl of Gloucester, who was related to him through his grandmother. In a gesture to Edward, Bruce sent their bodies back to the king, with two prisoners without ransom, Sir Marmaduke de Tweng and Edward's brother-in-law, Ralph de Monthermer, who returned Edward's seal.[41] Yet all these great displays of chivalry counted for little in the long term, Robert Bruce was unable to capitalise on his triumph. While Stirling Castle fell and was demolished in case it fell back into English hands, Bruce continued with his guerrilla tactics. He was not in 1314 recognised as king by Edward or the pope. Edward and his court still saw the political landscape in Scotland through the same lens; Scotland, they believed, belonged to the English crown and so, therefore, the campaigns would continue much as before.

For Edward, the defeat can only have been unexpected, overwhelming and shameful. Having been so determined and committing so much time, money and men to bring Bruce to heel in the summer of 1314, the speed and scale of the unexpected defeat was magnified. Edward and his military council were capable military leaders, and had the battle been fought on different territory the likely outcome would have been different,[42] something that both Edward and Bruce knew all too well. However, it had not. It had been fought at a place that Edward had not chosen nor, indeed, had he or Bruce expected. Bruce's sudden opportunity presented by Seton had secured the day, because even the lessons at Falkirk could not work at Bannockburn given the constricted space, which did not allow Edward to re-deploy his lines in time when Bruce attacked unexpectedly and from the left flank. It was such a daring, bold move. As Edward, Pembroke and the army left camp that morning, the formations chosen to reach Stirling Castle were tactically sound, especially when benchmarked against previous known campaigns. Against such odds, the outcome – with the benefit of hindsight only – often leads historians down the wrong path, as Nusbacher so clearly demonstrated in his recent work dispelling long outdated myths. Calling Edward 'military incompetent' or a 'coward', as has been the case, is misguided and inaccurate.[43]

What remains true, however, is that the defeat and the loss of so many high-ranking magnates and knights shocked contemporaries, especially those who had fought in the battle. Following English disaster in sight of the walls of Stirling Castle, Edward had once more to turn back south to England and face the likes of Lancaster and Warwick, who would now only grow stronger in the face of Edward's military defeat. Life for the king was about to become very difficult indeed.

15

Disputes and Discord

Thomas of Lancaster blamed the king's defeat at Bannockburn on one simple fact; he failed to observe the Ordinances.[1] God, Lancaster decided, was angry and a king who sat idle and refused baronial sanctioned reform would only suffer great personal ignominy. Although the enormity and scale of the defeat at Bannockburn was not primarily of Edward's making, he had failed to produce any success either; he was, unlike his council and by virtue of his position, accountable.

From Dunbar, the king reached Berwick on 27 June and moved to greater safety at York on 17 July, accompanied with his closest companions, Aymer de Valence, the Earl of Pembroke, Hugh Despenser, Henry Beaumont and Bartholomew Badlesmere. The latter was a leading retainer of the late Gilbert de Clare, Earl of Gloucester. In his painful humiliation Edward was only too aware of the need to discuss the crisis in Scotland and to meet his English opponents head on. The king summoned parliament on 29 July to meet at York in less than six weeks' time.[2] The prospect must have been stomach-wrenching. When the time came, Edward was absent for the start, appointing Pembroke, Beaumont and the Bishop of Exeter to act in his stead until he arrived, claiming he was preoccupied 'with arduous and special affairs touching the king'.[3] What these affairs were is unknown, but the prevarication would only delay the inevitable. Edward was clearly expecting confrontation with Lancaster and Warwick. He was careful at the last minute to remove Henry de Beaumont knowing full well that his presence would only antagonise his cousin, Lancaster.

Edward was right to feel anxious. Just as expected, once sat in the chamber, a triumphant Lancaster demanded that Edward reissue and uphold the Ordinances, which had been in abeyance for nearly two years. Unfortunately for the king, there were many others in parliament who supported reform, if not holding Edward solely responsibile for Bannockburn. Without any platform on which to counter the argument, Edward accepted.[4] The stronger position he had built up since Gaveston's murder began to quickly disappear.

As in 1311, the king's household under the auspices of the Ordinances was singled out for purge, but interestingly the men who were ushered in were mostly sympathetic to the king. John Sandale, who had been temporary treasurer of the household since 1312, was appointed chancellor on 26 September, replacing Walter Reynolds who, now being Archbishop of Canterbury, probably benefitted from his relief from office. Sandale was replaced with Walter of Norwich. Ingelard Warley was replaced by William Melton; Melton had been a loyal supporter of Edward since his time as Prince of Wales. The law enforcers of the time, the sheriffs of England, were replaced between 8 October and 16 January 1315.[5] The appointment of these men to key positions made clear that while Edward was forced to uphold the Ordinances he was able to influence the makeup of the executive and bureaucracy to his liking. Lancaster and Warwick demanded the removal of Hugh Despenser and Henry de Beaumont, but Edward was able to stoutly resist.[6] The mood in parliament was not, therefore, openly hostile, and the king still had far more support than he had enjoyed in 1310 when he was faced with a blanket wall of opposition. The legacy of Bannockburn was unfolding but the king was certainly far from facing political or personal ruin.

As parliament drew to a close, attention turned to negotiation with the Scots to release those English hostages caught up in the aftermath of Bannockburn. After Edward retreated south, the Bruce brothers immediately invaded northern England, harrying the local population as before, stealing livestock and causing general destruction. In August and September, Edward received word from Robert Bruce, who was seeking peace and recognition of his gains. While an English acknowledgement of Bruce's crown was not forthcoming, the dialogue provided a window for limited negotiation, headed up by John Botetourt and the Archbishop of York, lasting for the rest of the year. Edward may have been influenced by Philip IV to come to some terms of truce; Philip died as a result of a hunting accident in France on 29 November 1314 and so this influence would soon disappear.[7] In the face of such overwhelming defeat the English negotiating position was limited. In return for Bruce's wife Elizabeth de Burgh, his daughter Marjorie and his sister Christine, held captive in England since 1306, Robert returned the Earl of Hereford, which no doubt pleased his wife, Edward II's sister, Elizabeth. Robert Wishart, the Bishop of Glasgow, was also returned north of the border.[8] Roger Northburgh, the shield bearer who had been captured in the thick of the fighting while defending Edward, was released and returned to England to resume his office as keeper of the privy seal; this was apparently not objectionable to Lancaster or Warwick.

As winter 1314 drew to a wet, cold close (it rained most of the latter part of the year), Edward reflected on his misfortunes. Although far from desolate, he was nevertheless a long way off the freedom he believed he should enjoy as king. Vengeance for Gaveston's murder was looking remote, even impossible. As the Christmas festivities drew closer, he decided to bury the embalmed body of Piers Gaveston, still lying wrapped in cloth of gold at the Dominican House at Oxford since June 1312. 'For the king had proposed,' as the *Vita* records, '... first to avenge Piers' death, and then consign his body to the grave. But already, those have been readmitted to friendship from whom the king seeks vengeance.'[9] While the price of peace was a necessary artificial veneer of public forgiveness, in private Edward had certainly neither forgiven nor forgotten.

The ongoing deep love he held for Gaveston was made plain in the careful attention to detail Edward gave to Gaveston's mortal remains and his immortal soul. During the king's sixth regnal year, which ran from 8 July 1312 to 7 July 1313, he paid for 5,000lbs of wax to be used to burn candles around the body.[10] In 1313, Brother Walter de Ashridge, a Dominican friar, was given a very personal commission from the king that lasted 122 days; he travelled around the country asking for prayers from other religious institutions to ease Gaveston's soul.[11] Even after burial, Edward marked the anniversary of Piers' death as well as 18 July, which may have been Gaveston's birthday. Prayers would be said for the dead Earl of Cornwall right up until the end of Edward's reign, with the last entry in the official rolls on 28 June 1326.[12]

If Edward could not yet enact his revenge he could still make a point. The date for the funeral at the Dominican House at Edward's residence at Langley was set for 2 January, which fell within the octave of the Holy Innocents.[13] The symbolism could not have been plainer. Those in attendance included the Archbishop of Canterbury, the bishops of London, Winchester, Worcester and Bath & Wells; thirteen abbots, and many Dominican friars from beyond Langley. The presence of such a number of prelates and members of religious abbeys and houses suggests but does not confirm that some time before Gaveston's burial, the sentence of excommunication had been lifted; either by Clement V before his death in April 1314, or by the Archbishop of Canterbury who, during the papal interregnum before a successor was found, was in a position with support from his bishops to bring it about.[14] Edward would not have buried Gaveston otherwise. The earls of Pembroke and Hereford also attended, with Henry de Beaumont and Hugh Despenser the Elder, who was accompanied by his son and namesake. The chancellor John Sandale and the treasurer Walter of Norwich were also present along with a multitude of household knights and royal household officials.[15] Not all those invited, however, according to Trokelowe, attended, some preferring to stay away. Even in death, Gaveston still deeply divided opinion.[16]

When the time came to bury him, an emotional Edward ensured Gaveston's burial was as splendid as the earl had been in life. The embalmed body, moved from Oxford, was re-wrapped in three cloths of gold, which the king paid for at a cost of £300. After the interment, the congregation feasted, the king having ordered twenty-three tuns of wine for the occasion. With Gaveston's body interred, that chapter of Edward's life was far from over. From the grave, Piers Gaveston would continue to influence the political agenda.

The weather in 1315 was wet, both in England and across northern Europe. It rained relentlessly, especially from May until October. As fields became waterlogged and trackways impassable, rivers burst their banks and villages groaned under the weight of rainwater. Crops failed, livestock perished. The same happened again in 1316, and under such awful conditions, the population began to suffer terribly. Failed crops drove up the price of wheat, and other mainstay foodstuffs simply became out of reach for many.[17] Where wet conditions prevail, pestilence and disease follow.[18] The death of cattle, and sheep in particular, caused a major depletion in meat production and collapse of the buoyant wool market, England's main export. Income into Edward's royal coffers from exported wool dropped from £12,000 in 1312 to £7,000 in 1315–16.[19] Malnutrition meant the death toll rose and as much as five per cent of England's population was lost to famine. For those living through the time, it may well have felt apocalyptic, and the legacy it created ate away at the population for years to come, despite improved weather in 1317. The Black Death, which swept across Europe in the early 1340s was so savage because of a generally weakened population, which suffered as a result of a series of bad weather periods throughout the first half of the fourteenth century.

For those of a superstitious mind, the bad weather could be blamed on Edward himself. The dearth of resources in 1315–16 presented a major problem to the king and his government. Still dogged by his poor financial inheritance, the king's debts remained substantial and spare cash was hard to come by. The taxation used for the Scottish campaign was gone and the extensive loans agreed with the French crown, the papal curia and Antonio Pessagno were also spent, and now required repayment. The threat of a full-scale Scottish invasion was serious, feared the most of course in northern England, and the need to keep the castles in the region garrisoned and fed was a huge challenge. Rumours reached the king and his court that the populace had turned to eating dogs, horses, and, in the case of some whispers, children.[20]

In January 1315 parliament met at Westminster.[21] Lancaster used it to consolidate his position but with limited success. Unlike in 1310, he was no longer the popular leader of a loosely united cause. He was quarrelsome and difficult and his betrayal of Pembroke was not forgotten at court. Lancaster broadly failed to inspire loyalty.[22] Few were his direct allies, saving Warwick, who was already seriously ill and who subsequently died in August that year at Warwick Castle, which must have pleased Edward – at least one of Gaveston's killers had finally met his end.[23] However, Lancaster could still make his presence felt. Hugh Despenser was again his target and this time Edward was forced, temporarily at least, to retire his old ally from court, along with Walter Langton, Bishop of Coventry and Lichfield, who was detested by the former Ordainers but who had regained the king's favour after his fall in 1307.[24] Household expenditure was to be reduced and the Ordinances were again discussed, publicised and observed, as ordered on 14 February by the king. Finally, parliament agreed to a grant of much-needed taxation for war in Scotland, but with the rain falling and crops destined to fail, collecting this revenue would prove difficult. With a threat of increasingly destabilised prices, which forced many into starvation, Edward and parliament passed an act to control the cost of basic foodstuffs. Although well intentioned, it was met with outrage by traders selling their limited wares. In protest, they simply refused to part with what little they had and yet more of the population starved.[25]

In December 1314, the chancellor of Oxford University in his Christmas sermon declared that the ill created by Henry II's murder of Thomas Becket in 1170 would be visited on the fourth generation. The fourth generation was Edward II.[26] As Parliament was in session in Westminster the following month, news arrived that John Bonaventure, a London goldsmith, was accused, but later found not guilty, of speaking out against the king. This theme increasingly built momentum through the year and can be seen in official records, as a population burdened by wet weather, growing famine and continued threats of Scottish invasion looked to lay blame somewhere. Edward, they felt, was not taking their issues seriously, failing to act in any meaningful way that made a difference where hardship was at its worst. Yet the truth remained that the king simply had no money with which to respond. In August 1315, he ordered the magnates to limit the number of courses they served at their tables on account of those who went hungry. However poignant and heartfelt the move, it missed the point and clearly angered his magnates in the process.[27] Small gestures like this with his lesser subjects in mind were typical of Edward; at least he showed concern, the vast majority of his nobles would barely have raised an eyebrow.

To ease the Scottish situation, Edward held an assembly at Lincoln at the end of August, attended by the earls of Lancaster, Hereford, Richmond and Surrey, the Archbishop of Canterbury and the bishops of Carlisle and Norwich. Also in attendance was Roger Mortimer of Chirk, Justice of Wales. News had reached court that in a bid to place yet further pressure on the king of England following his defeat in the previous year, and because Edward still failed to recognise Robert Bruce as king, the Bruce brothers had opened up a second, more dangerous front in Ireland. Landing at Larne on the Antrim coast, where the Bruce family held lands and were long associated with the native Irish, Edward Bruce commenced a brutal and highly effective military campaign specifically intended to overcome and seize control of the English-held lordship there, centred on Dublin.[28]

Edward II was tall, strong and handsome, as noted by contemporaries. In war he fought like 'a lioness protecting her cubs'. He was loyal to his friends, intimate with his favourites and conventionally pious. He could also be unforgiving, vengeful and over-protective. He was, in short, both complex and full of contradictions.

It was at Lanercost Priory in February 1307 that Edward and Piers Gaveston were forced by Edward I to promise under oath on holy relics to agree to and maintain Gaveston's first exile. His departure was brief; he returned in August that year, following Edward II's accession.

Philip IV of France, with his wife and children Louis, Philip, Charles and Isabella. All three sons would become kings of France and his daughter the queen of England following her marriage to Edward II. This marriage was designed to cement political relationships between England and France.

Isabella married Edward II at Boulogne on 25 January 1308. Among her wedding gifts was a silver-gilt casket from her aunt Marguerite of France, who was the second wife of Edward I and stepmother to Edward II.

The coronation of Edward II, on 25 February 1308, was a lavish but controversial affair. Edward would inherit a toxic legacy of war, debt and baronial demands for reform from his father that would overshadow the best part of his reign.

Edward II was the first king crowned sitting on the Coronation Chair housing the confiscated Stone of Destiny taken by Edward I from the Scots in 1296. All monarchs crowned since have sat on this chair, including Elizabeth II in 1953.

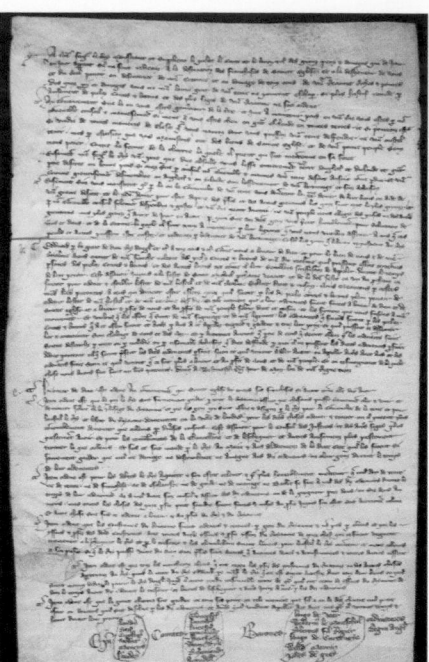

Baronial demands for reform dominated Edward II's reign. In 1310 he received this petition and six preliminary Ordinances seeking the king's authority to establish a commission of Lord Ordainers who would, within a year, produce forty-one clauses of reforms, one of which demanded the third and final exile of Piers Gaveston.

Edward was conventionally pious and his household accounts list records of devotions and pilgrimages. He favoured the murdered English saint, Thomas Becket, whose feast day fell on Edward II's accession, 7 July 1307. The king would later become embroiled in a medieval hoax connected with the alleged Holy Oil of St Thomas, which would cause him much embarrassment.

Knaresborough Castle in Yorkshire was gifted to Piers Gaveston, who remodelled the keep prior to his death in 1312. The king later granted it to another close favourite, Roger Damory, until he fell from favour and died opposing Edward in 1322.

In the summer of 1312, Piers Gaveston, his brother and sister, held out at Scarborough Castle against the forces of the Earl of Pembroke and Surrey, following Piers' return to Edward after the publication of the Ordinances. Gaveston surrendered the castle in return for a promise of protection. It was one of many mistakes that would bring about his end.

Above: Following his capture, Gaveston was seized at Deddington by the Earl of Warwick and imprisoned and tried at Warwick Castle by his peers. The mock trial in which Gaveston was not allowed to speak had no legal foundation but nevertheless resulted in a death sentence.

Left: Gaveston was brutally murdered on 19 June 1312 at Blacklow Hill, between the mighty castles of Kenilworth and Warwick. This Victorian monument marks the spot. He was handed over to two Welshmen, run through with a sword and beheaded.

Right: The battle of Bannockburn was a significant English defeat during the First War of Scottish Independence. Edward II fought fiercely but both he and his captains had not expected to be fighting that day. Restricted space and a change of Scottish tactics saw the English outmanoeuvred to devastating effect.

Below left: The counter seal of Edward II shows the king in a martial pose. Seals were used to authenticate royal documents in an age before signatures. Edward had many seals including the Great Seal, which was used for the most important of documents.

Below right: A silver penny of Edward II, found in London. Coins were an important way of disseminating the image of royal power across the kingdom. The head, while stylised, was a potent reminder that a king ruled, not reigned, in the fourteenth century.

Left: Edward's cousin Aymer de Valence, Earl of Pembroke, was, from 1312, a close confidant of the king whose moderating influences over Edward II did more than anyone's to maintain a fragile peace in England until he lost favour after 1322. He died in 1324 and is buried at Westminster Abbey.

Below: In the autumn of 1321, Edward II sent his wife, Isabella of France, to Leeds Castle. After the queen was violently turned away, and six of her party killed, Edward had his pretext for war against the contrariants.

Edward II exercised his long-awaited vengeance with the execution of his cousin Thomas of Lancaster on 22 March 1322 outside the walls of the earl's favourite castle at Pontefract. This act marked the highest point in the king's reign but also sowed the seeds for his eventual downfall less than five years later.

Shortly after Lancaster's execution, miracles were reported both at Pontefract and in the churchyard of St Paul's in London. Pilgrims flocked to these sites and purchased a variety of secular pilgrim badges, which depicted his life and death. Here the earl is beheaded with a sword and his soul can be seen rising up to Heaven.

Edwardus III Rex
Anglia et Isabelly
filia Philippi Pulchri

After 1322, the successful marriage of Edward II and Isabella of France began to fall apart. Edward's propensity for male favourites, especially following the rise of Hugh Despenser the Younger, did much to alienate Isabella in the 1320s. The effect would be devastating for all of them.

Isabella of France is received at the gates of Paris. The queen was sent on a diplomatic mission by her husband to the court of her brother Charles IV to reach agreement over English-held territories in France, including Gascony, confiscated by the French king in June 1324.

The mighty fortress of Caerphilly Castle was gifted to Hugh Despenser the Younger as part of his wife's inheritance. The castle would become a temporary refuge for Edward and his favourite as they fled west in 1326, attempting to raise an army to overcome the invading force led by Queen Isabella.

Above left: Isabella of France lands at Orwell in Suffolk at the head of a small army of English exiles, foreign mercenaries and men-at-arms. The fleet was procured as a result of a marriage betrothal in which her eldest son, later Edward III, was contracted to marry Philippa, daughter of the Count of Hainault.

Above right: The execution of Hugh Despenser the Younger at Hereford was both bloody and symbolic. First he was drawn through the town wearing a crown of nettles, strapped to a 50-foot ladder, asphyxiated but not to the point of death; his genitals were cut off and burned in front of him, after which he was then disembowelled, beheaded and his body quartered.

Below: Kenilworth Castle in Warwickshire became a temporary prison for Edward II following his capture on 16 November at Llantrisant. On 20 January 1327 he was forced to abdicate, the first English king to do so since the Norman Conquest, thereby setting a precedent that would reverberate through the centuries to come.

In April 1327, Edward was forcibly removed from the custody of his cousin Henry of Lancaster and transferred to Berkeley Castle in Gloucestershire, on the orders of Roger Mortimer and Queen Isabella.

Edward II was held captive in this cell from April until September 1327. Despite its location in the strongest part of the castle, there were numerous attempts to rescue him, one succeeding in the summer when he temporarily escaped. According to tradition, he was murdered in this room on 21 September 1327, but that tale has since been disproved.

The Dominican Order, whose friars wear distinctive black-and-white habits, was shown particular favour by Edward II and they, in turn, remained fiercely loyal to him. Both in 1327 and 1330 Dominican friars were implicated in plots to rescue the captive king.

The majestic Gloucester Cathedral was chosen for the burial of Edward's body. The cathedral, then known only as St Peter's Abbey, already housed the remains of Robert Curthose, eldest son of William the Conqueror, and was the place of coronation for the young Henry III in 1216.

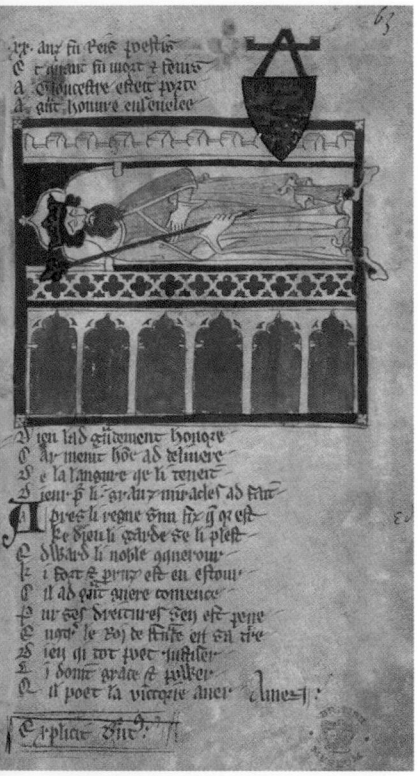

Above: The Shrine of the Three Kings in Cologne was an international place of pilgrimage. Edward visited it on more than one occasion, most notably described in Manuele Fieschi's letter, to pray at this sacred place.

Left: The only image of Edward's tomb to appear in a late fourteenth-century manuscript from the Romances in French verse. Given its detail, the illuminator may well have visited St Peter's Abbey before completing his work.

Following his secret removal from Berkeley Castle in September 1327, Edward was held for two-and-a-half years at Corfe Castle until his half-brother, Edmund of Woodstock, Earl of Kent, became aware of his whereabouts and attempted a rescue. Kent was executed and Edward moved to Ireland.

The Earl of Ulster, Richard de Burgh, who had supported Piers Gaveston when he was Lieutenant of Ireland in 1308–9, met Edward Bruce in battle at Connor-in-Down on 1 September 1315. Unbeknown to Edward II during his assembly, as they sat in discussion at Lincoln, de Burgh was routed and forced to flee into the west of Ireland. Edward's second hope, Roger Mortimer of Wigmore, who had spent considerable time in Ireland managing his vast estates there, was also resoundingly defeated in battle at Kells in Meath, and forced to retreat. Following these routs, there was a real danger that Edward Bruce would take Dublin and overrun Edward II's lordship entirely, affording him a springboard for the invasion of England through the principality of Wales. Edward Bruce's progress was made all the more worrying when he was crowned high king of Ireland on 6 June 1315, with the support of Donald O'Neill of Tyrone.[29]

These significant advances in Ireland coincided with attacks from Robert Bruce in the summer of 1315 on Carlisle. The castle held fast and within ten days Bruce was sent packing 'in great confusion' as a result of the defence mounted by the sheriff of Cumberland, Andrew Harclay.[30] As Edward II's assembly at Lincoln drew to a close, the king declared that he intended to remain in the north throughout the winter with those present. He also strongly encouraged sixty-six other magnates to move north for the duration, and, like everyone assembled, suffer the cost of guarding the north at their own individual expense. While no advances were made into Scotland, for the northern populace the presence of the king and wider court with the likes of Maurice de Berkeley at Berwick must have given at least some short-term comfort.[31] Edward was certainly trying to do what he could with what he had available.

The criticism of the king continued, however. In autumn, Edward embattled by the strains of governing the kingdom, spent a month in the Fens in Cambridgeshire and Norfolk. Always fond of water and highly athletic as noted by contemporaries, he spent his time swimming and rowing, in what must have been freezing waters. Nearly drowning, he had to be rescued by one of the 'common people' he was with, as derisively noted by the writer of the *Flores Historiarum*.[32]

The king always demonstrated a care for his untitled subjects and spending time with them in the Fens was just one of the many things contemporaries found out of step with his royal dignity. For Edward this was part of who he was, happy to share the company of people who made him laugh; fond of theatricals, music and sport. He often gave gifts, sometimes quite large, in exchange for the company or services of commoners. For the everyday people he came into contact with, it must have been a strange but nevertheless welcome interaction, and for Edward, a relief from the constant battle at court. For his magnates, living in a strict hierarchical society, the king's fraternisation with his lesser subjects was disgraceful and would later feature in the articles of deposition against him in January 1327.

Despite his common touch, not all his subjects were supporters. As 1315 drew to a close, a clerk named Thomas de Tynwelle was arrested for claiming that Edward was not his father's son. Whether he meant Edward was illegitimate or simply not the reflection of his father in terms of reputation or career, he was expressing a disgruntled opposition to Edward's kingship from the lower strata that may have been more widespread.

The rain continued to fall. As in 1315, the following year opened with a meeting of parliament on 27 January.[33] Lancaster, in the latter part of the previous year, had been growing in confidence and Edward is seen from the records referring items and decisions to him for consultation. It quickly went to his head. The day after parliament opened, Edward, through his spokesperson, the justice William Inge, announced that he wished to keep the session short, partly to ease the burden on the local populace of the town where they and their extensive retinues were assembled during such a period of famine. Unfortunately for the king, it was not to be, as an over-confident Lancaster failed to arrive until two weeks after parliament first opened. Lancaster was flexing his muscles. Edward was furious, but without his cousin the key business of the session, namely Scotland and what official political role Lancaster would hold, could not be considered.

When Lancaster finally arrived on 9 or 10 February the main business got underway. Edward agreed to not just uphold, but specifically to enforce the Ordinances, as well as observing the perambulation of the forest undertaken in 1300 during his father's reign; in short, ensuring royal control of large areas of England, which came with strict royal rights that were not being enlarged as they were wont to be in the past. On 24 February, Lancaster was given a formal position in the king's government. Edward reluctantly offered his cousin the position of head of a new King's Council. Its stated purpose was to control major decision-making; in practice it could impose further limits on the king. Collectively it was envisaged Edward and the council would work together and any of its members who gave bad advice was to be removed at the request of the king, and Lancaster, as its joint head.[34] Lancaster agreed, so long as he could withdraw without ill-will should he feel the need to if Edward failed to take his advice. Further reforms imposing limits on the king's authority were still sought by many of the magnates, a desire born in part from the overbearing policies of his father Edward I towards the end of his reign. Once again, Edward II's inheritance was casting a shadow over his own reign.

The council was in fact to be filled by moderates with royal sympathies and alongside this, Edward established a commission, probably while under pressure to further reform his household. Again, the commission was filled with moderates including the Archbishop of Canterbury, the earls of Pembroke, Hereford, Richmond and Bartholomew Badlesmere.[35] If Edward had lost his power temporarily and suffered the great indignity of not being trusted to rule with the same freedoms that his father had exercised, he had clearly not lost everything.

As Lancaster rose to a position of unprecedented power, it can be argued that there were almost two kings in England at this point; something that contemporaries had said when Gaveston was alive. However, it soon became apparent to Lancaster that he had been given a position he could not fulfil. Within two months of his appointment the earl, as head of the King's Council, unofficially retired from it. While he had been active for the first few months, actually dealing with the problems of famine, war in Scotland and Ireland, and hard economic pressure was beyond his capacity. Lancaster had exposed his own shortcomings. He had spent so long campaigning for the implementation and observance of the Ordinances but once he had won and was in a position to bring about more detailed reform, he could not deliver. He was a one trick pony better suited to bullying, rather than getting round the table and actually initiating real change. Sitting in council was simply not his style. He had unwittingly outmanoeuvred himself and so left the council. Whether he did so expecting his departure to be permanent or not is hard to determine, but he did formally hold onto the role. After meeting the king at Langley, Lancaster retired to his estates at Donnington in Leicestershire and later Pontefract in Yorkshire.[36] While no clear evidence exists, it may be that Edward and Lancaster had a disagreement at Langley, creating yet more difficulty.[37] Without Lancaster in council but holding onto office, government business became impossible to deliver and a political vacuum opened up.

Edward was not given much respite by Lancaster's self-exile from court. The year 1316 was filled with crises that challenged the king in maintaining law and order across his kingdom. Trouble began in Wales, which, given the threat of a Bruce invasion through the principality, needed to be resolved quickly. In December, Edward, hoping to maintain the loyalty of his Welsh subjects, placed the great northern castles in Gwynedd into a state of defensive readiness.[38] At Lincoln, while waiting for Lancaster to arrive at parliament, the king was careful to listen to and answer the petitions specifically made from his Welsh subjects. The care and attention he showed at this time proved to be an astute policy and north Wales in particular remained loyal and in a state of relative peace.

When revolt came, it was to be found in the lordship of Glamorgan in the south, formally held by Gilbert de Clare, the late Earl of Gloucester. Since his premature death at Bannockburn, most of Gloucester's estates, including Glamorgan, were brought under the king's control and royal officials were drafted in to administer them on the king's behalf. Payn Turberville was Edward's representative in Glamorgan but his heavy-handed, arrogant behaviour disgruntled the local inhabitants. Llewelyn Bren, who held high office during Gloucester's time and was the grandson of the former Lord of Senghenydd, was deprived of his office by Turberville. According to the *Vita*, Llewelyn took umbrage and threatened to put an end to Turberville's insolence. Unfortunately for Bren, it was reported to Payn who in turn reported his sedition to the king.[39] Edward, fearful that his officials were at risk of being undermined by the local populace, ordered Bren to attend upon him at the Lincoln parliament, adding that if his threat proved true, he would be hanged. It may seem odd today that to keep the peace Edward threatened the very man who was likely to rebel, but in the bigger picture the king needed to maintain the authority of his royal officials in the principality. If he allowed such behaviour to go unchecked, even if his officials were corrupt, law and order would crumble altogether.

Unfortunately for Edward, tired of yet more internal dispute, he was faced with just that. Failing to attend parliament, Bren and his men instead launched an attack on the constable of Caerphilly Castle who was holding court just outside the walls of the great fortress. Kidnapping him, they also managed to overcome the garrison at nearby Llantrisant Castle. Edward responded quickly before trouble could spread, and on 6 February ordered William Montacute and Hugh Audley into the area to restore peace. Five days later, Edward upped the ante and sent his brother-in-law, the Earl of Hereford who was also lord of neighbouring Brecon, to lead the force. The earl, Montacute and Audley were later joined by Roger Mortimer of Wigmore, now back from Ireland, with Henry of Lancaster, Thomas's brother; and John Giffard, as well as 150 men-at-arms and 2,000 infantry.[40] It was an impressive show of royal authority.

Through such a concerted and well thought out response from the king, Llewelyn Bren was quickly brought to heel and in his submission offered to give up his life if his men could be spared. It won the respect of Hereford and Mortimer, who petitioned Edward to show leniency. Edward granted it, after all, clemency was a sign of good kingship, and instead Bren, his wife and their five sons, among others, were sent to the Tower.[41] Edward had narrowly missed a wider confrontation but the expense of drafting in men to confront Bren was high and not well timed.

The bad news continued. In early May, word reached court that Edward's sister, Elizabeth, closest in age to the king and also born in Wales during their father's conquest there, had died during her tenth confinement. Elizabeth was thirty-three. No reaction from Edward is recorded, but the loss of another sister, and one he knew well and saw often as she was the wife of the Earl of Hereford, must have been another sad and bitter blow; 1316 was proving to be a tough year.

Further problems arose in the West Country as a long-standing feud between the citizens of Bristol and the constable of Bristol Castle and warden of the town, Bartholomew Badlesmere, erupted shortly after the Bren revolt was quelled. As three years of internal disaffection spilled over into open defiance, the royal justices were forced to flee in fear of their lives. Edward again had to act quickly to prevent a wider uprising. On 20 June, the king ordered Pembroke and William Inge to resolve the situation. By 7 July, the defiant Bristolian townsfolk barricaded the town gates and forced Pembroke to lay siege in order to gain access. On 19 July, after time away, Badlesmere returned and was accompanied by Roger Mortimer and Maurice de Berkeley whose seat was just north of Bristol at Berkeley Castle. As mangonels were used on the town walls, the inhabitants, realising the futility of their situation, quickly surrendered on 26 July.[42]

It had been a tough two years. Since Edward's defeat at Bannockburn, his position had weakened and he had been forced to accept a council to help govern the kingdom; with Lancaster as head of it, giving him a political office from which to challenge or even rival the king. Scottish raids in the north of England and invasion of Edward's lordship of Ireland threatened Edward's borders and revenues. Even the weather seemed to conspire against him and he narrowly escaped death as nature seemed to want to drown him. Yet in among all this hardship there were the odd rays of hope. While his household had been purged and his new council set up, he had enough influence to fill those positions with men for the most part sympathetic to his cause or at least moderate enough to ensure sensible policies. He had tried but failed to ease the burden of famine, but he cared enough about his subjects to show concern for their welfare. The attempt to fix prices was repealed at the Lincoln parliament, only a year after they had been implemented. He had the common touch, even if this led to derision from noble contemporaries and chroniclers.

At last some good news arrived in August 1316, when word reached Edward at York that Isabella had given birth to their second son, John, at Eltham Palace on the 15th. He had been conceived sometime shortly after Edward's holiday in the Fens, when he and Isabella spent the winter together at Clipstone in Nottinghamshire. Edward gave the enormous sum of £100 to the queen's steward who personally rode north to give Edward the news.[43] He also sent delicate fabrics, including cloth of gold, for his second son's baptism. Amidst this sea of troubles at least Edward had secured the future of the Plantagenet dynasty.

16

New Favourites

The relationship between the king and his over-mighty cousin was set to deteriorate even more. With Lancaster remaining at his estates in the north, Edward was given respite from having to deal with him in person. However, this was not particularly helpful for daily government. For Edward, like it or not, Lancaster was head of the newly formed council and his continued presence in London was essential if effective government was to continue. Thomas remained the premier earl in England, his wealth enormous, drawn from his five earldoms. This coupled with his blood royal ensured that he was too significant, too powerful to be ignored, no matter how much Edward tried. For the king this was entirely frustrating. He needed Lancaster's co-operation and yet in his heart, all Edward wanted was his destruction for murdering Piers Gaveston. Edward wrestled daily with an ongoing grief that was turning into steely, vengeful hatred.

Open conflict with Thomas at this stage may not have produced a conclusive result anyway, given the king's limited finances and the general lack of appetite among many to see Lancaster fall. An ensuing civil war would endanger the very fabric of the country and Edward himself had no appetite for such internal widespread strife – only the end result, Lancaster's death. The ever-present threat from the Scots was real and felt daily by the king's subjects in the north, and their advances into Ireland was yet another ongoing reminder that a full-scale Scottish invasion into England could be not entirely ruled out. All knew, and a few counselled the king, that a divided kingdom in the face of its enemies within and without could not hope to prosper. Edward listened but everyone knew of the hatred the king and Thomas held for one another. Hatred in any sense, can blind anyone when they are consumed by it, yet Edward held his emotions in check enough to stay his hand. For now the voices of moderation proffered by the likes of Pembroke and Hereford held sway at court.

Dark rumours sprang up that Lancaster was in league with Robert Bruce, made more plausible when the frequent Scottish raids into

England left Lancaster's vast estates untouched.[1] Yet nothing could be proved for certain, no action could be taken and so Edward waited. The cousins' enmity for one another was felt throughout the country and no more so than at court. The author of the *Vita* wrote:

> Whatever pleases the lord king the earl's servants try to upset; and whatever pleases the earl the king's servants call treachery; and so at the suggestion of the Devil the familiars of each start meddling, and their lords, by whom the land ought to be defended, are not allowed to rest in harmony.[2]

On 9 October 1316 Richard Kellaw, the Bishop of Durham, died. Ten days later two monks sought out the king at Crayke in Yorkshire for a royal licence to elect a successor, which was duly granted. As with all important offices, the king would seek to have his candidate nominated and secured in office, thereby guaranteeing a supporter. Achieving this could result from the application of gentle persuasion or something a little more direct, if necessary, during the election. Edward had his man, Thomas Charlton, keeper of the privy seal, put forward as his own candidate. Thomas was the brother of John Charlton, who had for many years been at odds with Lancaster's retainer Gruffudd de la Pole. The king's choice could not have been more calculated and all knew it. Isabella too offered an alternative candidate and was determined to see her close friend Louis de Beaumont, brother of Henry, appointed. Isabella's choice was also far from palatable to Lancaster, as he despised the Beaumonts as much as he did the king, and had singled them out in the Ordinances of 1311. Not to be outdone, Lancaster hit back and presented his own candidate, John de Kinardesey. The Earl of Hereford, just to complicate matters, suggested a fourth, John Walwayn, who may have been the author of the contemporary *Vita*.[3] As all four parties sent representatives to Durham to apply the necessary pressures on the monks prior to their election, the monks nevertheless held out and elected their own, a fifth candidate named Henry de Stamford. Edward must have been amused in the end by the whole affair, as he appeared prepared to allow the monks their decision. Yet Isabella was determined to see Louis de Beaumont gain the see, and with the support of her husband who wrote to the pope in November, she got her way in December. Pope John XXII, who had been elected in August 1316, quashed the monks' vote and duly provided Beaumont with his new position.[4] The royal gifts sent to the pope following his election, which included two embroidered copes, one studded with large white pearls, a gold ewer and matching basin, and thirteen gold salt cellars, must have done the trick.[5] Lancaster had been outmanoeuvred and quite possibly brooded all the more for it.

One of the most dangerous aspects of this bitter hatred was the inability of Edward and Thomas to work together to overcome the Scots. The campaign scheduled for 1316 was abandoned for the year. Following the expense of putting down localised revolts in Glamorgan and Bristol, and with the country impoverished and malnourished from another year of famine, the small receipts received in the exchequer from taxation proved too meagre for any meaningful campaign. As with winter the year before, the north was strengthened as well as it could be in order to hold the line, culminating in the appointment of the Earl of Arundel as warden of the Scottish March on 19 November. The king appointed Roger Mortimer of Wigmore as Lieutenant of Ireland on 23 November, in a bid to overcome the continued advances made by Edward Bruce. Mortimer's appointment was further bolstered by the king's demand that those magnates holding lands in Ireland ought to head there with all due speed to protect them.[6]

The late appointment of a new pope, following the long interregnum created by the death of Clement V in April 1314, had robbed Edward for nearly two years of a useful ally. The king had proved that he was adept at foreign diplomacy and could rally the support of the papal curia and the French crown when he needed it most. In early 1317, Edward sent a high-profile delegation to the papal palace at Avignon headed by the Earl of Pembroke, who was accompanied by Bartholomew Badlesmere, the Archbishop of Canterbury, Walter Reynolds, John Sandal the chancellor and newly appointed Bishop of Winchester, Edward's treasurer Walter of Norwich, and many clerks and officials.[7] It was to be an all-out charm offensive and £7,800 was borrowed from Italian bankers the Bardi to help cover the enormous expense of the trip, which in the end cost £3,800, of which £1,904 was used to purchase royal gifts from Edward and Isabella.[8]

To all intents and purposes their three-month diplomatic mission paid off. On 28 March 1317 the pope agreed to Edward's request to postpone his crusade to the Holy Land, which he had made on oath with his late father-in-law during his visit to France in 1313. Even better, John XXII granted the king permission to levy a tenth on the English clergy, which yielded £19,500. Edward was also able to borrow for five years £18,500 from another source of papal revenue, from the crusading tax imposed in 1311. Repayment of the loan drawn up between Edward and Clement V for the sum of 160,000 florins (£25,000) was also renegotiated, freeing up to eighty per cent of Edward's revenue from his duchy of Aquitaine, which had been fixed to the loan as collateral.[9] A need to beg and borrow from creditors remained one of Edward II's key challenges as a result of the debts bequeathed to him by his father, even ten years into his reign.

More significantly for the king, his embassy to Avignon was able to secure papal support against Scotland. On 28 March, the pope excommunicated Robert and Edward Bruce and on 1 May issued a bull ordering the Scots to cease their attacks on Edward's dominions. The pope also proclaimed a truce, which neither of the two Bruce brothers acknowledged.[10] Once again, Edward's efforts through his embassy on the foreign stage had paid off. Religious appointments made during the papal interregnum were also confirmed, although the king was thwarted in securing the bishopric of Hereford for his failed candidate at Durham, Thomas Charlton. Instead, and much to Edward's annoyance, Adam Orleton, previously a clerk, secured the lucrative position on his own volition while himself at Avignon.[11] Despite this small setback, relations with the papal curia looked as strong as ever, at least for the moment.

While there are no official records that exist reporting that the embassy discussed the Ordinances, the well-informed author of the *Vita* suggested that Edward had used the opportunity to discuss the possibility of revoking them. The *Vita* noted:

> To this the pope replied that the king of England ought not to be absolved from the observance of the said Ordinances since they had been drawn up, as he had been informed, by the care of trustworthy persons, and it was not likely that they had ordained anything to the prejudice of the kingdom or the church.[12]

If these discussions did indeed occur, the outcome allowed Edward, at the very least, to gauge the papal position. Disappointed with the result, the king could nevertheless now work on developing support from the Holy Father over the coming years, guaranteeing absolution from his oath and finally consigning the Ordinances to the midden.

With success achieved in the main, the English embassy left Avignon in early April. Pembroke left the main party to see to affairs on his estates at Montignac and then headed north to Orléans. Before he reached Paris he was ambushed on the road and held to ransom at Étampes either by Jean de la Moilière, or more likely a man named Jean de Lamouilly, who was a vassal of Edward II's nephew, Henry, Count of Bar. Kept in an unidentified location, Pembroke's capture was followed by a ransom demand for the enormous sum of £10,400.[13] The capture of one of Edward's principal advisors sent the king and court back in England into a panic. Without Pembroke, Lancaster would gain ground.

So what was it all about? De Lamouilly claimed he was due unpaid wages from his service in the English army, however this may have been something of a cover story. Pembroke was the unfortunate bystander to a bitter dispute between Edward II's niece, Joan de Bar, sister to Count Henry and wife to Earl Warenne in England since 1306. Their marriage had been stormy and by 1313 had broken down entirely as the earl had long since taken a mistress, Maud Nerford, and fathered many children with her. The ensuing marital drama, in which Warenne sought an annulment shortly after their separation, placed the king in a delicate situation. Edward initially supported his niece where he could and paid her expenses once she moved away from her husband. The drama tipped over into court and may account for Warenne's absence during the Bannockburn campaign in 1314 when his relationship with Edward temporarily became strained.

By 1316 the king had realised that there was little hope of reconciliation between the earl and his wife and so agreed to recognise Warenne's two illegitimate sons, John and Thomas, as the earl's heirs despite him still being married to Edward's niece Joan. Warenne surrendered his lands to the king in July that year, who immediately granted them back to him with the reversion to Maud and her two boys.[14] Joan was desperately upset and in August the king paid her expenses of £166 to leave England and return to her brother's court.[15] The Count of Bar shared his sister's distress and quite possibly through de Lamouilly, took the opportunity to ransom the Earl of Pembroke, thereby securing a large sum of money for his sister. All of this, of course, needed to be dealt with with a degree of discretion, which de Lamouilly could provide as front man.

Aymer de Valence entered this drama at the eleventh hour. It is highly likely that Pembroke was tasked with presenting Warenne's request for an annulment to the pope during his diplomatic mission and, given his position at court, as a cousin to the king, his capture would prove lucrative. While no direct evidence exists that shows Henry ordered his vassal Jean de Lamouilly to capture the earl, the facts and events as they unfolded look like more than pure coincidence.[16] The kidnap had its desired effect. Edward and his government worked hard to raise the money to secure the earl's release, the king himself putting up £2,500 of the £10,400 needed. The earl was free by early June.[17] The episode proves the king's reliance on him for counsel and good government. Pembroke, Badlesmere and Antonio Pessagno, who had remained in France during the last few months, re-joined Edward at Northampton on 4 July 1317.

During the six-month absence of Edward's chief counsellors, Scotland continued to dominate the king's thinking and the paralysis in government during Lancaster's absence had become evident. Everyone, including the king, knew something needed to be done about it. On 28 January Edward sent out writs of summons to the bishops of Salisbury and Exeter, the Earl of Hereford, and the king's half-brother Thomas, now Earl of Norfolk, Hugh Despenser, as well as thirteen clerks, for a 'colloquium' to be held at Clarendon starting on 9 February.[18] Lancaster, who was summoned to attend, refused to grasp the olive branch and remained absent. The king was angry but probably not disappointed. Those around him began to speak openly of Lancaster as a traitor.[19] With the absence of moderates like Pembroke to keep order, these voices became louder. Thinking Lancaster was a traitor was one thing, but to openly voice such an opinion in the formal setting of council was quite another and required a formal defence.

Those voices at Clarendon included three of the king's new favourites: Roger Damory, William Montacute and Hugh Audley the Younger. A former retainer of the Earl of Gloucester, Damory had caught Edward's eye during or shortly after the battle of Bannockburn. Whether Edward was impressed by his martial skill or because of a physical attraction it is not clear, but by the end of 1314, on Christmas Eve, Damory was granted custody of Gaveston's former castle at Knaresborough in Yorkshire.[20] Potentially this was emotionally significant. The following month, Edward ordered that Damory was to remain at court and in his company there grew an attachment that brought about a sudden rise in the fortunes of the knight. The gifts continued. The next month Damory obtained the lucrative wardship of the manor of Foston in Leicestershire, and a further wardship on 24 January 1317 while the king was at Woodstock.[21] Examining the chancery writs it becomes clear that Damory was often in the king's presence, making suggestions or seeking patronage for his followers, which Edward duly granted.[22] By 1317 at the Clarendon colloquium, Roger Damory had become Edward's principal favourite and was gaining significant power in and beyond the court.

William Montacute too was close to the king and soon a boon companion of Damory. A royal household knight since 1312, Montacute rose in position, replacing John Cromwell as steward of the royal household in November 1316. Months earlier he had been appointed captain of Edward's household knights during the Llewelyn Bren uprising and was also present at Bristol during the recent siege. In 1317 he received the lands of a northern rebel, William de Karliolo, who had turned coat with the Scots and lost his estate, and possibly his life as a result.[23] Much like Damory, Montacute was also given other financial benefits, receiving the wardship of the estates of the late Herbert de Maresco on 2 August 1317.[24] This elevated status positioned Montacute in the inner circle of the king. In January 1317, both Damory and Montacute contracted with the king to serve him for life in return for an annuity of 200 marks each.[25] The bonds between these men were made deliberately strong.

Hugh Audley, much like Montacute, had been a royal household knight, taking his position slightly earlier, during the time of Gaveston's third exile from England in 1311. Audley's father, also called Hugh Audley, was well known and an experienced knight at Edward's court. Collectively the three men secured such affection from Edward that the *Flores Historiarum* records they rose up 'in the king's shadow', and rather more pointedly accused them of seizing 'other men's goods'. They were 'more wicked than even Gaveston'.[26]

These 'wicked men' certainly grew in confidence. Their elevation at court was widely noted and by 1317 the three men, with the steadfast Hugh Despenser the Elder, felt strong enough to accuse the Earl of Lancaster of treason at Clarendon. Edward was willing to let them off the leash and if anything appeared to actively promote their dissent. With the absence of Pembroke and his senior councillors abroad in France, Edward's bitter hatred of Lancaster was being stoked by men who weighed the threat differently from England's senior advisors. It must have felt to observers that the king was preparing to go to war with his cousin. The Earl of Hereford, Edward's brother-in-law, still encouraged moderation and so, with the failure of Clarendon, another council meeting was proposed to meet at Westminster for 15 April.[27] This time Hugh Despenser the Younger was also summoned to attend to discuss the Gloucester inheritance, which still needed to be settled. As before, Lancaster and his retainer Robert Holland, who had also been invited, failed to show up.[28]

What happened next poured fuel onto the fire. On 9 May, Earl Warenne's retainer, Richard Martin, abducted Lancaster's wife, Alice de Lacy, from her manor at Canford in Dorset and spirited her away into the night to Warenne's manor at Reigate in Surrey. Alice appears to have been a willing victim, or rather accomplice, as her marriage to the difficult Thomas of Lancaster was far from successful; they had no children together and lived apart. Warenne certainly had no desire to marry her, as he was happy with his mistress Maud Nerford, so his motives were clearly to cause trouble with Lancaster.[29] It was poking a bees' nest. The event was an outrage and Lancaster was determined to bring Warenne and those involved to book, by violence preferably, which was Lancaster's way. For now, he bided his time. Thomas suspected Edward was behind the whole affair and it is most likely that he was. While Warenne and Lancaster had often been in dispute with each other, Edward, encouraged by Damory, Montacute and Audley, and without voices of reason to restrain him, most likely knew of, or gave unofficial support to, the abduction. The king's hostility during the first half of 1317 would certainly make it more than plausible, and for Warenne to act without the king's knowledge seems unlikely.

To make matters more fractious, Edward II finally agreed to the partition of the second largest earldom in England, Gloucester, on 17 April 1317, nearly three years after the late Earl of Gloucester was killed at the battle of Bannockburn. It had long been accepted that the late earl's wife Maud was not pregnant with Gilbert's child as she was still claiming to be some eighteen months after his death! Edward had been in no hurry to partition the land either, the revenues instead flowing into his coffers, but a long overdue settlement was being often pressed by an increasingly irritable Hugh Despenser the Younger, son and namesake of Edward's close and ever loyal counsellor.

The earldom had four beneficiaries, the earl's widow who was entitled to one third of its £6,500 value. The remaining two thirds were to be divided equally among Gloucester's three sisters; Eleanor, Margaret and Elizabeth, all nieces of the king. Through them, their husbands, if they had any, would become both wealthy and powerful overnight. Eleanor had since 1306 been married to the ambitious but not rich Hugh Despenser the Younger, and his desire to secure land and wealth drove him to pursue the partition. He first appeared in chancery in 1315 and by 1316, was directed to the Lincoln parliament to press his wife's rights there. Edward and his advisors deferred the decision and an irate Despenser lashed out, attacking John Roos, who had married his late brother's widow, while in the presence of the king, in Lincoln Cathedral. Roos had earlier attempted to arrest one of Despenser's knights, Ingelram Berenger, and as Despenser's hot temper boiled over, his common sense evaporated. He was fined for his actions, eventually receiving a pardon in January 1320.[30]

Margaret de Clare was the widow of Piers Gaveston and had not remarried since his murder in June 1312. Her sister Elizabeth was herself twice widowed. Her first husband was the young John de Burgh, heir to the earldom of Ulster but who had died young. On 4 February 1316, Elizabeth was abducted from Bristol Castle by Theobald de Verdun and married without the king's licence. Edward was furious and unable to do anything about it; de Verdun was set to become wealthy and powerful overnight. However, his designs fell apart with his sudden death in July the same year leaving behind a daughter, named Isabella in honour of the queen, who was sent to Amesbury Abbey and watched over by her aunt Mary, Edward II's sister.[31] Elizabeth was once more a widow and back on the medieval marriage market.

On 12 May formal orders were made by the king with support from his council to begin the process of partition.[32] Edward did not want a repeat of the Verdun abduction and so applied pressure on his nieces to marry quickly. As with most, if not all, marriage alliances of this importance in the Middle Ages, Edward arranged husbands that he felt suitable and the two sisters agreed to the proposals. To this effect and to cement the position of the king's favourites at court, Margaret married Hugh Audley the Younger on 28 April at Windsor. Edward provided three pounds of coins to be thrown over their heads during the ceremony.[33] The king's principal favourite Damory was married to Elizabeth sometime shortly afterwards.[34] These marriages, and the eventual partition of the earldom, which was concluded on 15 November 1317, thrust Damory, Audley and also Hugh Despenser the Younger into the forefront of the baronage. While none of them could call themselves Earl of Gloucester and join the highest levels of the nobility, their annual incomes were sufficient to underpin their position at court and make them forces in their own right. For Edward, this only strengthened his own position while for Lancaster, the threat was great.

Lancaster was not the only one who felt that the rise of the royal favourites was becoming too much to bear. On 22 May, while feasting during Pentecost, a woman mounted on a charger rode through the doors of Westminster Hall and approached the dais. There she presented a letter to the king and then left, possibly without speaking a word. Edward, ever fond of theatricality, took the letter and either he or another began to read it out aloud to those dining in the hall. He must have quickly wished he hadn't. The letter was a bitter remonstrance aimed at the king for allegedly neglecting his royal household knights, especially those of long-standing service by promoting those who had barely 'borne the heat of the day'.[35] To wit, Damory, Audley and Montacute, all royal household knights, who had risen fast and far beyond the expectations of any of their peers. The woman was promptly hunted down and under pressure, gave the name of the household knight who had put her up to it. He was arrested and when questioned claimed he had done it 'for the honour of the kingdom'.[36]

Nine days later, with the apparent mutterings at court still rife, Damory, Montacute, the two Despensers and Hugh Audley the younger, bound themselves together in a mutual bond in the presence of the king who was still at Westminster. The purpose of this bond is not clear, but given recent events and the bold claim of Lancastrian treachery at Clarendon months earlier, all five men knew they were dangerously exposed. It is most likely that these recognisances, made to the sum of £6,000 each, bound them together against any future action that would most likely be taken against them similar to that which Edward had experienced first-hand with Gaveston. If they were to be forcibly removed from court by others applying pressure on the king, they would act together to overcome their enemies and in turn protect the king .[37] If this is true, then this was Edward applying the lessons of the past in order to best protect those now closest to him. Tension at court was once again mounting fast.

The political environment in England was becoming dangerously overheated by the time Pembroke and Bartholomew Badlesmere returned from France in early July. The rapid decline in the already extremely strained relationship between Edward and Lancaster became openly acknowledged at Nottingham, when Lancaster again failed to attend after a summons to a third council meeting that year. Edward had been determined to force Lancaster's hand by summoning all of his councillors, including the Archbishop of Canterbury, the bishops of Winchester, Ely, Norwich, the earls Pembroke and Hereford, as well as leading barons like Badlesmere, and the two Despensers. Lancaster's failure to show up smacked of contempt and open defiance of a direct royal order.[38] This was Edward's intention and the earl walked into the trap.

On 21 July the king sent two letters to his cousin via his messenger William de Dene, firstly repeating the summons to council, while secondly accusing the earl of gathering armed men in the north and scaring the people as a result.[39] To this Lancaster finally responded declaring that if the council meeting was discussing matters of such importance it ought to be in parliament, which he would attend if called. With regard to armed men, he was simply raising them for the forthcoming campaign against the Scots; the whole army was due to muster on 11 August at Newcastle-upon-Tyne, and for no other reason.[40] He went on to declare that he had withdrawn from the council because the king had failed to accept the suggested reforms presented to him, possibly at Langley immediately before Lancaster first left for his northern estates. He also noted that the king failed to observe the Ordinances and made gifts to people in contravention of the same. Lancaster, according to Murimuth, stated, 'you have held them dearer than they were before, and others you have newly taken to you, which are of the same condition, and do give them your substance daily, so that little or nothing remaineth to you.'[41] This was a reference to Damory and the others as well as the Beamounts, especially Louis, now elected as Bishop of Durham, and Earl Warrenne, now Lancaster's bitterest enemy.

Thomas also went on, claiming via a messenger that his prolonged absence was brought about by '...fearing the deadly stratagems of certain persons who thrive under the protection of the royal court. Their enmity is already a matter of public knowledge; they have already carried off the earl's wife to his disgrace and shame'.[42] The threats at Clarendon had certainly found their way to Pontefract. Lancaster demanded that Edward purge his household and hold a parliament, upholding and enforcing the Ordinances. The king was, of course, furious; 'I will avenge the despite done to the earl when I can; I refuse to expel my household; for the abduction of his wife let him seek remedy in law only.' Damory and others exhorted Edward either to exile or imprison his cousin for such open defiance.[43] The restraining hands of Pembroke, Hereford and Badlesmere calmed the king down making him again see that to act against Lancaster now would end in calamity for the kingdom and victory for the Scots, who were again raiding northern England.

Instead, Edward was persuaded to head north towards York and to attempt to treat with Lancaster. To this effect Pembroke and Hereford took the lead and were supported by the archbishops of Canterbury and Dublin as well as the bishops of Winchester, Llandaff, Salisbury, Norwich and Chichester. The large size of the delegation demonstrates the widespread feeling that a speedy resolution was now long overdue and certainly desired by many at court. Lancaster responded positively, initially agreeing to meet the king in person rather than act through mediators. However, news soon reached him that Edward had allegedly threatened to imprison or kill him should Lancaster appear in person. Whether true or not, Thomas believed it and the talks collapsed. From here on, Lancaster would only approach the king with protection.[44]

Edward continued to head to York, but possibly under advice, travelled far around Lancaster's castle of Pontefract to avoid any open confrontation with the now nervous and isolated earl. Since the middle of 1316, Lancaster had no real political allies to count on, and certainly no friends at court following the death of the Earl of Warwick the year before. His withdrawal from court meant he was in no position to enforce his will. He was left skulking in the north, resorting to threats and the same demands for reform, which had grown tiresome to many. Lancaster's demands had cloaked his ambition for royal power and as time went on this became ever more transparent and distasteful to those at court. Nevertheless, peace in England could only be achieved by amends being made between the king and the earl.

Lancaster took the opportunity to openly defy Edward once more, reacting to the threats of violence against him, which had been bandied around all year. As Edward moved north with a large retinue of 1,500 men-at-arms, Lancaster and his own men swarmed across the roads and bridges to the south of Pontefract, cutting them off so the king could not pass south again or be relieved by armed men travelling north to meet him for the proposed Scottish campaign, now due to muster on 15 September. Justifying his action through his office of Steward of England, Lancaster claimed the king was required to consult with him before taking up arms against an enemy.[45] It was a peculiar and petty challenge and one which only further angered and alarmed the king and his council. The situation, with armed men on both sides in the mix, made open confrontation perilously close.

As Lancaster was flexing his muscles, a further crisis was emerging at Rushyford near Durham. Louis de Beaumont was on his way to his consecration as Bishop of Durham, with his brother. In their company were the two papal legates, the cardinals Luke Fieschi and Gaucelin d'Eauze, who had arrived in England in consequence of the English embassy to Avignon earlier in the year. They were there after the consecration to deliver the papal bulls of excommunication to Robert Bruce and had, like all foreign diplomats, received grants of royal protection to ensure they could move freely and with safety through Edward's kingdom. During their journey the whole party were set upon and robbed and all but the cardinals were thrown into Mitford Castle at the hands of Sir Gilbert de Middleton and his colleague Sir John de Lilburn, among others; Middleton and Lilburn were both disgruntled royal household knights.[46] Sir John de Lilburn was soon in Lancaster's employ and the whole affair had a whiff of Lancaster's involvement. His hatred for the Beamounts was all too evident and his violent action in closing off the roads to the king during the same week confirmed his guilt. Edward certainly thought so. Whatever the motivations and exact involvement of the earl, for Lancaster it was a diplomatic disaster that the papal legates were present in the entourage. Violence against papal envoys caused enormous outrage, and upsetting the pope was not something either Edward or Lancaster wanted or could afford. Thomas acted quickly, meeting the shaken cardinals at Durham the day after their ordeal, when he personally escorted them south to Boroughbridge in Yorkshire, where he handed them over to the safe escort of the earls of Pembroke and Hereford, who took them to the king at York.[47] Edward, highly embarrassed, wrote to the pope on 10 September expressing his horror at events and true to his word hunted down the now excommunicated Middleton after a protracted siege at Mitford Castle and had him hanged, drawn and quartered on 18 January 1318.[48]

Some good came of the debacle. As civil war looked imminent, the cardinals understood first-hand the dangers of this bitter hatred between Edward and Lancaster. With Pembroke, a temporary dialogue was opened between the king and his cousin. Edward agreed to take no action against Thomas or his men, while Lancaster agreed in turn to attend the next parliament, wherever and whenever the king chose to hold one. With the cardinals involved, both parties had to seek compromise.[49] Lancaster dismissed his armed men and Edward disbanded some of his. Parliament was duly summoned to meet at Lincoln for 27 January 1318, the first in two years.[50] Reconciliation took precedence and so Edward at the last hour abandoned the muster for the Scottish campaign. Once more the divisive relationship between king and cousin had restricted the ability to take the fight to the Scots.

While the immediate threat of internal war had dissipated, things were far from calm. As Edward left York and began his journey back to Westminster, Lancaster had cleared the bridges and roads to ensure the king's way was now open and unopposed. As Edward took the direct road south from York, which ran under the walls of Pontefract Castle, he was cajoled by his hotheaded favourites to seize his opportunity. Surrounded by men who told the king what he wanted to hear, Edward felt strong enough to challenge his cousin directly. Gaveston had, after all, been dead for more than five years. As he approached Pontefract, still with a sizeable force, the king ordered them into battle array. Lancaster and his much smaller garrison jeered as Edward prepared to attack. Pembroke pleaded with the king to stand down, reminding him that he had sworn not to act against Lancaster or his supporters and to put any differences aside until the next parliament. If the king failed now, the kingdom would be ruined. Edward declared that he had heard Lancaster was out to ambush him. At the eleventh hour the king listened to wiser council and stood down his men, instead marching on to the sound of Lancaster's men jeering their king.[51]

It was Thomas of Lancaster's turn to be angry and on this occasion he focused his vehement dislike firmly on Damory, whom Lancaster must have blamed for leading the king to arms. A week after events outside the walls of his favourite castle, Lancaster employed Sir John de Lilburn, who had been involved in the abduction of the Beamounts, to seize Knaresborough and Alton castles, both constabled by Damory. The attacks were quick and calculated. As Damory's estates were attacked, Edward commanded Lancaster to desist, which he simply ignored. In an attempt to force his hand, the king took Damory's lands back into royal custody. Lancaster could not attack royal property directly without his actions being considered treason, which would give Edward the legal justification to move against him.[52] Thomas reacted by moving against Earl Warenne, attacking his extensive Yorkshire estates and seizing his castles of Sandal and Conisborough, as well as damaging his wider property.[53]

Edward was forced to defend himself. On 1 November, the king took the precaution of securing key strategic castles for defence, re-appointing Pembroke to Rockingham Castle near Lancaster's own castle at Leicester, while Badlesmere was given Leeds Castle in Kent.[54] On 7 November, the king secured yet another loan, this time of 10,000 marks from his Italian bankers the Bardi and appointed Antonio Pessagno, his chief personal financier, as seneschal of Gascony with the aim of raising more funds there.[55] In all, between April 1312 and January 1319, Pessagno would loan the king more than £144,000.[56]

As tension grew before the forthcoming parliament, Pembroke and Badlesmere knew they needed to do everything possible to regain control of the king. Moderation was going to be the only way forward and men like Damory were far from moderate. On 24 November, Pembroke and Badlesmere secured an agreement in the form of an indenture whereby Damory would promise to be guided by the two men. He also agreed not to procure or consent to gifts from the king above the value of £20 without first discussing it with Pembroke and Badlesmere. Importantly, Damory also promised not to act in a prejudicial way to the king or his crown or persuade the king into rash action. If he discovered that anyone else was encouraging Edward to take such a course that was prejudicial to him or his crown, Damory was to immediately inform Pembroke and Badlesmere. In return, the two men agreed to defend Damory against his enemies, saving only the king. Damory sealed the agreement with a pledge of £10,000 and Pembroke and Badlesmere with all their moveable and immoveable goods. This is an extraordinary document and highlights the lengths to which Pembroke and Badlesmere were prepared to go in order to gain control of the situation and to protect the king, both from ill counsel and his own rash judgement, which he had displayed through most of 1317. The security of the realm and the crown demanded that Edward did not seek his revenge and this was a clever way in which to keep those around the king in check.[57]

By the close of 1317, England had narrowly avoided outright civil war, but nevertheless armed men headed by Lancaster were wreaking havoc in the north. Edward had become openly vengeful and in this his favourites only encouraged him. Yet despite this, the king commanded a wide degree of loyalty from his nobles and ecclesiastical magnates. He was working well with his council, listened to the more moderate among them when it mattered most, and presented himself as one seeking to confront the threat from the Bruce brothers. Yet for all that, he could also be rash and allow himself to be led by men he had raised about him, if their opinions were shared with his own. Edward was complex, a man of contradictions. Lancaster, on the other hand, was isolated, friendless and resorting to open violence to bully his way through events, seeking policies that many now considered unachievable. For Edward, he might not yet have his vengeance, but he had achieved much greater control and freedom than at any time since the English defeat at Bannockburn three-and-a-half years earlier.

17

Hollow Treaty

The leading magnates at court were worn out with the on-going feud between the king and Lancaster. The inability of either side to find a compromise had placed English government under enormous strain. In order to overcome the threat posed by the Scots, internal division needed to be put aside or, better still, mended. Edward too must have been exhausted. The hours, days and years spent waiting for the moment that he could exact his revenge must have been emotionally debilitating. For Lancaster, the never-ending threat of royal attack was equally draining.

As patience among courtiers became threadbare, it fell in the main to the prelates led by the Archbishop of Canterbury, Walter Reynolds, with the support of the earls of Pembroke and Hereford, to break the stalemate and seek, if possible, a lasting reconciliation. Edward trusted them and they in turn understood the king's position. They felt that for the king and Lancaster to meet in parliament in January would only breed further confrontation, either directly between themselves or certainly between their large retinues obliged to reside in the town during proceedings. It was asking for trouble.

On 4 January 1318 Edward was persuaded twice to postpone parliament, finally settling on 19 July at Lincoln, allowing a delegation time to seek out Thomas at Leicester and begin the unenviable job of reopening a constructive dialogue.[1] Matters became all the more pressing when news arrived at court that the English garrison at the border town of Berwick had been betrayed by one of their own, a man named Peter Spalding who, bribed by the Scots, allowed the enemy over the walls unchallenged to take the town; the castle fell eleven weeks later. Despite all the money, men and armour ploughed into its defence to counter years of Scottish naval blockades, Edward's preparations had proved futile in the face of treachery. The loss of Berwick, allowing Robert Bruce a foothold on the doorstep of England, was a shock, which Bruce quickly capitalised on, moving to capture the castles of Wark, Harbottle and Mitford soon after.[2] If a united government did not act now, of which Lancaster with his large retinue and riches was a critical element, a full-scale Scottish invasion of England was likely. Edward again needed to put aside his personal feelings.

Pembroke, Badeslesmere, Walter Reynolds and John Sandale, with Edward's authority, arrived at Leicester in early April and began to treat with Lancaster. While much of the detail of this early meeting seems confused among the chroniclers, what is clear is Lancaster quite predictably held fast to his policy of Edward's full observance of the Ordinances and reform of the royal household. Behind this demand lurked the desire for the removal of the royal favourites, in particular Damory, whom Lancaster now considered his bitterest enemy.[3] Those earlier recognisances and indentures, taken among the king's favourites and promoted by Edward the year before, suddenly looked like a wise investment.

By June, Edward convened a meeting with many of his prelates, the two cardinals, Gaucelin d'Eauze and Luke Fieschi, who were still in England, Pembroke, Hereford, and his favourites, Damory, Montacute and the two Despensers, with the aim of setting out his own position. It was ostensibly agreed that it was Lancaster's failure to co-operate, especially since his withdrawal from the council in 1316, that had fundamentally weakened government and deprived Edward of counsel, which Lancaster as his vassal was bound to give him. The earl's behaviour, raising armed men and spreading fear among the populace, needed to cease. Specifically, Lancaster would be asked to stop using the Ordinances as a pretext for raising bands of men-at-arms and that he should not use force to impose his will. Notably, the attendees also demanded that when Thomas presented himself in parliament 'he does not try to claim superiority for himself over others.'[4] Even the earl's peers had had enough of his general behaviour. As the meeting drew to a close, Edward declared that in return for these concessions he would uphold the Ordinances.[5] He had no intention of enforcing them.

With Edward's bargaining position clarified and the magnates behind him, the king was in a strong position. Understanding Lancaster's sensitivity to men like Damory and Despenser the Elder, Edward ensured his favourites were constrained by making all swear an oath not to threaten Lancaster or his supporters when the time would come for the two parties to meet.[6] Peace looked possible.

While Edward was working with those around him to seek a political compromise, he heard in late June that the son of a tanner, John Powderham, had arrived in Oxford declaring himself to be the one true king of England. He alleged that he and Edward had been switched at birth. Two days later the arrested Powderham found himself in the presence of the king, who with his characteristic humour, greeted the imposter as 'brother'. When Edward asked him if such claims were true, Powderham, not remotely intimidated by his royal audience, simply repeated his claim. What happened next says something about Edward's character. Whereas most kings would have been apoplectic with rage, the king, still in a playful mood, laughed and suggested John be given a 'bauble' and allowed to go around the country as a fool.[7] In the end, the king's patience ran out and Edward's Plantagenet temper flared; he ordered that Powderham's parents be brought to court, then at Northampton, to be questioned by William Montacute, who led the trial.[8] Montacute of course sentenced Powderham to death. Isabella was angry over the whole affair; she rightly saw such claims as a dangerous affront to Edward's dignity. Powderham was hanged on 23 July.[9] The whole affair was an embarrassment for Edward at a time when he needed it least.

Two days after Powderham's confrontation with the king, Edward heard good news. Isabella had given birth to their first daughter and third child at Woodstock on 28 June. In honour of his mother, the long departed Eleanor of Castile who had died in 1290, and following the tradition of the time, the baby was named after her paternal grandmother. The birth of another child, coming at such a time when the magnates were demonstrating their unified support for the king can only have empowered Edward for what lay ahead. The Plantagenet dynasty remained secure and any future confrontation with Lancaster could not change that.

As was expected, Lancaster, who was still in the north, refused to agree to the king's terms, which had been decided upon at Westminster; above all that Edward refused to remove men like Damory from court. As ever, Edward remained determined to keep those he chose and trusted closest to him. Lancaster declared his distrust of the king but this gambit ultimately fell on deaf ears. The delegation remained unmoved on the principal points and by the end of July, the earl had been worn down. On 7 August, as noted in a letter by the Archbishop of Canterbury, Edward met Lancaster somewhere between Loughborough and Leicester and formally exchanged the kiss of peace in the presence of a large part of the court.[10] Either at this meeting, or two days after, 'Roger Damory and the rest, except Hugh Despenser the Elder and the Earl Warenne, humbly presented themselves before the earl, [and] were received into his grace.'[11]

The absent Earl Warenne had been hung out to dry for the sake of wider peace. Thomas, still seething about the affront to his dignity, was given a free hand to pursue the earl privately in revenge for the abduction of Lancaster's wife, Alice de Lacy. For Lancaster this must have been enormously satisfying. For Surrey, it proved costly. Hunted down and imprisoned by Thomas in his castle of Pontefract, Warenne was beaten into submission and to secure his freedom gave up forever castles and estates in Yorkshire and lands in North Wales. Perhaps feeling some sense of guilt having being in collusion with the plan to abduct Alice, in January 1319 Edward altered Surrey's grant to ensure that Lancaster could only hold onto his gains during Surrey's lifetime, the reversion passing to Warenne's heirs upon his death.[12]

On 9 August the final details of the peace agreement were marked down in an indenture at Leake, the document later becoming known as the Treaty of Leake.[13] Among its terms, royal pardons were granted to men who had committed offences as a result of the hostility between Edward and Lancaster.[14] In order to facilitate the future workings of government, a small standing council was established, which would consist at any one time of five people; two bishops, one earl, one baron and one bannerette of Lancaster's choosing out of a pool of eight bishops, four earls, four barons, four Lancastrian bannerettes, each taking their position for one quarter in every year.[15] The earl himself was not to take any role in the council and his former position as head of council was dissolved. For Lancaster, this was a face-saving way to withdraw from daily government, something for which he had demonstrated little ability. For Edward, it can have only been a welcome relief knowing that he would at least not need to work with the earl face-to-face on a regular basis.

The creation of a small standing council proved an effective compromise, given that the pool of men identified to join its body were all people trusted by the king, who had worked with him previously and who had good relationships with him, with the exception of the Lancastrian bannerettes who had yet to prove themselves. Edward was conscious, like the rest of the body, that these bannerettes were there in reality to report back on the machinations of the court more broadly to Lancaster, but it was a small price to pay. However, for both men this reconciliation was nothing more than a public facade. While the need for unity was essential in the face of the Scottish threat, there still remained Edward's burning desire for revenge and Lancaster most certainly knew it. It would not take much to break the delicate peace that had taken the court months to bring about.

On 20 October, parliament, which had been summoned on 25 August to convene at York, got underway.[16] The Treaty of Leake was confirmed in full, the Ordinances were reissued and Magna Carta reconfirmed in its most recent form. Early into proceedings, rather dramatically, a head arrived in a basket from Ireland. Edward Bruce had given battle against English forces under the command of Sir John Bermingham on 14 October at Faughart near Dundalk, but on this occasion Bruce's luck ran out. He fell during the battle and was killed, his head cut off and body dismembered, parts being sent to the four chief towns of Ireland and his head to Edward at York.[17] At a stroke (of sword or axe), the Scottish threat from Ireland, which had loomed large over England since 1315, had been subdued. Buoyed by the news, parliament supported Edward's call for a unified campaign against Robert Bruce in Scotland; which it was agreed forces would muster at Newcastle on 10 June the following year.

For the king the York parliament proved a great success. The grants he had made to his court, especially to his favourites since 1316, were mostly confirmed, albeit with some small adjustments. Key appointments, which were acceptable to Edward, were also made. Hugh Despenser the Younger, who had been appointed by the council as chamberlain three months earlier, was confirmed in this post without any opposition. Surprisingly, Lancaster who was openly hostile to Hugh's father, did not feel the same about the younger man, as he made no objection. Despenser the Elder prudently kept away from York, being sent on a foreign mission to Edward's mother's homeland of Castile.[18] Bartholomew Badlesmere, who had been a key member of the inner court working alongside Pembroke since 1314, was made Steward of the Household in place of William Montacute, who became seneschal of Gascony.[19] The position took Montacute to France and away from court, which can only have pleased Lancaster. John Sandal, who had previously been chancellor, became treasurer, while his former position was filled by John de Hothum, Bishop of Ely. Edward was pleased.

As Montacute was quietly removed from court following his appointment on 20 November, Damory and Audley were temporarily retired. All three men made peace with Lancaster on 23 November, paying compensation to the earl for their previous misdemeanours. Damory paid 906 marks 7s 4d; Audley 1,229 marks 6s 6d, while Montacute handed over 413 marks 4s.[20] The removal of the royal favourites from court should not be overplayed, for they were still in Edward's favour but temporarily sent away to maintain the public peace with his cousin. It was not long before they were back. Edward had spent a great deal of time over the previous two years building up men close to him whose loyalties were to him alone. He would still require men of his making around him to counter Lancaster, and so a temporary exit was just that, temporary. In the case of Montacute, he would not see Edward again, dying in Gascony within a year, but the king still looked out for William's son and namesake who in the future was to play a significant role in bringing down Roger Mortimer at Nottingham in October 1330.

At this juncture Edward was very well aware that he had been beset by challenges almost immediately since his accession in July 1307.

Many he had inherited but many more had come about as a result of his own actions and of those around him. Throughout his life, he had always demonstrated his piety and had a particular fondness for the cult of St Thomas Becket, often going on pilgrimage to Canterbury. Edward looked to a Dominican friar, Brother Nicholas, who claimed since 1317 to know of a Holy Oil, which could solve all of the king's problems. The oil, it was claimed, was delivered to Thomas Becket in 1164 during his exile in France after the Virgin Mary appeared before the archbishop prophesying that the king, five generations on from then, if anointed from this phial of oil, would go on to be a champion of the Church and would recover the Holy Land for Christendom. The king mentioned in the prophesy was Edward II. For the king, this must have been incredibly tantalising for not only did it offer a potential solution to his many troubles, but it was a direct connection to the saint he was devoted to. The oil had ended up in the possession of Edward's brother-in-law, the late Duke of Brabant, who had brought it with him to Edward's coronation in 1308. The king had not been anointed with it, but with the traditional English Holy Oil used in all previous coronations on the advice of those around him. By 1319, Edward had regrets. He began to be seduced by the words of Brother Nicholas. In late 1318, the king sent Brother Nicholas to the pope at Avignon asking for his permission to be anointed with it. Adam Orleton, Bishop of Hereford, was also sent with a small English delegation to support the king's request. In the end it all counted for nothing as John XXII refused to believe that the oil was of any significance and that if Edward did indeed want to be anointed with it, he should do so privately, and not by the hands of a bishop, thereby avoiding scandal.[21] If this was not embarrassing enough, the pope ended his letter with a particular sting in the tail, adding that by undertaking re-anointing, the king would not solve his troubles but instead needed to look to God, as should the people of his kingdom.[22] Edward was humiliated and within a month wrote to the pope admitting 'his weakness' in being duped by Brother Nicholas, who had taken advantage of his 'dovelike simplicity'.[23] Nicholas was arrested, but escaped shortly afterwards. The whole affair, while unfortunate, reveals the depths of Edward's religious beliefs and his devotion to St Thomas Becket.

With a peace settlement in place, attention turned to Scotland. This was the first opportunity since the defeat at Bannockburn to raise an army of sufficient scale to undertake a full campaign against the Scots. Berwick was the starting point, given that the English no longer held castles beyond the border in which to position themselves before going on the offensive.[24] Orders given at York for a muster at Newcastle for 10 June were extended to 22 July, allowing time for the necessary men, equipment and supplies to be assembled.[25] Parliament granted taxation for the war effort, levying an eighteenth on the value of moveable goods on the people of England, while the Church granted the king a subsidy. The combined revenue raised a staggering £53,062 and was topped up with 10,000 marks, which the king borrowed from the Bardi.[26] The appetite for war was widespread. Famine, which had plagued England since 1315, had abated by 1318 and greatly aided in the collection of taxes as harvests were bountiful, although the north was to experience a great mortality of cattle and oxen in 1319.[27] Writs of summons went out and by July approximately 10,000 men assembled; 1,400 cavalry, 1,200 hobelars and 7,500 foot soldiers and other men-at-arms.[28] Just as Edward had been knighted before his fourth campaign to Scotland in 1306, the king now knighted his half-brother Thomas of Brotherton, Earl of Norfolk.[29]

Edward's force, with Lancaster in company, arrived below the walls of Berwick at the start of September 1319, beginning their assault on the 8th. The assembled navy of seventy-seven vessels under the command of Simon Driby, which cost £1,725, was immediately put to use.[30] In an attempt to scale the walls before the necessary siege engines arrived, a small boat was somehow fixed to the mast of a ship and, when filled with men, was hoisted up to the height of the wall with the aim of lowering a ramp or bridge over the parapet. This endeavour failed, with the ship running aground, which the Scots promptly attacked and set alight.[31] The fighting was fierce on both sides and shortly after, a five-day respite ensued while Edward and his war council called up the necessary siege engines from nearby Bamburgh and further afield.[32] While the men sat idle, news arrived in camp that the Scots had crossed the border and were harrying villages around Carlisle hoping to draw the English away from Berwick. In response, Edward sent 1,200 hobelars under the command of Sir Andrew Harclay to track them down while the siege continued.[33] Fighting resumed on 13 September and the garrison was nearly overcome but in the end the English were beaten back by fierce resistance. Just before a third assault could take place, more disturbing news arrived at camp.

Sir Andrew Harclay had failed to capture his quarry. Instead, the Scots contingent under the command of Thomas Randolph and Sir James Douglas, had slipped south of Carlisle and marched through County Durham into Yorkshire heading under the cover of darkness each night towards York.[34] Perhaps on a tip-off from Edmund Darel, a royal household knight but now a turncoat, the Scots appeared to have one mission in mind, the abduction of Queen Isabella.[35] The plot was prematurely sprung when a spy caught at York and placed under interrogation, confessed to William Melton, Archbishop of York, and the chancellor, John de Hothum. With the cream of the York garrison fighting with the king at Berwick, the queen was brought behind the safety of the walls but it was quickly decided to send her further south by water to the relative safety of Nottingham Castle.[36] Isabella had a lucky escape.

With the queen safely south, it fell to the Archbishop of York, the chancellor who was also Bishop of Ely and the town mayor, Nicholas Fleming, to raise what men they could find among the clergy and peasantry to head off the advancing Scots. The brave but doomed English found the heavily armed and well-trained Scots 12 miles beyond the town at Myton. The subsequent clash quickly turned into a massacre as clergy and peasantry alike were slaughtered, with the mayor cut down and dismembered, while Melton and Hothum narrowly escaped back to York.[37] Such was the slaughter that the whole event became known as the 'chapter of Myton' on account of the large numbers of clergy killed while defending their town.

The events at Myton threw Edward and the war council at Berwick into confusion with division immediately opening up about what to do next. Lancaster had already grown intolerant of his cousin, who had rashly declared that he intended to give custody of the castle of Berwick to Hugh Despenser the Younger and the town to Roger Damory before he had actually secured it.[38] With the Scots at large in England, many men, including Lancaster who held northern estates which were now vulnerable to attack, wanted to break the siege and head south to defend their property. The remaining war council, led by the king, wanted to continue the siege, Edward himself suggesting that they divide their forces, one continuing at Berwick while the other would hunt down the Scots as they returned to their homeland.[39] As the debates became heated, tempers flared and Lancaster and Edward clashed, the king reportedly being overheard to say that he still sought revenge for Gaveston. Appalled at Edward's favouritism of Damory and Despenser the Younger, and threatened by the gossip of the camp, Lancaster promptly packed up and he and his men left the army, returning to their estates without Edward's permission.[40]

No sooner had the earl left than heated debate turned to bitter resentment. Hugh Despenser the Younger, writing to his sheriff of Glamorgan on 21 September went so far as to claim that Lancaster was in league with Robert Bruce and together had orchestrated the recent events at York.[41] This feeling was widely shared. Without Lancaster and his men, Edward had no alternative but to break the siege, which had started with much enthusiasm, and turn his whole army south again to secure northern England. The accusations against Lancaster continued to grow as a despondent and frustrated army failed to understand why the campaign had ended before it really began. Even the chroniclers felt there was truth behind the rumours, the *Vita* lamenting, 'O noble earl, why do you not recall to mind the chosen generation, the royal stock which you disgrace ... how great a charge is the crime of broken faith!'[42] Lancaster, desperate to curb the gossip, hit back. 'I cannot stop up the mouths of men, but I can offer to clear myself either by the decision of a good man, or if it be necessary, by the white-hot iron, or if an accuser shall appear and wish to put himself on record, I shall offer my innocence by legal process.'[43] No accuser dared come forward and in the end Lancaster was able to purge himself on oath alone rather than through trial by ordeal. Edward had little choice but to sue for temporary respite with Robert Bruce, securing a two-year truce, which commenced on 29 December 1319.[44]

The York parliament opened in January 1320 filled with men frustrated – like their king – at the lack of progress in Scotland. Lancaster refused to attend claiming petulantly that parliament was being held in secret, despite the attendance of 157 people who responded to the summons, including nine earls and seventy-three barons. Any threads of peace made through the treaty of Leake were now evidently broken. Against such criticism during and after the siege, Lancaster lost all patience, declaring to anyone who would listen that the king and his followers were his enemies.[45] These were dangerous times.

Edward, who felt equally vindictive, hit back and made changes to his household without his cousin's consent. John de Hothum, who had survived the clash at Myton, was removed from the role of chancellor and replaced by the Bishop of Norwich, John Salmon. Walter Stapledon, the Bishop of Exeter, took the vacant role of treasurer following the death of the last incumbent John Sandal in the summer of 1319. Lastly, Robert Baldock became keeper of the privy seal.[46] Shortly afterwards, Edward announced that he was drawing parliament to a close early, given his need to leave for France with Isabella to perform his long overdue homage to the king of France, Philip V, who had succeeded to the throne following the death of his nephew in 1316. On 24 February, Edward made Pembroke *custos regni*.[47] Leaving parliament at York, Edward and Isabella made for Westminster, passing along the road under the walls of Pontefract Castle. Without any pre-emptive move from the king, Lancaster's garrison again jeered from the castle walls as the royal party passed south. Edward and his queen were furious and this event, as with the previous episode, was not to be forgotten.[48] Such was the open hatred between them that there was now no hope of reconciliation. While neither knew it, their ultimate reckoning was fast approaching.

Edward and Isabella departed for France on 19 June, taking with them Damory, Hugh Despenser the Younger, the chancellor and treasurer and William, the son of William Montacute, who had died eight months earlier in Gascony. The royal favourites were, literally, still close to the king. On the 30th, Edward performed his act of homage for Aquitaine, Ponthieu and Montreuil in the cathedral at Amiens. A few days later, when Edward and Philip came to reconfirm the 'perpetual friendship' that their fathers had concluded in 1303, Edward rather unexpectedly was challenged by a French councillor who suggested that as well as homage he should also perform fealty, effectively rendering him unequal and subservient to the king of France. Edward, visibly angered by the suggestion, did not wait for his councillors to advise him, but instead shot back that he remembered the homage he had performed in 1308 to Philip IV and no one could compel him to do otherwise, adding that 'he certainly [did] not intend to do so'. Fealty, the king ended by saying, was not on the agenda nor would it be.[49] The French councillor fell silent as did the rest of those in the room. Edward was quick-witted and could hold his own when it mattered most, no more so than when someone attempted to encroach upon the royal dignity.

Shortly after, Edward departed the company of the king of France and his court and headed to Abbeville in Ponthieu to restore order among his lands, now owned by Isabella as part of her dowry. On 20 July, the king and queen attended, along with the bishops of Exeter, Norwich and Hereford, the consecration of Henry de Burghersh as Bishop of Lincoln.[50] With homage performed and affairs settled in Ponthieu, the royal party finally left France towards the end of July, arriving in the city of London to pageantry and much revelry put on by the mayor, alderman and guilds of London on 2 August.[51]

Two months later, Edward settled into another parliament, this time held at Westminster. At some time during the year, the king, who had a generally curious nature as well as the common touch, lent those traits expression. He acquired a cottage surrounded by a ditch with a large garden located in the grounds of Westminster Abbey, which he would stay in when the mood took him. This retreat may have been reminiscent of his childhood days spent at Langley, which, although still in his possession, was away from London. This type of behaviour was again at odds with the strict hierarchical order of medieval society and contemporaries scoffed at his temporary respites in environments considered far below his royal dignity.[52] Edward refused to listen.

The king returned from France with determination to apply himself to the details of government, which were ordinarily left to his councillors. During the Westminster parliament, 141 petitions were answered, and rather than just stay for the opening, Edward remained throughout proceedings answering them and dealing with general business. The Bishop of Worcester, Thomas Cobham, captured this moment in a letter to Pope John XXII writing '...he arranged what business was to be dealt with, discussed and determined. Where amendment was necessary he ingeniously supplied what was lacking, thus giving say to his people, ensuring their security, and providing hope of an improvement in his behaviour.'[53] It was highly unusual for any king to stay in the presence of his magnates in the chamber for the duration of parliament, and as the king's behaviour was out of character it certainly was enough to be noted. It also demonstrated that Edward was adept at conducting business, but chose when to apply this skill more publicly.

Judging the king's reign to date, Edward could, when he needed to most, galvanise himself in defence of his rights, excel on the foreign stage or in bringing about compromise with his cousin when it became absolutely critical in defence of the realm; although at Berwick his temper and his behaviour only reignited conflict. However, this burning desire for revenge and his coalition of favourites kept close at court made Edward's style of government challenging, or challengable. Lancaster was not a man to forgive either. From Edward's perspective the royal favourites bolstered his position and gave him intimates who were solely reliant on him. One intimate in particular was about to enter the stage, his impact growing steadily from 1319. He would prove irresistible to Edward. What was yet to unfold would be more tragic than anyone at the time would have thought possible.

18

A Wolf in the Fold

Hugh Despenser the Younger had risen in both position and power since his marriage to Edward II's niece, Eleanor de Clare, in 1306. Although the marriage arranged by Edward I was a great match and an acknowledgement of his father's loyalty to the late king, it did not come with great tranches of land or any significant titles. For the best part of the next decade, the younger Despenser relied on income from his father's estates and through his wife's dower, which frustrated his burning ambitions to achieve greater position and wealth. During the middle years of Edward II's reign, Hugh began to play a more direct role, present among the royal favourites but in the shadow of his father Hugh Despenser the Elder, who remained unswerving in his loyalty to Edward I's son and heir. This loyalty allowed his own son to gain position at court and when the lands of the earldom of Gloucester were partitioned by the king in 1317, Despenser and his wife inherited the most important elements, which centred on the lordship of Glamorgan and included key castles like Caerphilly, Cardiff and many smaller manors. Despenser had become a wealthy man. Other grants soon followed. In the autumn of 1320 he was made constable of Bristol Castle.[1] By 1319 the magnates of England, including the Earl of Lancaster who had held back his characteristic hatred for the Despenser family, supported the younger Hugh's promotion to the role of chamberlain of Edward's household, which was confirmed in the parliament of 1319. Despenser was now moving in the highest of circles.

The warning signs, with the benefit of hindsight, had been there from the start. His hotheaded action in attacking John Roos in Lincoln Cathedral in the very presence of the king in 1316 was both unbecoming and also an infringement of the rules. The resulting fine, which Despenser never paid, demonstrated both his attitude and overweening pride. He had a violent temper and was unafraid to express it in order to achieve his aims. What both the king and the magnates of England had not appreciated, however, was this behaviour was typical rather than extraordinary, and unwittingly they had invited a wolf in among the sheep; and this wolf in particular was calculating, highly manipulative, dangerous to those around him and to Edward in particular.

Despenser the Younger did not rest after his wife inherited part of her late brother's estates. He soon devised a plan to acquire lands adjacent to his lordship in Glamorgan in South Wales to consolidate his power and all but set himself up as a new Earl of Gloucester. His modus operandi rested on coercion, bribery and open violence. He soon singled out the king's favourite Hugh Audley the Younger, who was the husband of his wife's sister Margaret, the widow of Piers Gaveston. The area of Gwynllwg, which sat in south Glamorgan and valued at £458, was a prize possession and Despenser wanted it. Before Audley had the opportunity to secure the homage of his inherited tenants, Despenser raced to Gwynllwg and received the homages himself, effectively forcing Audley off the land. Audley turned to Edward for help, who commanded Despenser to hand the land over to his favourite, but Despenser prevaricated and the king failed to pursue the matter with any sense of urgency. Under pressure, Despenser turned to rough diplomacy to seal the deal. Audley and Margaret eventually agreed to hand over Gwynllwg in return for six manors in England, the bargain very much in Despenser's favour.[2] Other lands quickly fell under his control as he extended his hold to the west of Glamorgan when Edward granted him the Cantref Mawr and other lands. When the Dowager Countess of Gloucester died on 2 July 1320, he also inherited the town of Tewkesbury and more, while all the time setting his sights on castles associated with the lordship of Brecon, which had been given to Roger Mortimer of Wigmore in 1316.[3] His ambition was self-evident; his tactics dangerous.

The Marcher lords, who were magnates with lands along the Welsh border and in South Wales, held a greater degree of autonomy and power in this area than magnates elsewhere in England, a hangover from the time of the Norman Conquest when subduing the Welsh was a priority delegated by the monarch to robust and aggressive lords. After Edward I's conquest of Wales at the time of Edward II's birth, the original role of the Marcher lord became less important, but their independent authority remained potent. As Despenser began a calculated campaign to build up both land and titles in South Wales, he too amassed significant independent powers in the region by virtue of his acquisitions, which began to rival and threaten the established Marcher lords who, for generations, had nursed their own ambitions. The Marches were ruled by a strict code, by close family ties and age-old custom. Despenser was an outsider.

By 1320, Hugh Despenser the Younger, not content with his lot, turned to the lordship of Gower, owned by William de Broase who, with no male heir, had settled the lordship on his daughter's son, John de Mowbray. However, the avaricious William subsequently spent years undermining his own settlement, offering the reversion of his estates to anyone who would pay the highest fee. The fee kept changing. With serious interest shown by the Earl of Hereford and Roger Mortimer of Wigmore, negotiations had been underway for years. In the autumn of 1319 Hugh Despenser entered talks with de Broase and either offered the highest price to date, or applied other forms of bargaining, and soon looked to be on a winning pledge. Securing Gower, with its administrative centre based at Swansea, would make Despenser uncomfortably powerful in the region.

Nerves began to fray and before long the Marcher lords, including Roger Damory, Roger Clifford and John Giffard, felt the need to band together to counter the threat posed by Despenser. In a moment of pique, John de Mowbray took the initiative and seized the lordship before his unscrupulous father-in-law could give away his wife's inheritance. Despenser, unaccustomed to failure, was furious and turned to Edward claiming that Mowbray had entered the lordship without the king's royal licence. The Marcher lords reminded the king that in the March his licence was not required, following ancient law and custom, but under Despenser's influence, Edward decided otherwise. On 26 October, at the Westminster parliament following his return from France, Edward ordered that Gower be taken into royal hands.[4] For now, the king would hold it – and determine who should possess it in future. The king's decision was highly unusual and royal officials led by Richard Foxcote were fiercely resisted by the inhabitants of Gower who remained loyal to Mowbray.[5] Under the threat of local aggression, Edward began to waver in his conviction and was prepared to grant the lordship to Mowbrary after all but, under Despenser's influence, changed his mind at the last minute.[6] As chamberlain, Despenser had the benefit of being always in Edward's presence and was therefore best placed to control the situation, influencing the only man who could settle the issue. Edward's brother-in-law and long serving councillor the Earl of Hereford, with Mowbrary, pleaded with the king to reconsider, but Edward refused their petition, removing at a stroke any further legal recourse. Despenser was pulling the strings and began threatening those about him. He openly spoke of treachery against the king and was overheard saying that he would avenge the death of his grandfather, who was killed at the battle of Evesham by the Mortimers in 1265.[7] Beyond his land grab, Despenser clearly had some axes to grind.

Just what was Edward doing? Since the start of 1320 the king quickly began to alienate those who were closest to him. The two royal favourites, Roger Damory and Hugh Audley the Younger had, since 1315, been drawn into Edward's inner circle, his need to counter the threat of Lancaster meant having such men at court. Yet as Despenser the Younger assumed the role of chamberlain in the summer of 1319, the immediate position and power of Damory and Audley quickly began to wane. If Despenser was to gain power and position, he knew that Damory and Audley stood in his way. He was a cuckoo in the nest. It is striking that Damory and Audley soon became powerless to prevent this reversal of fortune. Given Edward's earlier reliance on them both to counter Lancaster and the years spent nurturing and ennobling them, his withdrawal from the royal favourites was both quick and out of character. The threat imposed by Despenser in South Wales, where both Damory and Audley held lands, began to drive them into frustrated opposition. On 5 November, perhaps aware of their growing detachment, Edward reconfirmed Edward I's grant of the Gloucester earldom on the heirs of his late sister Joan. It was a move designed to offer security to the disaffected former favourites, effectively providing a safeguard that their wives' share of the Gloucester inheritance would not be further usurped.[8] It was a hollow and long-overdue gesture that did little to help. Damory and Audley had realised, with others at court, that Edward was now infatuated with Despenser and was increasingly being isolated by him.

This infatuation was both quick in the coming and intense in its degree and has been noted by contemporaries then and historians ever since. However, why was Edward infatuated at all? What drove the king's behaviour? Many think it was not unusual for this king, whose reliance on male favourites dominated his life, but a closer look reveals something out of character. Edward had always had royal favourites, Piers Gaveston being the man he loved the most and was closest to. Their bond had been forged as teenagers, long before Edward assumed the throne in 1307 and was unequivocally sexual as demonstrated by their actions. Edward's preoccupation with Gaveston's soul and his burning desire for revenge are the clearest proofs. The rise of Damory, Audley and Montacute in the middle years of his reign was driven by his need to counter the position of his over-mighty cousin and bring about his revenge for Gaveston's death. Damory seemed to head the group and may have been the more attached to the king, possibly sexually but this is speculative. By 1319, these bonds were strong, but by 1320 they were frayed and almost broken.

When all these royal favourites were at court, Edward never cut himself off from his wider council to the degree that those around him feared he would. Pembroke had, since Gaveston's murder, been the king's chief councillor and a voice of moderation. But in 1320 Pembroke spent a great deal of time away from Edward's company, visiting France in order to arrange his second marriage to Marie St Pol. Without Pembroke at court, Despenser had the added opportunity to exert his influence over the king. As Despenser's influence grew, so did Edward's isolation and his behaviour changed, pushing those about him away. The Brut chronicle noted that Despenser 'kept so the king's chamber, that no man might speak with the king ... the king himself would not be governed by no manner of man, but only by his father and him.'[9] Worse still, Baker declared Despenser the Younger 'to be another king, or more accurately ruler of the king'. Despenser 'frequently kept certain nobles from speaking to the king'.[10]

For all of the criticisms laid at Gaveston's door, isolating the king from his entire court was not one that stands up to scrutiny; for Despenser, it does.

Despenser the Younger was also possessive and domineering. By the end of 1320 he had become so confident of his hold over Edward that he was able to demonstrate his control during public audiences. Murimuth noted 'If the magnates were allowed to talk to the king, Despenser would listen to the conversation and reply freely on his [Edward's] account.'[11] While it was customary for the king to speak through another, Murimuth implies that Despenser did not wait to find out the king's will, but rather made the decisions himself and answered for the king, Edward seemingly happy to allow this to happen, again a charge not levied at Gaveston. This behaviour is at odds with the character of the king who had even in his recent visit to France demonstrated his ability in government affairs, using his initiative and responding in public on the spur of the moment. This abdication of even basic responsibilities in favour of Despenser feels less about the king's idleness, more about Despenser's sinister influence. Prior to 1319, Edward, who knew Despenser from at least 1306, showed no great love or affection for him, yet within a year this had turned to apparent infatuation. Something is amiss here.

This infatuation looks like a man who had been drawn under the spell of Despenser's manipulation, ruthless domination and possessive behaviour. To modern eyes, this would be termed emotional abuse, where the victim either fears the abuser or becomes infatuated with them as a result of the constant barrage of carefully layered deceits built up around them. Despenser's violent behaviour, his aggression towards even the most established of royal councillors, which went unchecked by the king; the calculated way he appears to have isolated Edward from even his most recent favourites, his control of the king in pubic arenas and the speed with which it all happened over eighteen months; this is all significant. Despenser knew that Edward desired males, as he was himself the former brother-in-law of Piers Gaveston, as well as having information from his father Hugh Despenser the Elder. Despenser the Younger was certainly in a position to use this knowledge to pursue his own ends. In a letter to John Inge, his sheriff at Glamorgan, he remarked 'that the times changed from one day to another; envy was growing against him, and especially among the magnates, because the king treated him better than any other'. He went on to order Inge to watch his affairs so that 'we may be rich and may attain our ends'.[12] Gaveston may have been in Edward's company and controlled patronage, but he neither sought political power, nor the manipulation of the king. Despenser was proving to be ruthless in pursuit of his personal ambition and if controlling the king was the only way to secure it, he was both calculating and rapacious enough to bring it about.

The assumption that Edward was a victim may feel odd to some. The idea that a man in any age is subject to the domination of another, and especially one who was king, is hard for many people to accept. However, the king's gender is of little consequence and an infatuation built up at the hands of a known and calculated manipulator is a recognisable scenario. Despenser represented power and Edward needed men like that to overcome Lancaster, which Hugh knew all too well and played on. Edward may have been king and in a position to bring an end to such a situation, but he was being manipulated. He was unable to see the very dangerous situation in which he was now placed. By mid-1320 Despenser's undisguised behaviour only reinforced his confidence in his possessive control of the king as noted by contemporary chroniclers and members of the court. What happened next in Glamorgan and beyond was so violent that those loyal to the king felt the need to save both him and themselves. Through this lens, these events make more sense. The Marcher lords knew they had to break the spell, especially when Edward placed Gower in temporary safekeeping with Despenser. It was clear that the favourite was engineering a permanent settlement in his favour and after that, the Marcher lords could not be sure if their lands were next.[13] Edward removed their legal recourse in Gower leaving open rebellion as their only option and in the minds of the Marcher lords, responsibility lay firmly with one man. Despenser needed to be separated from the king before they were all consumed.

As the Christmas court broke up in early January 1321, the Marcher lords, which now included Roger Mortimer of Wigmore, recently returned from Ireland, retired to their estates and began preparations for open conflict. Edward, aware of the tension, was kept informed of developments through key officials such as Robert Baldock in the north, Despenser's sheriff in Glamorgan, and William de Aune, constable of Edward's castle at Tickhill. Despenser turned his immediate attention to his lands, instructing his sheriff to ensure their defence.[14]

Thomas, Earl of Lancaster, had remained on his estates throughout 1320 and had watched the situation unfold from behind his walls at Pontefract Castle. On 22 February he chose to step into the fray, albeit tentatively. A meeting was held at Pontefract, mostly attended by northern lords but which may have included the Earl of Hereford, Mowbray and others. On 24 May, still at Pontefract, Lancaster held another with northern barons, but they refused to join the conflict with the Marcher lords. For those in south Wales, attacking the Despensers was, they felt, their only option. By March, Edward must have heard that an attack was imminent. As a test of loyalty, the king ordered Roger Mortimer of Chirk, who was Justice of North Wales and the uncle of Roger Mortimer of Wigmore, to place Edward's castles into a state of defence.[15] The test worked. Mortimer joined his nephew Roger Mortimer of Wigmore in revolt.

The king could no longer trust those in the area and on 6 March, with Despenser the Younger at his side, set out from Windsor and travelled west to Gloucester, seizing one of the major royal armouries at the castle of St Briavel's as he went, from Roger Damory. In a pointed attack on his former favourite, the king confiscated all of Audley's estates, citing his broken faith, which had been laid out in contract only a few years earlier with the king. It was a highly provocative and arbitrary move that drove Audley further towards rebellion. As events became more intense, Edward ordered Hereford and the two Mortimers of Wigmore and Chirk, Roger Damory, John Charlton and others to attend a council meeting with him and Despenser in order to hear their complaints.[16] The Marcher lords declared that they would attend if Despenser was removed from the king's presence and placed in the custody of the Earl of Lancaster until a forthcoming parliament, where their charges could be safely put to him to obtain the king's justice.[17] For Edward, the mere suggestion of Lancaster was enough to render any potential compromise a dead letter. It had all the hallmarks of Edward's previous experience in 1312 with the capture of Gaveston at Scarborough Castle. That promise of safe custody had resulted in his brutal murder. Edward had learnt that lesson the hard way and so refused outright. Instead, the king was astute in his response, claiming that he could not hand Hugh over to Lancaster, citing his coronation oath, the Ordinances, Magna Carta and the common law, because Despenser had not been accused of a crime. Instead, those in opposition were ordered to attend the king to discuss a date for the next parliament.[18] Without any further opportunity to bring the Marcher lords to heel, Edward turned around and made his way back towards London in anticipation of a forthcoming parliament, ordering on 13 April that the Marchers keep the peace.[19] While in the city he spent six days, from 8 July, at the Tower of London with Isabella, who had given birth to their fourth and last child, Joan, on the 5th.

With Despenser still firmly at Edward's side, Hereford, the two Mortimers, Damory, Audley the Younger with his father, Roger Clifford and others turned to open conflict. The rebellion began on 4 May at Despenser's town of Newport in Glamorgan, which, after its fall, was handed to Audley. Cardiff and Swansea in Gower were captured in quick succession.[20] The rebellion was targeted, hard-hitting and brutal. Despenser's constable, captured as Neath Castle fell, was beheaded along with Philip le Keu.[21] Damage to over twenty manors, castles, towns and estates amounted to £14,000. The lust for Despenser's overthrow became even more insatiable. Encouraged by Lancaster sitting behind the walls of his castle at Pontefract, Despenser lands in England were also singled out. Hugh Despenser the Elder, tainted by his son's behaviour, saw his lands across seventeen counties attacked, the devastation amounting to £38,000 of damage.[22] The spoils were divided among the rebels.[23] According to the author of the *Vita*, Despenser's tenants appealed to the Marcher lords for clemency, claiming that they never liked their lord. The Marchers agreed to move on if 'they would wholly renounce their homage to Hugh Despenser, that they would never acknowledge him as lord, but remain faithful to the lord king in all things ... all these things they solemnly confirmed having touched and kissed the Holy Gospels'.[24] Edward had created a firestorm and was unable to do anything to quell it.

After two months of sustained attacks, which went largely unchecked, the Marcher lords, known to contemporaries in the rebellion as contrariants, headed north to Sherburn-in-Elmet to meet Lancaster. Damory and Audley attended. Despite their hatred for one another, the situation had become so grave and Despenser so dangerous, these men were willing to suspend their differences for a wider cause. Also in attendance was Edward's highly loyal Archbishop of York, as well as the bishops of Durham and Carlisle, who acted as mediators.[25]

The attacks on Despenser lands, which remained under the protection of the king, were acts of open defiance. The Marcher lords desperately needed legal justification for their actions and this meeting, divided into two sessions at Sherburn, set out to establish it. Lancaster, using his position as Steward of England and supported by the assembled prelates and the Earl of Angus, acted as an audience before which the Marcher lords could lay their grievances. The pretext that the Steward was second only to the king and was able to bring about redress if the crimes undermined the king, the kingdom, or if the king himself was unable to offer recourse, provided the loose legal framework on which to find the justification they needed. What followed was an indenture which set out this legal position claiming that the ever-increasing oppressions of the Despensers, the younger in particular, could only be met with force. Their response was designed to protect the king, the kingdom, the children of the king, the Holy Church and the honour of God.[26] Not all agreed. Despite the efforts of Hereford and Lancaster, the northern magnates stood by the king, their aims based solely on the defence of the north against the daily threats from the Scots. The concerns of the Marcher lords, they felt, where just that, concerns of the Welsh March, and this was echoed by the prelates, who were there as mediators only.[27] The Marcher lords had no choice but to agree among themselves to hold out alone and so they turned their attention to London and the king who was waiting for them at Westminster.

Edward had learnt his lessons from 1312. As revolt raged in South Wales, his council, which included Pembroke who was briefly back from France, met on 17 May and was immediately divided between those who favoured a martial response and the others who suggested redress through the application of a legal process in parliament.[28] In the end, the king, under the briefly restored influence of Pembroke, followed the moderate approach and on 15 May summoned parliament to meet on 15 July at Westminster in the hope that the summons would take the heat out of the situation.[29] The ploy failed as the Marcher lords through the remaining part of May and June continued to devastate the lands of the Despensers.

As the attacks continued, Edward took steps to ensure that this time his royal favourite could not fall into the hands of his enemies, and sent him either to sea or to France with Pembroke. Whether Despenser the Younger made it to France is unclear but what is certain is that from June through until the end of summer, he remained at sea under the protection of the Cinque ports and even captured and sequestered the goods of two Genoese trading vessels that may have belonged to Antonio Pessagno, his greed as insatiable as ever.[30] Years later, Edward III was obliged to make payment of 8,000 marks in compensation for the goods Despenser stole that summer. As Despenser left for the sea, the king removed Badlesmere as constable of the strategically important castle and town at Dover and replaced him with Edward's youngest half-brother Edmund of Woodstock.[31] Soon after, the king granted Edmund the earldom of Kent, which Badlesmere had long coveted. As the Sherburn meeting got underway in the north at the end of June, and with Despenser the Younger now safely out of the kingdom, the king sent another long-standing moderate councillor, Badlesmere, and Walter Reynolds to the gathering to insist that the attacks cease, at the same time inviting the magnates to parliament. At this critical moment, Badlesmere unexpectedly switched sides and took up with the rebels, being sorely disappointed with Edward's recent grants to his half-brother Edmund, and probably resentful over the influence Despenser now had over the king. Edward was shocked at this last-minute betrayal.[32] Betrayal, particularly when personal rather than political, was something that Edward never forgave or forgot.

Parliament opened at Westminster on 15 July; the Marcher lords with their 5,000 men-at-arms arrived at St Albans, north of London, a week later. Lancaster remained at Pontefract. Edward had taken the precaution of ensuring the loyalty of the city and its mayor Hamo de Chigwell. As the road to the city remained blocked, the Archbishop of Canterbury, the bishops of London, Salisbury, Ely, Hereford and Chichester, left the king to mediate with the earls. It was not long before Walter Reynolds returned with the expected news that the Marcher lords would accept nothing other than the permanent exile of the Despensers, which Edward flatly rejected, changing tack by refusing to meet with them.[33]

On 29 July the Marcher lords entered the city and took up key positions stretching east to west. As their demands remained unchanged Edward remained defiant, still refusing to meet them.[34] As a tense and dangerous stalemate followed, the Earl of Pembroke arrived back in London from France. He was one of the few remaining at court who still had a chance of countering Despenser's influence. With Despenser absent, Pembroke took his opportunity and with the remaining earls loyal to Edward, Arundel, Surrey and Richmond, met with the Marchers. Discussions were intense as the Marcher lords were keen to draw Pembroke over to their cause.

Returning with the remaining earls, Pembroke outlined the position to Edward. As *Vita* suggests, to best protect the king, they had taken an oath with the Marcher lords to defend their grievances against the Despensers to the death.[35] The gravity of Edward's situation became absolutely clear when Pembroke pleaded with him to exile the Despensers as the majority of his former supporters had asked for, rather than bring the country to ruin. Edward still stubbornly refused. Pembroke had no alternative but to make it clear that if the king did not change his mind, then the magnates would seek to depose him and in this Pembroke would also withdraw his homage to the king. Edward must have been devastated both by the threat of deposition and the loss of Pembroke's unwavering support. This had become the greatest crisis of his reign as those about him, including his former moderate councillors, were forced to make threats against the king in the face of Despenser's rapacity. The threats were far more real than during the crisis years with Gaveston, as Edward now had an heir. Though the option of installing a young king was fraught with difficultes, there were no legal precedents for deposition.

Edward was truly infatuated. Despenser had done his work well. Despite the threats, the king replied that he could not disinherit anyone without a hearing and attempted to buy time for Despenser, suggesting he leave temporarily for Ireland as Gaveston had in 1308. Edward acknowledged that the Despensers had behaved badly but on no account would he consider them traitors.[36] Pembroke sought the formal intercession of the queen; she implored her husband on bended knee to exile the Despensers and save his realm, giving Edward the face-saving opportunity to back down without loss of reputation.[37] Even his wife, Edward must have felt, had deserted him. Emotionally exhausted and with nowhere to go, Edward finally and reluctantly gave way.

On 14 August the king entered the hostile chamber at Westminster flanked by Pembroke and Richmond and there listened to the charges presented to him that indicted the Despensers for many perceived and some very real crimes.[38] Despenser the Younger in particular was accused of keeping his father at court when it was agreed he would not; of usurping the royal power; of leading the king to do his will under duress so that if Edward refused, 'he did not forgive him when he did not do it'. This curious statement is the clearest indication that Despenser used psychological pressure on the king to dominate him, underpinned by a carefully crafted infatuation. Despenser was accused of badly counselling the king and of 'not allow[ing] the great men of the realm, or the good counsellors of the king, to speak with or approach the king, to counsel him well nor the king to speak with them, except in the presence and hearing of the said Sir Hugh and Sir Hugh, or one of them, and at their will and bidding and as they chose'.[39] Despenser was accused of influencing the king to take possession of Audley's lands without due legal process, that he was plotting to overrun Damory's lands as well as Hereford's and Sir John Giffard's; that he had seized Gower from John de Mowbray through deceit and lastly had executed Llewelyn Bren at Cardiff Castle despite his surrender to Roger Mortimer and Hereford under the guarantee of their protection in 1316. The execution of Bren did much to discredit him in Wales and would later come back to haunt him in the autumn of 1326. The Despensers, Edward formally heard, were to be permanently exiled by the feast of the passion of St John the Baptist on 29 August, their children disinherited.[40]

Even at this stage the king made it clear he had no intention of upholding the charges through a parliamentary statute, which required his royal assent and so instead the magnates made a parliamentary award, which allowed them to bring about Despenser's exile without it. Edward was making a statement; if the Despensers were to be removed from him it was neither through his design nor with his blessing. After weeks of rough handling from those closest to him, the king left the chamber 'anxious and sad'.[41] Six days later, Edward issued formal pardons to all those who had been involved in the rebellion, later claiming he had only done so under coercion.[42]

For all those involved, the immediate threat was removed but the cost was great. Many of Edward's former supporters, whom he had taken so long to cultivate, had shown that they had little choice but to use force, or threats of deposition as a way to bring about the removal of the king's closest favourite. Edward was a man to hold grudges and Despenser had worked his way firmly into the king's affections. Now Edward, forever sensitive to his royal dignity and having been forced against the backdrop of very real threats of deposition to concede to baronial demands, wanted vengeance on an even broader scale than before. With his determination to reassert his prerogative and have the Despensers back at his side, it would only be a matter of time before the king would find a way of achieving his aims and, in doing so, tip England back towards war. Two days after parliament had brought about the exile of the Despensers at Westminster, the king dined with the Bishop of Rochester and complained that the Despensers had been unjustly condemned. Rochester replied that Edward could overcome the defeat, to which the king whispered 'that he would within half a year make such an amend that the whole world would hear of it and tremble'.[43] Any hope of peace was dead.

PART FOUR

Freedom Corrupts

When flatterers tickle the attentive ear
At once they conquer all who speak the truth.

Vita Edwardi Secundi

19

A Lover's Revenge

The appetite of the Marcher lords and their followers for violent confrontation to bring about the exile of the Despensers caught Edward by surprise. Even chroniclers of the day thought they had gone too far, the *Vita* recording 'though formerly their cause had been just, they now turned right into wrong'.[1] Their greed had got the better of them and the king's heart, as a result, 'was bursting with desire for vengeance'.[2] Edward had demonstrated time and again that when faced with a direct personal challenge he could galvanise those around him, build coalitions and bring about a counter-manoeuvre to outwit his opponents in some form or other. In addition, he would not suffer any encroachment on his royal dignity without a fight. The Marcher lords by forcing their will on the king had this time pushed him too far. It had become personal. Edward, embittered, was beyond anger and felt compelled to make the contrariants – and the population of England – 'tremble'. The king did not just want the Despensers back; he wanted revenge.

Planning began in September 1321. Edward had been careful to ensure that the Despensers were removed from England before the Westminster parliament so their capture, as with Gaveston in 1312, could not result. Hugh Despenser the Elder headed for Poitou, while the Younger remained at sea in the Channel, abusing his protection from the Cinque Ports to continue his short-lived career as a pirate, preying on ships off the English and French coasts.[3] Edward and Hugh were able to use the geographical proximity to meet at Minister-on-Thames and together sailed to Harwich in early September for further discussion.

By late September the king was back at Westminster building support from those who had opposed him only a month earlier. Pembroke was quick to return to the fold, taking up his natural position as trusted royal counsellor. The earls of Arundel and Surrey, neither popular with the likes of Lancaster, knew their position was stronger with the king. Not all the bishops had opposed the Despensers either, with the Bishop of Rochester remaining an outspoken confidant of the king, with the chancellor and treasurer, the bishops of Norwich and Exeter respectively.[4] As Edward's position grew stronger again, the king began to enact a cleverly designed plan. Much as in 1308, Edward sought to divide and conquer.

As September drew to a close, Edward ordered that the Despenser lands taken by the contrariants be returned to the crown.[5] The Marchers, withdrawn from London to Oxford, ignored the royal demand. Badlesmere refused to give up Tonbridge Castle and went further by placing his castles of Chilham and Leeds in Kent into a state of defence. It was exactly the kind of provocation that Edward hoped to prompt, giving the king the legitimate reason to take up arms to quash his over-mighty vassals. Badlesmere, now hated by Edward for his treachery, and by Lancaster since 1318, was imperilled, relying on the likes of the remaining Marcher lords for support. The king, and probably Despenser too, sensed the vulnerability and were quick to exploit it.

Badlesmere had walked headlong into the trap and now the jaws snapped shut. In early October, Edward and Isabella left Westminster for Canterbury on the pretext of a pilgrimage. As they neared Leeds Castle, the queen was sent with a small retinue to seek shelter behind the castle walls. Fearing a plot, Badlesmere's wife refused Isabella entry. The queen insisted and as an awkward standoff ensued, the Leeds' garrison, remarkably, fired their arrows on Isabella and her company. Six of her men were killed while the queen escaped with her life.[6] Edward publicly declared his fury and ordered on 16 October that Leeds Castle be besieged, which assault he himself would lead.[7] By the 31st of that month under bombardment the castle fell and the king the following day had twelve of the garrison hanged, while the commander, Walter Culpeper, was taken to Winchelsea and publicly executed.[8] Badlesmere's wife and children and his nephew Bartholomew Burghersh were dispatched to the Tower. On 15 November the king announced he was going to go about the country to deal with malefactors.[9] The gloves were off.

The Marcher lords were caught on the back foot. Badlesmere had been desperate to help raise the siege at Leeds, which initially Hereford and the Mortimers were proposing to support and began mediation with the Archbishop of Canterbury Walter Reynolds to that effect. However Lancaster intervened and convinced the contrariants that support for Badlesmere was nothing short of folly. Without support there was nothing Badlesmere could do but retreat with the Marchers, bitter at Lancaster's ongoing hostility towards him. Yet there were still many in the country who felt sympathy for the Marcher cause. The city of London secretly supported the removal of the Despensers and those in opposition sought to cultivate their public support, which was undermined by the arrival of the Earl of Pembroke on 17 November. He was able to retain the reluctant city for the king. As the situation began boil, Lancaster stepped into the fray.

On 29 November Lancaster held a meeting at Doncaster with the Marcher lords. The list of those invited included 103 names, many of royalist sympathies and men who were part of the king's household. If Lancaster was hoping to gain support from those who feared and despised the growing influence of the Despensers, he was soon to be disappointed.[10] Edward wrote a furious letter prohibiting those named from attending and on the next day gave orders for his assembling army to meet him at Cirencester on 13 December.[11] The Doncaster meeting did little to help the Marcher cause.

The petition which came out of Doncaster set out the same arguments as in 1321, that ultimately the Despensers were evil councillors who had encouraged the king contrary to his coronation oath, Magna Carta and the Ordinances to disinherit peers of the realm. They claimed that their noble rights to act in the king's interest in order to protect the crown had been removed, leaving them without recourse. They concluded the petition by demanding that Edward give them an answer by 20 December and not to take it amiss if they defended their rights by pursuing the named evil councillors.[12] The day after the petition was drawn up the king received another petition, this time from Hugh Despenser the Younger, which set out the illegality of his exile and sought Edward's annulment of it. He would surrender himself to the king for both justice and protection. Hugh Despenser the Elder's petition followed in quick succession.[13] The timing was perfect and of course planned. Edward's response to Lancaster was a simple one, condemning his cousin for treating him like his subject; the king would hear no more. The Marchers were out in the cold.

On 8 December, after the Despenser petitions had been presented to his council who approved their return, Edward granted safe conducts, first to the younger and three weeks later to the elder Despenser. Pembroke, Richmond and Arundel who had at the last minute sided with the Marcher lords in 1321, now claimed they had only done so under duress and begged for royal forgiveness, which the king duly gave. It was clear to Pembroke and his peers that the return of the Despensers was now inevitable and they needed to manage it as best they could. With his council behind him, which included the Archbishop of Canterbury, the bishops of London, Ely, Salisbury and Rochester, as well as the support of his two half-brothers, the earls of Norfolk and Kent, Edward headed west to meet his army at Cirencester, taking Pembroke with him.

The contrariant lords divided their army. The Earl of Hereford had taken Gloucester, while the Mortimers kept to the northern area of the Welsh March. Between them they guarded the crossings of the River Severn, which divided the king from the March.[14] As Edward arrived in Gloucestershire and stayed at Cirencester for Christmas, he sent men against John Giffard of Brimpsfield. It was the first skirmish and success went to the king. On 27 December, Edward moved north towards Worcester, reaching it on New Year's Eve, seeking out a crossing over the river Severn, which still remained blocked to him. To break through, the king sent Fulk fitz Warin, Oliver Ingham, John Pecche and Robert le Ewer to capture the crossing at Bridgenorth, which they duly did.[15] On 1 January, Walter Reynolds on Edward's command made his way to St Paul's in London and publicly proclaimed that the exile of the Despensers was held unlawful.[16] Everything was suddenly moving at great pace.

The Mortimers understood the need to keep the king from crossing the Severn and on 5 January during the night swept into Bridgenorth, seizing the town, burning the bridge and violently attacking the king's advanced guard.[17] The action forced Edward to leave Worcester on 8 January, a day after Hugh Despenser the Younger's return into the king's peace was publicly declared to the citizens of London. No sooner had Edward left for the crossing at Shrewsbury than Roger Damory took Worcester behind him. These were to be their last real victories. Edward had thought ahead. To counter Mortimer confidence, the king had called upon the support of Gruffydd Llwyd, who was put to work in the northern March to capture the key Mortimer strongholds of Chirk, Welshpool and Clun. With such a raid against them, the two Mortimers began to waver, and when Edward's army crossed the Severn at Shrewsbury, their confidence evaporated. On 10 January Lancaster foolishly threw the dice and began to besiege Edward's castle at Tickhill near Doncaster rather than come to the Mortimers' rescue. They were left without hope of victory. On the 13th they began talks under safe conduct with the king's men to surrender, doing so on the 22nd.[18] Edward was in no mood for compromise and instead of welcoming them back into the fold immediately imprisoned them.[19]

The king's attention now turned to his brother-in-law, the Earl of Hereford, who was ensconced at Gloucester. Hereford, desperate not to be cut off from Lancaster, fled north before Edward, who turned south of Shrewsbury, and reached the town. There the king found and upbraided Adam Orleton, Bishop of Hereford, for supporting the rebels.[20] On 6 February, he arrived and recaptured Gloucester, finding Maurice de Berkeley and Hugh Audley the Elder. Again following their surrender, the king threw them into prison and Berkeley had his castle confiscated. Three knights who had supported the barons were hanged.[21] Edward's harsh dispensation of justice was a sign of what was to come. For the king, quashing this rebellion was personal. On 13 February, to ensure the Mortimers were more secure, Edward ordered the Earl of Surrey and Robert le Ewer to escort them to the Tower.

The Marcher lords confederacy was quickly disintegrating in the face of the speed and efficiency of Edward's campaign. Hereford, Damory, Audley the Younger, Badlesmere and Clifford remained at large and fled north to meet up with Lancaster at Pontefract. Edward sent word to his cousin not to harbour the Marcher rebels, to which Lancaster replied that he knew of no rebels and would kill any should he find them.[22] The message was clear. In Lancaster's mind, the contrariants were acting in self-defence, and as Steward of England he felt he had the right to support them. Yet this time Lancaster had overestimated the strength of his position. His action in moving against the king at Tickhill now gave Edward the much-needed excuse to turn his army north and destroy his cousin once and for all. Vengeance, Edward's personal motivation since the murder of Piers Gaveston in June 1312, was now firmly fixed at the forefront of the king's ambition.

Edward needed to keep up the pace before the rebels had a chance to move further north. News had reached him that the Scots had once again invaded northern England, and the years of suspicion that Lancaster was in league with the Bruce aroused Edward's fears that they might unite against him.[23] The timing was too much of a coincidence. All his gains to date might be for nothing. Edward ordered Andrew Harclay, sheriff of Cumberland, to raise his hobelars and protect the north. Harclay, the king commanded, could begin temporary truce negotiations with the Scots, should this be required.[24] On 14 February Edward ordered at least 15,000 infantry, mostly made up of 12,000 men from Wales, to muster by 5 March at Coventry.[25] To block aid from abroad, Edward wrote to the pope and the king of France to inform them of events in England. Those who criticise Edward's strategic martial ability do him a great injustice. The planning and the speed with which the king commanded events from September 1321 is breathtaking and highlights Edward's capabilities in campaigning – when he could command the support of men behind a single cause.

As February drew to a close, Edward heard via William Melton, Archbishop of York, that letters had come into the archbishop's possession, written between a man named as 'King Arthur' and Sir James Douglas and Thomas Randolph. It was political dynamite. The mysterious King Arthur was Lancaster, who had adopted the mythical king's name as a not particularly effective cover. Finally it could be proved that Lancaster had been in league with the Scots all along. It was treason. Edward seized upon the opportunity and immediately ordered the archbishop, bishops and sheriffs across England to publicise the letters.[26] It had the desired effect. Men across the country began to lose faith in the treacherous earl and his powerful retainers, such as Fulk Lestrange and Peter de Mauley, began to desert him, taking their large retinues with them as Edward mustered at Coventry.[27]

On 3 March the king was rejoined by both Despensers at Lichfield, who brought with them a large force. Kenilworth Castle, Lancaster's mighty Midland fortress, surrendered as Edward arrived in the region. As the king marched north, Lancaster broke off his siege at Tickhill and with Hereford and the remaining contrariants moved to the river crossing at Burton-on-Trent near Lancaster's castle of Tutbury to prevent Edward from crossing. Lancaster made the fateful decision to unfurl his banner, which legally proclaimed his stand as rebellion rather than mere opposition. With the Scottish correspondence, this had now become a fight that Lancaster could no longer afford to lose. This stand was shortlived, and by the third day of fighting, Edward and his army were able to outflank the rebels.[28] The remaining contrariants fled to Pontefract Castle leaving behind a mortally wounded Roger Damory. On 13 March, slowly dying of his wounds, Damory was tried and sentenced to death as a traitor. Yet despite his actions, Edward could not bring himself to see Damory hanged, drawn and beheaded and so he was allowed to die of his wounds in the nearby abbey.[29] This act of mild compassion from Edward despite Damory's treachery is unusual from a king who never forgot a personal injury. It may indicate the sadness Edward felt about Damory's disloyalty, when he had done so much to raise the latter from the dust and hints at the closeness that these two men had once enjoyed. Either way, Edward knew Damory would die of his wounds.

The king declared that the remaining rebels were traitors and ordered his half-brother the Earl of Kent and the Earl of Surrey to capture Lancaster's mighty fortress of Pontefract.[30] At the last minute, Lancaster's retainer Robert Holland deserted the earl, leaving him unable to organise a substantial defence.[31] Lancaster and the rebels decided to flee north, only after Roger Clifford threatened the Earl of Lancaster with an unsheathed sword, demanding that they go.[32] They did not get far. As the king's army marched to Pontefract, Isabella had written to Andrew Harclay and Simon Ward, sheriff of York, commanding both men to cut off the rebels' retreat north. The queen's demand had done its work and Harclay appeared at the head of 4,000 men at the river crossing at Boroughbridge.[33] The rebels were trapped. Determined to break through, Hereford commanded two columns of men on foot to cross the narrow bridge, while Lancaster attempted to ford the river under a hail of arrows. As Hereford began to walk across the bridge with his men, he was skewered by pikes thrust from underneath between the gaps of the wooden planks by some of Harclay's men hiding there in secret.[34] Lancaster retreated to the bank and made a truce with Harclay to keep the peace until the following morning. Harclay agreed but could not be bribed to let the earl and the rebels across the bridge. With little hope of crossing and cut off from retreating south by Edward's advancing army, men began to desert the rebel army overnight, especially those in the retinue of the now dead Earl of Hereford.[35] As dawn approached on 17 March, Harclay, now joined by Simon Ward, charged into the rebel camp and captured Lancaster and the leading men and removed them to York Castle.[36] Badlesmere escaped but was captured days later at Stowe Park.

The day after Boroughbridge, Edward arrived outside the walls of Pontefract and accepted its surrender from the constable of the castle. What a moment of gratification for the king, to accept the surrender of the garrison that had on two separate occasions jeered at him from those mighty walls. They were not jeering now. On 21 March, Lancaster was transferred from York Castle to Pontefract. There he was presented to the king and the Despensers, and according to the *Anonimalle* chronicle, a shorter version of the Brut, he was 'contemptuously insulted to the face' and then locked up in a new tower the earl had recently built, as the gossip went at the time, to imprison the king.[37] Lancaster's fall was complete. The next day would be his trial.

For ten years Edward had sought revenge for the murder of his lover Piers Gaveston. The fierce desire had dominated the core part of his reign and had dogged his ability to rule as effectively as his position should have allowed him to. His personal desires had directed his policies. Now on 22 March, Edward stood in Lancaster's own great castle of Pontefract and was determined to do to him what his cousin had done all those years ago to Gaveston.

Lancaster was brought before Edward, both Despensers, the earls Pembroke, Kent, Richmond, Surrey, Atholl and Agnus as well as the royal justice Robert Mablethorp. Much like Gaveston's mock trial at Warwick castle, Lancaster was forced to listen to the accusations levelled against him. The indictment was lengthy, including the seizure of the king's jewels and property at Newcastle in 1312; bringing armed men to parliaments; the siege of Tickhill; holding up the king's army at Pontefract and the behaviour of the garrison from its walls; and more damning than the rest, treasonable correspondence with the Scots. The evidence for which was not just the letters published in March, but also an indenture found on the dead body of the Earl of Hereford at Boroughbridge, which promised Lancaster and Hereford aid from Robert Bruce.[38] Just as at Gaveston's trial, Lancaster was not given permission to speak, though he attempted to.[39] Lancaster was found guilty of treason and, like Gaveston, was condemned to be hanged, drawn and beheaded. The sentence was commuted because of Lancaster's royal blood and on the intercession of the queen, who was the earl's niece. Once the sentence was passed, Lancaster was taken from the castle, where it had been snowing, mounted on a mule and taken to a nearby hill in front of an assembled crowd, much like Gaveston had been forced to when taken from Warwick Castle to Blacklow Hill. There, Lancaster was handed over to an executioner, forced to kneel facing towards Scotland as a pointed reminder of his treason and clumsily beheaded. It took two or three blows of a sword to sever his head from his neck.[40] On that cold day in March 1322, Edward finally had his long awaited revenge.

Revenge is an act of passion; vengeance of justice. Injuries are revenged: crimes are avenged.[41]

20

Wheel of Fortune

'O Calamity! To see men lately dressed in purple and fine linen now attired in rags, bound and imprisoned in chains!'[1] For contemporaries this was a shocking turn of events. Nor was Thomas of Lancaster the only man to meet his maker by the king's command. On the same day, perhaps even before the earl lost his head, six of his satellites, including William Tuchet, Henry de Bradbourne and Thomas Maudit, were also executed.[2] The following day Roger Clifford, John de Mowbray and Gaucelin d'Eyville were hanged outside the gates of York Castle.[3] Justices were granted powers to try contrariants around the country. To hammer home the futility of their rebellion, each of those rebels assembled before the judges were in mockery forced to wear their green and yellow tunics, last worn as a symbol of their unity during the rebellion in 1321.[4] Sir Roger Elmbridge and John Giffard of Brimpsfield were dragged out of their cells and hanged at Gloucester.

The most savage punishment of all was reserved for Bartholomew Badlesmere. He was hauled through the streets of Canterbury to the Blean and eventually, while still conscious, was hanged, drawn and beheaded. The dire end was punishment for fleeing the king as a traitor after Edward crossed the river at Burton-on-Trent at the beginning of March. Badlesmere's head was impaled on the Burgate so all those entering and leaving the town could see what happened to those who opposed their king.[5] Out of the other twenty-one rebels executed across the country, only Lancaster's body was buried immediately, all the other corpses were left to rot were they hung until the bishops petitioned the king to take them down and permit Christian burial two years later.[6]

Not all the rebels were executed. Many were received into the king's peace including a fair number of Lancaster's former retainers. Hugh Audley, Edward's former favourite, was spared on account of his marriage to Margaret de Clare. He was promptly imprisoned at the Tower, while his father Hugh Audley the Elder and Maurice de Berkeley were sent to cells at Wallingford castle. The Rogers of Chirk and Wigmore, who had surrendered to Edward at Shrewsbury on 22 January, were taken for trial at Westminster Hall where on 2 August they were found guilty of treason for their roles in seizing Gloucester from the king and attacking his army at Bridgenorth. On 22 July, the king had already ordered the judges to commute any future sentence, but on 2 August they were nevertheless condemned to death in Westminster Hall. In a moment of clemency, Edward kept to his earlier decision and on the following day commuted the Mortimers' sentence to imprisonment.[7] As they were transported to the Tower of London, so too were another fifteen people including Thomas Gurney – who still had a role to play in Edward's life – and the sons of Badlesmere and John de Mowbray.[8]

The wives and children of the rebels were rounded up and held at castles and convents around England. Perhaps the most notable confinement is that of the wife, sons and daughters of Roger Mortimer of Wigmore. Their long captivity was no doubt made worse by the future actions of Roger Mortimer himself.[9] The majority, but by no means all, of those imprisoned were reduced to living off a meagre daily allowance of 3*d*, which barely sustained them.[10] Adding to the heartache, the pope John XXII excommunicated those rebels who had 'attacked the king and his realm'.[11]

The execution of men on this scale shocked contemporaries. It was highly unusual during times of opposition to the crown that the malefactors would or could expect to face the ultimate sanction. Imprisonment, exile and forfeiture of lands was the accepted convention, however, Edward was proceeding on the assumption that these men were beyond the law, traitors since mid-March who had chosen to remain beyond the king's peace.

The execution of the Earl of Lancaster was the most shocking of all. While Edward's burning desire for vengeance had ultimately driven the king and determined Lancaster's fate, Thomas had not been tried in parliament by his peers. While Edward had been keen to ensure the judges at Pontefract were his peers, the failure to present the earl for trial in parliament to a much larger body and in which he could raise a defence made many in England uneasy. His royal blood and position as premier earl in England had not saved him. From here onwards, at the moment of Edward's greatest and most spectacular victory, the king had fundamentally, and perhaps not unwittingly, altered the game. Those around him were no longer able to oppose him without the threat of royal aggression, which could see them lose everything, even their lives. Edward must have felt in a position of great strength, but shadowing this, as would soon become apparent, was the notion that opposition to the king now meant that there was no going back. The stakes had just been increased considerably. In these unprecedented times, while Edward appeared to have the full support of the most important of his magnates in March 1322, fear would almost certainly have quickly crept into the court. For the first time in his reign Edward was free to rule unrestrainedly; but at what cost?

Edward was quick to reward those who had stood by him during his finest hour. The largest endowments were made to Hugh Despenser the Elder who gained the earldom of Winchester, while Sir Andrew Harclay who had been instrumental in the capture of Lancaster and the death of the Earl of Hereford at Boroughbridge received a new creation; the earldom of Carlisle.[12] Along with the title came lands worth £2,000. Hugh Despenser the Younger did not receive the earldom of Gloucester, which he greatly coveted, as Edward clearly understood the sensitivity of such a grant. Instead, the king restored all the lands Despenser had acquired in Glamorgan and extended his reach by giving Hugh Roger Damory's former lordship of Usk, among other gifts.[13] It was a great gift and one that continued to consolidate the younger Despenser's powerbase in the region. He was also restored to the office of chamberlain, giving him complete control over access to the king, and his annual revenue rose to £5,000 a year, making him one of the richest men in England.[14]

Pembroke received Lancaster's former house at New Temple in London as well as the honour of Higham Ferrers.[15] The Earl of Kent was granted three castles; John of Eltham, Edward's youngest son who was six years old, gained Tutbury castle. Many others such as the earls of Surrey, Arundel and Richmond received gifts from the king for services and support during the campaign. Edward always rewarded personal loyalty. Interestingly, no gifts were given to Isabella and this may be one of the earliest signs that their marriage was under strain.

The king was able to turn rebel catastrophe into a lucrative financial opportunity, using precedents set down by his father Edward I. In July that year, Edward decided former rebels could buy back their lands on payment of a fine as well as extracting an oath of further fines or payments, the amount determined by the king, should the respective landholder ever rebel again. It was an insurance policy designed to crudely bind his subjects to him as well as fill his long-empty coffers. In the end, the fines raised £15,000 and were paid, more often than not, by instalments to the treasury.[16]

Edward took pains to ensure that his victory would be cemented for posterity. As early as 14 March, the king sent out writs summoning parliament to meet at York on 2 May.[17] In attendance were his brothers Kent and Norfolk, his son, Edward, Earl of Chester, with Richmond, Pembroke, Arundel, Surrey, Angus and Atholl and seventy-two barons.[18] As parliament opened, the first piece of business confirmed the legality of Lancaster's execution and the confiscation of his estates. Immediately afterwards, the action taken against the Despensers at the Westminster parliament of 1321 was formally annulled. But perhaps the most satisfying outcome of the York parliament for Edward, beyond the formal recognition justifying Lancaster's demise, was the universal support for the repeal of the Ordinances. With Edward's new found position, no one was willing to step up to defend Lancaster's former calling card. In a show of compromise, Edward actually declared that he would reissue six of the forty-one clauses that dealt with old bones of contention including prises and confirming the scale of the forest, which had been reconfirmed in the time of his father. Expansion of areas of England defined as the royal forest threatened to usurp the rights of nobles and communities alike, as forest laws restricted usage considerably in the king's personal favour.

As parliament drew towards a close the body confirmed support for an immediate Scottish campaign that Edward had called for on 25 March, which for the first time in the reign would not be dogged by internal English division. The army was to muster on 24 July at Newcastle. Emboldened by his recent victory Edward summoned unsustainable numbers of men from England, Ireland, Wales and Gascony, an unprecedented 40,000.[19] He was clearly attempting to capitalise on the current momentum and indicates the emotional high he was on. In the end, approximately 20,000 men, 2,100 hobelars and 1,250 cavalry mustered for the forthcoming campaign.[20]

No sooner had Despenser regained his role as chamberlain than he again began exerting his manipulative influence over the king. For Edward having the Despensers by his side had given him the position, the confidence and the excuse to bring about his longed-for revenge. With such a heady mix of cause and effect, Edward's affection for Despenser the Younger must have only deepened. Hugh must have been aware that his position at Edward's side now made him unassailable.

To be certain, Despenser now acted. This time his target was the moderate Earl of Pembroke who was, until 1321, one of few men still able to influence the king. Pembroke's role in Despenser's exile needed to be addressed and so Hugh convinced Edward to have the earl arrested shortly after the York parliament broke up. Only after the earl's peers rallied to his defence was Pembroke able to receive Edward's pardon after he made personal pledges of loyalty, which echoed the former indenture that existed between them since November 1317.[21] It was an ugly affair but one designed to send out a clear signal to the court; Pembroke was a spent political force.

The campaign in Scotland of 1322 was to be Edward's last. Leaving Newcastle on 10 August, the king led the army into Scotland reaching the outskirts of Edinburgh on the 19th. Bruce resorted to his age-old tactic of avoiding open battle, despite his earlier victory at Bannockburn. Instead he withdrew his men and cleared the lands of Lothian of all livestock, denying the English army the ability to feed itself: scorched earth. With the absence of any English-held castle north of the border, the army was forced to keep on the move, without a central base to rest. Edward had pre-empted the move and ordered about thirty-six ships to bring supplies up the north coast. However, harried by storms out in the North Sea, and dogged by Flemish mercenaries who turned pirate, the majority of the ships failed to make it through.[22] As a result the army, 20,000 strong, quickly began to starve.

Within less than three weeks, without the hope of food or further supply, Edward was forced to break up the campaign. His hopes of a glorious victory that would rival his father's achievements were gone, along with the triumphant feeling of invincibility that most likely had set in since the spring of that year. It was a failure that the king most certainly did not want to acknowledge and was quick to blame on the Flemish attacks. As in previous years after 1314, Edward decided to spend the winter in the north guarding the border from Scottish assault.

But the Bruce was not yet done – he turned the hunter into the hunted. As Edward's army began the retreat south at the end of August, Bruce set off in pursuit and surprised Edward's army near Melrose Abbey, inflicting serious injury during the clashes.[23] The Scots raided into Northumberland and on 30 September, the Bruce himself crossed into England – reaching as far south as Northallerton in Yorkshire on 12 October. Edward, who was a mere 15 miles away at Rievaulx Abbey, was caught off guard and was suddenly in grave danger.[24]

In a bid to stave off capture, the king sent word to Pembroke to take his forces and meet the Earl of Richmond and Henry de Beaumont at Byland and there they should meet the Scots, now headed by Sir James Douglas and Sir Thomas Randolph. Pembroke obliged but what followed on 14 October was an English rout at Blackhow Moor, which saw Richmond captured and Pembroke narrowly escape back to the comparative safety of York.[25] More worryingly, as Edward and Despenser were having breakfast at Rievaulx Abbey, frantic news arrived of the recent defeat and their imminent risk of capture. Edward, Despenser and their households were forced to flee 50 miles south to Bridlington Priory on horseback before arriving at York, leaving all their belongings behind, including the king's privy seal, which was again returned to him by Bruce as it had been after Bannockburn.[26] It was deeply humiliating. Chroniclers poured scorn on the king calling him 'chicken-hearted and luckless in war', but Edward's retreat was essential given his army had been earlier disbanded.[27] Capture by the Scots was something that the king and his government could not afford and would, in an instant, bring about the end of all English hopes of ruling over Scotland. For the king, the humiliation was great and cut deep for now he was acting like a fugitive in his own kingdom.

It didn't get any better. In all the confusion, Queen Isabella, who had been placed in the comparative safety of Tynemouth Priory, now found herself cut off behind enemy lines. As her husband was retreating to the south, the English countryside around her was teeming with the Scots, who may have been aware of her presence. With Despenser's wife, Eleanor de Clare, Isabella and her retinue were forced to make a break for it, first by commandeering a ship in waters full of Flemish pirates, and then being forced to continue the last of their journey by horse. The retreat itself may have been dramatic and quite possibly subject to Scottish attack as one of her ladies was allegedly killed. Another went into premature labour, dying shortly afterwards.[28] Before her flight, Edward, desperate to avoid catastrophe, attempted to rescue his wife by sending Henry de Sully, the butler of France, who was participating in the campaign, to her aid – but he was captured at the rout near Byland. Edward also sought to provide Isabella with protection by commanding the constable of Norham Castle to raise a defence for the queen. Whatever the outcome, Isabella took matters into her own hands. However, after her ordeal, the queen became so aggrieved by this incident that she would later claim that Despenser himself had imperilled her safety and that of her household by counselling the king to abandon her.[29] It may be pure exaggeration, years later, but it is noteworthy that the queen fell back on this event in her not too distant memory. Whatever her view, Despenser was unlikely to be complicit as his own wife, who was probably pregnant, was also with the queen at the time. As the signs of strain began to emerge in the royal marriage, this incident may well have been a significant turning point that would put Edward and Isabella on separate but equally dangerous paths.

The year 1323 did not get much better. As Edward grew in political power, he would no longer entertain direct challenge to his rule. As Despenser and those at court began to enact reforms to the king's household, which Edward himself approved of, the king was finally able to overcome the doomed financial inheritance passed down to him by his father Edward I. The king retained much of the lucrative income from estates confiscated from the contrariants, most notably Lancaster's five earldoms, and in 1323 he would receive £42,000 in taxation receipts from parliament. Soon Edward would be more or less in credit and, ironically, would spend less on his household than in any other time during his reign, which had always been an aim of the Ordainers.[30]

Yet despite his new-found wealth, Edward was unable to bring about conquest in Scotland, another critical legacy inherited from his father.

Those around him became increasingly frustrated with this and in early January that year, the Earl of Carlisle, new into his position as earl, overstepped the mark and secretly began negotiating with the Bruce. Harclay's aim was most likely a settlement that he hoped would bring peace to northern England and would, in itself, be favourable enough to Edward for the king to support it. Harclay did not yet know Edward well enough, who despite the years of setbacks, had never once given up hope of winning in Scotland. Given his father's mighty reputation and that Scottish conquest was now a question of English national pride, failure could not be countenanced. Edward never entertained the prospect of giving up and so when the king got wind of Harclay's actions on 7 January, he immediately sent out letters prohibiting the earl and others from engaging in talks of truce or settlement with the Scots.[31] Despite the warning, Harclay thought he could win the king over so the secret talks with Bruce continued, resulting in a furious Edward ordering Harclay's arrest and branding him a traitor. Three weeks later, the earl was caught by Sir Anthony Lucy at Carlisle Castle and on 3 March his jury, which consisted of the earl of Kent, John Hastings, three royal household knights and a royal justice, condemned Harclay to death. Despite holding the rank of earl for less than a year, he was stripped of the title, degraded from the rank of knight, and hanged, drawn and quartered. His body parts were placed at Carlisle, Newcastle, York and Shrewsbury.[32] As ever, Edward made it clear that he valued loyalty above everything else. He had become ruthless.

In the end Harclay's treason was futile. On the back of the ferocity of Scottish invasion following Edward's campaign of 1322, it was clear that success in Scotland was still far beyond reach, despite the support of a seemingly unified nobility. Shortly after Harclay's dismembered body parts arrived in various towns, Edward opened negotiations with Bruce, which by May resulted in the sealing of a thirteen-year truce, which at the very least gave the north of England respite from further Scottish attacks. Edward was still able to refuse to acknowledge Bruce as king and Bruce had time to continue to consolidate gains in his own kingdom.[33] It was a sensible policy for all involved and the best the parties were likely to achieve at that moment. When Isabella and Mortimer's regime came to power they, unlike Edward, agreed to the Treaty of Northampton in 1328, otherwise known as 'The Shameful Peace', which granted Scotland its independence and formally recognised Robert Bruce as an independent king. Edward, despite all his setbacks in Scotland, is often judged too harshly for being meek in war. Such accusations fail to take account of much of the evidence or the context.

Edward's mood was sour for the most part of 1323. Long gone was the jubilant atmosphere of victory. As Harclay's treachery came to light, so too came disturbing news from the south that some of the imprisoned contrariants were hatching plots to gain their freedom. Worse, it looked as if various pockets of rebels were in communication with each other – as as well building surreptitious support from places like London.

The first of the major plots occurred at Wallingford Castle, where Maurice de Berkeley and Hugh Audley the Elder were imprisoned. Building up trust with the constable and the guards, Maurice was able to invite his squire and a few men to dinner, which the castle constable and his gatekeepers attended. During the meal, the squire and guests rose up and at swordpoint demanded that the guards hand over the keys, which they did. Twenty more men loyal to Berkeley and Audley arrived shortly afterwards. Just before the castle could be overwhelmed, their plot was foiled when a boy living within the castle grew suspicious and managed to raise the alarm with the mayor who, in turn, raised the local sheriff. Berkeley, Audley and the men were unable to escape and instead hunkered down and held Wallingford against the sheriff. Edward and Despenser were quick to act, and the new Earl of Winchester and Edward's half-brother the Earl of Kent arrived and threatened to storm the castle. Fourteen days after the whole debacle began, Berkeley's men surrendered and as Winchester and Kent entered the castle, they found Berkeley and Audley locked in their cells and the rest of the conspirators in the chapel pleading sanctuary.[34] It did them little good as the ringleaders Roger Wauton, Sir Edmund de la Beche and Sir John de Wilyngton were taken to the king at Pontefract where the former was hanged and the latter two thrown into prison.[35]

During the hiatus at Wallingford, the king had called on the mayor of London, Hamo de Chigwell, to send fifty crossbowmen to help break the siege, which they refused claiming that as the queen and the heir to the throne, the Earl of Chester, were residing at the Tower, they were needed to protect her. Edward was both suspicious and furious and on 4 April intervened in London's fiercely independent politics and removed the mayor from office, replacing him with Nicholas de Farndon. The king also removed others from their offices.[36] To make an example of the discredited mayor and his men, they were forced to accompany the king and queen on pilgrimage to Canterbury before finally being allowed to leave the court as Edward moved to York in May. The net effect was to harm relations with the city and put Edward on a path of conflict he would never step off. From here onwards, he may have maintained the support of the city on the surface, but he had most certainly lost hearts and minds.

To compound the king's growing unease, reports began to surface that miracles had occurred at the very spot on which Thomas of Lancaster had been executed. By May 1323 further miracles allegedly occurred at the location of the stone tablet in London, which had been erected at St Paul's by Lancaster in 1311 to commemorate the publication of the Ordinances. The date of the alleged London miracles falls shortly after Hamo de Chigwell was removed from office and can be taken as a clear sign of the growing distaste Londoners felt towards Edward and the Despenser regime. The Despensers had never been popular in the city and were blamed for the London Eyre (circuit court) of 1321, which had encroached upon the city's liberties when Edward took it back into royal hands in February that year. To quell the chance of a growing cult around his dead cousin, the king ordered Robert Baldock to remove the stone tablet and the candles which had sprung up around it.[37] Orders were given that anyone visiting the site of Lancaster's execution was to be imprisoned. The popular mood was beginning to turn against the king and by September, in Bristol, a town that had already rebelled in 1316, riots broke out around the gallows of the long-dead contrariants Henry de Monfort, and Henry de Wilyngton, a relation of one of the ring leaders of the Wallingford castle plot.

As August began, further conspiracies made themselves manifest as Roger Mortimer of Wigmore dramatically escaped from his confinement in the Tower of London. The plot, with distinct echoes of the Wallingford escape attempt, saw Mortimer with the aid of the deputy constable of the Tower, Gerard d' Alspaye, drug the constable and guards while they were dining. Once incapacitated, d'Alspaye was able to spring Mortimer from his cell and both escaped via the kitchen and over the outer walls with rope. They both made it to the bank of the River Thames and to an awaiting boat, kept safe by other conspirators. Rowing to the south side of the river, Mortimer, d'Alspaye and the others then fled to a mill owned by John de Gisors, who had suffered at the hands of the king by losing office in the city earlier in May.[38] Other Londoners, such as Richard de Béthune and Ralph de Bocton, were also complicit. With a well thought out plan that must have taken some time to arrange, Mortimer was able to make it to the south coast where he took ship to France.

Edward was right to be disturbed by the prison break. Mortimer was a senior baron and the calculated plan to rescue him, which had support from disgruntled Londoners, demonstrated to Edward that popular opinion was turning against him, at least in the city. On 6 August, five days after Mortimer's escape, the king sent Walter Stapledon, treasurer and Bishop of Exeter, to relieve the constable of his duties. So concerned were the king and the Despensers that they could lose control of the Tower, Stapledon was told not to make his intentions known until he was beyond the gates and within the inner walls of the mighty fortress.[39] It worked and Edward was able to change the constable. The king and the Despensers, who had a long-standing feud with Mortimer whose ancestor had killed Despenser the Elder's father at the battle of Evesham in 1265, were keen to see him recaptured. They thought his likely route would have taken him to his estates in Ireland but news arrived that he had been seen in France.

Plots, riots and further plots did little to alleviate Edward's ever-blackening mood. As pressure began to build and the king continued to rule with an iron grip, which was encouraged by his chamberlain, Edward began to fall out with those around him, most notably his bishops who, for the better part of the reign, had supported him at times of grave crisis. As failure in Scotland had brought about successive raids into England, Edward lashed out in a fit of pique against Louis de Beaumont, Bishop of Durham, whom the king claimed had done little to defend the north through 'laziness and neglect', despite Beamount's claims that he would raise a noble defence if elected to the bishopric.[40] Worse still, Edward quarrelled heatedly with the bishop's brother Henry during the peace negotiations with the Scots, during which the king had Henry temporarily imprisoned. The Beaumont brothers, who had always remained fiercely loyal to the king, now found themselves at the sharp end of his condemnation and this quite possibly placed further strain on Edward's relationship with Isabella, who was a close friend and advocate of the Beaumont family.

Edward quarrelled with John Droxford, Bishop of Bath & Wells, and Henry Burghersh, Bishop of Lincoln, who had sympathised with his late uncle, Bartholomew Badlesmere during the events of 1321–22. The king had confiscated Lincoln's temporalities, meaning he was financially constrained. By 1323, Edward was so incensed by these two men that he wrote to Pope John XXII demanding they be translated from their sees, citing that they were 'descended from the race of traitors'.[41] The pope disagreed and refused to budge. To add insult to injury, the pope declined to support Edward's candidate to the vacant see of Winchester. Instead, he granted it to one of Edward's clerks, John Stratford, who happened to be at Avignon on the king's business and was able to advance his own credentials. Edward was furious as his own candidate, Robert Baldock, was left out in the cold. When Stratford returned to England he was treated to three separate interrogations, the final one with the king himself on 7 December 1323. The details of these meetings are unclear but, despite the storm, Stratford remained in his bishopric. In the end, Edward was forced to back down and by the summer of 1324, he appeared to be reconciled with the bishop.[42]

This trend continued into early 1324. Since Adam Orleton's elevation to the bishopric of Hereford, Edward had taken a real dislike to him. The king had heavily criticised his appointment, which, much like Stratford, had been achieved by persuading the pope in person of his credentials without royal backing. Orleton, Edward believed, had been and continued to be an active supporter of those who had rebelled in 1321. When the king's army had travelled west in January 1322 reaching Hereford, he had found the bishop there and upbraided him for supporting the barons.[43] Now the king suspected that Orleton was secretly supporting Mortimer, and later events would prove him right. Against the growing miasma of suspicion in England, Edward moved against the bishop, ordering him to appear before the justices on 23 January 1324. After two more meetings, where Orleton refused to bend and was eventually claimed by the Archbishop of Canterbury for the Church, meaning he was under papal protection, Orleton was eventually convicted of conspiring with Mortimer on 19 March 1324 by a jury of men from Hereford. Although the king was unable to exercise capital punishment as Orleton belonged to the Church, the king confiscated his lands and temporalities and ordered Walter Reynolds, Archbishop of Canterbury, to hold him in custody.[44] This whole affair created in Orleton an enemy that Edward II would later have to come face-to-face with in the most extraordinary of situations.

Since achieving his greatest victory by overcoming the Earl of Lancaster, Edward was able to secure great political freedom. He became both extremely powerful and also financially independent, something that had long held him back. Yet in his moment of greatest victory, the king had also created a universal fear that lingered in the shadows of the court and across the magnate class. He had changed the political landscape and the magnates' ability to stand in opposition to the crown in ways that made previous customs and conventions now moribund. With the Despensers by his side, and the Younger manipulating the king, Edward became increasingly isolated and ignorantly self-assured. As 1323 showed, that self-assurance created enemies and began the breakdown of his marriage and long-standing loyal relationships. With the escape of Mortimer from the Tower, increasing disaffection among the Londoners, and riots in Bristol, these had become dangerous times. England, and her king in particular, was again careering towards disaster.

21

Wife, Queen, Rebel

Open conflict began in 1324, not in England, but in Edward's English-held territories in France, in the duchy of Aquitaine. Aquitaine had come to the English crown through the marriage of Eleanor of Aquitaine to Henry II in 1152 and the king's later accession to the English throne in 1154. Although successive monarchs had fought bitterly with the French king, the duchy, albeit it much smaller than in the twelfth century, now centred on Gascony. The relationship between the kings of England and France had long been a difficult one. In France, the king of England was simply the Duke of Aquitaine and therefore owed homage to his overlord. For Edward II and his predecessors, this created a significant imbalance in status between two persons who were kings in their own right and therefore equals on the political stage. Status governed the medieval mind. The thorny subject of homage, in which the king of England would kneel and pledge his alliance to his overlord for his French domains, rankled with the English. When another of Philip IV's sons perished after a short rule without male issue, his final heir, Charles IV, took the throne in January 1322. Homage was once more due from Edward II.

Charles, unlike his brothers, was calculating and unbending, like his father Philip IV. Initially the king of France relented, allowing Edward time to postpone his homage for the duchy on account of the turmoil in England as the king was focussed on bringing down his over-mighty vassals and securing the northern border from the Scots. However, once Edward and Bruce had agreed to the thirteen-year truce, Charles moved quickly – demanding Edward cross to France and perform homage in the customary way. Edward did what he and his father Edward I had always done, he played for time, which Charles must have expected.

However, events beyond Edward's control soon altered the political tempo. On 15 October 1323, a French royal serjeant in the duchy was found hanging from a post under a flag flying the fleur-de-lys, the royal coat of arms. Rather provocatively Charles IV was determined to build a royal bastide in an area known as the Agenais, which formed part of Edward's duchy, and this wooden post had earlier been driven into the ground to mark its future location. The siting of a bastide in such a sensitive area rankled with the local populace and was cause for concern to Edward, his council in England, and his seneschal in the duchy, Ralph Basset. As tensions ran high, someone unknown chose to act and news of the murder of a French royal serjeant reached Charles IV at Angers on 1 November. He was quick to blame both the local lord Raymond-Bernard of Montpezat and Ralph Basset. Charles IV used this incident and Edward's excuses to delay performance of his homage as a pretext to confiscate the duchy, which remained his right as overlord. As later events would demonstrate, the king of France certainly had ambitions to keep the Agenais all along and so could have engineered a situation that would allow him to achieve his end.

A diplomatic incident had erupted, made worse as Edward's messengers had recently left England seeking a further postponement of his homage shortly before the murder had taken place. The timing could not have been worse. Edward immediately grasped the delicate nature of the situation and was quick to try and calm the choppy political waters, writing to his brother-in-law on 7 December reassuring Charles that he was outraged by the murder and had not ordered it. Charles responded by exiling Montpezat and Basset from France, who fled back to England and were received by Edward, which only angered the king of France more.

Edward's hastily dispatched envoys were getting nowhere and so, on 13 June 1324, the king and his council dispatched the Earl of Pembroke to the French court, Pembroke was a veteran of Anglo-French politics. Just when Edward needed him to engineer a solution, Pembroke failed to reach Charles' court, dying shortly after dinner on 23 June near Boulogne.[1] News of the loss of his cousin reached Edward on 26 June and in the following month the earl's body was returned to England and at the request of his widow, was buried in some splendour at Westminster Abbey alongside the growing royal mausoleum.[2] His career was outstanding and his determined support of Edward following Gaveston's murder in 1312 had been instrumental in preventing civil war on numerous occasions during Edward's clashes with his other cousin, Thomas of Lancaster. Although Pembroke lost his influence from early 1321 onwards in the often threatening presence of Hugh Despenser the Younger, the loss of Pembroke must have been felt by Edward on a personal level. They had been through much together. With Pembroke no more, Edward had lost yet another voice of reasonableness, intelligence and downright common sense.

Charles IV's patience was fast running out. Just before Edward's fortieth birthday, the French king had summoned an army to muster on 10 June. On 24 June he formally confiscated the duchy from the king of England, the first time it had been lost since the last war in Gascony between Edward I and Philip IV, which ran from 1294 to 1303.[3] A month later, Edward turned to his inexperienced twenty-two-year-old half-brother Edmund, Earl of Kent, appointing him his lieutenant in the duchy and dispatched him with Alexander Bicknor, Archbishop of Dublin, to begin raising a defence against the threat of French military action.

In England a now frustrated Edward lashed out, much like his father had done in the 1290s, ordering the arrest of all French citizens currently living in his kingdom as well as preparing his own military response.[4] In September, rumours swept the south-west that the French would invade and to better protect the coastline, Edward, under the influence of Hugh Despenser and Walter Stapledon, treasurer and Bishop of Exeter, took Queen Isabella's lands back into his custody.[5] It was an unprecedented move, differing from the confiscation of lands from French aliens in the 1290s.[6] The lands confiscated from the queen also included those in inland counties. On 28 September, as further French arrests were ordered, the queen's household was purged of its French members.[7] In return for the loss of her income of £4,500, Isabella received a reduced but by no means paltry income of £2,613 6s 8d. paid for from the Exchequer.[8] Nevertheless, Isabella must have been outraged. So what was driving this?

Although the relative successful marriage of Edward and Isabella since 1308 appears to have begun to cool after March 1322, the confiscation of the queen's lands may be less about Edward and Isabella, and more about Edward and Isabella's brother Charles IV. At this moment, Edward was unaware of the Earl of Kent's truce at La Réole. In short, he was hitting back, only in the most personal way, reminding Charles that his marriage to Isabella had since 1303 been a cornerstone of the agreement to return the duchy to his father Edward I in that year. He had kept his side of the bargain. It had the desired effect, for Charles later informed Edward's envoys during tortuous negotiations that he was far from happy about the dismissal of the queen's French household servants. Edward had shot an arrow and it had found its mark. This in itself feels petty and vindictive, and given that Isabella herself blamed Despenser and Stapledon for Edward's decision, it is all too clear who lay at the heart of such an ill-advised strategy.[9]

By August the French army numbering approximately 7,000 men under the command of the king of France's uncle Charles of Valois, swept into the duchy and seized Agen, the chief town in the Agenais, before moving on La Réole which, on 22 September, was handed over by the Earl of Kent on the advice of Alexander Bicknor, or so Edward thought. In return, both parties gained a six-month truce following heavy fighting.[10] Kent's self-made truce gave Edward time to negotiate but his position was ultimately a weak one. He needed allies and so, from September, began marriage talks with the kings of Aragon and Castile. Edward, himself half-Castilian through his mother Eleanor, abandoned talks with King Jamie III of Aragon in February 1325, instead pursuing an alliance with the regents of the twelve-year-old Alfonso XI, king of Castile.[11] The plan was simple. Alfonso would marry Edward's daughter Eleanor, while the king of Castile's sister Eleanora would marry Edward and Isabella's eldest son and heir, Edward, Earl of Chester. It would not only continue ties between England and Castile, which Edward was keen to promote, but would also give the king support in the region against Charles IV. The king of France, nervous at the suggestion, hit back at Edward and his council accusing him as Duke of Aquitaine of having treasonable dealings with the king of France's neighbours.[12]

News of the truce at La Réole reached the royal court and Edward called an assembly, which met in London on 20 October. Shortly afterwards, the king was advised to go in person to the duchy, armed with 1,000 men-at-arms and 10,000 infantry and resist Charles of Valois. Before Edward set sail, the nobles felt there should be a ceremony, similar to the one in which Edward himself had taken part in 1297 when his father departed for Flanders; the nobles felt Edward II's son and heir should be presented and receive fealty from them.[13] As before, this would achieve two things – firstly, confidence that should Edward II not return because of capture or death, the country would rally behind his son and heir, while secondly, during a regency while the king was absent, the country would rally behind the young Edward and stave off any attacks from the Scots while the king was absent.

Emboldened by widespread support, Edward sent out orders on 17 November for a general muster at Portsmouth for 17 March 1325, which he himself would lead.[14] However, subsequent peace negotiations, encouraged by Pope John XXII, meant that by February, Edward appointed the earls of Surrey and Atholl to lead the army in his place.[15] The army did not sail until May, partly due to inclement weather and poor winds, but during the interval the infantry remained unpaid and began to get restless, plundering and rioting through Portsmouth and the surrounding area and again, once they had arrived at Bordeaux in Gascony.[16]

The peace negotiations had begun soon after conflict looked imminent. The pope was quick to send his envoys Hugh, Bishop of Orange, and Guillaume de Laudin, Archbishop of Vienne, to England; they dined with Edward on numerous occasions through November before setting off to the French court.[17] Joining them on the 15th were Edward's own envoys, the bishops of Norwich and Winchester and Henry de Beaumont.[18] Their mission was a simple one, which not only included the return of the duchy, but also proposals that the young Edward be made Duke of Aquitaine in his father's place and therefore able to perform homage; as well as possible talks of marriage.[19] For Edward, the suggestion of passing on the title to his son before his own death was in keeping with his own inheritance, when the dukedom was granted to him by his own father in 1306. In the political game, it was also wise for Edward to simultaneously propose a number of possible marriages for his son before finally committing to one, be it with France, Castile, Aragon or elsewhere. Yet Edward remained nervous of Charles and expected some kind of duplicity and so ordered that his envoys, while empowered to negotiate, could not finalise anything without first consulting with the king himself. It was a shrewd move on Edward's part, for he realised soon enough that the king of France was very much cut from the same cloth as his late father-in-law, Philip IV.

Charles, in a position of political and military strength simply rejected the offer, but did eventually propose to receive the young Edward to perform homage as duke, and his mother, Queen Isabella, to help negotiate a permanent settlement. Edward, his council, and a further assembly held at Westminster in February 1325, suspected a ruse and refused to send both queen and the heir to the throne into a country that was currently at war with England. The chances that both parties may be taken hostage or kept as security in a diplomatic game were far too high. In the end, it was suggested that Isabella herself should go, without the young Edward, to begin the process of negotiation. Fearful that Roger Mortimer, who was at large in northern France, might capture Isabella en route to Paris, Edward requested Charles expel Mortimer and his adherents from France altogether lest harm befall Charles' sister.

Anxieties about Mortimer's motives were ever-present at Edward's court. Only months earlier, Walter Reynolds, Archbishop of Canterbury, had secured intelligence that led him to believe Mortimer and his allies were attempting to raise an invasion fleet with the support of the Count of Hainault and the king of Bohemia, with troops and mercenaries from Germany, France and Hainault to swell their numbers. Their aim, at the very least, was the removal of their long-standing and now bitterest of enemies, the ever unpopular Despensers, if not the king himself.[20] This rumour has an uncanny resemblance to the actual invasion that did materialise eighteen months later. But in 1325, Mortimer, who had a plan to invade, was not sufficiently resourced to pull it off. Although many modern historians have seen Isabella and Charles IV in collusion with Mortimer at this time, there is no firm evidence of it.

On 16 February 1325, Edward was informed that his brother-in-law would receive his sister, Queen Isabella, at the French court to begin peace negotiations.[21] Preparations were hastily arranged and the queen, with thirty well-chosen people joining her retinue, set off for the diplomatic trip.[22] According to the *Vita*, Isabella 'departed very joyfully', reaching Wissant on 9 March and Pontoise by the 20th where, the following day, she was joined by the three English envoys who had long since laboured against Charles IV and his advisors.[23] To help ease her travel, Edward had ensured the queen left with £1,000 in ready cash and freedom to draw on the bank of the Bardi, if required.

Despite her efforts Isabella found her youngest brother to be 'harsh'. Whatever she tried to do to ease the diplomatic tension, Isabella wrote that Charles was ultimately 'unyielding'.[24] Yet despite her frustrations, the queen remained resolute and continued to try to broker a peace alongside Edward's other English envoys. By the start of April, terms for a settlement were reached and on 30 May, Isabella discussed with her brother the final settlement, which was agreed in the following days amongst the English, French and papal envoys.[25] It had been a tortuous few months in which Isabella herself had taken an active part.

The terms were far from comfortable. Edward was to surrender the duchy to Charles until homage could be performed personally. The cost of the conflict was to be picked up by the English crown and Charles would retain permanent possession of the Agenais, which was his intention all along. Refuse outright and war would follow, and given the threat of the Scots on the northern border in England, a war on two fronts would cripple Edward, militarily, financially and politically – as it had his father towards the end of his reign. To accept meant the loss of the Agenais and humiliation in still having to personally perform homage to what must have seemed a vitriolic Charles IV. The king complained he was being disinherited by the settlement and so turned to those around him for advice on 2 May.

Since their return from exile, Hugh Despenser and his father, now Earl of Winchester, with the treasurer Walter Stapledon, Bishop of Exeter, and Robert Baldock, chancellor, were Edward's principal advisors. The author of the *Anonimalle* chronicle calls Baldock 'a false and evilly inclined man' while Lanercost calls him 'pernicious' going on to exclaim that Edward was under his influence to such an extent that he was 'controlled in everything'.[26] The *Vita* claimed Baldock 'brought about the ruin of great men', which the evidence would suggest is true.[27] The same chronicler also claims that the Earl of Winchester was 'hated by everyone', while his son was 'arrogant'.[28] When Edward sought advice on how to proceed with Charles's settlement, Despenser was fearful that by accepting it, the king would need to leave England to perform homage. To ensure those on the council could not undermine him, Despenser challenged them declaring 'now we shall see who will advise the king to cross over to his enemies; he is a manifest traitor whoever he may be.'[29] Despenser was afraid. Unwelcome in France, and hated at home, he was only too aware that his power rested with the presence of Edward himself. Without the king by his side, Despenser was at risk and feared for his life. Yet threatening the council demonstrated his overconfidence. His emotional manipulation of Edward now ran so deep he was capable of threatening all those around him at court without fear of losing royal support. It had a dual effect. While it made Despenser all powerful and rich, which was his ambition, it also made him deeply hated. He was a threat to the nobles' own survival as they were cut off from their natural recourse to their king. By 1325 Despenser, his father, Stapledon and Baldock were detested, and their widespread influence was so negative and hostile that it had all the hallmarks of tyranny. Edward, under Despenser's influence, was now too invested in him to see the damage or to separate himself from this toxic political clique.

Despenser's threats played out and the assembled prelates and magnates informed Edward that the settlement was too significant for them to judge what was reasonable and instead it required parliamentary involvement. Parliament was summoned to meet on 5 June at Westminster where it agreed that Edward should accept the settlement, which the king confirmed on 13 June.[30] Despenser had been temporarily outmanoeuvred.

During these intense months, Edward had taken an active role in the Gascon crisis. He was as determined as ever to protect his rights and inheritance. He was at his best politically when he personally felt affected by grave injustice. The pressure on him, though, was significant and it is no surprise to find that he spent a great deal of time in 1325 in his small dwelling at Westminster, which he affectionately called 'little Burgundy'.[31] This gave him time away from the daily pressures of the court while he still remained close to the hub of political life. But even this respite was not sufficient to improve his mood to any measurable degree.

In the last three years, the king's temperament had grown more irascible and less tolerant of those who criticised him or opposed his policies. Years of ad hoc political opposition from his magnates from his accession until 1322 had made him increasingly sensitive to criticism. Despenser had helped heighten that by isolating the king from his nobility. In 1323–4 Edward spent much of his time 'making war against the ministers of Holy Church'.[32] He remained vehemently opposed to Adam Orleton, the disgraced Bishop of Hereford, believing, perhaps rightly, that Orleton was in some way connected to Roger Mortimer. Given anxiety at court about Mortimer's activities on the continent,

Edward was in no mood for reconciliation with his bishop. The bishop's temporalities remained confiscated, including his favourite manor of Shinfield.[33] Yet by 1325 Orleton reached out to Edward's cousin, Henry of Lancaster, brother and heir to the late Thomas. Henry replied to Orleton in sympathetic terms and when the king was handed copies of the letters in May, while staying at Winchester, Edward's temper boiled over. He accused his cousin of treason, throwing in that Henry's recent use of his brother's coat of arms was without his permission and therefore provocative.[34]

Henry, who had always remained loyal to Edward, was forced to defend himself claiming the use of the coat of arms was his hereditary right derived from his father, the late Edmund of Lancaster, the king's uncle, and not his own brother Thomas.[35] Making matters worse, Henry had recently erected a cross in Leicester in remembrance of his dead brother. He was earl there and Leicester was the only title he had been given by Edward after Thomas' execution in 1322. Given Edward's sensitivities in 1323 about the increasing number of pilgrims venerating the place of Thomas' execution and in St Paul's in London, it hardly helped quell the growing pro-Lancastrian tide. There were even secular pilgrimage badges made for those making trips to either site. For Edward it was all too much, and against a backdrop of intense pressure over Gascony, the king had little patience with his magnates. The result was to alienate one of his natural supporters, and the most senior earl currently living in England by virtue of his royal blood. During the year, Edward also fell out with his long-serving friend Walter Reynolds, Archbishop of Canterbury, over an internal dispute the archbishop had with William Melton, Archbishop of York.[36] The king quarrelled with Alexander Bicknor, Archbishop of Dublin, for, as Edward saw it, giving his half-brother the Earl of Kent poor advice about handing over the castle at La Réole in 1324. By May, Edward had written to John XXII requesting he be removed from office.[37] Internal division between Edward and his prelates and lay magnates had become a modus operandi and, with the clique at court led by Despenser, the atmosphere in England was both dangerous and divisive. The *Vita* lamented:

> The harshness of the king has today increased so much that no one however great and wise dares to cross his will. Thus parliament, colloquies and councils decide nothing these days. For the nobles of the realm, terrified by threats and penalties inflicted on others let the king's will have free play.[38]

As part of the Gascon settlement, Edward, according to the advice of parliament, suggested and secured a postponement for delivering homage for his French territories until 29 August.[39] By mid-August preparations were ongoing for Edward's crossing to France, but throughout the month, the king seemed indecisive in his commands as to whether he was going in person or not. Edward reached the Abbey of Langdon near Dover and while being hosted by his long-time friend William who was abbot, the king wrote to Charles IV claiming he suddenly felt unwell and was therefore unable to make the date for his homage but was still determined to do so soon.[40] The illness, certainly a ruse, gave Edward more time as he thought about sending his eldest son in his place. On 5 July the king resurrected the suggestion that the young Edward receive the duchy of Aquitaine and the County of Ponthieu, his oldest title, and head in his place to France. On 2 September the Bishop of Winchester was able to propose the option again to Charles, who accepted. The king was concerned for his own safety, anxious as ever that Roger Mortimer, who may have posed a risk to Isabella on her journey to Paris, would likewise attempt to capture or kill him.[41]

Unlike 1324 when the idea had first been mooted, England and France now had a workable peace accord. For Edward, sending his son removed the humiliation of bending the knee to the French king. It also allowed him to remain in the country protecting the Despensers, who were terrified of the king's absence.[42] The king swayed between sending his son and going in person, as is seen by his often conflicting instructions sent out through the month of August. Still uncertain of Charles' intentions and wary of the Capet reputation for political duplicity, Edward was right to be nervous. In the end, Despenser 'who was greatly hated by several great lords of the land and also by all of the commonalty, was very distressed and complained piteously to the king'.[43] His complaints worked for in the end, Edward fatefully decided to send the heir to the throne to France.

Even before Charles IV had sent his response, Edward had granted Ponthieu to his eldest son on 2 September. Eight days later, the young Edward was invested as Duke of Aquitaine. At Dover, Edward lectured his son about his duties and told him to follow the advice he had given. This included not marrying anyone without the king's express permission. Clearly Edward remained suspicious about the machinations of the king of France. On 12 September, the young Edward boarded a ship and crossed the Channel, arriving in Paris ten days later. In a great ceremony at Vincennes, the future Edward III, in the presence of his mother Queen Isabella and his uncle Charles IV of France, the young Duke of Aquitaine and Count of Ponthieu gave homage for his French territories. It was a lavish affair and attended by the English and papal envoys as well as the Duke of Burgundy.[44] In October, the duchy was formally restored by the king of France. Peace had been restored between the two countries.

Edward and his parliament had been conscious as far back as 1324 that sending both Isabella and the heir to the throne to France was a risk.

Now that peace had been restored the king expected Isabella and the Duke of Aquitaine to return to him immediately. However, before long it became apparent that Isabella was in no mood to leave her brother's court. Since 1322 her marriage had become increasingly strained and the central figure lurking behind this marital divide was Hugh Despenser the Younger. Isabella had been careful to hide her personal view but the confiscation of her lands and the reduced living standards she was made to endure were sufficient to outrage her. While historians have often claimed that her children, John of Eltham, Eleanor and Joan were removed from her by Despenser, this is not true. All royal children were given their own households at a very early age, sometimes shared between siblings but overseen by someone who was not their parent. This was true of Edward's own childhood. It was unfortunate timing that Isabella's children were given their own households at the same time that her lands were confiscated. The move may have been designed actually to ease the financial burden and Isabella herself did not, at the time or after, complain about the arrangement.

What was an issue was Despenser's usurpation of royal authority and his overarching influence. As that leverage over Edward became stronger and more threatening, Isabella was unable to influence her husband in a personal way or in her political role as principal intercessor. In royal correspondence issued in the name of the king, Despenser often wrote statements like 'it seems to the king and to us'.[45] It must have felt to some as if there were two kings, one in power and one in name only.

Rumours of a possible annulment to the royal marriage began to circulate and are found in some chronicles, but they were nothing more than hearsay. Such an action would only have resulted in war with France, something that Edward and his council had spent eighteen months trying to prevent.[46] Isabella's longstanding lady of the chamber since 1311, Eleanor de Clare, wife of Despenser, may have begun to spy on her if the Lanercost chronicler is to be believed.[47] If true, Isabella may have become aware of it. Edward and his queen appeared to spend more time apart. For Isabella, it was an affront to her dignity: and the subsequent breakdown of a previously successful marriage was to be principally laid not at Edward's door, but at Despenser's, as the queen herself made clear. Edward did nothing to retrieve the situation.

Against a backdrop of intimidation and general fear in England, the French court must have felt like a welcome retreat. It was, after all, her ancestral home. Isabella's brother may have promoted her concerns, and so when Edward began to demand Isabella's immediate return, Charles simply replied that the queen was there of her own volition and that he would not dismiss her for the love he bore her. Edward began to cut off Isabella's financial resources, the last payment from the Exchequer was made on 17 June, but her brother loaned her money to cover the shortfall to pay her living expenses.[48]

On 22 September, Walter Stapledon was sent with money and a simple message. The queen was to return immediately and if she did, she would be paid her expenses. Stapledon was ill-chosen to deliver such a sensitive message, given Isabella's feelings towards him, which Edward himself probably did not know at the time. As Stapledon announced his message to the queen in front of the royal French court, a furious Isabella retorted:

> I feel that marriage is a joining together of man and woman, maintaining the undivided habit of life, and that someone has come between my husband and myself trying to break this bond; I protest that I will not return until this intruder is removed, but, discarding my marriage garment, shall assume the robes of widowhood and mourning until I am avenged of this Pharisee.[49]

It was political and personal dynamite. Isabella's words caused panic back in England and a confused and no doubt humiliated Edward called for parliament to meet on 18 November.[50] Stapledon, horrified by Isabella's response determined that the French court was plotting against him and so, dressed as either a merchant or a pilgrim, fled to the coast without Isabella's permission, sailing back to England where he arrived on or before 29 September.[51]

In parliament Edward attempted to persuade those around him that the queen's behaviour was irrational and influenced by people around her in France. In a speech given at the opening of proceedings at Westminster the king said,

> You know all the long-standing disputes and processes between the king of France and us over the land of Gascony, and how providently, as it then seemed, the queen crossed to France to make peace, being told that when her mission was accomplished she should at once return. As and this she promised with good will. And on her departure she did not seem to anyone to be offended. As she took her leave she saluted all and went away joyfully. But now someone has changed her attitude. Someone has primed her with inventions. For I know that she has not fabricated any affront out of her own head. Yet she says that Hugh Despenser is her adversary and hostile to her ... it is surprising that she has conceived this dislike of Hugh, for when she departed, towards no one was she more agreeable, myself excepted. For this reason Hugh is much cast down; but he is nevertheless prepared to show his innocence in any way whatsoever. Hence I firmly believe that the queen had been led into this error at the suggestion of someone, and he is wicked and hostile whoever he may be.[52]

Edward pressed for advice from parliament, which suggested that each of the bishops write to the queen, urging her to return, highlighting that Hugh Despenser had proved his innocence and that he had only ever

> ...done anything in his power to help her; and that he will always in future do this, he has confirmed by his corporeal oath ... that he could not believe that these threats ever proceeded from your head alone, but that they came from some other source, especially as before your departure and during it you showed yourself gracious to him, and afterwards sent him friendly letters.[53]

The bishops' letters went on to implore Isabella not to invade as she had appeared to suggest in order to remove Hugh Despenser, as civil war in England could only lead to disaster.

On 1 December Edward began writing to Isabella, to her brother Charles IV and sixteen French bishops.[54] The king stated that he was surprised by Isabella's opposition to Hugh and that she was afraid of him, given her behaviour around him. Edward made clear that he had only ever treated his wife with honour and he expected her to return to him. The next day, the king changed tack and after sleeping on it, decided to write to his son to see if he could persuade him to return either with, or without, his mother.[55] All those frantic letters reveal Edward's deep unease about this hugely embarrassing and very public expression of their marital breakdown. However much he wrote, it was all too late. He had lost control of his wife and now his son. The combination was dangerous and given that Isabella remained at her brother's court and now in open defiance of her husband and Hugh Despenser in particular, what happened next could only be catastrophic for one or all of them.

22

Bloodletting

Roger Mortimer of Wigmore was never far from Edward's mind. After his escape from the Tower of London news reached the king as early as 10 August 1323 that the rebel lord had fled to France. Fear quickly spread through royal circles, quite possibly fuelled by the Despensers, who were the Mortimer family's long-standing enemies since the 1260s. Reports about Mortimer's potential whereabouts and plans conflicted. First he was said to be heading to his extensive estates in Ireland,[1] then that he planned to murder Edward, his favourites and chief ministers; and then, by December 1323, that the Lord of Wigmore was heading to Germany.[2] Edward became obsessed with security. If Mortimer remained at large, the king decided that he was a threat to him personally. Edward did as much as he could to isolate 'the Mortimer' as he took to calling him, writing to his brother-in-law in 1323 asking him to remove the rebel lord from France. With hindsight, Edward was right to feel the way he did.

Isabella's determination to hold out at the court of her brother Charles IV with her son, the young Edward, now Duke of Aquitaine, was borne out of one simple fact. The Despensers had to go, in particular Hugh Despenser the Younger. The queen had hoped that her dramatic speech would shame her husband into giving up his favourite. Yet Despenser's grip was so tight and Edward's affection so intense that even this failed to break the spell. If Isabella herself could not bring about the end of Despenser's dominance, no earl, prelate or baron in England could do so either. Edward had apparently called her bluff; but on this occasion it was no bluff at all. What would become deadly for the king was Isabella's next move.

On 8 February 1326, Edward publicly acknowledged a rumour that he now understood to be fact. The queen, he made clear, was now adopting the counsel of Roger Mortimer and his confederates.[3] When this began is unclear but from November 1325, a significant proportion of Isabella's household such as the marshals of her hall, Robert Sendal and Geoffrey

Mildenhale, began returning from France either because the queen could no longer pay their wages or because they feared Edward's wrath at the queen's refusal to return home. It is highly likely that some reported the alarming news of this new alliance. This immediately drove Edward to further panic and anger. The combination of losing control of his wife and his son, who were now working with his principal enemy, suddenly exposed his vulnerabilities and that of his regime.

Isabella wrote to Walter Reynolds on 5 February claiming she was afraid of Despenser, especially as he 'governs our lord and his entire kingdom' and declared that she could not return to her husband, which she desired, because her life was in danger due to the royal favourite.[4] Edward took to penning his own letters and on 18 March wrote to Charles IV imploring him in good faith to return his wife to him. The same day he wrote directly to his son reassuring him that his mother need not fear Despenser, but then more pointedly went on to accuse the queen of keeping Mortimer 'within and without house'.[5] This may be a euphemistic reference to a much greater fear: Isabella and Mortimer may have become lovers.

So is it true? We can never know for sure but it is certain that Isabella and Mortimer were united by a single common cause, the destruction of the Despensers. They most likely met up at Reims where Isabella, under the pretext of a pilgrimage, had travelled, close to the border with Hainault where Mortimer was residing.[6] After the queen's dramatic refusal to return to England, Mortimer must have quickly heard about it and made contact through a third party. Rumour had long persisted that he was attempting to raise a fleet in Hainault to invade England, but he lacked both the capital and the justifiable cause to attain his goal. Isabella's new position changed the game. Together they could overthrow the Despensers now that Edward had refused to give them up. Whatever the truth of it, Isabella and Mortimer from here on in certainly formed a mutually beneficial alliance. Any suggestion this began much earlier is impossible to substantiate and does not fit with Isabella's character or the evidence. Yet still, in these extraordinary times, Isabella and Mortimer's business-like relationship could easily have spilled over into something more intimate, given how closely they worked together under the intense pressure of the situation they found themselves in. They needed each other because a failure of one would destroy the other. Edward appeared to believe himself cuckolded. He realised he now faced a likely invasion. Once more he was called upon actively to defend his favourites, only this time it would be for all or nothing.

During the first few months of 1326, Edward's nerves were raw. The country became restless and the fear that Charles IV would support his sister and invade the south coast while the Scots would break their truce and invade from the north gripped the government. Threats became real, when on 19 January the chief baron of the exchequer and key Despenser associate, Robert Belers, was stabbed to death at Rearsby in Leicestershire. The murderers fled to France and quite possibly joined Isabella's growing group of discontented exiles.[7] The rebel captives of 1321–22, who were still in prisons around the country, were swiftly relocated to different castles and abbeys in case they were communicating with the enemy or at risk of being sprung. Roger Mortimer's mother, the redoubtable Margaret de Fiennes, was moved to Elstow Abbey in Bedford.[8] News continued to arrive, this time that the king's half-brother, the Earl of Kent, had remained in France with Isabella, as had the Earl of Richmond, Henry de Beaumont, and William Airmyn, Bishop of Norwich. The many people the king had clashed with since 1322 were now choosing sides; mostly, the other side. Hatred of the Despensers was so widespread and fear that the king was so under the influence of a malevolent man like Hugh led many to decide they had no alternative. At this moment the rallying cry of opposition was a simple one – removal of the Despensers and those evil councillors who surrounded the king, but not the king himself. He was, after all, anointed by God. Only if they acted together, could they achieve this – given that the fall of Lancaster in 1322 now meant rebellion would be punishable by death. There was safety in numbers.

Charles IV did little to dissuade his sister from her chosen course of action. Mortimer had been readmitted to the French court, despite Edward's earlier pleas to have him removed. On 11 May the Lord of Wigmore attended the coronation of Charles IV's queen, Jeanne of Évreux, at the Sainte Chapelle in Paris, wearing, rather provocatively, Edward's livery. While Isabella and Mortimer may not have been open about any intimacy, the fact Mortimer was present and allowed to stay is striking and symbolic. Charles was playing the game too. After Gascony, he could well afford to encourage political dissent in England, which could only weaken Edward's position.

By June, as Edward took back direct control of Gascony from his runaway son, Charles ordered French troops, who were in the process of withdrawing from the duchy, back in to secure key positions for his nephew. In August, Charles expelled or imprisoned English aliens in France, leaving Edward to reciprocate in England.[9] The whole Gascon crisis was once again on the verge of erupting into war. In January 1326, Edward heard from the Archbishop of Canterbury that the king of France had approached Count William of Hainault for his daughter's hand in marriage to Edward, Duke of Aquitaine, a proposal set in motion by Isabella. Given the threat of Mortimer's earlier presence in Hainault, and the rumour of a potential foreign invasion, the marriage of Edward's son could prove catastrophic to Edward II's position. On 3 January, he angrily penned a letter to Pope John XXII asking him to deny the papal dispensation necessary for the marriage, a requirement in canon law given that the potential bride and groom were too closely related.[10] Sending his son unmarried to the Continent was, in hindsight, proving to be a critical mistake and had been a risk Edward undoubtedly was aware of even before he sent him. Given his options in 1325, his decision was the best option from a bad set of cards he had left to play. The king was now fighting an uphill battle. With Isabella in opposition, Mortimer in alliance and possibly having an affair with Edward's wife, disgruntled exiles flocking to Isabella's banner, Charles IV rattling his sabre and the threat of Scottish invasion rumbling in the north, Edward can only have felt overwhelmed and mistrustful of everyone.

On 15 February the pope grasped the enormity of what was at stake and took pains to act as mediator. He wrote to Edward and Isabella, dispatching two papal envoys, the Archbishop of Vienne and the Bishop of Orange, who had only a year earlier helped to bring about some semblance of peace in Gascony. Two days later, the pope wrote to Hugh Despenser the Younger suggesting that he ought to retire from court, given that he was the sole reason why the queen was refusing to return to her husband.[11] Despenser ignored the request. On 19 May the envoys arrived in England and after a two-day conference with the king and his favourite but no one else, they departed for France.[12] The day after, Edward wrote to the pope insisting that the queen should return to him, adding that he was now aware that his wife planned an invasion into England.

Even at this juncture Edward still refused to give up the Despensers and those around him, though this would, at a stroke, remove the tenuous legitimacy and *primum mobile* of Isabella and Mortimer's opposition. Even a friendly but nevertheless direct challenge from Hamo de Hethe, the aged Bishop of Rochester, one of the few men from whom Edward listened to criticism, could not persuade the king to change course.[13] Hethe made it clear he thought Despenser should step away from court. As always, it is a mark of Edward's character that he held out against those who told him what to do or in his eyes impinged upon his royal dignity. He may well have believed that there was no going back anyway.

By June, invasion seemed almost inevitable. In a last attempt to avoid conflict, Edward wrote to his brother-in-law and the Bishop of Beauvais declaring his shame and humiliation at Isabella's behaviour and her ongoing association with 'the Mortimer'. On 19 June he wrote yet another letter to his son. The tension jumps off the page as Edward begs him to return home; but then his impatience appears to get the better of him. He ends by threatening the young Edward that if he continues to disobey his father's command 'he would for the rest of his life be an example to all other disobedient sons'.[14] Such a letter would hardly encourage obedience. By this time the king was utterly exasperated.

For Edward there would be but a small ray of light. By the summer, Charles IV began to fall ill and grew increasingly uncomfortable with the ongoing position of Isabella at his court. With papal envoys now involved, Charles could no longer be seen to actively support his sister's unconventional stance and her ongoing open association with Mortimer, which was now an embarrassment. Despenser's spies may have sensed the mood: Hugh sent large sums of money to the French court in a bid to convince Charles' councillors to withdraw their support for England's queen.[15] With her welcome fading fast, Isabella had no choice but to leave her brother's court, heading for Hainault and taking with her the young Edward, the Earl of Kent and Mortimer. Those other associates now in her service soon followed.

Edward and Despenser had spent much of the year preparing for a possible invasion. As early as February the king had ordered that the south coast be carefully guarded and in the same week further orders were given to search everyone entering and leaving the country to ensure they were not carrying subversive letters to the king's enemies or removing money, weapons and other such items that would aid Mortimer and his allies.[16] At the end of June, despite the pressure of the unfolding crisis, nine days later than usual, Edward took the time to pause and mark the anniversary of Piers Gaveston's murder, something that he did every year, both on the day of his lover's demise and his birthday. The grief still real. On 28 June, he asked the Convent of Leeds in Kent to remember to pray for Gaveston's soul.[17] The following month, he gave Hugh Despenser his copy of the tragic and doomed love story *Tristan and Isolde*.[18] The choice of subject matter makes clear Edward's deep attachment to him.

In early August, Isabella confirmed Mortimer's agreement with Count William for 132 ships and eight warships, underwritten against loss by her revenues from the county of Ponthieu that she had pledged two months earlier.[19] The real prize for the Count of Hainault came on 27 August when a betrothal was agreed between the young Edward and Philippa, one of the count's daughters. Isabella had secured her invasion force by offering her son as collateral. Edward pledged to marry his potential bride within two years, to provide her with the necessary dowry traditional for the queens of England and that he would secure the required dispensation from the pope who, it seemed, had heeded Edward II's plea not to grant one without his prior consultation. If their invasion failed and the marriage came to nothing, the young Edward was liable to a fine of £10,000. The deadly deal was done. Isabella gained her fleet.

As events in Hainault were unfolding, Edward and Despenser were continuing with preparations to defend the coast, and the country more widely. Hugh spent a great deal of time away from Edward, travelling about in the west, making plans which included Edward and the immediate court moving towards Wales, which echoed the strategy of 1321–22 that had proved so successful. In Wales the king could guarantee support and Despenser held his principal estates there, so felt he could rely on his tenants to rise up in his defence. As yet, they did not have good intelligence indicating from which direction an invasion fleet would come. As a result, through August, a complex plan was drawn up in which the largest ships were ordered to assemble at Portsmouth to repel a French invasion or to attack Normandy, while the smaller ships were ordered to protect the east coast from London up to Orwell in Suffolk.[20] Robert Waterville, a man who had previously been in the service of Bartholomew Badlesmere before 1321, was given command of the eastern fleet. Waterville had quickly gained a royal pardon following his master's fall and since then had shown the king nothing but loyalty and so was beyond suspicion. Beacons were erected to speed any word.

To escape the pressures of war planning, Edward joined a group of labourers at his palace at Clarendon to make hedges and dig a ditch.[21] While this kind of behaviour evoked scorn from the chroniclers and his contemporaries, it was something the king continued to do. He found great relief with his common subjects and his chamber accounts are littered with thousands of entries where he handed out money in person, or through his valets. He also went rowing, swimming or played games with his subjects whenever he could. He had a genuine affection for those he met, being enormously generous with his gift giving. While digging the ditch, he borrowed twelve pence, a week's wage for a well-paid labourer, so he could give it to one of the workers to buy shoes.[22] Despite the trouble with his enemies and unrest in parts of the country, Edward himself must have believed that the people of England were still with him as he himself knew and spoke to some of them frequently. What he may have failed to appreciate was that those in front of him would not have been prepared to tell him what others were saying.

War planning continued. On 2 September, 1,300 archers and 700 infantry were ordered to muster at Orwell and the king's half-brother, the Earl of Norfolk, was appointed to protect East Anglia.[23] Other key officials were given defence of various parts of the kingdom, including Henry Percy and Thomas Wake, who were to hold the north, while Henry of Lancaster was to hold the Midlands with the Earl of Winchester. Edward and Despenser may have been blind as to the direction of the invasion fleet, but they were taking no chances. They had a concrete plan, their bases were covered; on paper, this was sufficient to overcome the threat. All that remained, by September 1326, was for each man to play his role and the kingdom would be secure.

There was not long to wait. On 21 September Isabella had assembled her invasion fleet. Her army was between 1,000 and 1,500 men, of whom 700 were paid mercenaries, and included key English exiles.[24] Despite their small number and the enormous risk they now faced, Isabella, Mortimer, Kent and others must have been confident they would soon be joined by men in England if they landed safely. It is likely that despite Edward and Despenser's best efforts, Kent and others were in communication with sympathisers inside Edward's kingdom. The small invasion force set sail either from Dordrecht or Brill.[25]

After a three-day voyage, Isabella's force landed at the small port of Orwell in Suffolk. Edward's fleet, commanded by Robert Waterville, failed to appear and given that Waterville soon found favour with Isabella, it is likely he had been bribed to stay away or convinced to join her cause. Had he not, the fleet could have easily overpowered her army. Shortly after landing, Isabella and her men moved to Bury St Edmunds, where she was soon joined by Edward's half-brother, the Earl of Norfolk – the man who had been made responsible for protecting East Anglia. Norfolk, despite his blood tie to his half-brother, despised Despenser. Norfolk had been recently forced to sell to Despenser his lordship of Chepstow for an insultingly low price and Edward was deaf to his brother's complaints. In this, Norfolk was like so many others among his peers, secretly alienated men who wanted to see the Despensers fall from power.[26] As Isabella continued west through Cambridgeshire, then south to Hertfordshire and on to Dunstable in Bedfordshire, she was joined by Henry of Lancaster and, shortly after that, by Henry Percy and Thomas Wake. Edward's plan was rapidly falling apart as the leaders responsible for its delivery went over to the queen's side. As the queen moved around the Home Counties, people flocked to her. If there was any resistance, there is none recorded.[27]

Added to antagonism felt against the Despensers, fear of the king himself was growing. While none of those who opposed the Despensers at this stage sought Edward's deposition, his rule since 1322 had called into question many long-standing loyalties. Edward had systematically alienated many of his prelates, something which before 1322 was out of character with his rule. The effect was felt now during his moment of greatest need. As his key magnates began to melt away, so too did those prelates who had come face-to-face with Edward's Plantagenet rage. Henry de Burghersh, Bishop of Lincoln; John de Hothum, Bishop of Ely; and Alexander Bicknor, Archbishop of Dublin, quickly declared for the queen and made their way to join her.[28] As did Adam Orleton, Bishop of Hereford, who had felt Edward's wrath the most. He galloped from Hereford at great speed to join the queen at Oxford.[29] Edward's long-standing suspicions of Orleton may have been well founded after all and his later behaviour would suggest some connection with Mortimer since possibly before, and probably after, his escape from the Tower.

News of the landing reached Edward on 27 September, three days after the queen had disembarked. One of the ships in her invasion fleet, returning to Hainault, had been captured, or may have deserted, and headed up the Thames taking the news to the king, who was at the Tower.[30] Edward immediately sent out orders to muster his forces, all the while being careful to stress the safety of Isabella, his son and the Earl of Kent.[31] The next day he offered the massive reward of £1,000, equivalent to about half the annual income of a small earldom, to anyone who brought Mortimer's head to him. This only caused further resentment, which had been simmering under the surface in London. Shortly afterwards, a letter arrived in the capital from Isabella and the young Edward, explaining why they had come.

On 2 October Edward and both the Despensers kept to their plan and left London, heading into the west where the latter had been making preparations throughout the year. They took with them the enormous sum of £29,000 to aid them in raising a defence and left the much-loathed Walter Stapledon as keeper of the city alongside the mayor, Hamo de Chigwell.[32] Robert Baldock also followed the king, but Despenser's wife Eleanor was left at the Tower to guard Edward's youngest son, the ten-year-old John of Eltham.[33]

As the king moved west he was kept informed of the many defections of those who had been appointed to raise a defence. With the king now absent from London, a second letter arrived in the city on 9 October, again from Isabella and her son, imploring those within the city to support their joint cause and bring about the destruction of the Despensers.[34] The effect was electrifying. London quickly erupted into an orgy of violence. Hamo de Chigwell, the mayor, lost control of the city as the mob forced him to swear loyalty to Isabella despite the fact that in 1322 Chigwell had been one of the men who had adjudged Mortimer guilty of treason and sentenced him to death; a sentence Edward had commuted to life imprisonment. Chigwell gave way but was soon replaced by Richard Béthune because the city and the queen were unsure of his loyalties. Geoffrey le Scrope, the chief justice who had been raising troops for the king, became a target but managed to escape the mob by fleeing across the river to the south. Two days earlier, Walter Reynolds, the Archbishop of Canterbury, had called conclave at Lambeth to discuss Isabella's invasion. The conclave was attended by the bishops of Rochester, Winchester, Worcester, Exeter and London and by the 15th, Exeter and Rochester were in the city itself, caught up in the violence. Reynolds lost his nerve and fled into Kent, taking with him all of the

Bishop of Rochester's horses in his desperation to get away, leaving the aged bishop to escape the city on foot.

Walter Stapledon, Bishop of Exeter and until recently the greatly detested treasurer, attempted to make his way to the Tower but given the ensuing riot, cut short his journey across the city seeking sanctuary at St Paul's instead. He never made it past the north door as the angry mob caught up with him and dragged him to Cheapside where his head was cut off with a bread knife. John Paddington and William Attewelle, unfortunate enough to be in his company, were also beheaded, most likely in the same fashion.[35] John Marshal, a renowned ally of Despenser, was hunted down and beheaded. Looting and violence washed over the city like a wave and to mark their support for the queen, the mob sent Stapledon's head in a basket to Isabella who was shortly to arrive at Gloucester.[36] The following day, the Tower of London fell to the mob after they pressured constable John Weston to hand over the keys. Edward's prisoners, held there since 1322, were released. Roger Mortimer's uncle, Roger Mortimer of Chirk, was not among them. He had died there on 3 August. Eleanor Despenser was suddenly at great risk, as was Edward and Isabella's ten-year-old son John of Eltham, who was forced to swear loyalty to a hostile crowd and become the nominal guardian of the city, sworn to hold it for his mother, to which he duly agreed.[37] In another act of defiance, the Londoners dug out the plaque that had been erected commemorating the Ordinances in 1311, which Edward had removed the year after Lancaster's execution, and redisplayed it. For the city, Edward, as much as the Despensers, had become tyrannical.

As London descended into anarchy, the king, the Despensers, Baldock and others continued to move west with their household knights and retainers. By 9 October, seven days after leaving London, they had reached Gloucester while Isabella remained at Dunstable. There Edward ordered Henry of Lancaster's lands to be taken into royal custody, appointing Despenser's son, also called Hugh, to take possession.[38] Without his key nobles the game was fast shifting away from the king and he must have known it. Frantic attempts were made to raise yet more troops, but as events were moving so swiftly it was hard for anyone to either know where the king was or have the time to assemble to meet him. His Welsh supporters, the staunch leaders Rhys ap Gruffudd and Gruffydd Llwyd, were struggling to reach him. On top of this, Edward may have been popular in Wales throughout his reign but Despenser was certainly not. His grasping policies and actions in Wales since 1317 had alienated many – including his tenants. The Welsh had long memories and Despenser's brutal execution of Llewelyn Bren now came back to haunt him. As Edward and Despenser's plan fell apart, they knew they needed to enact a contingency. On 16 October they arrived at the mighty fortress of Chepstow, the castle that had set Norfolk against Despenser and lost Edward his half-brother's support. They needed to move to safety and fast.

Isabella was careful to follow in her husband's wake, at a distance, until she was sure of her numbers. The subsequent support of key nobles and prelates gave the queen and Mortimer confidence. Isabella published a letter while at Wallingford, where Edward had been only ten days earlier, confidently setting out why she and her army were present in England and in a state of array. Being careful to avoid any mention of Mortimer, Isabella's open letter was issued in the name of herself, her son and the Earl of Kent, which immediately gave legitimacy to their cause, guaranteeing a positive reception from most of those who read it.

The content was cleverly worded propaganda and placed the blame for all of the kingdom's poor government squarely at the door of the Despensers and men like Baldock. Edward was omitted and instead addressed as one who had been disinherited. The letter claimed the Church and the kingdom had been greatly diminished by the machinations of those evil councillors; that Hugh Despenser himself had set out to usurp and appropriate royal power; that the great men of the realm had been shamefully put to death, imprisoned, banished or exiled. The implied reference to men like Lancaster would resonate, as many still saw the dead earl as something of a champion. Isabella even threw in widows and orphans, who had been wrongly deprived of their rights.[39] It was powerful and it worked. Such an approach ensured the widest possible sympathy. The letter ended by saying that they – Isabella, her son, and Kent – had been deprived of Edward's goodwill and that they had come to relieve the realm and its people of all recent oppressions. It was to be a critical turning point. From here onwards, Edward had no hope of stemming the tide. Adam Orleton took to the pulpit at Oxford and began preaching one of many sermons, this one from Genesis, 3:15, 'I will put enmity between thee and the woman, and between thy seed and her seed; it shall bruise thy head and thou shalt bruise his heel.'[40]

On 20 October the king, Despenser the Younger, Baldock and a few others set sail from Chepstow, possible heading for Lundy Island in the Bristol Channel or to Ireland. Despenser the Elder was not among them, having stayed at Bristol Castle when the king and the party had passed through there to defend it. Ireland was a sensible option for there, with support from key magnates like John d'Arcy, Justiciar of Ireland, Edward would have been well received. He also had the support of Rhys ap Gruffudd and Gruffydd Llwyd in Wales, and hope, therefore, in a secure place, of raising an army.[41] Edward had the means financially to do it. But it seemed fate conspired against them, for the winds were contrary. Edward paid Despenser's confessor, who was on board, to pray to St Anne for fair winds, as all sailors of the period were wont to do, but it had no effect. On the 25th they had no alternative but to put in at Cardiff and make a dash for Despenser's mightiest fortress, the almost impregnable Caerphilly Castle.[42] Three days later, attempting once more to raise men, the king sent out urgent writs of summons to those in the south and west of Wales to ride to him and meet the invasion.[43] They were ineffective.

Edward's attempted flight had backfired. Whenever the king left England he was, by way of custom, obliged to appoint a *custos regni* to hold the administration and act in his stead while absent. Edward had done this many times, most controversially with Gaveston in 1308, who was given extensive powers, which the earl used conservatively. As Edward boarded his ship and sailed into the Bristol Channel it gave the queen, who had now arrived at Bristol on 18 October, the chance to seize royal power without ever meeting Edward or the Despensers in arms, which constituted treason and had posed a real risk of delegitimising their action.

On 26 October, the queen issued a document stating that as Edward had abjured the realm, leaving the country without government, the queen, therefore, had been advised by those prelates and nobles around her to appoint her son as guardian who would govern the country until the king's return.[44] The document carried no legal weight, but these were extraordinary times and with no one to stop her and most of the country with her, this simple declaration handed Isabella the kingdom. Two days later, the young Edward summoned a 'parliament' to meet at Westminster for 14 December.[45] On the same day the queen turned her attention to her secondary prize. Shortly after her arrival at Bristol, the castle garrison had refused to support the Elder Despenser and so the castle fell after a very brief siege. Hugh Despenser, 1st Earl of Winchester was hauled before a court presided over by the judge William Trussell, which included Henry of Leicester, now styled, for the first time, as Earl of Lancaster. The earls of Kent and Norfolk also sat in judgement, with Mortimer, Thomas Wake and others. In a mock trial, which mirrored that of Lancaster's, and Gaveston's before that, Winchester was given no defence or right to speak. He was accused of treason for usurping royal power, for ill advising the king and encouraging Edward to act against his prelates after 1322.[46] His sentence was a foregone conclusion but unlike Lancaster, there would be no leniency. The sixty-five-year-old, who had remained loyal to Edward throughout his reign, and his father before that, was drawn through the streets of Bristol, hanged until near-dead, his body mutilated and then beheaded in front of a jeering crowd. His head was taken to Winchester and put on display, while his body was fed to the dogs.[47]

News reached Edward shortly afterwards. The loss and brutality of Winchester's execution must have been devastating for the king, given that the elder Despenser had been at his side since before 1307. Perhaps he had been something of a father figure to him and now, in this moment of utter desolation, Edward must have realised the game was up. Capture now meant almost certain death for those in his company and, without an army, he had no way of protecting them; something he always did for his friends. With this in mind, the movements of the king in the first two weeks of November become somewhat erratic and make little sense. Edward and Despenser left the safety of the walls of Caerphilly Castle, leaving £13,000 behind them as well as the privy seal, and headed to the Cistercian abbeys of Margam and Neath. They arrived at the latter on 5 November, depositing items from Edward's baggage including money and jewels. There they paused for at least four days, no doubt frantically and chaotically planning their next move. On 10 November Edward carried out his last official act as king, appointing Rhys ap Gruffudd who had now reached him, and his nephew Edward de Bohun, to meet with Isabella and arrange a conference.[48] Whether they set out on their mission is not known but it soon became apparent that the queen had sent a formidable search party after the king and they were about to be captured.

In one final panic, Edward, Despenser and Baldock left Neath on 11 November to make the short journey back to the comparative safety of Caerphilly Castle. The journey was slow going and during or shortly after a storm on the 16th, Edward separated from the party as they passed through Llantrisant through what later became known as the Vale of Treachery. He may have been trying to give the others, including Despenser, the best possible chance of escape, believing that he was the principal prize. Such an act of loyalty at this desperate hour would not be atypical. That same day he was captured, apparently betrayed by a group of Welshmen and handed over to his cousin, Henry of Lancaster. His sacrifice – if such it was – achieved nothing. Despenser, Baldock and others did not get much further. They were captured, allegedly by men who included the sons of the murdered Llewelyn Bren, and were handed over to Henry Leyburne and Robert Stangrove, who escorted them in chains to Hereford and the waiting Isabella.[49] Edward was taken by Henry of Lancaster first to Monmouth Castle and then on to Kenilworth Castle, where he arrived on 5 December. Edward had earlier spent the whole month of April in 1326 at Kenilworth preparing to fight the anticipated invasion. He now returned a prisoner.

The king's humiliation continued. On 20 November, Adam Orleton was specifically selected to attend on Edward at Monmouth Castle and recover the great seal, which the king still had in his possession. The seal was essential for authenticating royal documents and its possession gave the owner the practical tools for the exercise of royal power. Of all the people to request this of the king, Orleton was the last that Edward could wish to see. He loathed the bishop and now, as they stood across the room from each other, all Edward's long-held suspicions about Orleton's conspiracies were confirmed. For Orleton, this must have been satisfying as the shoe was now on the other foot; something neither party had expected two years earlier. Edward refused to surrender the seal but after days of bullying he relented.[50] Official record claimed the king decided voluntarily to agree but this seems very unlikely and out of character, especially given it was Orleton who was doing the asking. By the end of November, all the mechanisms of government had been wrestled from the king.

The last grisly step for Isabella and Mortimer was now to make good on the queen's promise when she first resisted Edward's summons to return home to England. The fate of Despenser and those that supported him were long ago sealed. The bloodletting, which had begun in London shortly after the invasion, followed by the execution of Winchester at Bristol, now arrived at Hereford. Robert Baldock, the former chancellor, was, as a member of the clergy, beyond Isabella's grasp and so was handed over to Orleton, who imprisoned him in his London house. Soon Baldock was seized by a group of Londoners and thrown into the infamous Fleet Prison, to die on 28 May the following year.[51] The Earl of Arundel, who had supported the king and whose son was married to Despenser's daughter, fell afoul of his cousin Roger Mortimer, in particular. Arundel seems not to have had any trial but nevertheless fell victim to the new regime. On 17 November the forty-one-year-old earl was taken out into the streets of Hereford and there, and possibly deliberately, beheaded with a blunt axe or sword; it took twenty-two blows to finally severe his head.[52] Executed alongside him were John Daniel and Robert de Micheldever.

The bloodiest act was saved for Hugh Despenser the Younger. Anticipating his fate Despenser attempted to starve himself rather than give the queen, who wanted him executed in London, the satisfaction of his death.[53] As he weakened, Isabella was forced to execute him at Hereford. A travesty of a trial was arranged in which William Trussell, Lancaster, Norfolk, Kent, Mortimer and others were appointed to sit in judgement. As with his father's trial, and in mimicry of that of Lancaster's in which Despenser himself had sat as one of the judges, he was not allowed to speak.[54]

The accusations presented to him were extensive and comprehensive, many true, with some trumped up for good measure. In essence, Despenser was declared a traitor, a usurper of royal power and a tyrant.

He was charged with evil counsel, of working against the magnates and prelates of England, bringing about their destruction, including Thomas, Earl of Lancaster. His various and many land grabs and usurpation of people's rights, titles and liberties were noted, as was the death of so many men during the Scottish campaign of 1322 from starvation. He was accused of imprisoning Mortimer and of abandoning the queen, who was in danger at Tynemouth Priory in 1322, and attempting to send great sums of money to France to bring about Isabella's destruction. In all, he was told that all the good people of the kingdom, great and small, at all levels of society, thought him a traitor and a robber.[55] His sentence was to be predictably savage.

On the same day as his trial, 24 November, he was dragged through the streets of Hereford while wearing a crown of nettles and then partially hung on a 50-foot gallows.[56] After this part of his ordeal, and still very much alive, he was castrated, his genitals burnt in front of him, a reference to his alleged sodomitic relationship with the king. The chronicler Jean Le Bel who was present, went so far as to call Despenser a sodomite and heretic. Until this point, Hugh Despenser seemed determined not to make a noise or give his audience the satisfaction of seeing his pain. But as his abdomen was cut open and his entrails pulled out, the pain overcame him and he cried out in agony. Lastly, his head was cut off and his limbs quartered from his body. His head would be sent to London for display and his four quarters to the towns of York, Bristol, Dover and Carlisle.[57]

The orgy of violence into which the country had now descended was drawing to a short-term close. For Edward, news about Despenser's death would have reached him soon enough. In the space of only two months, the king had gone from a position of strength and freedom to a prisoner in his own kingdom, stripped of his dignity and the ability to exercise his royal power. Those closest to him had been savagely put to death including Despenser, a man he relied on for almost everything. His emotional state of mind at the end of the year can only be guessed at. It is not hard to think that he was utterly broken, overwhelmed by the enormity of it all and vulnerable to anything that now lay ahead. These were dark days but soon enough, they would become darker still.

23

End of All Things

While Edward spent Christmas alone at Kenilworth in 'great sadness', his enemies gathered at Wallingford Castle to begin planning the final act required to secure their extraordinary gains.[1] Since 1325, Isabella had suggested that she would return to Edward once Despenser was removed. Her earlier suggestions were now exposed as hollow. Through her actions, Isabella had humiliated Edward in front of the French court and the whole of Europe. Edward believed she had made him a cuckold. Isabella had defied his orders and betrothed their son to the daughter of the Count of Hainault in order to secure an invasion fleet and an army. The queen had turned or destroyed Edward's closest circle of councillors, men he thought of as friends; one most likely his lover. On Isabella's orders Hugh Despenser the Elder had been savagely put to death, a man whom Edward had by his side since before he became king. The following execution of Hugh Despenser the Younger and the king's incarceration meant one thing. For Edward and Isabella, there would be no chance of reconciliation and Isabella would do everything in her power to avoid it. Isabella and Mortimer were now most likely lovers. Reconciliation was out of the question. Adam Orleton, Bishop of Hereford, preached a sermon in which he claimed the king's cruelty prohibited the queen's return to her husband's side. Orleton luridly claimed that Edward carried a knife in his hose, ready to kill his wife whenever the opportunity arose. However theatrical and untrue this may have been, it silenced the debate.[2]

All that now remained was what to do with the king himself? Most agreed that Edward could not simply be released and allowed to continue to govern. Given the king's taste for holding grudges and propensity for revenge, coupled with his expert ability in sowing discord between his enemies, most at Wallingford feared a repeat of 1322. They suspected, and not without good reason, that their lives would be in danger if Edward regained his royal power. Death was out of the question, especially for the prelates who refused to consider such a course of action. There was only one solution: deposition. But this dramatic step was of course beset with problems. No king had ever been removed from the throne before. Edward had been anointed by God at the ancient ceremony of the coronation. It set him spiritually above his people. There was no precedent. There was no legal process. In order to bring it about, a clever scheme of smoke and mirrors and calculated theatre would need to be devised. Roger Mortimer, his cousin Thomas Wake, and the Bishop of Hereford, now came into their own. Their united determination, with that of Isabella herself, was the driving force that would bring about what until now had been unthinkable. The propaganda machine continued in its work. While at Wallingford, Orleton took the opportunity to preach a further sermon which accused Edward of sodomy and tyranny. The reference to sodomy was a clear indication that rumour, or simply knowledge of the king's relationships with his male favourites, was something to capitalise on in order to blacken his character and it was quickly seized upon. It was also typical in this period to associate sodomy with tyranny in order to damage the reputation of an enemy, whether the party was guilty of sodomy or not.[3]

Deposition, it had been decided, would be enacted in parliament, which the young Edward had called in his father's name on 28 October, and which had been delayed on 3 December until 7 January at Westminster.[4] All that remained was for the king to attend in person, and Orleton and perhaps the Bishop of Winchester were dispatched to Kenilworth to bring the king south. They arrived on 4 January. Edward, despite his emotional fragility, had enough of the Plantagenet rage in him to lambast his enemies, 'curs[ing] them contemptuously, declaring that he would not come upon his enemies – or rather, his traitors'.[5] The king realised he still had one card to play. Without the king present at parliament then the body, in law, was no parliament at all. Any gathering of the prelates, nobles, barons and representatives of the towns and boroughs was merely an assembly, without power and legal definition. By staying away, Edward could outmanoeuvre his opponents. It was an apparently clever strategy but, at this stage, one that missed the point. The determination of his enemies was so great that they would carry on regardless. Edward's absence also deprived his few remaining supporters a platform upon which to create wider sympathy. The king's presence could have tipped the balance making his deposition all the harder to enact. The king had unwittingly outmanoeuvred himself.

The 'parliament' did not officially begin until 12 January, when the delegation returned from Kenilworth with news of Edward's defiance. If Isabella and Mortimer were expecting a speedy result, they were to be disappointed. As Orleton asked those who had assembled whether Edward should remain as king, the body showed they were divided. The enormity of the decision in front of them, great unease at the absence of the king, and the knowledge that this action was unprecedented, all played their part. The king still had support. William Melton, Archbishop of York, the bishops of Rochester, London and Carlisle, and possibly more, stood by Edward in his greatest hour of need. It was soon apparent to Orleton that this was going nowhere, and so the assembly was dismissed for the day.

Roger Mortimer and Isabella changed tack. If there was suspicion and unease in the assembly, then Mortimer would do everything to exploit it. He called upon the support of his ally, the recently appointed mayor of London, Richard de Béthune, who wrote to the assembly inviting them to swear to maintain the queen, the heir to the throne and more pointedly to bring about the deposition of the king in an oath to be given publicly at the Guildhall after the following day's session in parliament.[6] Given recent events in the city, where prelates as much as laymen were hunted down and executed, the threat was far from subtle. Fear of the London mob was sufficient to begin to silence voices loyal to the king and slowly but surely Mortimer and Isabella were shifting the balance in their favour. That evening, Mortimer met with the earls and principal barons in Westminster Hall, at which it was unanimously agreed that the king should lose his crown in favour of his son.[7] With a key body of support among the nobles, the threat of the London mob behind them, and leading prelates like Walter Reynolds, Archbishop of Canterbury, now with them, there was enough support to bring about their plans.

The date 13 January 1327 should perhaps be remembered in English history as much as 1066 and 1215. As the body of parliament assembled, a coup de théâtre was expertly managed. First Roger Mortimer took to his feet, declaring that he was merely the messenger and he could inform those assembled that the magnates had unanimously agreed Edward II should be removed from power. Edward's rule, Mortimer said, was 'inadequate'; he had broken his sacred coronation oath, taken evil counsel, destroyed the Church as well as his rightful counsellors.[8] At this, Mortimer's cousin Thomas Wake, primed in his role, jumped to his feet echoing the remark that the king should be removed from power.

Next it was Adam Orleton's turn. He began a sermon taken from the Book of Proverbs, preaching 'where there is no governor the people shall fall'.[9] It was well selected. Orleton explained the details of his visit to Kenilworth, how he had made it clear to the king that the people had given up on his misrule and his 'intolerable defects'. Edward, Orleton declared, had fought back, insisting that he had followed the council ordained and given to him.[10] As Orleton sat down, it may have been at this stage that the articles of deposition were read out to the gathering.

The articles of deposition set out the grounds for the king's removal. He was accused of being personally incapable of governing his people; of allowing himself to be advised by evil counsellors; of losing Scotland, parts of Gascony and lands in Ireland, which had come to him in peace. The latter, in particular, is, of course, far from the truth. Edward was also accused, among other things, of destroying the Church, imprisoning churchmen as well as exiling, imprisoning, disinheriting or putting to death the great men of the kingdom. The king's unusual habits or 'occupations', especially fraternising with his subjects, were marked out as reasons for his removal, especially because the king devoted time to these rather than governing the kingdom. He was accused of abandoning his country and his people when he set sail in 1326 with Despenser and his followers. Importantly, as at other times during his reign, Edward was accused of failing to observe his coronation oath and ultimately, and damningly, of being incorrigible and therefore without hope of improvement. It was held that these alleged failings were so notorious and widespread that there was no way of denying them and so, implicitly, that there was no other course of action for those assembled to take.[11] Interestingly, nowhere in the articles was Edward accused of tyranny, a claim reserved for Hugh Despenser the Younger. This suggests a view that Edward had been under Hugh's emotional manipulation and therefore not the perpetrator of many of the events that would bring the downfall of both.

The Bishop of Winchester then stood up and preached, taking as his lesson 'my head hurts' from the Book of Kings.[12] The suggestion was another simple one. Edward he said was head of the kingdom, and if the head was corrupted by weakness then so was the kingdom. The head therefore had to be changed and for this, the young Edward should become king. The spectacle was building. Thomas Wake, on cue, jumped up again to rally the assembly and demanded to know if they agreed. A wave of support flowed through the room; the tide was quickly turning and those too afraid to oppose, now very much in the minority, stayed quiet. Lastly Walter Reynolds, the former friend of Edward II, who like Despenser the Elder had been at Edward's side when he was the Prince of Wales, now did the only thing left open to him. In fear of Isabella and Mortimer, and therefore in an act of self-preservation, Reynolds declared that 'the voice of the people is the voice of God'; in essence that God willed it and, through those assembled, had empowered them to bring about change to save the kingdom.[13] Thomas Wake finished by shouting 'let it be done, let it be done' and many of those in the chamber joined in, swept up in the growing fervour. The young Edward was ushered into the chamber and presented as the new king, which was then followed by the singing of 'Glory, laud and honour'.

Not all there were caught up in that heady moment of political drama. The aged Bishop of Rochester was later accosted for his failure to participate in the singing.[14] Fear in the chamber was real. Over the next few days, the Londoners extracted their requested oath at the Guildhall, Roger Mortimer being the first to take it. When it came to it, the Guildhall oath now excluded the demand for deposition, the very thing parliament had been induced to deliver by the implicit threat of retaliation if they had failed. The threat had been nothing but a ruse, and Mortimer and de Béthune had played their parts well. They had secured what they needed and that was sufficient.[15] That said, the records show there were many who subsequently failed to take the oath, no doubt angry at such duplicity. In the end it mattered not. The deed was done. Edward II was about to lose his crown.

The end came on 20 January. Edward received the Bishop of Winchester and Lincoln in his chamber at Kenilworth Castle.[16] There they delivered the news privately to the king, which Edward by now must have suspected and spent days working himself up to resist. Given his lifelong determination to protect his royal dignity, even now he must have fought hard against the suggestion that he should voluntarily give up his throne, making way for his son. He held firm. They tried to assure him that he would be treated with the utmost respect for the rest of his life. It was a poor argument. The two bishops resorted to threats. If he did not relinquish his crown he could, according to the colourful account in le Baker, be replaced with someone not of his direct line. That implied Mortimer. While the notion of replacing Edward with anyone other than his heir would not have been conceivable or acceptable to anyone in England at the time, least of all Isabella, or leading magnates like Lancaster, Norfolk or Kent, it may have been used as a tool to force Edward to abdicate. The king, locked away and starved of information at Kenilworth, would have had no sense of the political climate in England following the invasion. The threat, as far as the king knew, magnified by his earlier preoccupation that Mortimer was dangerous beyond measure to everyone, even Isabella, was believable.

The two bishops were not alone. Shortly after their conference with the king, the rest of their delegation, which included another twenty-two men, representative of the prelates, earls, priors, justices, knights of England, citizens of London and the Cinque ports, then arrived. By this stage the king was utterly exhausted, highly emotional and battleworn. Everything he knew, everything that characterised his life, was in the balance and he knew it. Eventually Edward entered the adjoining chamber dressed in a black robe to hear their commission. He could barely stand and may well have fainted, being helped to his feet by his cousin, Henry of Lancaster, and the Bishop of Winchester.[17] Adam Orleton, one of Edward's bitterest enemies, stepped forward and informed the king of why they were there and demanded that he abdicate. Edward must have refused. He began to weep, perhaps he also became angry, again it is not all that clear. But in the end he could not hold out against such overwhelming and widespread resistance to his rule. At some point he must have given in. William Trussell, the man who had pronounced judgement on both the Despensers, then stepped up and formally renounced homage on behalf of the entire kingdom.[18] Finally, Sir Thomas Blount, the steward of the royal household, symbolically broke his staff of office.[19] Edward had been forced to abdicate, but it was more deposition than abdication. He lost his throne only a few miles away from where Gaveston lost his life.

Edward was no longer king but Edward of Caernarfon, the title of his birth. Occasionally in official records he would also be called 'Edward, the king's father'. On 24 January, a general proclamation was made in London, announcing that Edward II had renounced his throne and that his son, the young Edward, was now to wear the crown.[20] Shortly afterwards, on 2 February, Edward III was hastily crowned at Westminster Abbey, although he was soon to discover that he was far from inheriting the royal power. For the next three years, until October 1330, it would be Isabella and Mortimer who would rule in Edward's name.

On the same day as the coronation, Isabella received a self-made grant awarding her an annual income of £13,333 or 20,000 marks.[21] It was unprecedented and made her the richest person ever in England, except the king himself, and indeed the wealthiest throughout the medieval period as a whole. The queen also received the vast personal treasure of Hugh Despenser the Younger and the executed Earl of Arundel.[22] Mortimer initially received little in way of grants, beyond the restitution of his property, conscious that he should not be seen to behave like Edward II's royal favourites. However, what Mortimer lacked in grants he made up for in power. Through his relationship with Isabella, and the young age and inexperience of the new king, Mortimer had more than wealth could buy, so long as he could control the king. By the close of January 1327, Isabella and Mortimer had delivered a political coup that was more far-reaching than anything the Despensers had ever achieved. By the time of their fall from power in 1330, the enormous treasury that Edward II had amassed was entirely spent, the magnates of England were sickened and on occasion, victims of Isabella's and Mortimer's widespread misrule and tyranny. These were extraordinary times that turned even the most reasonable individuals into tyrants.

Edward remained in the custody of his cousin, Henry of Lancaster, until 3 April. Little is known of his stay at Kenilworth but he certainly would have had the freedom of the castle and was to all intents and purposes treated kindly.[23] The king's state of mind is hard to determine, but the stress he had gone through since September 1326 must have been taking a heavy toll. By the end of March, Lancaster and Mortimer had clashed over a renewal of the war in Scotland and the queen and her lover were all too aware that Lancaster, like his brother before him, was the premier earl in England. They needed to wrestle Edward from him, otherwise, should Lancaster have a change of heart and restore Edward to the throne, they were all in danger. To this effect, while Lancaster was at court, formal custody of the king was passed to Thomas de Berkeley and his brother-in-law John Maltravers, neither man supporters of the former king.[24] The transfer was a duplicitous trick. Lancaster himself claimed later that Edward had been forcibly removed from his custody by Mortimer. True enough, the Baron of Wigmore was in the vicinity of Kenilworth at the time of the transfer with a large group of armed retainers to add leverage to the demand that the constable of Kenilworth hand over the former king. Edward was moved under heavy guard to Berkeley Castle in Gloucestershire, arriving there on 5 April.[25] It would later be claimed in 1330 in the charges levied against him that Mortimer had forcibly removed Edward in order to bring about his murder.[26] Whether this was true or not, Lancaster had been outmanoeuvred: but Edward himself, even from his prison, remained a real threat to the new regime.

At Berkeley he was kept in a room above the gatehouse of the keep, which was one of the strongest parts of the castle. Here, the chronicler Adam Murimuth who was in the south-west during the time of Edward's captivity, and who knew Isabella and Mortimer, thought that Thomas de Berkeley treated Edward humanely, Maltravers 'otherwise'.[27] At some point Thomas Gurney, a Somerset knight, was also appointed as a keeper of the king, alongside these two men. The close rolls show that his keepers were awarded the significant sum of £5 a day to maintain the king's welfare, so it is likely Edward did have some comfort, albeit possibly far less than that at Kenilworth.[28] His guards also received a further £500 in cash, which was taken from the treasure Edward and Despenser had stored at Caerphilly Castle.[29] Whether this money was spent on the king's personal welfare is uncertain, but there is little reason, after their wages had been deducted, to believe otherwise.

Tales of Edward's captivity have become the stuff of legend. No more so than the story that the king's room, which is indeed located next to a deep shaft or well, was filled with rotting animal carcasses to promote disease and bring about Edward's death. Such claims only appear in two places, the long version of the Brut chronicle and that of le Baker. The latter, writing in the 1350s and far removed from events was careful to depict Edward as a saintly martyr at a time when there were calls for the dead king's canonisation. It is safe to assume that such stories are fanciful. Just as was the equally spurious claim that while in captivity Edward penned a poem, lamenting his fate, which was most likely written about that time but by another, sympathetic to the king's cause.[30]

Certainly at the time of Edward's forced abdication not everyone in England supported the king's removal from the throne. No sooner had Edward lost the crown, than rumours were afoot in the Midlands, and more widely, that men were working to bring about his release from captivity. In March, a commission was appointed to look into reports that the Dunheved brothers from Dunchurch in Warwickshire and their accomplices were attempting to spring Edward from his prison. This may have been one of many reasons why the king was moved to the south-west. By July, another plot was hatched, involving the same group of people who had grown in number and had apparently, at least initially, succeeded in their plan. According to a letter written by Thomas Berkeley to the Bishop of Ely, Berkeley makes reference to an earlier letter where he described how a large group of men had approached Berkeley castle, seized the king and plundered the fortress.[31] It is unclear whether Edward got beyond the castle grounds itself; or if so, he must have been recaptured within days. For Edward it must have been a remarkable moment, a brief one, that gave him hope where there had only been months of darkness. He may also have learnt that not everyone in the country was against him.

Those who conspired to help the king were mostly Dominican friars and other members of the clergy. The ringleaders, the brothers Stephen and Thomas Dunheved, knew the king. The former had previously held the manor of Dunchurch, the latter had been one of Edward's personal confessors. Others in the party were thought to be Dominicans from Warwick, who may well have attended the body of Piers Gaveston following his murder in 1312, as well the knight, Edmund Gacelyn, who had previously been in the service of Hugh Despenser the Younger.[32] Orders for the arrest of the brothers went out in June, perhaps shortly after the attack on the castle.[33] Whatever their limited success, the official records remain suspiciously quiet, no doubt keen to avoid any public awareness that the king was not securely held. The Dunheved brothers and their comrades were hunted down and were imprisoned or escaped.

At the same time, Robert Bruce had invaded northern England shortly after Edward II's fall from power. Disturbingly for Isabella and Mortimer, in Bruce's retinue was Donald, Earl of Mar. Loyal to Edward throughout his reign, Mar may well have persuaded Bruce to invade. When Bruce travelled to Ireland in late spring, where Edward III's rule had not yet been proclaimed, the suspicion that Bruce was working to free Edward II sent hares running. Rhys ap Gruffudd joined Bruce's ranks. The former had been with Edward at Neath, just days before his capture in November 1326. Perhaps his parting mission, after all, had been another more desperate one; to rally support for the king beyond his borders, which would tie in with Edward's attempt to take ship with Despenser to Ireland. If true, Bruce could have expected Scottish independence as a price for Edward's restoration and for the first time in his life, Edward may have granted it, given he had no alternative. Whether this is true or not, and no direct evidence survives, the new regime saw Bruce's activities as a menace.

As a result of these plots, Isabella and Mortimer applied the same strategy that Edward and Despenser had deployed in the years after 1322. The king was temporarily moved from castle to castle, which probably included Corfe in Dorset as well as Bristol.[34] Travelling by night and being moved under heavy guard, the regime could feel safer in the knowledge that any attempt at rescue was now less likely. However, despite their efforts a third plot, and the most serious, was discovered. On 14 September 1327, Roger Mortimer's man in North Wales, William Shaldford, wrote to his master reporting that Rhys ap Gruffudd and Gruffydd Llywd in North Wales were working together to seize Edward from Berkeley and restore him to his throne.[35] The threat was real, underpinned by their influence in Wales. Given the number of plots that had sprung up since the late spring, it must have felt to Isabella and Mortimer that they were facing the hydra. Something had to be done and quickly, before they lost control of Edward entirely.

That something was yet another strand of the same policy of smoke and mirrors, which had been applied since before the invasion. Edward needed to disappear and death was the best option available to them, or at any rate the perception that the king was no longer alive. William Ockley was dispatched while Mortimer was conveniently in the south-west to deliver a letter to John Maltravers and Thomas Gurney at Berkeley Castle. The letter came with a message, which simply requested they 'acquaint themselves with its content and find an appropriate remedy to avoid peril'.[36]

On 22 September Thomas Gurney sped away from Berkeley Castle, heading eventually for Lincoln where he arrived late in the evening on the 23rd. There he presented a letter to the king, who was in the town holding parliament, which had been in session since 15 September. Edward III was informed that his father was dead. Within hours, possibly in the early morning of 24 September, Edward III wrote to his cousin, the young Earl of Hereford, informing him that his father had died but also that England was on the brink of being invaded by the Scots.[37] Four days later, a formal announcement was made in parliament that Edward had succumbed to death by natural causes on the feast of St Matthew the Apostle and Evangelist, that is to say, on 21 September. For those gathered at parliament, it must have been a surprise and while no one at this stage raised any suggestions of foul play, it must have quickly crossed the minds of many. It was all too convenient. Edward I had died at the age of sixty-eight, Edward III himself would die at the age of sixty-five. Edward II, whose constitution was more than robust, was apparently dead of natural causes at forty-three.

Contemporaries and those writing within a few years after the king's pronounced death were increasingly suspicious. The *Anonimalle* chronicle, one of the short versions of the Brut, thought Edward had 'become ill and died'.[38] The annalist of St Paul's did not think to offer a suggestion simply stating that Edward 'died at Berkeley … where he was held prisoner'.[39] Others, however, become increasingly more vocal. Lanercost thought the king had died naturally or because of the violence of others.[40] Murimuth initially wrote that the king died at Berkeley, but by the time he writes of the fall of Mortimer in 1330, the chronicler goes so far as to record the common perception that he had been murdered and the chosen method was suffocation.[41] The French *Chronicle of London* stated that the former king was 'vilely murdered' while the formal accusations presented against Mortimer in November 1330 accuse him of 'falsely and traitorously' murdering the prisoner.[42] As the century wore on, the long version of the Brut and the colourful account of le Baker claim that Edward's death was something far more lurid and violent. The Brut states:

> After dinner when the king had gone to bed and was asleep, the traitors … went quietly to his chamber and laid a large table on his stomach and with other men's help pressed him down … the tyrants, false traitors, then took a horn and put it in his fundament as deep as they could, and took a spit of burning copper, and put it through the horn into his body, and often times rolled it there within his bowels, and so they killed their lord and nothing was perceived.[43]

Such lurid tales were also taken up by le Baker and the *Polychronicon* nearly thirty years after the event, influenced by a copy of the Brut. The story of the red-hot poker fails to hold up to any real scrutiny. According to le Baker the screams Edward made as he was subjected to such torment were heard over a mile away. Such an act of barbarity, while seen by some as poetic justice playing on the king's reputation as a lover of men, are surely invention.[44] If the murder of the king was carried out that night, it most certainly would have been done quietly. Any likely cause of death would have been something far more simple and is suggested early enough in the chronicles, who themselves were relying on gossip and hearsay. The method of violence deployed would most likely have been suffocation, one that could be easily carried out. Roger Mortimer, through his agents William Ockley and Thomas Gurney, was held to be culpable by 1330. After Mortimer's fall, Edward III offered a reward for the capture of Gurney and Ockley; Gurney at £100 and Ockley at 100 marks if caught alive. If dead, the king would pay 100 marks for the head of the former and £40 for the latter.[45]

All that now remained was for the burial of the king's body. Much as with his father Edward I in 1307, the body could not be buried immediately given Edward III's preoccupation with fighting a war against the Scots. Edward's body therefore lay in the chapel at Berkeley Castle until 21 October, when it was moved to the Benedictine Abbey of St Peter's, now the magnificent Gloucester Cathedral. During this time, it was watched over by Sir William Beaukaire, whose presence at Berkeley is suspicious. While Beaukaire had formerly been in Despenser's service right up until the latter's execution, he arrived at Berkeley on 21 September, before the death of the former king. He was an odd choice of guardian, given his former association with the king. There the body was quickly eviscerated and embalmed by a local woman and not the king's physician, which was the usual custom. In preparing the body, first the king's heart was removed and placed into a silver vase, for which expenses of 37s 8d were later claimed from the Exchequer by Thomas Berkeley.[46] The vase was then given to Isabella, who had it included inside the breast of the effigy of her tomb when she herself died in 1358.[47] Edward's body was wrapped carefully from head to toe in cerecloth, heavily impregnated with wax to seal the corpse and prevent further corruption. If there were any marks of violence upon the body then they were not visible by the time anyone else saw it. After this point, abbots, priors, knights and burgesses from Bristol and Gloucester were invited to view the body, but given that the embalming had already taken place, could only view the corpse 'superficially'.[48]

By mid-October it was decided that the body should rest at St Peter's Abbey, which itself had close royal connections as the burial place of Robert Curthose, eldest son of William the Conqueror and place of the coronation of Henry III, Edward II's grandfather in 1216. Westminster, while increasingly used as the Plantagenet royal mausoleum, was too close to London where the populace had so recently violently revolted. Gloucester was safe, prestigious enough, and only 15 miles from Berkeley. On 21 October, the abbot John Thokey received the corpse, which had been carried on a richly decorated hearse sent from London and received by the local populace in a great procession as it approached the abbey.[49] Once there, more watchers were appointed, including John Eaglescliff, the Bishop of Llandaff, and Hugh de Glanville, who remained with the coffin until the funeral on 20 December.[50] The hearse was later replaced and Edward was surrounded by four gilded lions supporting mantles bearing the royal leopards of England, as well as statues of the four Evangelists, eight angels and two lions rampant.[51] In all, it was a symbol of royal majesty. Again, while the coffin sat in the abbey, the body was not visible, wrapped in cerecloth; and for the first time in royal funerals a wooden effigy was carved of the image of the king dressed in his coronation robes from 1308 and placed on top of the coffin. This image itself may have later been used to craft the magnificent alabaster effigy that now adorns the king's tomb.

The funeral took place on 20 December 1327 and was attended by Edward III, Isabella, and Roger Mortimer, who was dressed in new clothes of rich black; he would later be executed in them. Other than that, and assuming all the prelates, magnates and important civic representatives would have been present, little more is known. It would have been a grand affair designed to impart the symbolic moment of the old king's passing and the beginning of the new king's rule. The coffin was interred under an arch on the north side of the Presbytery adjacent to the Ambulatory, up near the high altar and initially a plain Purbeck marble slab was placed over it. However, beyond this, there is nothing of the funeral in any official record, which is out of character for royal funerals before and since. It was almost as if the whole event was yet one more smokescreen.

The reality, at least to Isabella and Mortimer, was that the funeral was indeed one more piece of theatre. For despite the grand show at the abbey, Edward of Caernarfon was alive.

24

Redemption

On 19 March 1330, Edmund of Woodstock, Earl of Kent, stood in a crowded market place at Winchester. He had been waiting for hours. But this delay was more than a mere inconvenience, for Kent awaited his execution. Found guilty of treason by Robert Howell, the king's coroner, on accusations brought by Roger Mortimer with a kowtowing parliament in support, the appointed executioner refused to cut off the earl's head. In the end, a latrine cleaner, himself facing punishment, was granted a pardon in exchange for dispatching the earl. The twenty-eight-year-old Edmund was beheaded before an ominously silent crowd. Half-brother to Edward II and son of Edward I, Kent's crime struck at the very core of Isabella and Mortimer's regime. Kent's transgression was extraordinary; not only did he believe that Edward II was alive, but that he had attempted to free his half-brother from his secret prison at Corfe Castle – some three years after the king's apparent funeral – a funeral that Kent himself had attended.[1]

In a terrified confession it had emerged that the earl was unequivocal in his belief, and that he had the support of nearly forty others, including high-profile members of the court such as the Archbishop of York, the Bishop of London and the mayor of London, Simon Swanland.[2] Kent had learned of Edward's whereabouts and spent 1329 building a secret coalition of supporters to bring about Edward's release. William Melton, Archbishop of York, had written to the mayor of London organising provisions and money, up to £5,000, in preparation for the king's escape.[3] The plan was well thought out. After Edward was sprung from his gaol, he was to board one of three awaiting ships commandeered by John Gymmynges and a monk of Quarr Abbey on the Isle of Wight. He and his party were to sail along the south coast to Kent's castle at Arundel; after which, he would be taken to the Continent, perhaps to Brabant were his nephew was duke and his sister Margaret still alive. There the king could recover, rebuild his forces and launch an invasion to reclaim his kingdom.

Support for Kent's action had grown wider through 1329. Kent's supporters certainly believed his claim, for they threw in their all to bring about the former king's release. If they failed, they could expect the same punishments as those caught up in the bloodletting of 1326. Kent eventually lost his life, while his family were placed under strict house arrest. Other supporters lost lands and were imprisoned or exiled. In this endeavour these men and their families were not acting on a mere whim. They would not gamble with their own freedom or worse still their lives, those of their families and their right to their possessions and inheritances, unless they were utterly convinced.

The regime of Isabella and Mortimer had become at least as avaricious and dangerous as that which it had replaced. As time wore on, Roger Mortimer looked more like Hugh Despenser the Younger, acquiring lands and power. A reluctant Edward III invested Mortimer with the newly created title of Earl of March in October 1328. Mortimer's wealth and possessions now eclipsed Despenser himself. Isabella continued with her own landgrab and Edward III found himself a king in name only. In 1328, Isabella and Mortimer had agreed to the unthinkable, a peace settlement with Robert Bruce in which the latter's claim to the Scottish crown and therefore Scottish independence were duly recognised. Although Edward II lost the battle of Bannockburn, and battles thereafter in his conflict with his Scottish enemies, he had always held out against this, even when faced with war on multiple fronts. Isabella and Mortimer simply surrendered English claims in a treaty that became known as 'the Shameful Peace'. Henry of Lancaster began raising troops later that year to challenge Mortimer, but in the end, civil war was narrowly avoided. Against such a backdrop, those supporters of Kent certainly had a motivation for opposition to the regime, but such an opposition was only going to be successful if Edward of Caernarfon could be produced at the end of it. Anything else would not have bound the party together sufficiently to bring about the fall of Isabella and Mortimer. Edward III himself was still untried and unable to stem the tide. Edward II had to be alive and therefore returned to his throne, thereby restoring the natural order of succession.

So was it true? Was Edward II alive? Those involved in Kent's plot certainly believed so. The list of supporters included high-profile names such as Henry Beaumont and Thomas Roscelyn, both recent Mortimer supporters, but now themselves in exile on the Continent following Lancaster's action in 1328. Edward II's close friend William, Abbot of Langdon, Donald, Earl of Mar who was in Scotland, and the Earl of Buchan, were party to the design. Ingelram de Berengar, Fulk fitz Warin, and Thomas Wake, the man who had taken an active part in persuading parliament in January 1327 to depose Edward II and now in exile, were also all involved. Rhys ap Gruffudd in Wales continued to be restless. Donald of Mar was allegedly raising as many as 40,000 men, an unlikely figure, in order to come south with Beaumont and Roscelyn, who were in advance to land a force from Brabant in Scotland to bring about the restoration.[4] The number of Dominicans and men of different religious orders caught up in the plot was significant, and may even have included Thomas Dunheved, Edward's former confessor who had attempted three years earlier to rescue him from Kenilworth and Berkeley castles.[5]

Like so many plots of this magnitude, it began to unravel before the release could be enacted. Kent had asked his wife, Margaret Wake, to pen a letter that he could deliver to his half-brother. Travelling to Corfe Kent was refused admission and instead was persuaded by John Deveril and Bogo de Bayeux to hand over the letter, which they promised to give to their prisoner; they promptly informed Mortimer who, at Winchester, had Kent arrested as parliament got underway.[6] The plot fell apart, many but not all of those involved fled, Mortimer had Edward of Caernarfon removed from Corfe and Kent promptly sent to his death. For Mortimer and Isabella it had been a close call and one that warranted an extreme response to avoid a repeat. For now, Edward again falls back into the murky shadows.

Shortly after Kent's death, proclamations were issued threatening arrest for anyone caught stating that the former king was alive. Many fled to the Continent while the Dominicans and their fellow friars were rounded up and thrown into prisons.[7] William Melton was interrogated and revealed that he had heard of Edward's secret captivity from William Kingsclere on 10 October 1329, but denied that he sought to have Edward III removed from his throne.[8] Kent claimed in his confession that even the pope, John XXII, had instructed him to follow up on his conviction and bring about the release of the former king, which he himself would fund. After Kent's fall, John XXII refuted this in a letter to Edward III and Isabella in September 1330.[9] While this letter may be taken at face value, it is just as likely an attempt at distancing himself from a failed plot. Papal involvement with the plan would have created a scandal and undermined Edward III at a time when the pope was in private correspondence with the king – just before the fall of Mortimer the following month. He could not afford to make Isabella and Mortimer suspicious, as it would compromise Edward III.

Much was made, then and for centuries later, of Kent's assertion in his confession that he had come to hear of his brother's survival and whereabouts through a Dominican friar, possibly Thomas Dunheved. This friar had claimed he had learnt of Edward's whereabouts from a devil that appeared out of a burning fire.[10] As a result, Edmund has been viewed as gullible or simply stupid. Belief in the supernatural was a mainstay of the medieval mind, but it is likely Kent fabricated a story to protect his source, which may have been Edward III, or someone in a position that needed further protection after the plot failed, perhaps in the hope that the king could be rescued from elsewhere at a later date.[11] How many of Kent's supporters would have followed him on such a dangerous mission on the back of such a claim? Kent had conviction and those about him, far from unintelligent, understood the gravity of their actions and must have followed him on something more concrete than an apparition.

There are other indications that Edward was at Corfe at this point. Among Kent's supporters was John Pecche, former constable of Corfe Castle who had held the position since December 1325. It is unclear when exactly Pecche was replaced; he certainly had been removed by September 1329 when John Maltravers was formally appointed. Edward was, possibly, in captivity during Pecche's constableship. Pecche was also a Warwickshire man and had a number of connections with the Dunheved brothers. John had a previous dispute with Margaret Dunheved, his neighbour before 1326, and had turned to Hugh Despenser the Younger for help.[12] It is quite possible that Pecche saw Edward at Corfe and this motivated him and his son to join Kent and the growing group of conspirators.[13]

Kent's subsequent execution shocked contemporaries and was a critical turning point in the regime of Isabella and Mortimer. Six months later, Mortimer was seized by the eighteen-year-old Edward III and a few trusted men at Nottingham Castle on 19 October 1330. He was executed by hanging at Tyburn a month later. Isabella was sent into short-term retirement while Edward III asserted his long overdue sovereignty. Those associated with Mortimer and the apparent murder of Edward II began to fade away.

Thomas Berkeley was brought before the same body that tried Roger Mortimer, the day after Mortimer had been sentenced to death. There, under questioning, Berkeley made the most remarkable statement when answering the accusation of complicity in the death of Edward II. He declared that 'he never consented to it, helped with it, or procured it, *and nor had he ever heard of his death* until this present parliament'.[14] This was more than three years after Edward's funeral, at which Berkeley had been present, and it was on Berkeley's orders that news of Edward's death had been sent to his son at Lincoln. I believe this statement was not just Berkeley resurrecting Kent's recent plot seven months earlier as a possible, rather desperate defence, but a genuine conviction that Edward was still alive.[15] Berkeley did not flee after Mortimer's fall, which is, in itself, telling. Amazingly, he was acquitted of the murder but nevertheless was charged with appointing the two men held by the court to be responsible for Edward's death, Thomas Gurney and William

Ockley. The court did not believe the king lived. This charge hung over Berkeley's head until parliament, in 1335, declared Thomas 'quit of the death of the king his father and without culpability' and he was formally pardoned in 1337.[16]

Thomas Gurney remained in England during Berkeley's trial but only after the latter was charged with Gurney's appointment did Gurney flee, with financial aid offered by Thomas Berkeley. As mentioned earlier, Edward III offered a reward of £100 for the return of Gurney alive, or 100 marks for his head. Within a year, he was caught in Burgos in Spain. He managed to escape, only to be recaptured two years later in the Bay of Naples by William de Tweng. On their return journey to England, Gurney died at Bayonne.[17] Ockley fled shortly after Mortimer's arrest with a similar bounty offered for his arrest or death. Despite the incentive, Ockley disappears from the records and history altogether.

The other man most associated with events at Berkeley in September 1327 and with Kent's fall in March 1330 was John Maltravers. He fled as soon as Roger fell from power via Mousehole in Cornwall, with the aid of Benedict Noght and John le Taverner.[18] Strangely, the order for his arrest did not follow for six weeks giving Maltravers plenty of time to flee. He was tried in his absence and sentenced to be hanged, drawn, and beheaded, not for killing Edward II, but for his part in the death of the Earl of Kent in 1330.[19] A conviction for regicide was not pursued, perhaps through a lack of evidence – or because the king secretly knew that his father was still alive. It is possible that Edward III knew all along, but could never reveal the secret without endangering his own position. Through his mother, he had gained his throne through force and could easily be viewed as a usurper, guilty of treason should his secret ever be revealed and his father restored to power. Isabella and Mortimer used this knowledge as a means to control the young king as outlined so well by historian Ian Mortimer.[20] Edward was forced to accede to Mortimer's and Isabella's actions, including Kent's execution, which Edward III had reluctantly agreed to, under the threat of Edward II's restoration.[21]

Anointed kings had rarely been deposed across Europe, let alone murdered. Patricide was seen as abhorrent, just as it is today. Edward III was paralysed by his knowledge that his father was alive and he was unable to set him free, or kill him. It suited Edward to have his father locked away but since Kent's failed plot in March 1330, Edward of Caernarfon had disappeared from Corfe and his son did not know where Mortimer had transferred him. Isabella is also unlikely to have had her husband killed. Although she certainly had no intention of returning to her marriage after November 1326, killing her husband, an anointed king and father of her children, was arguably a step too far. It also set a precedent for the future, which endangered the royal line Isabella was attempting to protect. Mortimer may have had the same convictions, but even if not he was ruled by Isabella in this. Without the queen, Mortimer was nothing.

Maltravers appears again in March 1334, when he wrote to Edward III claiming to have knowledge relevant to the 'well being of the realm', quite possibly information on Edward II's whereabouts since his disappearance from Corfe. Edward sent William Montacute, a close personal friend and the man who had helped the king bring down Roger Mortimer, to the Continent to hear the information.[22] Whatever he heard is unrecorded. By 1339, Maltravers appears to have been in the employ of Edward III, serving in Ireland in 1344. A year later he submitted to the king and was given leave to return to England to face trial.[23] Maltravers, for whatever reason, delayed his return until 1352, when he finally faced the court and was acquitted of his involvement in Kent's death.[24] It was extraordinary that someone who the chroniclers see as being complicit in the alleged murder of Edward II would not only find himself in the service of Edward II's son towards the end of the 1330s but later acquitted of any crimes. What had changed?

Something extraordinary. In early 1336, Nicholinus de Fieschi, an envoy of Genoa, arrived at the court of Edward III carrying letters. Among them was one of particular importance, for it contained a message written by a third party, Manuele Fieschi, purporting to be a report of a confession from Edward II himself. In it, Manuele gives a detailed account of the events from 1326 up until 1335 as told to him by someone who, Manuele believed, was Edward II.[25] It's explosive stuff, for many of the details given fit the known evidence, some of which were known to only a handful of contemporaries, adding significantly to its veracity and historical value. The letter is translated in full in the appendices of this book and a facsimile is provided on the half-title page.[26]

Fieschi, in relaying Edward's confession, states that following Isabella's invasion, the king fled west through England, there taking ship from Chepstow to Glamorgan. In Glamorgan he was captured by Henry of Lancaster and was deposed at Kenilworth and incarcerated at Berkeley. Sometime later, Edward was told by a servant that Thomas Gurney and Simon Bereford, another Mortimer adherent, were on their way to kill him and that he could escape by switching clothes with the servant who gave him that information. He then escaped at twilight, killed a porter at one of the castle doors and made away with someone described as his 'keeper', or sometimes his 'companion', but who is never named in the letter. He was then taken by his keeper to Corfe and there he resided for a year and a half in secret, without Maltravers' knowledge, until the Earl of Kent's plot came to light. When Kent's plot was discovered and the earl beheaded, Manuele wrote, the former king was moved to Ireland, with his companion. Edward remained there for nine months where, after taking the habit of a hermit, he returned secretly to England, travelled to Sandwich and sailed to the Continent.

The letter goes on to claim that Edward, arriving at Sluys, went to Avignon and gained an audience with the pope, John XXII, staying there for fifteen days. Finally 'after various discussions' Edward, with papal approval, went to Paris, then to Brabant, and on to Cologne to see the shrine of The Three Kings. After which he travelled to Milan in Lombardy, and beyond; he eventually entered a hermitage at the castle of Melazzo, where he stayed for two and a half years. He moved on, because of war in the region, to the castle of Cecima in the diocese of Pavia, still in Lombardy, where he remained a hermit and a recluse and presumably gave his confession to Fieschi or someone else.[27] The detail in the letter is remarkable. It may be the only account of Edward II after 1327. Equally it may be the work of an imposter, or a simple forgery. However, research has demonstrated that the letter is not forged and was written by Manuele Fieschi in or just before 1336.[28]

Manuele was a papal notary from 1329 and a collector of papal taxes in Melazzo and Cecima. In 1343 he became Bishop of Vercelli until his death in 1348, in the region where Edward was said to be residing. The Fieschis, distantly related to Edward II, were a powerful family, two of whom were made popes in the thirteenth century and they had contacts at the English court, holding benefices there during the reign of Edward II.[29] The letters came from a family with extensive connections in the region.

It is unlikely that Fieschi made up the content or heard it from an imposter. The value of the letter is increased by its detail. Only Edward and a handful of his followers who were still with him during his flight from Isabella knew he sailed from Chepstow, an unlikely port. This fact is only confirmed because it survives in the king's chamber account, which was with him when he sailed and which was rescued after the fall of Caerphilly Castle in 1327. It would have been accessible to very few contemporaries.

The major events of 1326–1327 are briefly outlined and were more or less common knowedge. The timeline in the letter is slightly out of step in relation to Edward's incarceration at Corfe, as it would have been for two and a half years, not the one and a half outlined in the letter. However, this is the only place where the timeline appears out of sync and it may simply be scribal error, especially as Manuele was most likely writing this letter sometime after the king had made his confession. The castellan is also described as someone called 'Thomas' and not John Deveril, John Maltravers or John Pecche, who had all been keepers of the castle. Ian Mortimer believes that Edward was told a false name in order to confuse him and make him believe that he was being helped rather than held captive by men associated with Roger Mortimer.[30] The presence of Edward at Corfe also makes sense as according to Murimuth, Edward had been moved there and to Bristol in secret during the night in the summer of 1327 to prevent plotters rescuing him; something Edward II had done with contrariant rebels after 1322. It may have been at this moment, in the summer of 1327, that Edward's gaolers – and Mortimer in particular – appreciated the importance of keeping Edward's location and his future captivity a secret. That, and the growing plots to free him, made what was later claimed by Fieschi in 1336 all the more likely.

Edward's stay in Ireland makes sense as Roger Mortimer held extensive estates in Ireland and so Edward could be safely ensconced there, being unrecognisable to many as the king had never visited Ireland during his reign. For Mortimer and Isabella, this was a safe, secret prison for the former king, which allowed them to maintain their hold over Edward III at home. The young king would be unable to help his father, even if he had wanted to. Furthermore, a nine-month stay in Ireland after his removal from Corfe outlined in the letter aligns neatly with the period between the execution of Kent, the fall and execution of Roger Mortimer, and time for news to reach Ireland. The 'companion' mentioned in the letter who appears to accompany Edward from 1327–1330, is no longer mentioned. It is likely that this companion was in fact a man in the employ of Mortimer and Maltravers, and he seems to disappear after Roger's fall.[31] It is possible that Edward either knew his companion was a Mortimer man and he was treated well by him, or that he believed this man was helping him, keeping him secure and safe beyond Roger's machinations; the former seems more likely.

The arrival of the Fieschi letter appeared to have an impact. Shortly afterwards, on 4 July 1336, Edward III granted 8,000 marks to the community of Genoa in compensation for the actions of piracy committed by Hugh Despenser the Younger as far back as 1321, when he was exiled from England following the rebellion in the Welsh March that year. It is strange that for fifteen years, the requests for compensation had been turned down but after Edward III received this letter, the compensation was immediately paid to the community in the area where Edward II was said to be a hermit.[32] Nine months later, at the first parliament since the letter arrived, Thomas Berkeley was acquitted of all the charges against him. Isabella, who had returned to the usual role of dowager queen with her vast possessions stripped from her in 1330, suddenly found her income doubled in 1337.[33] As noted earlier, Maltravers begins to appear in the employ of Edward III. These may just be coincidences but it would appear that Edward III believed in the content of the letter that Nicholinus Fieschi showed him.

Lastly, in September 1338, Edward III himself may have held an audience with his father at Koblenz. We can see from official records that there the king of England met one William le Galeys or 'William the Welshman' who appeared to claim that he was the king's father. Wales being the place of Edward of Caernarfon's birth, it was a fitting surname if this was in fact Edward II himself. This William le Galeys had been arrested at Cologne and brought to the king at Koblenz but arrived under the guard of a Lombard, not a man from Cologne. Edward's hermitage was in Lombardy. The arrest, therefore, was a smoke screen. The expenses of their travel, 25s 6d were also covered by Edward III. According to the official record, the king then travelled with William to Antwerp, where he was entertained for three weeks in December, just after Queen Philippa had given birth to her second son, Lionel.[34] It is likely Edward II was able to see his grandson. When the visit was concluded, 'William le Galeys' returned to Lombardy.

What is striking about this visit is that if William le Galeys, who is noted as purporting to be the king's father in Edward III's wardrobe book, was in fact a royal imposter, he would most certainly have been imprisoned or, more likely, executed. Again, as Ian Mortimer has noted in the last decade, the keeper of wardrobe accounts had also known Edward II personally and there are no disparaging remarks about the claim in the entries made. Edward II himself had followed this more brutal course of action when an imposter, John Powderham, appeared before his court in 1318. Yet this man in 1338 was taken into the royal household, entertained by the king for three weeks, and then simply allowed to roam free after the event. It is unfathomable, unless we come to the conclusion that William le Galeys was Edward II. His treatment and freedom to return to Lombardy, the place Fieschi claimed was Edward's place of residence at Cecima, is all too coincidental.

Edward of Caernarfon, after December 1338, disappears forever from the record. His life, feigned death and subsequent survival until this date reads like a conspiracy theory or a romance. However, the evidence is compelling. Ian Mortimer has demonstrated that the actual death of Edward II was most likely sometime around 1341. From that date, Nicholinus Fieschi received a sum of one mark a day, sent from Edward III's treasury to 'divers parts beyond the sea on certain affairs'.[35] These certain affairs may have been the return of Edward's body, which could have been embalmed and preserved and brought back in secret to England. Once there, it is highly likely the body of the late king was then interred at Gloucester, after the body of the porter noted in the Fieschi letter was removed. Shortly after, a magnificent tomb in the court style was erected, most likely on the orders of Edward III himself.

The image of the king is saintly, and when viewed today, it still captures all the magnificence that Edward III intended to give his father in death, despite its loss of colours over the last 700 years. In March 1343, a year or more after the real burial, Edward III himself visited Gloucester and after this date, but not before, many senior members of the royal family began to visit the abbey.[36]

While there is no single revelation that can prove beyond all doubt that Edward II was alive until 1341, the various pieces of circumstantial evidence are overwhelming. Edward II lived on as Edward of Caernarfon or William le Galeys for many years after his deposition and alleged demise in 1327. For nearly 700 years the tale of Edward's brutal murder has been accepted as fact; and yet, like those living at the time and until very recently, we have been duped by Isabella and Roger Mortimer.

Epilogue: 'Edward the Man'

Edward II was a man of great complexity and contradiction. His character defined his rule. Above all, he cared deeply for and was motivated by those immediately around him, no more so than the small group of intimates he kept at court. He could be generous, as his household accounts testify. He frequently handed out gifts, either through others or in person. He was equitable in his gift-giving in the sense that all levels of society benefitted, even if his exercise of patronage among his nobles was dangerously unbalanced. He had a unique common touch, which meant a close familiarity with his subjects. He holidayed in the Fens in 1315, he would dig ditches, go rowing, swimming, or simply stand at the riverbank. He invited people into his personal chambers so he could talk to them – sailors, labourers and others – because he appeared genuinely interested in their daily lives. He was intensely curious; it is difficult to communicate just how unconventional all this was for a medieval king. The familiarity with his common subjects singled Edward out for accusations of degeneracy. Today he would be seen as a 'man of the people'.

He could love intensely, as his relationship with Piers Gaveston, which was undoubtedly sexual, demonstrated. His reliance on favourites such as Roger Damory, Hugh Audley, William Montacute and the Despensers was driven by his affection. He was loyal and used his position to protect those who meant the most to him. Edward would not suffer betrayal, taking any slight as a great offence. He was intensely protective of those he cared for, and vindictive to those who threatened or turned against him or his friends. The fate of Bartholomew Badlesmere is one of the more unfortunate examples of what happened to anybody who betrayed the king's confidence. Yet even at the highest point of his reign, as he overcame his enemies in 1322, Edward chose not to execute the defeated Roger Damory – perhaps because he was slowly dying anyway, or perhaps because in that moment Edward took pity on someone he may well have loved beyond friendship. We will never know for sure.

Edward could be vengeful. The murder of Piers Gaveston at the hands of Thomas of Lancaster would dominate his thinking for ten years. He had a long memory and was never more determined in action than when he felt personally aggrieved. He had no qualms in locking up the wives, sons and daughters of rebel contrariants or leaving the executed unburied for two years. He could allow his personal passions to overrule sound judgement. His intense desire for Gaveston and determination to destroy Lancaster were two sides of the same coin. His resolution to keep Hugh Despenser the Younger with him in 1326 brought about his ultimate undoing. His passions could make him determined and ultimately intractable.

Edward was also shrewd and diplomatic when he most needed to be. Much like his father, Edward II understood the need to accept political reforms when there was no other way, only to attempt to revoke them at a later date. This was most clear in his determination to avoid the Ordinances in order to preserve the dignity of the crown. This 'accept now, rescind later' policy would infuriate his magnates, especially his cousin Lancaster, yet the king's ability to play for time, undermine actions which encroached upon his royal sovereignty and build support for his cause, was one of his key skills as a leader. In an age when baronial opposition was based on an individual's needs or desires over any great constitutional principle or a united desire for reform for the benefit of the kingdom, Edward could be tactful in building diplomatic bridges, drawing supporters to his cause and outmanoeuvring his opponents as a consequence. But he could also fail to make those relationships binding, often distrusting the chief counsellors of the crown.

He understood the importance of building international support too, and could call upon these relationships during times of political crisis. Edward's relationship with two successive popes, Clement V and John XXII, proved invaluable during his turbulent reign. He could, at times, even call upon the support of his father-in-law Philip IV and that of successive kings of France (with the exception of Charles IV), when the need was greatest and used such influences astutely for his own gain.

Edward was pious in a conventional way. His account books are littered with devotions made to saints, to his deceased parents, lost sisters and, of course, Gaveston, throughout his lifetime. This no doubt continued after he became a hermit in Italy. He could inspire loyalty, especially from the Dominicans who did so much to try and bring about his release from captivity through various plots from 1327 to 1330. Even after his fall from power, Edward continued to command the loyalty of men across society, from Donald of Mar in Scotland and Rhys ap Gruffudd in Wales, to knights, friars, preachers and sailors. He could be widely hated, but he was also loved.

He was gregarious and full of humour. He loved music including the crwth, watched many theatrical performances, founded colleges at

Oxford and Cambridge and joined in the pageantry of his court. He even had a pet lion. Equally, he enjoyed his privacy and his acquisition of a little moated manor house or cottage at Westminster, which he affectionately called Little Burgundy, allowed him to escape the politics and pressures of his court. He found solace in his own space and comfort among his people; the former undoubtedly helped in his later vocation as a hermit. He would have adapted well into his unexpected 'second life'.

He loved his family. He cared for his wife, possibly even after the rise of Hugh Despenser the Younger, but his judgment was clouded by the latter's flattery and manipulation. Edward could allow those closest to him to dominate him when he chose, but perhaps Despenser, with all his clever emotional manipulation, was too strong for Edward to control. He could be short-sighted, easily led if he agreed in part with an opinion, and could make decisions that he would later regret. He would also listen to and act on reason when he needed it most, and could hear sound advice from men like Aymer de Valence, even when the latter's view was different from his own, at least until March 1322.

He was also capable in arms and continued his father's policy in Scotland. Despite the significant failure of Bannockburn, Edward refused to acknowledge defeat. He was not afraid of war, would fight fiercely in battle and pursue his enemies, as events in 1322 clearly show. The fall of the contrariants and the execution of Thomas of Lancaster were personal triumphs in Edward's life. Ironically, they also contributed to his fall from power.

In an age when a king ruled and did not merely reign, his personality ultimately defined his kingship. With the heady mix of his doomed inheritance, his determination to keep those he cared for closest to him, and his unconventional style of kingship, at odds with the expectations of those around him, Edward II was unable to prevent his fall, which was after 1326 the only possible outcome for those in opposition to him. To restore the king to his power in January 1327, given his propensity for vengeance, was simply not an option his opponents could countenance. Edward had demonstrated what his revenge could deliver and after the execution of his cousin Lancaster, the king had raised the political stakes too high.

Edward was a man born to be king, who ruled like a king out of his age, and ultimately paid a high price because he exercised his power in the only way he knew how. He is more than history has for so long declared him to be.

Appendices

Appendix One

Entered onto the Close Rolls for the years 1325 and 1326 are some of the extraordinary letters Edward sent to his wife, his son and brother-in-law, the king of France, as the breakdown of his marriage with Isabella became something of a European public scandal. As the months passed and the king was unable to bring about reconciliation and wrest back control of his son and heir, the letters become flooded with anxiety, increasing frustration, and outright anger. The danger that this rift presented is all too apparent with the frequent mention of 'the Mortimer'. The intensity and pressure of the situation Edward now found himself in leaps out from the pages.

Letter from Edward II to his wife, Isabella of France, written at Westminster on 1 December, 1325.

To the queen. The king has frequently ordered her, both before and after the homage, to come to him with all speed, laying aside all excuses; but before the homage she was excused by reason of the advancement of the affairs, and she has now informed the king by the bishop of Winchester, with her letters of credence, that she will not return now for danger and doubt of Hugh le Despenser. The king marvels at this to the extent of his power, especially as she always behaved amiably to him, and he to her, in the king's presence, and particularly at her departure by her behaviour, and after her departure by very special letters sent to him, which he has shown to the king. The king knows for truth, and she knows, that Hugh has always procured her all the honour with the king that he could; and no evil or villainy was done to her after her marriage by any abetment and procurement, unless peradventure sometimes the king has addressed to her in secret words of reproof, by her own fault, if she will remember, as was befitting, without other hardship, and she ought not, for God and the law of the church and for the honour of the king and of her, to transgress the king's commands for anything on earth, nor leave his company. It will much displease the king if now, after homage has been done to the king of France, and the king and the king of France are in such a good way of love, she, whom the king sent for peace, should be the reason of any difference between the king and the king of France, and especially for feigned and untrue reasons. He therefore orders her to put aside all such feigned reasons and excuses, and to come to him with all speed, especially as the king of France has, according to the bishop's report, said, in the bishop's presence, that she shall not be molested nor delayed from coming to the king contrary to her safe-conduct, since the king is her husband and she is his wife. As to her expenses, the king will, when she had returned to him as a wife ought to do to her husband, ordain so that she shall have no lack of things appertaining to her, whereby neither the king nor she may be dishonoured in any wise. The king also wills and orders that she suffer and make Edward, his son, return to him in as much haste as possible, according to the king's orders to him, and this she is in no wise to neglect, since the king has a great desire to see and talk with him. And whereas lately, when Walter, bishop of Exeter, was with the queen, the king was informed that some of the king's banished enemies lay in wait for the bishop to have done him harm of his body if they had seen a fitting time, and the king, to eschew such perils and by reason of the great affairs of the king's that the bishop had to do, ordered him to hasten home in the most secure manner possible, putting aside all other matters, in order to save himself; the king therefore wills and orders her to excuse the bishop for coming to him so suddenly from those parts, and she is to understand that the bishop did so for no other reasons than those aforesaid.[1]

~

Letter from Edward II to his brother-in-law, Charles IV, king of France, written at Westminster, on 1 December 1325. Copies of this letter were also sent to sixteen French magnates, lay and ecclesiastical, including the Archbishop of Rheims, the Duke of Burgundy and the Count of Flanders.

To the king of France. The king has received and understood his letters, delivered by the bishop of Wyncestre [Winchester], and has also understood what the bishop has told him by word of mouth concerning the matters contained in the letters. As to the king of France's information to the king that he understood from trustworthy men that the queen of England durst not come to the king for peril of her life and for the doubt that she has of Hugh le Despenser, it is not fitting that she should doubt Hugh or any other man living in the king's realm, since if either Hugh or any other man in the realm wished her evil, and the king knew of it, he would chastise them in such manner that others should take example; and such is, and has been, and always will be the king's will, and he has sufficient power therefor. He wishes the king of France to know that he could never perceive that Hugh privately or openly, in word or deed, or in countenance did not behave himself in all points towards the queen as he ought to have done to his lady; but when the king remembers the amiable countenances and words between the queen and Hugh that he has seen and the great friendships that she held to him upon her going beyond sea, and the loving letters that she sent him not long ago, which Hugh has shown to the king, he cannot in any manner believe that the queen by herself can understand such thing concerning Hugh, whoever has out of hatred made her so understand, and the king cannot believe it of Hugh in any manner, but he believes that, after himself, Hugh is the man of his realm who wishes her most honour, and this Hugh had always shown, and the king testifies it in good truth. He prays the king of France not to give credence to those who would make him understand otherwise, but that he will believe the king's testimony, because the king has, and of reason ought to have, much greater knowledge of this matter than others. He therefore prays the king of France as especially as he can, that he will, for the honour of him, the king, and of the king's wife, do so much that she shall come to the king in such haste as she can, because the king is rendered very uneasy because he has such loss of her company, and he would not have deprived himself thereof of it had not been for the great trust that he had, and has, in the king of France and in his good faith that she would return at the king's will. The king also prays the king of France to expedite and cause to be delivered Edward, the king's eldest son, nephew of the king of France, and to render to him the lands of the duchy that the king of France holds, for the love and affection that the king of France has to Edward, and so that he shall not be disinherited, which the king does not think the king of France wishes. He also prays the king of France to suffer Edward to come to him with all possible haste, as the king has ordered him, as the king has a great will to see and speak with him, and it was always his will that he should return to him so soon as the homage was done and when the king should order him. Whereas when Walter, bishop of Exeter, was with the king of France, the king was given to understand that some of the king's enemies lay in wait for the bishop to do him harm of his body, and the king, to eschew such perils and for the great affairs of his that the bishop had so ordered him to hasten home in the most secure manner, putting aside other matters, to save himself; the king prays the king of France to excuse the bishop for his sudden return from those parts, and to understand that he did so solely for the aforesaid reasons.[2]

~

Letter from Edward II to his son Edward, Duke of Aquitaine, written at Lichfield on 18 March 1326.

To Edward, the king's son. The king understands what Edward has answered by his letters, and that he remembers what he was charged by the king concerning his not marrying without the king and concerning other matters, and what he said to the king at his departure from Dovre [Dover], and that he would always obey the king's orders and pleasure with all his power. If he do so, he will do wisely and will do his duty, and will have the grace of God, the king, and of all men; if he do not, he cannot avoid great dishonour and damage to God and all men, and the king's wrath and indignation: the king therefore charges him, to the best of his power, and under pain of forfeiting all he may to the king, to remember well the matters aforesaid, and that he do not marry, or suffer himself to be married, without the king's assent, or before he have returned to the king, and the he do nothing else that may [be] to the king's damage, in anger of heart. Regarding what he has informed the king, that is seems to him that he cannot come to the king so speedily as the king has ordered him by reason of his mother, who is, as he says, in great uneasiness of heart, and that he cannot leave her until she be in such point, out of affection and to do his duty ... to leave [her] in such unhappiness for long; he knows how the king has loved and cherished her, and, truly, if she has conducted herself towards the king as she ought to have done towards her lord, the king would be much harassed to learn of her grief or unhappiness, but as she feigns a reason to withdraw from the king by reason of his dear and faithful nephew Hugh le Despenser, who has always served the king well and faithfully, Edward can see and everybody can see that she openly, notoriously, and knowingly, contrary to her duty and the estate of the king's crown, which she is bound to love and maintain, draws to her and retains in her company of her council the Mortimer, the king's traitor and mortal enemy, approved, attainted, and adjudged in full parliament, and keeps his company within and without house, in despite of the king and of his crown and of the rights of his realm, which Mortimer the king of France had banished from his power as the king's enemy at the king's request at another time, and now she does worse, if possible, when she has delivered Edward to the company of the king's said enemy, and makes [him] Edward's councillor, and causes Edward to adhere to him openly and notoriously in the sight of everybody, to the great dishonour and villainy of the king and of Edward, and in prejudice of the king's crown and of the laws and usages of the realm of England, which Edward is bound to save and maintain before all things. For these and many other reasons Edward's stay in those parts, which is so shameful and may be perilous and damaging to him in many ways, does not please the king, and ought not to please Edward, either for his mother or for any one else. The king therefore orders and charges him to come to him as speedily as possible, notwithstanding the above or any other excuses, since his mother has written to the king that she will not disturb his returning if he wish to return, and the king does not think that the king of France will detain him contrary to his safe-conduct. He is enjoined not to omit coming to the king speedily, either for his mother or for any other reason, or for going into the duchy [of Aquitaine], concerning which the king will soon make ordinance for Edward's honour, or for any other cause or excuse, if he wish to escape the king's anger and indignation and forfeiture of what he can forfeit to the king; so that the king may make ordinance concerning him and his estate, as well in the duchy as in other lands that Edward has on this side. If John de Bretaigne [earl of Richmond] and John de Crombwell [Cromwell] wish to come in his company, they will do their duty. He is enjoined not to transgress the king's orders, because the king is much troubled that he has done what he ought not to have done.[3]

~

Letter from Edward II to his son Edward, Duke of Aquitaine, written at Westminster, on 19 June 1326.

To Edward, the king's son. Although he has written to the king that he remembers what the king enjoined upon him at his departure from the king at Dovre [Dover], and that he would not transgress the king's commandments in any point, but would execute them to the best of his power, it seems to the king that he does not keep the covenant, and does not obey his commands, as a good son should do, since he has not come to the king to be under his government as he ought to be and as the king has ordered him to do by other letters under his benison, but has notoriously kept company with and adhered to Mortimer, the king's traitor and mortal enemy, in the company of his mother and elsewhere, Mortimer having publicly borne at Parys [Paris] Edward's suit at the coronation at Whitsuntide last, in great despite of the king, and to the great dishonour of the king and of Edward, whereas Edward has informed the king untruly that Mortimer is not an adherent of the queen or of him; whereby the king considers himself very evilly paid. The king also understands that Edward has, by counsel contrary to the king and contrary to his own profit, made many orders, ordinances, and divers things, without advising the king and contrary to the king's orders and will, concerning the duchy of Guyenne [Gascony] given to him by the king; Edward ought to remember the manner of the gift and his answer to the king at Dovre when the king made the gift: which matters are unbecoming and may be very damaging. The king therefore orders and charges him, by his duty and the king's blessing, and under pain of forfeiture, and as he wishes that the king shall hold for his dear and well loved son, as he has always done, to come to the king with all speed, laying aside all excuses, from his mother or from other, or other excuses that he has written to the king heretofore, so that the king may ordain for him and his estate as befits, especially as Edward ought not to have, nor to wish to have, by right and reason any other governor than the king. Moreover, the king charges him, in like manner, not to marry until he have returned to the king, or without the king's assent and command, and not to do anything touching the duchy or elsewhere contrary to the king's orders and will, or without first advising the king and having his assent, and to cause anything that he may have done to be revoked as befits. He is enjoined to take these commands to heart, although he be of tender age, and to execute them humbly and completely, if he wishes to avoid the king's anger and indignation, and as he loves his own profit and honour. He is enjoyed not to trust to any counsel contrary to his father's will, as the wise king Solomon teaches him, and to inform the king speedily of his proceedings; understanding for certain that if the king find him contrary or disobedient thereafter to his will, by what counsel soever it may be, he will ordain in such wise that Edward shall feel it all the days of his life, and that all other sons shall take example thereby of disobeying their lords and fathers.[4]

~

Letter from Edward II to his brother-in-law, Charles IV, king of France, written at Westminster, on 19 June 1326.

To the king's brother. The king reminds him of what he wrote to him at another time concerning the unbecoming conduct of his wife, the sister of the king of France, in withdrawing herself so shamefully from the king, and in not returning at his order, and in attracting to her company and adhering to the Mortimer, the king's traitor and mortal enemy, and the king's other enemies on that side, and in causing Edward, the king's son and heir, to adhere to the king's enemies aforesaid, to the great dishonour of the king, and of all her blood, and that the king of France ought to have been well-wishing, for his and the king's honour, that such matters should be duly redressed; and the king requested him by the said letters to send to the king the latter's son, who is of such tender age that he cannot and knows not how to govern or guide himself, and ought therefore to be under the king's government and under that of no other, according to right and reason and the covenant between the king and the king of France, so that the king might ordain concerning him and his goods and estate, as befits; and that, as the king's son had done homage to the king of France entirely for the whole of the duchy, the latter would render to the king's son aforesaid in full the lands of the duchy, without having regard to the strictness of the words of any covenant that, in the opinion of some, seem to be intended for the king's disinheritance; as it more fully contained in the king's letters aforesaid. As yet nothing has been done concerning these matters, but the adherence of the king's wife and son to his said traitors and mortal enemies on that side is continued notoriously, in so much that the said traitor, the Mortimer, publicly bore at Parys [Paris] the suit of the king's son [at the coronation] of the queen of France at Whitsuntide last, to the great dishonour and despite of the king. The king therefore prays the king of France from his heart, for the nourishment of right and peace and of affection and friendship between them, which the king desires above all things, that he will understand and fulfil the king's requests aforesaid with good will and speedily, for the king's profit and honour and so that he may not be dishonoured, nor he and his son disinherited, which he does not think the king of France desires, but that the king of France may understand well from the king, as from every man of his estate, that he is and ought to be much aggrieved by suffering so long such shameful despites and great damages, and, indeed, he will be unable to suffer them for long.[5]

Appendix Two

The Fieschi Letter written by papal notary Manuele de Fieschi to Edward III some time in early 1336 (see half-title page). The letter outlines the survival of Edward II after September 1327, starting with the king's movements in the autumn of 1326 through to his subsequent flight to the Continent and life as a hermit thereafter.

In the name of the Lord Amen. Those things that I have heard from the confession of your father I have written with my own hand and afterwards I have taken care to be made known to Your Highness. First he says that feeling England in subversion against him, afterwards on the admonition of your mother, he withdrew from his family in the castle of the Earl Marshal by the sea, which is called Chepstow. Afterwards, led by fear, he took a barque with the lords Hugh Despenser and the earl of Arundel and several others and made his way to Glamorgan on the sea, and there he was captured, together with the said Lord Hugh and Master Robert Baldock; and they were captured by Lord Henry of Lancaster, and they led him to the castle of Kenilworth, and others were elsewhere at various places; and there he lost the crown at the insistence of many. Afterwards you were subsequently crowned on the feast of Candlemas next following. Finally they sent him to the castle of Berkeley. Afterwards the servant who was keeping him, after some little time, said to your father: Lord, Lord Thomas Gourney and Lord Simon Barford, knights, have come with the purpose of killing you. If it pleases, I shall give you my clothes, that you may better be able to escape. Then with the said clothes, at twilight, he went out of the prison; and when he had reached the last door without resistance, because he was not recognised, he found the porter sleeping, whom he quickly killed; and having got the keys of the door, he opened the door and went out, and his keeper who was keeping him. The said knights who had come to kill him, seeing that he had thus fled, fearing the indignation of the queen, even the danger to their persons, thought to put that aforesaid porter, his heart having been extracted, in a box, and maliciously presented to the queen the heart and body of the aforesaid porter as the body of your father, and as the body of the king the said porter was buried in Gloucester. And after he had gone out of the prisons of the aforesaid castle, he was received in the castle of Corfe with his companion who was keeping him in the prisons by Lord Thomas, castellan of the said castle, the lord being ignorant, Lord John Maltravers, lord of the said Thomas, in which castle he was secretly for a year and a half. Afterwards, having heard that the earl of Kent, because he said he was alive, had been beheaded, he took a ship with his said keeper and with the consent and counsel of the said Thomas, who had received him, crossed into Ireland, where he was for nine months. Afterwards fearing lest he be recognised there, having taken the habit of a hermit, he came back to England and proceeded to the port of Sandwich, and in the same habit crossed the sea to Sluys. Afterwards he turned his steps in Normandy and from Normandy, as many do, going across through Languedoc, came to Avignon, where, having given a florin to the servant of the pope, sent by the said servant a document to pope John, which pope had him called to him, and held him secretly and honourably more than fifteen days. Finally, after various discussions, all things having been considered, permission having been received, he went to Paris and from Paris to Brabant, from Brabant to Cologne so that out of devotion he might see The Three Kings, and leaving Cologne he crossed over Germany, that is to say, he headed for Milan in Lombardy, and from Milan he entered a certain hermitage of the castle of Melazzo, in which hermitage he stayed for two years and a half; and because war overran the said castle, he changed himself to the castle of Cecima in another hermitage of the diocese of Pavia in Lombardy, and he was in this last hermitage for two years or thereabout, always the recluse, doing penance, and praying God for you and other sinners. In testimony of which I have caused my seal to be affixed for the consideration of Your Highness.

Your Manuele de Fieschi, notary of the lord pope, your devoted servant.[1]

Notes

Abbreviations

Ann Lond: *Annales Londonienses*, 1195–1330
Ann Paul: *Annales Paulini*, 1307–1340
Anonimalle: *The Anonimalle Chronicle* 1307–1334 (ed. Wendy R. Childs and John Taylor)
Aymer: J.R.S Phillips, *Aymer de Valence, Earl of Pembroke, 1307–1324*
Bruce: John Barbour *The Bruce* (ed. A.A.M Duncan)
Brut: *The Brut Chronicles of England* (ed F.W.D Brie)
Buck: Mark Buck, *Politics, Finance and the Church in the Reign of Edward II*
CCR: Calendar of Close Rolls
CChR: Calendar of Charter Rolls
CCW: Calendar of Chancery Writs
CFR: Calendar of Fine Rolls
Chaplais: Pierre Chaplais, *Piers Gaveston: Edward II's Adoptive Brother*
CIM: Calendar of Inquisitions Post Mortem
Cockerill: Sara Cockerill, *Eleanor of Castile: The Shadow Queen*
CPL: Calendar of Papal Letters
CPR: Calendar of Patent Rolls
Doherty: Paul Doherty, *Isabella and the Strange Death of Edward II*
Flores: *Flores Historiarum, vol. iii* (ed H.R Luard)
Foedera: *Rhymer's Foedera, Conventiones, Litterae, 1307–27, vol i and ii*
Fryde: Natalie Fryde, *The Tyranny and Fall of Edward II*
Gesta Edwardi: *Gesta Edwardi de Carnarvon Auctore Canonico Bridlingtoniensi* (ed. W. Stubbs)
Guisborough: *The Chronicle of Walter of Guisborough* (ed. Harry Rothwell)
Haines: Roy Martin Haines, *King Edward II*
Hamilton: J.S. Hamilton, *Piers Gaveston Earl of Cornwall, 1307–1312*
Intrigue: Ian Mortimer, *Medieval Intrigue*
Isabella: Kathryn Warner: *Isabella of France: The Rebel Queen*
Johnstone: Hilda Johnstone, *Edward of Carnarvon 1284–1307*
Knighton: *Chronicon Henrici Knighton, vol I* (ed. J.R Lumby)
Lanercost: *Chronicon de Lanercost, 1272–1356, vol ii* (ed. J. Stevenson)
Le Baker: *Chronicon Galfridi le Baker de Swynbroke* (ed. Thompson)

Letters: Hilda Johnstone, *Letters of Edward, Prince of Wales 1304–1305*

Maddicott: J.R. Maddicott, *Thomas of Lancaster 1307–1322*

McNamee: C. McNamee, *The Wars of the Bruces: Scotland, England and Ireland, 1306–1328*

Melsa: *Chronica Monasterii de Melsa, vol ii* (ed. E.A Bond)

Morris: Marc Morris, *A Great and Terrible King*

Mortimer: Ian Mortimer, *The Greatest Traitor*

Murimuth: *Adae Murimuth Continuatio Chronicarum* (ed E.M Thompson)

Nusbacher: Aryeh Nusbacher, *The Battle of Bannockburn, 1314*

Phillips: Seymour Phillips, *Edward II*

Polychronicon: *Polychronicon Ranulphi Higden, vol. viii* (ed. J.R Lumby)

Prestwich: Michael Prestwich, *Edward I*

PROME: The Parliament Rolls of Medieval England

PW: Parliamentary Writs

Sardos: *The War of Saint-Sardos, 1323–25* (ed. Pierre Chaplais)

Scalacronica: *Scalacronica by Sir Thomas Gray of Heton, knight, 1272–1363* (ed. Sir Herbert Maxwell)

Sempringham: *Chroniques de Sempringham: Livere de Reis de Britannie* (ed. J. Glover)

The National Archives (C: Chancery; DL: Duchy of Lancaster; E: Exchequer; KB: King's Bench; SC: Special Collections)

Trivet: *Nicolai Triveti Annalium Continuatio* (ed A. Hall)

Trokewlowe: *Johannis de Trokelowe et Henrici de Blaneforde Chronica et Annales* (ed. H.T. Riley)

Warner: Kathryn Warner, *Edward II: The Unconventional King*

Vita: *Vita Edwardi Secundi* (ed. N. Denholm-Young)

Preface

1. Prestwich, 565–6. Morris, 377.
2. Johnstone, Hilda. *Edward of Carnarvon, 1284–1307.*
3. Phillips, Seymour. *Edward II, Aymer de Valence: Earl of Pembroke, 1307–24.*
4. Mortimer, Ian. *Intrigues*, Introduction.

Part One: Heir Apparent

1. Born on a Field of Conquest

1. Johnstone, 7.
2. Flores, 61. Guisborough, 15.
3. E 101/351/15, m.2. Phillips, 33. Prestwich, 4.
4. Morris, 188–90. Bellamy, J.G. *The Law of Treason in the Middle Ages*, 23–6.
5. Morris, 191–2.
6. *Vita*, 40. Prestwich, 5, 44.
7. Cockerill, 348–9.
8. Phillips, 36. Johnstone, 9.
9. Morris, 190.
10. CPR, 1307–13, 448. Johnstone, 9.
11. CPR, 1307–13, 591. CCR, 1313–17, 86. Johnstone, 9.
12. CCR, 1279–88, 275.

2. A Happy Childhood

1. Cockerill, 309.
2. Parsons, *The Year of Eleanor of Castile's Birth*, 261–2. Cockerill, 310.
3. Johnstone, 24.

4. Ibid, 12. Green, M.A.E, *Princesses of England*, 459.
5. Howell, *Eleanor of Provence*, 300. Phillips, 42.
6. Prestwich, 128.
7. Phillips, 42.
8. Ibid, 42.
9. Morris, 227.
10. Parsons, *The Year of Eleanor of Castile's Birth*, 260.
11. Morris, 235–6.
12. Prestwich, 128.
13. Parsons, *The Year of Eleanor of Castile's Birth*, 260–2.
14. Flores, 71. Cockerill, 343. Parsons, *Eleanor of Castile*, 58.
15. Cockerill, 348.
16. Ibid, 344–45, 48–49.
17. C47/3/22, m.2
18. Prestwich, 307.
19. Cockerill, 359.
20. E 101/353/18, m.10. Johnstone, 11. Tout, *Chapters in Medieval Administrative History*, 366.
21. Duggan, A.J. *The Cult of St Thomas Becket*, 31.
22. Phillips, 50.
23. Ibid, 50.
24. Johnstone, 29.
25. Ibid, 30.
26. E 101/353/18, m.2.d, 3d, 4d. Phillips, 51.
27. E 101/353/18, m.6. Johnstone, 28. Phillips, 51.
28. Ibid.

3. Stepping out of the Shadows

1. Phillips, 78. Johnstone, 33.
2. Phillips, 78–79. Johnstone, 36.
3. Guisborough, 29. Phillips, 78.
4. Johnstone, 36.
5. Miller, Edward. *War and Economic Development*, 19.
6. *Annales Prioratus de Dunstapalia, Annales Monastici*, 392.
7. Miller, 11–13.
8. CPR, 1292–1301, 297. Morris, 306.
9. Morris, 305–6. Powicke, M. *The Thirteenth Century*, 682–83.
10. CCR, 1296–1302, 142.
11. CCW, 75.
12. Flores, 103.
13. Guisborough, 294.
14. Ibid, 3984–403.
15. Prestwich, 478.
16. PW, 62–3.
17. Morris, 312.
18. Johnstone, 32.
19. Foedera, I, ii, 894.
20. Morris, 319.
21. Johnstone, 44–5.
22. E 101/353/18,m.6 Johnstone, 45.
23. Johnstone, 46 citing St Edmundsbury Chronicle in English Historical Review, lviii, 75.
24. Johnstone, 51. Phillips, 82–4.

25. Roll of Arms of the Princes, Barons and Knights who attended Edward I at the Siege of Caerlaverock, 17–18.

4. Prince of Wales

1. Morris, 327–30.
2. CChR, 1300–26, 6.
3. Cockerill, 285.
4. CChR, 1300–26, 9. Johnstone, 57–60.
5. CChR, 1300–26, 6.
6. Ibid, 9.
7. Johnstone, 60.
8. Phillips, 86.
9. CPR, 1343–45, 227–34. Johnstone, 62.
10. Conway-Davies, *Conquest*, 386. Phillips, 86.
11. CPR, 1434–45, 228, 231. Johnstone, 63.
12. Letters, 11.
13. Ibid, 114.
14. Phillips, 37–8.
15. Ibid, 89.
16. Prestwich, 127.
17. CCR, 1288–1296, 502.
18. Letters, 135.

5. A Taste of War

1. Prestwich, 493.
2. Phillips, 89–90.
3. Johnstone, 73.
4. Ibid, 76.
5. Morris, 332–33.
6. Ibid, 333. Prestwich, 493.
7. Johnstone, 81.
8. Ibid, 85.
9. Cockerill, 339.
10. Johnstone, 85.
11. Ibid, 87. Phillips, 92.
12. E 101/363/18, ff.9d, 10.
13. E 101/363/18, f, 20.
14. Morris, 339.
15. *Chronicle of Peter Langtoft*, 255.
16. Johnstone, 92.
17. Morris, 343. Prestwich, 501.
18. Ibid.
19. Weir, 6. Phillips, 91.

6. Knighthood

1. Johnstone, 96–7.
2. Letters, 30. Hamilton, 31.
3. CDS, ii, 397.
4. Prestwich, 548–49.
5. Beardwood, A. *The Trial of Walter Langton*, 14–15.
6. Johnstone, 99.
7. Ibid, 99.
8. Morris, 343–44. Prestwich, 503.
9. Letters, 70.

10. Phillips, 107.
11. CPR, 1301–07, 428. CCR, 1302–7, 438.
12. Morris, 354.
13. Flores, 131. Johnstone, 107.
14. CCR, 1302–07, 434, 438.
15. CPR, 1301–7, 424.
16. Flores, 131. Hamilton, 32. Johnstone, 107.
17. Ann Lond, 146.
18. Johnstone, 108.
19. *Chronicle of Peter of Langtoft*, 260.
20. Phillips, 112.
21. Ibid, 112. Morris, 355.
22. Ann Lond, 146.
23. Hamilton, 33. Johnstone, 112.
24. Lanercost, 177.
25. Phillips, 113.
26. CDS, ii, 508.
27. Phillips, 114.
28. Lanercost. 179–80.
29. Morris, 357.
30. Phillips, 115–16.
31. Johnstone, 116. Hamilton, 33. Mortimer, 28.

7. An Errant Son

1. Guisborough, 382–3. Ann Paul, 255. Hamilton, 34–5.
2. Phillips, 121. Davies, R.R *The First English Empire*, 34–5.
3. CCR, 1302–07, 526–7. Hamilton, 34. Chaplais, 22. Johnstone, 123–24.
4. Phillips, 122–23. Haskins, *A Chronicle of the Civil Wars of Edward II*, 75.
5. Hamilton, 19–28. Chaplais, 4–5.
6. Phillips, 120–1.
7. Ann Paul, 255. Lanercost, 210.
8. Hamilton, 34. Johnstone, 123.
9. BL Add. MS 22923 f.14v. Johnstone, 123–4.
10. CCR, 1302–07, 506, 516.
11. BL Add. MS 22923 f. 7v, f12. Hamilton, 35.
12. Hamilton, 138.
13. BL Add. MS 22923 f.17v. Hamilton, 36.
14. Morris, 360.
15. Ibid, 360–1.
16. *The Song of Lewes*, 14. Edward I was called a 'leopard' in the contemporary song of Lewes.
17. Guisborough, 379. Prestwich, 556–7. Johnstone, 126.

Part Two: Love and Betrayal

8. The King's Favour

1. Lanercost, 182.
2. Guisborough, 379.
3. Seymour, 126 citing C 47/24/3, no 1b.
4. Chaplais, 27.
5. Lanercost, 184. *Vita*,1. Chaplais, 27.
6. Maddicott, 70–1. Hamilton, 37. Chaplais, 31.
7. *Vita*, 1.
8. Maddicott, 71.

9. Chaplais, 26 citing PRO E 101/373/15,f. 21v.
10. Ibid, 26.
11. Phillips, 127.
12. Hamilton, 39, 140.
13. Ibid, 43.
14. Aymer, 25.
15. Prestwich, *Plantagenet England*, 175–7. Phillips, 129.
16. Guisborough, 383. Phillips, 130.
17. Ann Paul, 257. Flores, 140.
18. Phillips, 130.
19. Prestwich, 558. Morris, 363–64.
20. Hamilton, 38. Chaplais, 34.
21. Hamilton, 38.
22. *Vita*, 2.
23. Weir, 16.
24. Foedera, 24. Ann Paul, 258. CPR, 1307–13, 31.
25. Foedera, 28, CPR, 1307–13, 43. Aymer, 133.
26. *Vita*, 3.
27. Boswell, J.B. *Christianity, Social Tolerance and Homosexuality* (Chicago, 1980), 298–300. Maddicott, 83. Hamilton, 110.
28. Ann Paul, 255, 259.
29. *Vita*, 30.
30. Burgtorf, J. *"With my life, his joyes began and ended": Piers Gaveston and King Edward II of England Revisited*, 31–51. Jochen Burgtorf sets out the context for the chroniclers' general writings and motivations in their work. However, I disagree with his overall conclusion that Edward and Gaveston were not in a same-sex relationship.
31. Guisborough, 382. Ann Paul, 258. Hamilton, 22. John Stowe made a reference to Claramonde de Marsan as a witch in his *Chronicle of England*.
32. Hamilton, 20–24. Sets out Gaveston's heritage in comprehensive detail.
33. Ibid, 23–4, 27.
34. Ibid, 19.
35. CPR, 1307–13, 43. PW, 18–19. Foedera, 27. Phillips, 133.
36. Weir, 16.
37. Costain, Thomas. *The Pageant of England, 1272–1377: The Three Edwards* (London, 1973).Weir, 27.
38. Phillips, 134–5.
39. Ibid, 135.
40. Trokelowe, 65. Hamilton, 47.

9. A Pariah at Court

1. Hamilton, 46.
2. Ibid, 46.
3. BL MS Harley 636, f. 232.
4. CPR, 1307–13, 34. Chaplais, 41. Hamilton, 45.
5. Foedera, 31. PW, appendix, 9–10. CFR, 1307–19, 14.
6. Guisborough, 383. Ann Paul, 257.
7. Murimuth, 11.
8. Ann Paul, 258.
9. Prestwich, 561–2. McFarlane, K.B. *Had Edward I a "policy" Towards the Earls,* 248–67.
10. Prestwich, 561–3.
11. Bod. Dugdale MS 18, f.80. Phillips, 316–17.

12. Select Historical Documents, 1–5. Strong, Roy. *Coronation: A History of Kingship and British Monarchy*, 92–3.
13. Ann Paul, 260.
14. Phillips, 143–5.
15. Ibid, 140, 144.
16. Flores, 141. Ann Paul, 260.
17. Foedera, 33–6.
18. Phillips, 145.
19. E 101/325/4, m2. E 101/373/15, F.51.
20. Ann Paul, 262.
21. Ann Paul, 262–3. Guisborough, 381–2.
22. CFR, 1307–19, 17–19. CPR, 1307–13, 51–52. Hamilton, 49.
23. Maddicott, 76.
24. CFR, 1307–19, 5. Hamilton, 49.
25. Phillips, 147.
26. Ann Paul, 263.
27. PROME, Parliament, March 1308.
28. EHD, 1189–1327, 525–6.
29. Phillips, 149.
30. E 101/373/7.
31. Foedera, 44. Ann Lond, 154.
32. Hamilton, 53.
33. Phillips, 150.
34. Foedera, 48. CChR, 1300–26, 111. Hamilton, 53–4.
35. Lanercost, 187.
36. CPR, 1307–13, 83, 93. Foedera, 51.
37. Hamilton, 57.
38. E 101/373/15 f. 47v.

10. A Time for Tact

1. Hamilton, 67.
2. Ibid, 68.
3. Maddicott, 71. Phillips, 127–8.
4. Ann Paul, 264. Maddicott, 90–2. Hamilton, 67–9.
5. Ann Paul, 264.
6. Phillips, 152. Maddicott, 90.
7. Ormrod, W.M. *Thomas of Lancaster's First Quarrel with Edward II*, 31–45.
8. Ann Paul, 264.
9. PROME, Parliament, April 1309.
10. Foedera, 53, 65. CPR, 1307–13, 94. Phillips, 153. Maddicott, 94.
11. Hamilton, 70.
12. E 101/373/24m. CPR. 1307–13, 94.
13. Foedera, 54, 63–4. Phillips, 152.
14. Foedera, 55.
15. Phillips, 153.
16. *Vita*, 6–7.
17. Phillips, 154.
18. Foedera, 69. Phillips, 154.
19. E 101/372/23.
20. Maddicott, 95–7. Hamilton, 72. Phillips, 155.
21. Maddicott, 97–8. Phillips, 156.
22. Foedera 51, Hamilton, 70.
23. *Vita*, 7. Chaplais, 58–9. Maddicott, 97.
24. Hamilton, 73.

25. CCR, 1307–13, 158–9. Phillips, 158.
26. Bod, MS Latin Hist 5, m10.

11. The Ordinances

1. PW, 37–8.
2. Select Historical Documents, 6–8. Maddicott, 103–4. Phillips, 159.
3. CCR, 1307–13, 225–6.
4. Hamilton, 74.
5. Warner, 55. Chaplais, 56–7.
6. *Vita*, 7–8.
7. Ibid, 16–17. Phillips, 161.
8. *Vita*, 8. Lanercost, 194. Haines, 74.
9. Guisborough, 384. Hamilton, 76–7.
10. PW, 40–2.
11. *Vita*, 8.
12. Ibid, 9.
13. CPR, 1307–13, 206–7. Phillips, 164.
14. Ann Lond, 167–8.
15. PROME, Parliament, February 1310.
16. Ann Lond, 168–9.
17. Ibid. Phillips, 165.
18. PROME, Parliament, February, 1310.
19. *Vita*, 10.
20. Phillips, 166.
21. Foedera, 113. Ann Lond, 173. Haines, 76–77.
22. Phillips, 167.
23. Ann Paul, 269.
24. Phillips, 168.
25. Hamilton, 81.
26. Trokelowe, 72–3. Hamilton, 85.
27. *Vita*, 21–3. Ann Lond, 174. Ann Paul, 269.
28. Phillips, 170.
29. Hamilton, 84.
30. Foedera, 129. Hamilton, 85.
31. Maddicott, 23. Hamilton, 40.
32. Lanercost, 215.
33. CFR, 1307–19, 92.
34. Phillips, 171.
35. Guisborough, 385. Murimuth, 15.
36. Foedera, 128–9.
37. PW, 44–56.
38. CDS, iii no177. Phillips, 174.
39. CFR, 1307–19, 73.
40. *Vita*, 23.
41. Ann Paul, 269. Hamilton, 87.
42. EHD, 1189–1327, 527–39.
43. Ibid, 532.
44. Phillips, 176–77.
45. Maddicott, 177.

12. Murder at Blacklow Hill

1. Ann Lond, 202. Ann Paul, 271.
2. Foedera, 144. Chaplais, 75.
3. BL Cotton MS. Nero C VIII, f. 83.
4. PW, 57–68. Parliament ran from 5 November until 18 December 1311.
5. Ann Lond, 198–202.
6. CPR, 1307–13, 397 in relation to the appointment of Gaveston's attorneys.
7. Phillips, 182.
8. Foedera, 151.
9. *Vita*, 21.
10. BL Cotton MS *Nero C VIII*, f.84. Given Philip IV's hostility to Piers, it would be unlikely that he would linger in northern France, so it is therefore likely he had indeed set himself up in the duchy of Edward's sister Margaret and the king's brother-in-law.
11. Phillips, 183. Chaplais, 78–9.
12. CCR, 1307–12, 448 –49. Foedera, 153–4.
13. CCR, 1307–12, 449.
14. BL Cotton MS Nero C VIII, f84v. Hamilton, 94. Phillips, 183.
15. CPR, 1307–13, 413.
16. Ann Paul, 271.
17. BL Cotton MS Nero C VIII, f84v. Phillips, 182. Maddicott, 124.
18. Hamilton, 93.
19. Ibid, 93.
20. *Vita*, 24.
21. CChR, 1300–26, 185–87, 189–91.
22. *Vita*, 22–3.
23. Hamilton, 95.
24. Ann Lond, 204. Aymer, 32. Phillips, 186.
25. CPR, 1307–13, 453.
26. Ibid, 454. CFR, 1307–19. 129.
27. *Vita*, 23. Foedera, 203.
28. Hamilton, 95–96. Phillips, 187.
29. Phillips, 188. Hamilton, 96.
30. *Vita*, 43. Ann Lond, 204.
31. Ann Lond, 204. Phillips, 188, Maddicott, 125–6, Aymer, 33–4.
32. Trokelowe, 76.
33. PW, 72. Flores, 150.
34. *Vita*, 25.
35. *Vita*, 27. Lanercost, 198. Trokelowe, 77. Flores, 152.
36. Ann Lond, 207.
37. Ibid, 207. *Vita* 27–8.

13. Fragile Peace

1. *Vita*, 26. Hamilton, 98.
2. Hamilton, 109–112. Excellent summary of Gaveston's changing position at court and suggested reasons for his demise.
3. Lanercost, 198.
4. *Vita*, 32.
5. Flores, 336. Phillips, 193.
6. Foedera, 173–4. CPR, 1307–13, 485–88. CCR, 1307–13, 428–29, 540, 542–43, 544.
7. The Political Songs of England. Ed. T. Wright, 259–261.
8. Hamilton, 168.
9. PW, 53. CPR, 1307–13, 489–90.

10. *Vita*, 29–30. Ann Lond, 208–10.
11. Ann Paul, 272. Ann Lond, 210. *Vita*, 33.
12. Ann Lond, 211. Maddicott, 135. Phillips, 199.
13. Maddicott, 140–141.
14. CPR, 1307–13, 508. Foedera, 184.
15. Warner, 78.
16. CCR, 1307–13, 558. Foedera, 187. Phillips, 201.
17. Ann Lond, 221. CPR, 1307–13, 395, 398. Warner, 79.
18. Phillips, 207.
19. Foedera, 203–205. Maddicott, 336.
20. Foedera, 203–205. Hamilton, 121–26.
21. Chaplais, 91–93.
22. Ann Lond, 225. *Vita*, 38.
23. CCR, 1307–13, 583. Foedera, 212–13.
24. *Vita*, 39.
25. Warner, 80.
26. Ibid, 80. Phillips, 210.
27. Phillips, 210.
28. *Chronique Metrique de Godfray de Paris*, ed J A Buchon, 194.
29. Warner, 81.
30. Ibid, 81. Phillips, 213.
31. Warner, 81.
32. Ibid, 81.
33. PW, 103.
34. Foedera, 230–3. *Vita*, 43–4. CPR, 1307–13, 21–26, 35–6.

Part Three: Overmighty Vassals

14. Bannockburn

1. McNamee, 131. Haines, 254.
2. McNamee, 59–60.
3. Ibid, 131. Phillips, 224.
4. Phillips, 219.
5. Haines, 93.
6. CPR, 1313–17, 49–51. Ann Lond, 227.
7. CCR, 1313–18, 86.
8. CCW, 395.
9. CCR, 1313–18, 95.
10. McNamee, 61.
11. Prestwich, Armies and Warfare, 117. Phillips, 226.
12. *Vita*, 50.
13. Meaux, 331–332 claims it was because the summons contravened the Ordinances, which had in fact been in abeyance since early 1312.
14. Knighton, 410. Flores, 156–7. Aymer, 73. Phillips, 227.
15. *Vita*, 50. Aymer, 157–8. Barrow, 206. Phillips, 227.
16. PW, 120–125. Writs of summons were issued on 26 November 1313.
17. Bruce, 376. Barrow, 209. McNamee, 60–1.
18. *Vita*, 50.
19. Ibid, 50–1.
20. Barrow, 208–9.
21. Nusbacher, 130.
22. Bruce, 496–7.
23. Flores, 158. *Vita*, 51. Haines, 259. Barrow, 217.
24. *Vita*, 51. Bruce, 448–51. Barrow, 216. Nusbacher, 111–12.

25. *Scalacronica*, 53–4. Bruce, 452–7. Barrow, 219–21.
26. Nusbacher, 96.
27. *Scalacronica*, 55.
28. Bruce, 456. Barrow, 222. Nusbacher, 122–123.
29. Nusbacher, 126. Phillips, 231.
30. *Vita*, 52.
31. Bruce, 442–4. Nusbacher, 130–1.
32. *Scalacronica*, 55. Nusbacher, 125.
33. Bruce, 472–3. Barrow, 225–6. Phillips, 232.
34. Bruce, 480–1. *Vita*, 52–3. Prestwich, Armies and Warfare, 223.
35. Trokelowe, 86. *Scalacronica*, 56.
36. Warner, 88–9.
37. Bruce, 494–7. *Scalacronica*, 56. Lanercost, 208–9. Phillips, 232–3. Barrow, 229. Aymer, 74.
38. *Vita*, 54. Bruce, 498–9. Lanercost, 227–28. Aymer, 74–5.
39. Ann Lond, 231.
40. Lanercost, 228. *Vita*, 55. Aymer, 75. Barrow, 231. Phillips, 236.
41. Phillips, 232. Barrow, 231.
42. Nusbacher, 125–6., 130.
43. Warner, 15, 87 claims Edward had a 'lack of military ability and experience', which is incorrect but refutes the claim of cowardice. Tout, 30 claims Edward was 'weak and feckless'; Hutchinson, 85 holds that it is 'unjust' to blame Edward for defeat at Bannockburn; Nusbacher, 130 refutes the claim that Edward was an 'idiot' in military matters.

15. Disputes and Discord

1. *Vita*, 57.
2. PW, 126–135.
3. CPR, 1313–17, 169.
4. *Vita*, 57. Lanercost, 229.
5. CCR, 1313–18, 197–8. CPR, 1313–17, 178. CFR, 1307–19, 220–1. Phillips, 239.
6. Flores, 173. *Vita*, 58.
7. Foedera, 254–6. McNamee, 77–8. Phillips, 240.
8. *Vita*, 58. Lanercost, 229.
9. *Vita*, 58–9.
10. Warner, 93.
11. Hamilton, 166. Phillips, 241.
12. CPR, 1324–27, 281.
13. Chaplais, 111.
14. Phillips, 241–42. Hamilton, 99–100.
15. Trokelowe, 88. BL Cotton, Cleoptra D.III, f56d. Phillips, 242.
16. Trokelowe, 88.
17. *Vita*, 69. Lanercost, 217.
18. *Vita*, 70–1.
19. Maddicott, 163. Phillips, 253. Jordan, W.C. *Great Famine*, 18–19, 194.
20. Trokelowe, 95. *Vita*, 70.
21. Ann Lond, 232.
22. Maddicott, 158–61. Phillips, 246.
23. CCR, 1313–18, 163.
24. *Vita*, 59.
25. Foedera, 263,266,268. *Vita*, 69.
26. Phillips, 278.
27. Warner, 97.

28. McNamee, 169–71.
29. Ibid. 171–75. Davies, R.R. *The Scots' invasion of Ireland*, 1315, 109–10. Lydon, J. *The Impact of the Bruce Invasion*, 196.
30. Lanercost, 213–16. *Vita*, 61–2.
31. Foedera, 275. Maddicott, 171. Phillips, 259–61.
32. Flores, 173.
33. PW, 152–58. Parliament had been summoned on 16 October 1315.
34. Maddicott, 181–2. Phillips, 267.
35. Gesta Edwardi, 50–2.
36. CPR, 1313–17, 476. CCW, 440.
37. Phillips, 276. Maddicott, 186–7.
38. CCR, 1313–18, 267.
39. *Vita*, 66. Smith, J.B. *The Rebellion of Llywelyn Bren*, 72–86.
40. *Vita*, 67. CCW, 437–39. Smith, *Rebellion*, 79–86.
41. Phillips, 272–73. Warner, 102.
42. *Vita*, 74. Phillips, 274. Aymer, 103.
43. Warner, 105.

16. New Favourites

1. *Vita*, 76.
2. Ibid, 75–6.
3. Maddicott, 24–5.
4. Foedera, 302. Phillips, 281–2.
5. Wright, *The Church and the English Crown, App II,* 283. Warner, 104. Phillips, 284.
6. CPR, 1313–17, 563. CFR, 1307–19, 312.
7. CCW, 450–9.
8. CPR, 1313–17, 608. Phillips, 286.
9. Foedera, 322–4.
10. Ibid, 321–2, 327–8. CPL, 1305–42, 127.
11. Foedera, 302–22. Phillips, 284. Haines, *The Church and Politics*, 16–19.
12. *Vita*, 79.
13. *Scalacronica*, 78–9. Foedera, 329. Aymer, 111–17.
14. Phillips, 289.
15. CPR, 1313–17, 12. CCR, 1313–18, 45–6.
16. Phillips, 288–9.
17. CPR, 1317–21, 6,9.
18. CCR, 1313–18, 451. Trivet, 20.
19. Flores, 178. Trivet, 20.
20. CFR, 1307–19, 225.
21. Ibid, 234, 237, 249, 316–17.
22. Maddicott, 193–4.
23. CChR, 1300–26, 361, 403. Maddicott, 194–5.
24. CFR, 1307–19, 337.
25. CPR, 1313–17, 609, 669–70. Maddicott, 194. Phillips, 294.
26. Flores, 78. Trivet, 20.
27. CCR, 1313–18, 449–56.
28. Maddicott, 191.
29. Meaux, 335.
30. Phillips, 270. Warner, 100.
31. Warner, 109. Phillips, 270.
32. C 81/100/4231
33. Warner, 110.
34. CPR, 1317–21, 641, 644.

35. Trokelowe, 98–9. Walsingham, 149–50.
36. Ibid.
37. CCR, 1313–18, 477. E 163/3/6, m1. Maddicott, 195. Phillips, 297.
38. CCR, 1313–18, 482.
39. Phillips, 293.
40. Gesta Edwardi, 50–2.
41. Maddicott, 196.
42. *Vita*, 80.
43. Ibid, 80.
44. *Vita*, 81. Phillips, 298.
45. Trivet, 23. *Vita*, 81.
46. Phillips, 299. Maddicott, 205.
47. Melsa, 334. Trivet, 23. Maddicott, 206–7.
48. Foedera, 341. Lanercost, 218. *Scalacronica*, 60. *Anonimalle*, 90–2.
49. Trivet, 23. Flores, 180. *Vita*, 81.
50. PW, 171.
51. Trivet, 23. Flores, 180. *Vita*, 82.
52. CPR, 1313–21, 34, 46, 58.
53. Maddicott, 207–8. Phillips, 302.
54. CPR, 1317–21, 46. CFR, 1307–19, 344. CCR, 1313–18,504–5. Foedera, 343.
55. Foedera, 346–7.
56. Phillips, 303.
57. E /163/4/6. Aymer, 135. Phillips, 303. Maddicott, 211–12.

17. Hollow Treaty

1. PW, 178. CCR, 1313–18, 590. CPR, 1317–21, 69.
2. Lanercost, 219–20. *Scalacronica*, 66. McNamee, 151–2.
3. Flores, 183–4. Gesta Edwardi, 54. Knighton, 413.
4. Phillips, 314.
5. Ann Paul, 282. Maddicott, 218–19.
6. Phillips, 315.
7. *Anonimalle*, 95.
8. Lanercost, 236.
9. Childs, Wendy. *Welcome my Brother*, 149–162.
10. Ibid, 319–20.
11. *Vita*, 88.
12. Maddicott, 235–6.
13. E/163/4/7/2. Foedera, 370. CCR, 1318–23, 112–114.
14. Foedera, 371.
15. Maddicott, 224–226. Phillips, 320.
17. PW, 182–95.
18. Lanercost, 225–6.
19. *Vita*, 93.
20. Foedera, 377.
21. CCR, 1318–23, 109–10. Phillips, 331. Maddicott, 233.
22. Foedera, 399 in connection to the English delegation's trip to Avignon.
23. Phillips, 324–5. Phillips, S, *Edward II and the Prophets*, 196–7.
24. Phillips, 341–2.
25. *Anonimalle*, 95–7. *Vita*, 94–5.
26. CCR, 1318–23, 141.
27. Phillips, 343.
28. Lanercost, 227–8.
29. Ibid. Maddicott, 244.
30. Ann Paul, 286.

31. McNamee, 218 citing BL MS Aff 17362, ff.25, 28.
32. McNamee, 218.
33. *Anonimalle*, 97.
34. Phillips, 349.
35. *Scalacronica*, 86–7. *Anonimalle*, 97.
36. Ann Paul, 287–8.
37. Ibid. *Vita*, 95. Flores, 189.
38. *Vita*, 96–7. Bruce, 646. *Anonimalle*, 99. McNamee, 94.
39. Flores, 188.
40. Lanercost, 227.
41. Melsa, 336. Gesta Edwardi, 57. Maddicott, 247. Bruce, 658.
42. Maddicott, 249. Phillips, 350.
42. *Vita*, 98.
43. Ibid, 102.
44. Lanercost, 228.
45. *Vita*, 104.
46. Phillips, 354.
47. CPR, 1318–21, 425. Aymer, 189.
48. Phillips, 355.
49. Vale, M. *The Princely Court*, 51.
50. Ann Paul, 289.
51. Ibid, 290.
52. Flores, 193. Warner, 133.
53. Haines, 45. Phillips, 358. Maddicott, 257. Warner, 136.

18. A Wolf in the Fold

1. CPR, 1317–21, 514.
2. CPR, 1317–21, 60, 103, 415, 456.
3. Pugh,T.B. 'Marcher Lords', 168. Phillips, 365.
4. CCR, 1318–23, 268.
5. CPR, 1317–21, 547. CFR, 1319–27, 41, 43.
6. Ann Paul, 237. Davies,J.C *Despenser's War*, 36–42.
7. *Vita*, 108–9.
8. Phillips, 386.
9. Brut, 212.
10. Le Baker cited in Haines, 124.
11. Murimuth, 33.
12. Philips, 367. Goronwy, J.Edwards, *Calendar of Ancient Correspondence*, 219–20.
13. *Anonimalle*, 92. Phillips, 368.
14. Phillips, 373. Maddicott, 264, 306.
15. CCR, 1318–23, 290.
16. CCR, 1318–23, 363–4. Maddicott, 265. Phillips, 375.
17. Maddicott, 265–6.
18. CCR, 1318–23, 367–8.
19. Ibid, 366.
20. *Vita*, 110. Davies, *Despenser's War*, 53.
21. CPR, 1321–24, 167–8. Warner, 142.
22. *Vita*, 111. Davies, *Despenser's War*, 56.
23. *Vita*, 110.
24. Ibid, 111.
25. Flores, 197. Gesta Edwardi, 62. Maddicott, 274–5.
26. Maddicott, 242–3. Phillips, 378–82.

27. Wilkinson, B. *The Sherburn Indenture and the Attack on the Despensers,* *1321,* 1–28.
28. CCR, 1318–23, 367–8. *Vita,* 112.
29. *Vita,* 112. PW, 234–43.
30. *Scalacronica,* 70. *Anonimalle,* 101. *Vita,* 115–6.
31. CFR, 1319–27, 62.
32. Flores, 199.
33. Ann Paul, 293–4. Trokelowe, 109.
34. Ann Paul, 294–6. *Vita,* 112.
35. *Vita,* 112.
36. Phillips, 287–8 citing the *Historia Roffensis in Parliamentary Texts,* 155–73.
37. Ann Paul, 297. Warner, 145.
38. *Vita,* 113–4. Ann Paul, 297.
39. Phillips, 392. PROME, Parliament of 1321.
40. Parliamentary Texts, 168–9.
41. Ann Paul, 207. *Vita,* 114–6. *Anonimalle,* 101. CCR, 1318–23, 494.
42. *Vita,* 116.
43. Phillips, 394. Warner, 146.

Part Four: Freedom Corrupts

19. A Lover's Revenge

1. *Vita,* 115.
2. *Anonimalle,* 103.
3. Ann Paul, 300. *Vita,* 115.
4. *Vita,* 117–18. *Anonimalle,* 105.
5. CCR, 1318–23, 402, 408.
6. Ann Paul, 298–9.
7. CCR, 1318–23, 504. Ann Paul, 299.
8. Ann Paul, 299. *Anonimalle,* 103.
9. Phillips, 400.
10. Maddicott, 299–300.
11. CCR, 1318–23, 408, 506, 508. CPR, 1321–24, 38.
12. Maddicott, 301.
13. CCR, 1318–23, 541–5. Phillips, 400.
14. *Vita,* 118.
15. Ibid, 118. Phillips, 402.
16. Ann Paul, 301. *Vita,* 121.
17. *Vita,* 118.
18. CPR, 1321–24, 47–51.
19. Murimuth, 35. Ann Paul, 301. *Anonimalle,* 105.
20. *Vita,* 119.
21. Flores, 203. *Vita,* 120.
22. Foedera, 472–3. Maddicott, 307. Phillips, 405.
23. Lanercost, 231–32.
24. Foedera, 473.
25. CPR, 1321–24, 73–4.
26. CCR, 1318–23, 525–6. Foedera, 463, 472, 474. Ann Paul, 302.
27. Maddicott, 295–6.
28. *Vita,* 122. Gesta Edwardi, 74. *Anonimalle,* 104–5.
29. *Vita,* 123.
30. CCR, 1318–23, 522. Phillips, 407.
31. *Vita,* 122–23.
32. Brut, 217. Maddicott, 311.

33. Flores, 205. *Vita*, 124. Ann Paul, 302.
34. Lanercost, 233. *Anonimalle*, 107.
35. *Vita*, 124. Lanercost, 233.
36. *Anonimalle*, 107.
37. *Anonimalle*, 107. *Vita*, 125.
38. Foedera, 478–9. Maddicott, 311–12. Phillips, 408–9.
39. Brut, 222–3.
40. *Vita*, 126. Ann Paul, 303. Gesta Edwardi, 76. Maddicott, 312.
41. Dr Samuel Johnson.

20. Wheel of Fortune

1. *Vita*, 124–5.
2. Foedera, 479. Haskins, 'A Chronicle of the Civil Wars of Edward II'. Sayles, 'Formal Judgement on the Traitors of 1322', 60.
3. Brut, 224. Gesta Edwardi, 78.
4. Trokelowe, 109.
5. *Anonimalle*, 109. Fryde, 61.
6. Murimuth, 43.
7. PW, 216. Mortimer, 126.
8. Fryde, 63.
9. Ibid, 63–4. Mortimer, 121.
10. E 403/207, mII.
11. CPL, 448.
12. CChR, 1300–26, 442–4, 448. CPR, 1321–24, 128. Foedera, 481.
13. CChR, 1300–26, 444, 448–51.
14. Phillips, 418.
15. CPR, 1321–24, 87. CChR, 1300–26, 441.
16. Fryde, 76–7.
17. PW, 245–60.
18. Ibid. Phillips, 422.
19. CPR, 1321–24, 96–8. Foedera, 482.
20. Prestwich, Armies and Warfare, 117. Phillips, 227–8.
21. CCR, 1318–23, 563–4. Aymer, 227–8.
22. Bruce, 680–1.
23. Phillips, 427.
24. Lanercost, 247.
25. Flores, 210. Lanercost, 246. Bruce, 684–8.
26. Lanercost, 240.
27. Ibid.
28. Doherty, 75–8. Isabella, 156.
29. Isabella, 156. Holmes, *Judgement on Despenser the Younger*, 265.
30. Phillips, 421–22.
31. Foedera, 502.
32. CPR, 1321–24, 260. Foedera, 509.
33. Phillips, 431–6.
34. *Vita*, 127–131.
35. Sempringham, 346. Phillips, 439.
36. Ann Paul, 305.
37. *Anonimalle*, 115. Flores, 213–14.
38. Ann Paul, 305–6. Flores, 217. Murimuth, 40. Phillips, 440. Mortimer, 1–2.
39. Phillips, 440.
40. Foedera, 506.
41. Warner, 172.
42. Phillips, 450–1.

43. *Vita*, 119.
44. Haines, 'The Church and Politics', 145–7. Phillips, 453.

21. Wife, Queen, Rebel
  1. Ann Paul, 307. Aymer, 233.
  2. Aymer, 233.
  3. Sardos, 188.
  4. Foedera, 560–2. Phillips, 463–4.
  5. CFR, 1319–27, 300. *Anonimalle*, 119.
  6. Phillips, 466.
  7. Foedera, 570. Buck, 151.
  8. Buck, 152, note 166.
  9. *Vita*, 142.
  10. Sardos, 61–3. Phillips, 464–66. Vale, 238.
  11. Foedera, 568–73. Warner, 182–3.
  12. Phillips, 469.
  13. Ibid, 467.
  14. Foedera, 580.
  15. *Anonimalle*, 119. Ann Paul, 308.
  16. *Vita*, 136. Sardos, 210, 220, 226. Buck, 150–1.
  17. Ann Paul, 308. Phillips, 468.
  18. Foedera, 579.
  19. Sardos, 193–6.
  20. Sardos, 59, 72–3. Warner, 184.
  21. Foedera, 599.
  22. CPR, 1324–27, 44.
  23. *Vita*, 135. Ann Paul, 308.
  24. Sardos, 199. Phillips, 472.
  25. Foedera, 601–2.
  26. *Anonimalle*, 115. Lanercost, 250.
  27. *Vita*, 142.
  28. Ibid, 140, 142.
  29. Ibid, 138.
  30. PW, 328–33. Phillips, 475.
  31. Warner, 188.
  32. Phillips, 448–54.
  33. CFR, 1319–27, 262, 269. Haines, *The Church and Politics*, 145–7.
  34. *Vita*, 136–7.
  35. Ibid, 137.
  36. Ibid, 139.
  37. Foedera, 600–1. Phillips, 477.
  38. *Vita*, 136.
  39. Foedera, 604–6.
  40. Ibid, 606.
  41. BL Cotton. MS Faustina, B.v, f45v. Phillips, 477.
  42. *Vita*, 140. Murimuth, 44.
  43. *Anonimalle*, 115.
  44. Sardos, 243–5. Ann Paul, 309.
  45. Warner, 187.
  46. Lanercost, 249. Ann Paul, 337.
  47. Lanercost, 249.
  48. Phillips, 481.
  49. *Vita*, 143.
  50. PW, 334–47.

51. Murimuth, 46. *Vita*, 142. Le Baker, 20. Buck, 157.
52. *Vita*, 143–4.
53. *Vita*, 144. See appendices of this book for letters from Edward II in 1325–26 to Isabella, Edward his son and heir and Charles IV of France.
54. CCR, 1323–27, 580–2. Foedera, 615.
55. Foedera, 616.

22. Bloodletting

1. CCR, 1323–27, 133–4.
2. Sardos, 2.
3. CCR, 1323–27, 543. Foedera, 619.
4. Phillips, 491.
5. CCR, 1323–27, 578.
6. Sardos, 270.
7. Warner, 205. Phillips, 492.
8. CPR, 1324–27, 206.
9. Fryde, 182.
10. Foedera, 618.
11. CPL, 1305–42, 473, 475.
12. Ibid, 473. Ann Paul, 312.
13. Phillips, 497–8 citing the Rochester Chronicle *Historia Roffensis*.
14. CCR, 1323–7, 576–8.
15. Brut, 234–5. *Scalacronica*, 90–3.
16. CPR, 1324–27, 208–210. CCR, 1323–27, 545–7.
17. Warner, 213 citing SAL MS 122, 75, 77.
18. Phillips, 57–8. Prestwich, *The Court of Edward II*, 69.
19. Phillips, 500.
20. Foedera, 636–9.
21. Warner, 214 citing SAL MS 122, 81.
22. Ibid.
23. CPR, 1324–27, 315–16.
24. Ann Paul, 312. Knighton, 431–2.
25. Le Bel, 18. Froissart, 66.
26. Fryde, 186.
27. *Anonimalle*, 123, 125.
28. Phillips, 504.
29. Haines, *The Church and Politics*, 165, 227.
30. Ann Paul, 315.
31. CPR, 1324–27, 327–31.
32. *Anonimalle*, 126–7. Fryde, 105.
33. Knighton, 434. Phillips, 505.
34. Ann Paul, 315. *Anonimalle*, 124–7.
35. Ann Paul, 315–6. *Anonimalle*, 129. Murimuth, 48. Buck, 220–1.
36. Buck, 221.
37. Knighton, 434. Phillips, 506.
38. CFR, 1319–27, 418–21.
39. Phillips, 509.
40. Haines, 165. Mortimer, 154–5. Phillips, 509. (According to the King James version of 285 years hence.)
41. Lanercost, 256–7.
42. Ibid, 256–7. *Anonimalle*, 131. Murimuth, 49.
43. CPR, 1324–27, 333–5.
44. CCR, 1323–27, 655–6. Foedera, 646.

45. PW, 350–66. The *custos regni* had no legal authority to request a parliament and without the presence of the king himself the body was not a legal entity or its decisions binding.
46. Ann Paul, 317–18. Phillips, 513.
47. Brut, 240.
48. CPR, 1324–27, 336.
49. Ann Paul, 319. Flores, 234. *Anonimalle*, 131. Phillips, 515. Fryde, 191–2.
50. CCR, 1323–27, 655.
51. Ann Paul, 321.
52. Ibid, 321. *Anonimalle*, 131.
53. Brut, 240.
54. Ann Paul, 32. Gesta Edwardi, 87. Holmes, *Judgement on Despenser the Younger*, 261–7. Phillips, 516.
55. Holmes, *Judgement on Despenser the Younger*, 261–7.
56. *Anonimalle*, 131.
57. Brut, 240. Knighton, 436. Ann Paul, 320. Le Bel, 28. Fryde, 192–3.

23. End of All Things

1. Flores, 235.
2. Haines, Death of a King, 32.
3. Mortimer, *Sermons of Sodomy*, 50–2.
4. PW, 350–66. CCR, 1327–30, 101–2.
5. Lanercost, 254.
6. Phillips, 526. Mortimer, 167. Valente, *Deposition*, 855–6.
7. Le Bel, 29.
8. Valente, 858–9. Phillips, 527.
9. Proverbs 11:14.
10. Phillips, 528.
11. Valente, 880–1. Mortimer, 169. Select Document, 37.
12. 2 Kings 4:19. Lanercost, 258.
13. Valente, *Deposition*, 871.
14. Mortimer, 168.
15. Ibid, 168. Doherty, 187. – Doherty claims de Béthune had overreached himself and so was forced to drop the deposition clause in the oath. This feels unlikely.
16. Le Baker, 27.
17. Ibid, 27. Warner, 14.
18. Foedera, 650. Ann Paul, 324. *Anonimalle*, 113. Select Documents, 38. Phillips, 536.
19. Valente, 880–1.
20. CCR, 1327–30, 1.
21. Murimuth, 54. Mortimer, 171. Doherty, 208–9.
22. Warner, K. Isabella, 215.
23. Ibid, 215. Fryde, 209.
24. CCR, 1327–30, 77.
25. Murimuth, 52. Ann Paul, 333.
26. PROME, November 1330 Parliament.
27. Murimuth, 52.
28. CCR, 1327–30, 77, 86.
29. Phillips, 541.
30. Valente, *The Lament of Edward II*, 422.29. Phillips, 541.
31. Fryde, 201. Phillips, 544. Tanqueray, F.J. *Conspiracies of Thomas Dunheved, 1327*, 119–24.

32. Phillips, 544. Warner, 237.
33. CPR, 1327–30, 99.
34. Murimuth, 52. Le Baker, 30–31.
35. Warner, 241. Phillips, 546–7.
36. Mortimer, 187.
37. Haines, *Afterlife*, 85. Phillips, 547–8. *Intrigue*, 68. Warner, 242.
38. *Anonimalle*, 135.
39. Ibid, 135.
40. Lanercost, 260.
41. Murimuth, 53–4.
42. French Chronicle, 58. PROME, November 1330 Parliament.
43. Brut, 253 as cited and translated in Mortimer, 190.
44. Ormrod, *The Sexualities of Edward II*, 37–9. Mortimer, *Sermons of Sodomy*, 53–6.
45. PROME, November 1330 Parliament.
46. Phillips, 552.
47. Ibid, 552. Blackley, F.D. ' The Tomb of Isabella', 161–4.
48. Murimuth, 52–3.
49. Historis et Cartularium, 44–5.
50. Mortimer, 186.
51. Phillips, 553.

24. Redemption

1. Murimuth, 60. Brut, 267. Foedera, 783, 787.
2. Brut, 255–6 for the Earl of Kent's confession. Warner, 250, confirms that a further thirty people were involved in Kent's plot, bringing the actual number closer to 70 than the 40 first suggested.
3. Warner, 248 citing CR136/C2027, Warwickshire County Record Office. *Intrigue*, 154–5.
4. Phillips, 566. Warner, 249.
5. Lanercost, 266. Phillips, 566. Warner, 250. Mortimer, 230–1.
6. Brut, 265. Mortimer, 229.
7. Murimuth, 60. Lanercost, 265. Le Baker, 44.
8. Phillips, 566–7.
9. Ibid, 570.. Phillips believes that the pope was not connected to the conspiracy, taking at face value the letter penned in September 1330. This fails to take into context the wider position that the pope found himself in, secretly supporting Edward III at a delicate time by corresponding with the king who secretly addressed his letters as 'Pater Sancte'. The pope could quite easily have been acting with more circumspection than his letter would otherwise indicate.
10. Lanercost, 265.
11. Mortimer, 230–1 believes it may have been Edward III who informed Kent of his father's secret whereabouts as a means of bringing Mortimer down from power.
12. Phillips, 568. Warner, 251.
13. Warner, 251.
14. PROME, November 1330 Parliament.
15. Mortimer, 248.
16. Foedera, 960. Phillips, 567.
17. Hunter, *Measures taken for the Apprehension of Sir Thomas de Gurney*, 274–97. Mortimer, 249.
18. CPR, 1330–34, 144.

19. PROME, November 1330 Parliament.
20. Mortimer, Chapter 12 Revised, 244–68 sets out comprehensive arguments for why Edward III must have known of his father's survival.
21. Brut, 267.
22. CPR, 1330–34, 535. Mortimer, 248.
23. Foedera, 56.
24. Phillips, 575. Mortimer, 248.
25. Appendix Two of this book – The Fieschi Letter. Mortimer, 251–52. Cuttino & Lyman, *Where is Edward II*, 544.
26. The letter was discovered in 1878 by a French archivist Alexandre Germain as he worked on the archives of the Bishop of Maguelone held in the *Archives départementales d' Hérault* at Montpellier. Since its publication, historians such as Frederick Tout, Cuttino and Lyman, Roy Martin Haines and more recently Ian Mortimer have hotly debated its contents.
27. Mortimer, 251–2.
28. Mortimer, Chapter 12 Revised, 244–68.
29. Phillips, 589. Mortimer, 254.
30. Mortimer, 258.
31. Ibid, 258.
32. Ibid, 259.
33. CPR, 1334–38, 489.
34. Mortimer, 260. Warner, 255.
35. CCR 1341–43, 83, 182. Mortimer, 263.
36. Murimuth, 135. Mortimer, 263.

Appendices

Appendix One

1. CCR, 1323–27, 580.
2. Ibid, 580–82.
3. Ibid, 578.
4. Ibid, 576–77.
5. Ibid, 577.

Appendix Two

1. Cuttino, G.P. and Lyman, Thomas W, *Where is Edward II*, Speculum, v. liii, 1978, 526–7.

List of Illustrations

23. The Execution of Thomas of Lancaster, March 1322 from the *Luttrell Psalter*, c1325–35 (© *The British Library Board*).
24. Secular or Pilgrim Badge depicting the execution of Thomas of Lancaster (© *The Trustees of the British Museum*).
25. An unhappy marriage. Edward II and Isabella of France from Walter de Milemete's *De Nobilitatibus, sapientiis, et prudentiis regum*, c14th (© *The Governing Body of Christ Church, Oxford*).
26. Isabella of France arrives at the gates of Paris, 1325 from the chronicle of Jean Froissart, c14th (© *Art Collection 3/Alamy Stock Photo*).
27. Caerphilly Castle, Caerphilly (*Creative Commons, Amanderson2*).
28. Isabella lands with her forces at Orwell, Suffolk in 1326 from Jean Fouquet's Chronicles of Saint-Denis, c15th (©Photo 12/*Alamy Stock Photo*).
29. Execution of Hugh Despenser the Younger at Hereford in 1326 from the chronicle of Jean Froissart, c14th (© *Photo 12/Alamy Stock Photo*).
30. Kenilworth Castle, Warwickshire (© *John Martin/Alamy Stock Photo*).
31. Berkeley Castle, Gloucestershire (*Creative Commons, Jeff Hart*).
32. Edward II's cell at Berkeley Castle, Gloucestershire (*Author's Collection by kind permission of the Berkeley Family*).
33. Dominican Friars; 'Jean de Vignay and his book', c14th (© *The British Library Board*).
34. Gloucester Cathedral, Gloucestershire (*Author's Collection*).
35. Manuscript depicting the tomb of Edward II from the *Romances in French Verse, Roman de Brut* (© *The British Library Board*).
36. Corfe Castle, Dorset (*Creative Commons, Andrew Campbell*).
37. Shrine of the Three Kings, Cologne (© *Interfoto/Alamy Stock Photo*).

Bibliography

Primary Sources

Adae Murimuth Continuatio Chronicarum, ed. E.M. Thompson (London, 1889).

Annales Londonienses 1195–1330, in W.Stubbs, ed. Chronicles of the Reigns of Edward I and Edward II, Vol I, Rolls Series, lxxvi (London, 1882).

Annales Paulini 1307–1340 in W.Stubbs, ed. Chronicles of the Reigns of Edward I and Edward II, Vol I, Rolls Series, lxxvi (London, 1882).

Annales Prioratus de Dunstaplia, Annales Monastici iii, ed. H.R. Luard (London, 1869).

Anonimalle Chronicle 1307 to 1334 from Brotherton Collection MS 29, ed. W.R Childs and J. Taylor (Yorkshire Archaeological Society Record Series 147, 1991).

The Bruce, ed. A.A.M. Duncan (Edinburgh, 1997).

The Brut, ed. F.W.D. Brie, Early English Text Society, cxxxi, part I (London, 1906).

Bodleian Library (esp Ms. Latin Hist).

British Library (esp Ads MS. 22923).

Calendar of Ancient Petitions relating to Wales, ed. J. Goronwy Edwards (Cardiff, 1975).

Calendar of Chancery Writs (London, HMSO, 1927).

Calendar of Charter Rolls, 1300–1326 (London, HMSO, 1908).

Calendar of Close Rolls (London, HMSO, 1898–1906).

Calendar of Documents Relating to Scotland, 1307–1357, ed. Joseph Bain (Edinburgh, 1887).

Calendar of Entries in the Papal Registers Relating to Great Britain and Ireland: Papal Letters, 1305–1341, ed. W.H. Bliss (London, HMSO, 1895).

Calendar of Fine Rolls (London, HMSO, 1911–13).

Calendar of Inquisitions Post Mortem (London, HMSO, 1898).

Calendar of Patent Rolls (London, HMSO, 1895–1903).

Chronicle of Peter of Langtoft in English Historical Documents, 1189–1327. ed. H.R. Rothwell (London, 1975).

Chronica Monasterii de Melsa, ed E.A Bond, vol ii, Rolls Series (London, 1867).

Chronicle of Walter of Guisborough, ed. H. Rothwell, Camden 3rd Series, lxxix (London, 1989).

Chronicon de Lanercost, 1272–1346, ed. Herbert Maxwell (Glasgow, 1913).

Chronicon Galfridi le Baker de Swynebroke, ed. E.M. Thompson (Oxford, 1889).

Edward II The Man

Chronicon Henrici Knighton, ed. J.R. Lumby, i. Rolls Series (London, 1889).

Chronique de Jean le Bel, ed. J. Viard and E. Deprez, i, Société de l'Historie de France (1904).

Chronique Metrique de Godfray de Paris. ed J A Buchon (Paris, 1827).

Chroniques de Sempringham: Livre des Reis de Britannie, ed. J.Glover, Rolls Series (London, 1865).

Cotton Manuscripts (esp Nero C.VIII).

Edward II, the Lord Ordainers and Piers Gaveston's Jewels and Horses, ed. R.A. Roberts. Camden 3rd Series, xli (London, 1929).

English Historical Documents, vol 3, 1189–1327, ed Harry Rothwell (London, 1975).

Flores Historiarum, vol 3, ed. H.R.Luard Rolls Series (London, HMSO, 1890).

Foedera, Conventiones, Litterae et Cujuscunque Generis Acta Publica, ed T.Rymer vol I, ii (London, 1816–20).

French Chronicle of London, ed. G.J. Aungier, Camden Society, xxviii (London, 1844).

Froissart: Chronicles, ed. Geoffrey Brereton (London, 1978).

Gesta Edwardi de Carnarvon Auctore Canonica Bridlingtoniense, in Chronicles of the Reigns of Edward I and Edward II, ii, ed, W.Stubbs, Rolls Seroes (London, 1882).

Johannis de Trokelowe et Henrici de Blaneford Chronica et Annales, ed H.T. Riley, Rolls Series (London, HMSO, London, 1866).

Nicolai Triveti Annalium Continuatio, ed A.Hall (Oxford, 1722).

Parliamentary Rolls of Medieval England, 1275–1504, vol iii, iv, ed. J.R.S. Phillips (Woodbridge, 2005).

Parliamentary Texts of the Later Middle Ages, ed N.Pronay and J.Taylor (Oxford, 1980).

Parliamentary Writs and Writs of Military Summons, Edward I and Edward II, ed F. Palgrave, Record Commission (London, 1827–34).

Polychronicon Ranulphi Higden, ed. J.R. Lumby, viii Rolls Series (London, 1882).

Roll of Arms of the Princes, Barons and Knights who attended Edward I at the Siege of Caerlaverock, ed. T. Wright (London, 1864).

Rotuli Parliamentorum Hactenus Inediti, ed. H.G. Richardson and G.O Sayles, Camden 3rd Series, li (London, 1935).

Scalacronica of Thomas Gray of Heton, ed. J. Stevenson, Maitland Club (Edinburgh, 1836).

Scotichronicon by Walter Bower, ed. D.E.R. Watt, viii, (Aberdeen, 1987).

Select Documents of English Constitutional History, 1307–1485, ed. S.B. Chrimes and A.L. Brown (London, 1961).

The National Archives: Chancery (C), Duchy of Lancaster (DL), Exchequer (E), King's Bench (KB) and Special Collections (SC).

The Political Songs of England from the Reign of King John to that of Edward II, ed T.Wright (London, 1839).

The Itinerary of Edward II and his household, 1307–27, ed. E.M. Hallam. List and Index Society, ccxi (London, 1984).

The Song of Lewes, ed. C.L. Kingsford (1890).

The War of Saint-Sardos (1323–25): Gascon Correspondance and Diplomatic Documents, ed. Pierre Chaplais. Camden 3rd Series, lxxxvii (London, 1954).

Trevet, Nicholas, Annales Sex Regum Angliae, ed. T. Hog, The English Historical Society Publications, ix, (London, 1845).

Vita Edwardi Secundi, ed. N. Denholm-Young (London, 1957).

Vita Edward Secundi, ed. W.R. Childs (Oxford, 2005).

Vita et Mors Edwardi Secundi in Chronicles of the Reigns of Edward I and Edward II, ii, ed W. Stubbs, Rolls Series (London, 1883).

Walsingham, Thomas. *Historia Anglicana,* ed. H.T. Riley, Rolls Series (London, 1863).

Walter of Frocester, Historia Monasterii Gloucestriae.

Secondary Sources

Barlow, J. Bryant, R. Heighway, C. Jeens, C. Smith, D. *Edward II: His Last Months and his Monument* (The Bristol and Gloucester Archaeological Society, 2015)

Barrow, G.W.S. *Kingship and Unity: Scotland, 1000–1306* (London, 1981).

Barrow, G.W.S. *Robert Bruce and the Community of the Realm of Scotland* (3rd ed. Edinburgh, 1988).

Beardwood, A. 'The Trial of Walter Langton, Bishop of Lichfield, 1307–1312' in *Transactions of the American Philosophical Society* (Philadelphia, 1964).

Bellamy, J.G. *The Law of Treason in the Middle Ages*, (Cambridge, 1970).

Benz St John, Lisa. Three Medieval Queens: Queenship and the Crown in *Fourteenth Century England* (New York, 2012).

Bingham, Caroline. *The Life and Times of Edward II* (Edinburgh, 1982).

Blackley, F.D. 'Adam, the Bastard Son of Edward II', *BIHR*, XXXVII (1964).

Blackley, F.D. 'Isabella and the Bishop of Exeter' in T.A. Sandqvist and M.R Powicke, ed, *Essays in Medieval History presented to Bertie Wilkinson* (Toronto, 1969).

Blackley, F.D. 'The Tomb of Isabella, wife of Edward II of England', *Bulletin of the International Society for the Study of Church Monuments*, viii (1983).

Boswell, J.B. *Christianity, Social Tolerance and Homosexuality* (Chicago, 1980).

Brown, Chris. *Bannockburn 1314: A New History* (Stroud, 2009).

Brown, Michael. *Bannockburn: The Scottish War and the British Isles 1307–1323* (Edinburgh, 2008).

Brown, Elizabeth. 'The Political Repercussions of Family Ties in the Early Fourteenth Century: The marriage of Edward II and Isabelle of France', *Speculum*, lxiii (1988).

Buck, M. Politics, *Finance and the Church in the reign of Edward II: Walter Stapledon Treasurer of England*, Cambridge Studies in Medieval Life and Thought, 3rd Series, xix (Cambridge, 1983).

Buck, M. 'The Reform of the Exchequer, 1316–26', *EHR*, 98 (1983).

Burgtoff, Jochen. 'With my life, his joyes began and ended': Piers Gaveston and King Edward II of England Revisited' in *Fourteenth Century England, V*, ed N. Saul. (Woodbridge, Suffolk & Rochester NY, 2008).

Chaplais, P. *Piers Gaveston: Edward II's Adoptive Brother* (Oxford, 1994).

Chaplais, P. *English Diplomatic Practice in the Middle Ages* (London, 2003).

Childs, Wendy. 'Welcome my Brother': Edward II, John Powderham and the chronicles, 1318' in *Church and Chronicle in the Middle Ages: Essays presented to John Taylor*, ed. I. Eood & G.A. Loud (London, 1991).

Childs, Wendy. 'England in Europe in the reign of Edward II' in *The Reign of Edward II: New Perspectives* ed. G.Dodd and A. Musson (Woodbridge, Suffolk & Rochester, NY, 2006).

Cockerill, S. *Eleanor of Castile: The Shadow Queen* (Stroud, 2014).

Costain, Thomas. *The Pageant of England, 1272–1377: The Three Edwards* (London, 1973).

Cuttino, G.P. and Thomas Lyman. 'Where is Edward II', *Speculum*, liii, (1978).

Davies, J.C. 'The Despenser War in Glamorgan' in *TRHS*, 3rd series, ix (1915).

Davies, J.C. *The Baronial Opposition to Edward II: Its Character and Policy* (Cambridge, 1918).

Davies, R.R. *The First English Empire: Power and Identities in the British Isles 1093–1343* (Oxford, 2000).

Davies, R.R. *Conquest, Coexistence and Change: Wales, 1063–1415* (Oxford & Cardiff, 1987).

Denholm Young, N. 'The Authorship of the Vita Edwardi Secundi' in *Collected Papers* (Cardiff, 1969).

Denton, Jeffrey H. *Robert Winchelsey and the Crown 1294–1313* (Cambridge, 2002).

Doherty, P. *Isabella and the Strange Death of Edward II* (London, 2003).

Doherty, P. 'The Date of Birth of Isabella, Queen of England', *BIHR*, XLVIII (1975).

Dryburgh, P. 'The last refuge of a scoundrel? Edward II and Ireland, 1321–7' in *The Reign of Edward II: New Perspectives*, ed. G.Dodd and A.Musson (Woodbridge, Suffolk & Rochester, NY, 2006).

Duffy, M. *Royal Tombs of Medieval England* (Stroud, 2003).

Duggan, A.J. The Cult of St Thomas Becket in the Thirteenth Century in *St Thomas Cantilupe, Bishop of Hereford*, ed. M. Jancey (Hereford, 1982).

Edwards, J. 'The Cult of "St" Thomas of Lancaster and its iconography' in *Yorkshire Archaeological Journal*, lxiv (1992).

Edwards, J.G. 'Sir Gruffydd Llwyd', *EHR*, xxx (1915).

Edwards, K. 'The political importance of the English bishops during the reign of Edward II', *EHR*, lix (1944).

Edwards, K. 'The Personal and Political Activities of the English Episcopate During the Reign of Edward II', *BIHR*, XVI (1938).

Evans, M. *The Death of Kings: Royal Deaths in Medieval England* (London, 2003).

Frame, Robin. 'Power and Society in the Lordship of Ireland, 1272–1377', *Past and Present*, lxxvi (1977).

Frame, Robin. *English Lordship in Ireland, 1318–1361* (Oxford, 1982).

Fryde, Natalie. *The Tyranny and Fall of Edward II, 1321–1326* (Cambridge, 1979).

Fryde, E.B. 'The Deposits of Hugh Despenser the Younger with Italian Bankers', *Economic History Review*, 2nd Series, iii (1951).

Gibbs, V. 'The Battle of Boroughbride and the Boroughbridge Roll', *Genealogist*, xxi (1905).

Green, M.A.E. *Lives of the Princesses of England*, ii (London, 1850).

Haines, R.M. *King Edward II: Edward of Caernarfon, His Life, His Reign, and its Aftermath, 1284–1330* (Montreal and London, 2003).

Haines, R.M. *The Church and Politics in Fourteenth-Century England: The Career of Adam Orleton c.1275–1345*, Cambridge Studies in Medieval Life and Thought, 3rd series (Cambridge, 1978).

Haines, R.M. *Death of a King* (Lancaster, 2002).

Haines, R.M. *Archbishop John Startford:Political Revolutionary and Champion of the Liberties of the English Church, 1275/80 – 1348* (Toronto, 1986).

Haines, R.M. 'Edwardus redivivus: the "afterlife" of Edward of Caernarvon' in *Transactions of the Bristol and Gloucestershire Archaeological Society*, cxiv (1997).

Haines, R.M. 'Roger Mortimer's Scam', *Transactions of the Bristol and Gloucestershire Archaeological Society*, cxxvi (2008).

Hamilton, J.S. *Piers Gaveston: Earl of Cornwall, 1307–1312: Politics and Patronage in the Reign of Edward II* (Detroit and London, 1988).

Hamilton, J.S. 'The Charter witness lists for the reign of Edward II' in *The Reign of Edward II: New Perspectives*, ed. G.Dodd and A.Musson (Woodbridge, Suffolk & Rochester, NY, 2006).

Hamilton, J.S. 'The uncertain death of Edward II' in *History Compass* (2008).

Hamilton, J.S. 'A Reassessment of the Loyalty of the Household Knights of Edward II' in *Fourteenth Century England VII*, ed, Mark Ormrod (Woodbridge, 2012).

Hamilton, J.S. 'The English coronation oath', *Speculum*, xxiv (1949).

Haskins, G.L. *A Chronicle of the civil wars of Edward II*. *Speculum*, xiv (1939).

Haskins, G.L. 'The Doncaster Petition of 1321', *EHR*, liii (1938).

Haskins, G.L. 'Judicial Proceedings Against a Traitor after Boroughbridge', *Speculum*, xii (1937).

Holmes, G.A. 'Judgement on the younger Despenser, 1326', *EHR*, lxx (1955).

Holmes, G.A. 'A protest against the Despensers, 1326', *Speculum*, xxx (1955).

Holmes, G.A. *The Estates of the Higher Nobility in Fourteenth Century England*, (1957).

Howell, M. Eleanor of Provence: *Queenship in Thirteenth Century England* (Oxford and Malden Mass, 1998).

Hutchinson, Harold. F. *Edward II: The Pliant King* (London, 1971).

Hunter, J .'On the measures taken for the Apprehension of Sir Thomas de Gournay, one of the Murderers of king Edward the second' in *Archaeologia*, xxvii (1838).

Johnstone, H. *Edward of Carnarvon, 1284–1307* (Manchester, 1946).

Johnstone, H. *Letters of Edward, Prince of Wales 1304–1305*. (Cambridge, 1931).

Johnstone, H. 'The eccentricities of Edward II', *EHR*, xlviii (1933).

Johnstone, H. 'Isabella, the She-Wolf of France', *History*, xxi (1936).

Johnstone, H. 'The Parliament of Lincoln, 1316', *EHR*, xxxvi (1921).

Johnstone, H. 'The County of Ponthieu, 1279–1307', *EHR*, xxix (1914).

Jordan, W.C. *The Great Famine: Northern Europe in the Early Fourteenth Century* (Princeton, 1996).

KcFarlane, K.B. *The Nobility of Later Medieval England* (Oxford, 1973).

Kershaw,I. 'The Great Famine and Agrarian Crisis in England 1315–1322', *Past & Present*, lix (May, 1973).

King, A. 'Bandits, Robbers and Schavaldours: War and Disorder in Northumberland in the reign of Edward II', *Thirteenth-Century England IX*. Ed Michael Prestwich, Richard Britnell and Robin Frame (Woodbridge, 2003).

King, Andy. 'Thomas of Lancaster's First Quarrel with Edward II' in *Fourteenth Century England*, iii, ed W.M. Ormrod (Woodbridge, Suffolk & Rochester, NY, 2004).

Lawne, Penny. 'Edmund of Woodstock, 1301–1330: A Study of Personal Loyalty' in *Fourteenth Century England VI*, ed. C. Given-Wilson (Woodbridge, 2010).

Lawrence, M. 'Rise of a royal favourite: the early career of Hugh Despenser the Elder' in *The Reign of Edward II: New Perspectives*, ed. G.Dodds and A.Musson (Woodbridgem Suffolk & Rochester, NY, 2008).

Lucas, H.S. 'The Great European Famine of 1315, 1316 and 1317', *Speculum*, v (1930).

Lydon, J. *The Impact of the Bruce Invasion' in New History of Ireland*, ii, ed. Art Cosgrove (Oxford, 1987).

Maddicott, J.R. *Thomas of Lancaster, 1307–1322: A Study in the Reign of Edward II* (Oxford, 1970).

Maddicott, J.R. 'Thomas of Lancaster and Sir Robert Holland: a study in Noble Patronage', *EHR*, lxxxvi (1971).

McFarlane, K.B. 'Had Edward I a "policy" towards the earls' in *Nobility of Later Medieval England in History*, l (1965).

McKisack, M. *The Fourteenth Century, 1307–1399* (Oxford, 1959).

McNamee, C. *The Wars of the Bruces: Scotland, England and Ireland, 1306–1328* (East Linton, 1997).

McNamee, C. 'The Scots' Invasion of Ireland, 1315' in *The British Isles, 1100–1500*, ed. R.R. Davies (Edinburgh & Atlantic Highlands, NJ, 1988).

Miller, Edward. *War and Economic Development* (Cambridge, 1975).

Moore, S.A. 'Documents Relating to the Death and Burial of Edward II', *Archaeologia*, L (1887).

Morris, M. *A Great and Terrible King: Edward I and the Forging of Britain* (London, 2008).

Mortimer, Ian. *The Greatest Traitor: The Life of Sir Roger Mortimer, Ruler of England 1327 to 1330* (London, 2003).

Mortimer, Ian. *Medieval Intrigues: Decoding Royal Conspiracies* (London, 2010).

Mortimer, Ian. *The Perfect King: The Life of Edward III* (London, 2006).

Mortimer, Ian. *Sermons of Sodomy* (re-issued in Intrigues).

Nusbacher, A. *The Battle of Bannockburn 1314* (Stroud, 2005).

Ormrod, W. M. 'The Sexualities of Edward II' in Dodd and Mussin, eds. *The Reign of Edward II: New Perspectives*. (2006).

Parsons, 'The Year of Eleanor of Castile's Birth and her Children by Edward I', *Medieval Studies*, xlvi, (1984).

Parsons, J.C. 'The Intercessory Patronage of Queens Margaret and Isabella of France' in *Thirteenth-Century England VI*, ed. Michael Prestwich, R.H. Britnell and Robin Frame (Woodbridge, 1997).

Parsons, John Carmi. *Eleanor of Castile: Queen and Society in Thirteenth-Century England* (Basingstoke, 1995).

Perry, R. *Edward the Second: Suddenly, at Berkeley* (Wotton-under-Edge, 1988).

Phillips, J.R.S. *Aymer de Valence, Earl of Pembroke, 1307–24: Baronial Politics in the Reign of Edward II* (Oxford, 1972).

Phillips, S. *Edward II* (New Haven & London, 2010).

Phillips, S. 'Edward II and the Prophets', England in the *Fourteenth Century: Proceedings of the 1985 Harlaxton Symposium*, ed W.M. Ormrod (Woodbridge, 1986).

Phillips, J.R.S. '"Edward II" in Italy: English and Welsh Political Exiles and Fugitives in Continental Europe, 1322–1364' in *Thirteenth-Century England X*, ed Michael Prestwich, , R.H. Britnell and Robin Frame (Woodbridge, 2005).

Prestwich, M. *Edward I, King of England* (new ed, New Haven & London, 1997).

Prestwich, M. *Plantagenet England, 1225–1360* (Oxford, 2005).

Prestwich, M. *The Three Edwards: War and State in England 1272–1377* (London, 1980).

Prestwich, M. *Armies and Warfare in the Middle Ages: The English Experience* (New Haven & London, 1996).

Prestwich, M. 'Gilbert de Middleton and the attack on the cardinals, 1317' in Warriors and Churchmen in *The High Middle Ages: Essays presented to Karl Leyser*, ed. T.Reuter (London, 1992).

Prestwich, M. 'Edward I and the Maid of Norway', *SHR*, lxix (October 1990).

Pugh, T.B. 'Marcher Lords of Glamorgan and Morgannwg, 1317–1485' in *Glamorgan County History, III: The Middle Ages*. (1971).

Prestwich, M. 'The Ordinances of 1311 and the politics of the early fourteenth century' in *Politics and Crisis in Fourteenth-Century England*, ed. J. Taylor and W.R. Childs (Gloucester, 1990).

Bibliography

Raban, S. *England under Edward I and Edward II, 1259–1327* (Oxford, 2000).

Rhodes, W.E. 'The Inventory of the jewels and wardrobe of Queen Isabella (1307–8), *EHR*, xii (1897).

Robinson, C. 'Was Edward the Second a degenerate? A consideration of his reign from that point of view', *American Journal of Insanity*, lxvi (1909–10).

Saaler, Mary. *Edward II 1307–27* (London, 1997).

Salisbury, K. 'A political agreement of June 1318', *EHR*, xxxiii (1918).

Saul, Nigel. 'The Despensers and the Downfall of Edward II', *EHR*, xcix (1984).

Sayles, G.O. 'The Formal Judgements on the Traitors of 1322', *Speculum*, xvi (1941).

Sadler, John. *Bannockburn: Battle for Liberty* (Barnsley, 2008).

Sandquist, T.A. 'The Holy Oil of St. Thomas of Canterbury', in *Essays in Medieval History presented to Bertie Wilkinson*, ed. T.A Sanfquist and M.R. Powicke (Toronto, 1969).

Smith, J.B. 'The Rebellion of Llywelyn Bren' in *Glamorgan County History, iii, The Middle Ages*, ed. T.B Pugh (Cardiff, 1971).

Smith, J.B. 'Edward II and the Allegiance of Wales', *Welsh History Review*, viii (1976).

Strong, Roy. *Coronation: A History of Kingship and British Monarchy* (London, 2005).

Stuart, E.P. 'The Interview between Philip V and Edward II at Amiens in 1320', *EHR*, xli (1926).

Tanqueray, A.J. 'The Conspiracies of Thomas Dunheved, 1327', *EHR*, xxxi (1916).

Tebbit, A. 'Royal Patronage and political alliance: the household knights of Edward II', *The Reign of Edward II: New Perspectives*, ed. G. Dodd and A.Musson (Woodbridge, 2006).

Tout, T.F. *The Place of the Reign of Edward II in English History* (Manchester, 1936).

Taylor, John. 'The Judgement of Hugh Despenser the Younger', *Medievalia et Humanistica*, xii (1958).

Vale, M. *The Princely Court: Medieval Court and Culture in North-West Europe* (Oxford, 2001).

Valente, C. 'The Deposition and Abdication of Edward II', *EHR*, cxiii (1998).

Valente, C. 'The "Lament of Edward II": Religious Lyric, Political Propaganda', *Speculum*, lxxvii (2002).

Warner, Kathryn. *Edward II: The Unconventional King* (Stroud, 2014).

Warner, Kathryn. *Isabella of France: The Rebel Queen* (Stroud, 2016).

Warner, K. 'The Adherents of Edmund of Woodstock, Earl of Kent, in March 1330', *EHR*, cxxvi (2011).

Waugh, S.L. 'The Profits of Violence: the Minor Gentry in the Rebellions of 1321–22 in Gloucestershire and Herefordshire', *Speculum*, lii (1972).

Weir, Alison. *Isabella, She-Wolf of France, Queen of England* (Jonathan Cape, London, 2005).

Wilkinson, B. 'The Sherburn Indenture and the Attack on the Despensers', *EHR*, lxiii (1948).

Wilkinson, B. 'The Coronation Oath of Edward II and the Statute of York', *Speculum*, xix (1944).

Wilkinson, B. 'The negotiations proceeding the "Treaty" of Leake, August 1318' in *Studies in Medieval History presented to Frederick Maurice Powicke*, ed. R.W. Hunt, W.A Pantin and R.W. Southern (Oxford, 1948).

Wright, J.R. *The Church and the English Crown, 1305–1334: Pontifical Institute of Mediaeval Studies* (Toronto, 1980).

Index

Also available from Amberley Publishing